Brief C++

Late Objects

3/e

Brief C++

Late Objects

3/e

Cay Horstmann
San Jose State University

WILEY

PUBLISHER	Laurie Rosatone
EDITORIAL DIRECTOR	Don Fowley
DEVELOPMENTAL EDITOR	Cindy Johnson
ASSISTANT DEVELOPMENT EDITOR	Ryann Dannelly
EXECUTIVE MARKETING MANAGER	Dan Sayre
SENIOR PRODUCTION EDITOR	Laura Abrams
SENIOR CONTENT MANAGER	Valerie Zaborski
EDITORIAL ASSISTANT	Anna Pham
SENIOR DESIGNER	Tom Nery
SENIOR PHOTO EDITOR	Billy Ray
PRODUCTION MANAGEMENT	Cindy Johnson
COVER IMAGE	© Monty Rakusen/Getty Images

This book was set in Stempel Garamond LT Std by Publishing Services, and printed and bound by Quad/Graphics, Versailles. The cover was printed by Quad/Graphics, Versailles.

This book is printed on acid-free paper. ∞

Founded in 1807, John Wiley & Sons, Inc. has been a valued source of knowledge and understanding for more than 200 years, helping people around the world meet their needs and fulfill their aspirations. Our company is built on a foundation of principles that include responsibility to the communities we serve and where we live and work. In 2008, we launched a Corporate Citizenship Initiative, a global effort to address the environmental, social, economic, and ethical challenges we face in our business. Among the issues we are addressing are carbon impact, paper specifications and procurement, ethical conduct within our business and among our vendors, and community and charitable support. For more information, please visit our website: *www.wiley.com/go/citizenship*.

ISBN 13: 978-1-119-40042-4

The inside back cover will contain printing identification and country of origin if omitted from this page. In addition, if the ISBN on the back cover differs from the ISBN on this page, the one on the back cover is correct.

Printed in the United States of America.

V10019577_070320

PREFACE

This book is an introduction to C++ and computer programming that focuses on the essentials—and on effective learning. The book is designed to serve a wide range of student interests and abilities and is suitable for a first course in programming for computer scientists, engineers, and students in other disciplines. No prior programming experience is required, and only a modest amount of high school algebra is needed.

Here are the key features of this book:

Present fundamentals first.

This book uses the C++ programming language as a vehicle for introducing computer science concepts. A substantial subset of the C++ language is covered, focusing on the modern features of standard C++ that make students productive. The book takes a traditional route, first stressing control structures, procedural decomposition, and array algorithms. Objects are used when appropriate in the early chapters. Students start designing and implementing their own classes in Chapter 9.

Guidance and worked examples help students succeed.

Beginning programmers often ask "How do I start? Now what do I do?" Of course, an activity as complex as programming cannot be reduced to cookbook-style instructions. However, step-by-step guidance is immensely helpful for building confidence and providing an outline for the task at hand. "Problem Solving" sections stress the importance of design and planning. "How To" guides help students with common programming tasks. Additional Worked Examples are available in the E-Text or online.

Tip: Source files for all of the program examples in the book, including the Worked Examples, are provided with the source code for this book. Download the files to your computer for easy access as you work through the chapters.

Practice makes perfect.

Of course, programming students need to be able to implement nontrivial programs, but they first need to have the confidence that they can succeed. The Enhanced E-Text immerses students in activities designed to foster in-depth learning. Students don't just watch animations and code traces, they work on generating them. The activities provide instant feedback to show students what they did right and where they need to study more. A wealth of practice opportunities, including code completion questions and skill-oriented multiple-choice questions, appear at the end of each section, and each chapter ends with well-crafted review exercises and programming projects.

Problem solving strategies are made explicit.

Practical, step-by-step illustrations of techniques help students devise and evaluate solutions to programming problems. Introduced where they are most relevant, these strategies address barriers to success for many students. Strategies included are:

- Algorithm Design (with pseudocode)
- First Do It By Hand (doing sample calculations by hand)
- Flowcharts

- Selecting Test Cases
- Hand-Tracing
- Storyboards
- Solve a Simpler Problem First
- Reusable Functions
- Stepwise Refinement
- Adapting Algorithms
- Discovering Algorithms by Manipulating Physical Objects
- Draw a Picture (pointer diagrams)
- Tracing Objects (identifying state and behavior)
- Discovering Classes

A visual approach motivates the reader and eases navigation.

Photographs present visual analogies that explain the nature and behavior of computer concepts. Step-by-step figures illustrate complex program operations. Syntax boxes and example tables present a variety of typical and special cases in a compact format. It is easy to get the "lay of the land" by browsing the visuals, before focusing on the textual material.

© Terraxplorer/iStockphoto.

Visual features help the reader with navigation.

Focus on the essentials while being technically accurate.

An encyclopedic coverage is not helpful for a beginning programmer, but neither is the opposite—reducing the material to a list of simplistic bullet points. In this book, the essentials are presented in digestible chunks, with separate notes that go deeper into good practices or language features when the reader is ready for the additional information. You will not find artificial over-simplifications that give an illusion of knowledge.

Reinforce sound engineering practices.

A multitude of useful tips on software quality and common errors encourage the development of good programming habits. The focus is on test-driven development, encouraging students to test their programs systematically.

Engage with optional engineering and business exercises.

Review exercises are enhanced with problems from scientific and business domains. Designed to engage students, the exercises illustrate the value of programming in applied fields.

New to This Edition

Updated for Modern Versions of C++

A number of features of the C++ 2011 and C++ 2014 standards are described either as recommended "best practice" or as Special Topics.

New and Reorganized Topics

The book now supports two pathways into object-oriented programming and inheritance. Pointers and structures can be covered before introducing classes. Alternatively, pointers can be deferred until after the implementation of classes.

A sequence of Worked Examples and exercises introduces "media computation"—generating and modifying images, sounds, and animations.

Lower-Cost, Interactive Format

This third edition is published as a lower-cost Enhanced E-Text that supports active learning through a wealth of interactive activities. These activities engage and prepare students for independent programming and the Review Exercises, Practice Exercises, and Programming Projects at the end of each E-Text chapter. The Enhanced E-Text may also be bundled with a print version of the book.

Interactive learning solutions are expanding every day, so to learn more about these options or to explore other options to suit your needs, please contact your Wiley account manager (www.wiley.com/go/whosmyrep) or visit the product information page for this text on wiley.com (https://www.wiley.com/en-us/search?pq=horstmann%7C relevance).

The Enhanced E-Text is designed to enable student practice without the instructor assigning the interactivities or recording their scores. If you are interested in assigning and grading students' work on them, ask your Wiley Account Manager about the online course option implemented in the Engage Learning Management System. The Engage course supports the assignment and automatic grading of the interactivities. Engage access includes access to the Enhanced E-Text.

Features in the Enhanced E-Text

The interactive Enhanced E-Text guides students from the basics to writing complex programs. After they read a bit, they can try all of the interactive exercises for that section. Active reading is an engaging way for students to ensure that students are prepared before going to class.

There five types of interactivities:

Code Walkthrough   Code Walkthrough activities ask students to trace through a segment of code, choosing which line will be executed next and entering the new values of variables changed by the code's execution. This activity simulates the hand-tracing problem solving technique taught in Chapters 3 and 4—but with immediate feedback.

Example Table   Example table activities make the student the active participant in building up tables of code examples similar to those found in the book. The tables come in many different forms. Some tables ask the student to determine the output of a line of code, or the value of an expression, or to provide code for certain tasks. This activity helps students assess their understanding of the reading—while it is easy to go back and review.

Algorithm Animation   An algorithm animation shows the essential steps of an algorithm. However, instead of passively watching, students get to predict each step. When finished, students can start over with a different set of inputs. This is a surprisingly effective way of learning and remembering algorithms.

Rearrange Code   Rearrange code activities ask the student to arrange lines of code by dragging them from the list on the right to the area at left so that the resulting code fulfills the task described in the problem. This activity builds facility with coding structure and implementing common algorithms.

Object Diagram   Object diagram activities ask the student to create a memory diagram to illustrate how variables and objects are initialized and updated as sample code executes. The activity depicts variables, objects, and references in the same way as the figures in the book. After an activity is completed, pressing "Play" replays the animation. This activity goes beyond hand-tracing to illuminate what is happening in memory as code executes.

Code Completion   Code completion activities ask the student to finish a partially-completed program, then paste the solution into CodeCheck (a Wiley-based online code evaluator) to learn whether it produces the desired result. Tester classes on the CodeCheck site run and report whether the code passed the tests. This activity serves as a skill-building lab to better prepare the student for writing programs from scratch.

A Tour of the Book

This book is intended for a two-semester introduction to programming that may also include algorithms and data structures. The organization of chapters offers the same flexibility as the previous edition; dependencies among the chapters are also shown in Figure 1.

Part A: Fundamentals (Chapters 1–8)

The first six chapters follow a traditional approach to basic programming concepts. Students learn about control structures, stepwise refinement, and arrays. Objects are used only for input/output and string processing. Input/output is first covered in Chapter 2, which may be followed by an introduction to reading and writing text files in Section 8.1.

In a course for engineers with a need for systems and embedded programming, you will want to cover Chapter 7 on pointers. Sections 7.1 and 7.4 are sufficient for using pointers with polymorphism in Chapter 10.

File processing is the subject of Chapter 8. Section 8.1 can be covered sooner for an introduction to reading and writing text files. The remainder of the chapter gives additional material for practical applications.

Part B: Object-Oriented Design (Chapters 9–10)

After students have gained a solid foundation, they are ready to tackle the implementation of classes. Chapters 9 and 10 introduce the object-oriented features of C++. Chapter 9 introduces class design and implementation. Chapter 10 covers inheritance and polymorphism. By the end of these chapters, students will be able to implement programs with multiple interacting classes.

Any subset of these chapters can be incorporated into a custom print version of this text; ask your Wiley sales representative for details, or visit `https://customselect. wiley.com/` to create your custom order.

Appendices

Appendices A and B summarize C++ reserved words and operators. Appendix C lists character escape sequences and ASCII character code values. Appendix D documents all of the library functions and classes used in this book.

Appendix E contains a programming style guide. Using a style guide for programming assignments benefits students by directing them toward good habits and reducing gratuitous choice. The style guide is available in electronic form on the book's companion web site so that instructors can modify it to reflect their preferred style.

Appendix F, available in the E-Text, introduces common number systems used in computing.

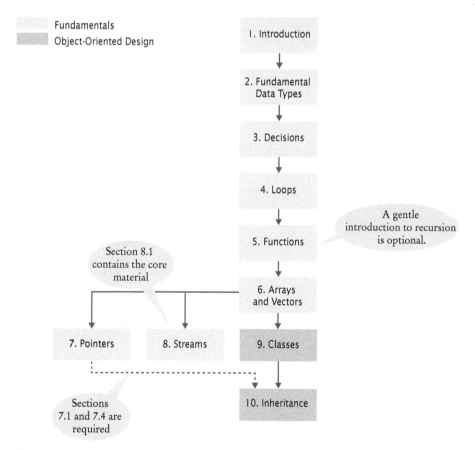

Figure 1   Chapter Dependencies

Web Resources

This book is complemented by a complete suite of online resources. Visit the online companion sites at www.Wiley.com. The online resources include

- Source code for all example programs in the book and its Worked Examples, plus additional example programs.
- Worked Examples that apply the problem-solving steps in the book to other realistic examples.
- Lecture presentation slides (for instructors only).
- Solutions to all review and programming exercises (for instructors only).
- A test bank that focuses on skills, not just terminology (for instructors only). This extensive set of multiple-choice questions can be used with a word processor or imported into a course management system.
- "CodeCheck" assignments that allow students to work on programming problems presented in an innovative online service and receive immediate feedback. Instructors can assign exercises that have already been prepared, or easily add their own. Visit http://codecheck.it to learn more.

Pointers in the print companion describe what students will find in their E-Text or online.

WORKED EXAMPLE 2.1
Computing Travel Time

Learn how to develop a hand calculation to compute the time that a robot requires to retrieve an item from rocky terrain. See your E-Text or visit wiley.com/go/bc1o3

Courtesy of NASA.

EXAMPLE CODE   See how_to_1/scores_vector in your companion code for a solution using vectors instead of arrays.

A Walkthrough of the Learning Aids

The pedagogical elements in this book work together to focus on and reinforce key concepts and fundamental principles of programming, with additional tips and detail organized to support and deepen these fundamentals. In addition to traditional features, such as chapter objectives and a wealth of exercises, each chapter contains elements geared to today's visual learner.

Throughout each chapter, **margin notes** show where new concepts are introduced and provide an outline of key ideas.

Annotated **syntax boxes** provide a quick, visual overview of new language constructs.

Annotations explain required components and point to more information on common errors or best practices associated with the syntax.

Analogies to everyday objects are used to explain the nature and behavior of concepts such as variables, data types, loops, and more.

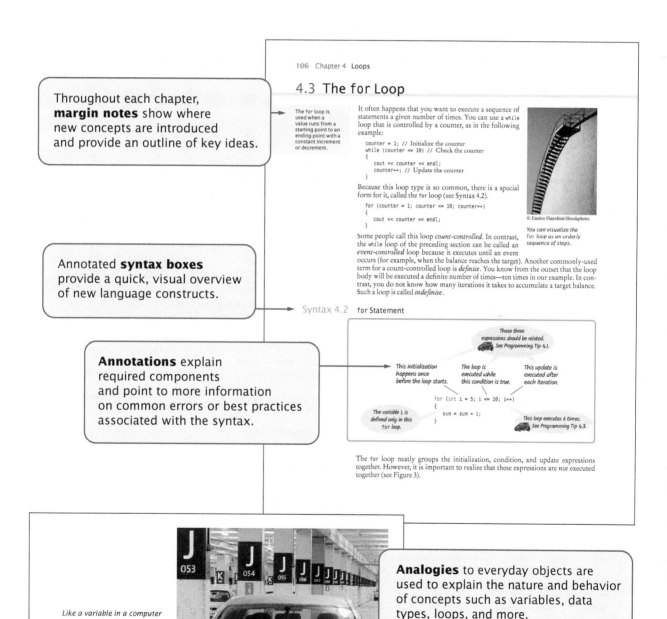

106   Chapter 4   Loops

4.3 The for Loop

The for loop is used when a value runs from a starting point to an ending point with a constant increment or decrement.

It often happens that you want to execute a sequence of statements a given number of times. You can use a while loop that is controlled by a counter, as in the following example:

```
counter = 1; // Initialize the counter
while (counter <= 10) // Check the counter
{
   cout << counter << endl;
   counter++; // Update the counter
}
```

Because this loop type is so common, there is a special form for it, called the for loop (see Syntax 4.2).

```
for (counter = 1; counter <= 10; counter++)
{
   cout << counter << endl;
}
```

© Enrico Fianchini/iStockphoto.

You can visualize the for loop as an orderly sequence of steps.

Some people call this loop *count-controlled*. In contrast, the while loop of the preceding section can be called an *event-controlled* loop because it executes until an event occurs (for example, when the balance reaches the target). Another commonly-used term for a count-controlled loop is *definite*. You know from the outset that the loop body will be executed a definite number of times—ten times in our example. In contrast, you do not know how many iterations it takes to accumulate a target balance. Such a loop is called *indefinite*.

Syntax 4.2   for Statement

These three expressions should be related. See Programming Tip 4.1.

This initialization happens once before the loop starts.

The loop is executed while this condition is true.

This update is executed after each iteration.

```
for (int i = 5; i <= 10; i++)
{
   sum = sum + i;
}
```

The variable i is defined only in this for loop.

This loop executes 6 times. See Programming Tip 4.3.

The for loop neatly groups the initialization, condition, and update expressions together. However, it is important to realize that these expressions are *not* executed together (see Figure 3).

Like a variable in a computer program, a parking space has an identifier and contents.

Memorable photos reinforce analogies and help students remember the concepts.

A recipe for a fruit pie may say to use any kind of fruit. Here, "fruit" is an example of a parameter variable. Apples and cherries are examples of arguments.

Problem Solving sections teach techniques for generating ideas and evaluating proposed solutions, often using pencil and paper or other artifacts. These sections emphasize that most of the planning and problem solving that makes students successful happens away from the computer.

6.5 Problem Solving: Discovering Algorithms by Manipulating Physical Objects 277

Now how does that help us with our problem, switching the first and the second half of the array?

Let's put the first coin into place, by swapping it with the fifth coin. However, as C++ programmers, we will say that we swap the coins in positions 0 and 4:

Next, we swap the coins in positions 1 and 5:

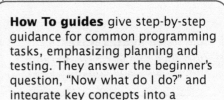

HOW TO 1.1
Describing an Algorithm with Pseudocode

This is the first of many "How To" sections in this book that give you step-by-step procedures for carrying out important tasks in developing computer programs.

Before you are ready to write a program in C++, you need to develop an algorithm—a method for arriving at a solution for a particular problem. Describe the algorithm in pseudocode—a sequence of precise steps formulated in English. To illustrate, we'll devise an algorithm for this problem:

Problem Statement You have the choice of buying one of two cars. One is more fuel efficient than the other, but also more expensive. You know the price and fuel efficiency (in miles per gallon, mpg) of both cars. You plan to keep the car for ten years. Assume a price of $4 per gallon of gas and usage of 15,000 miles per year. You will pay cash for the car and not worry about financing costs. Which car is the better deal?

© dlewis33/Getty Images.

Step 1 Determine the inputs and outputs.

In our sample problem, we have these inputs:

- *purchase price1* and *fuel efficiency1*, the price and fuel efficiency (in mpg) of the first car
- *purchase price2* and *fuel efficiency2*, the price and fuel efficiency of the second car

How To guides give step-by-step guidance for common programming tasks, emphasizing planning and testing. They answer the beginner's question, "Now what do I do?" and integrate key concepts into a problem-solving sequence.

WORKED EXAMPLE 1.1
Writing an Algorithm for Tiling a Floor

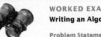

Problem Statement Your task is to tile a rectangular bathroom floor with alternating black and white tiles measuring 4 × 4 inches. The floor dimensions, measured in inches, are multiples of 4.

Step 1 Determine the inputs and outputs.

The inputs are the floor dimensions (length × width), measured in inches. The output is a tiled floor.

Step 2 Break down the problem into smaller tasks.

A natural subtask is to lay one row of tiles. If you can solve that task, then you can solve the problem by laying one row next to the other, starting from a wall, until

© rban/iStockphoto.

Worked Examples apply the steps in the How To to a different example, showing how they can be used to plan, implement, and test a solution to another programming problem.

Table 3 Variable Names in C++

Variable Name	Comment
can_volume1	Variable names consist of letters, numbers, and the underscore character.
x	In mathematics, you use short variable names such as x or y. This is legal in C++, but not very common, because it can make programs harder to understand (see Programming Tip 2.1).
⚠ Can_volume	**Caution:** Variable names are case sensitive. This variable name is different from can_volume.
🚫 6pack	**Error:** Variable names cannot start with a number.
🚫 can volume	**Error:** Variable names cannot contain spaces.
🚫 double	**Error:** You cannot use a reserved word as a variable name.
🚫 ltr/fl.oz	**Error:** You cannot use symbols such as . or /

Example tables support beginners with multiple, concrete examples. These tables point out common errors and present another quick reference to the section's topic.

Consider the function call illustrated in Figure 3:

```
double result1 = cube_volume(2);
```

- The parameter variable side_length of the cube_volume function is created. ❶
- The parameter variable is initialized with the value of the argument that was passed in the call. In our case, side_length is set to 2. ❷
- The function computes the expression side_length * side_length * side_length, which has the value 8. That value is stored in the variable volume. ❸
- The function returns. All of its variables are removed. The return value is transferred to the *caller*, that is, the function calling the cube_volume function. ❹

❶ Function call

```
double result1 = cube_volume(2);
```
result1 =

side_length =

❷ Initializing function parameter variable

```
double result1 = cube_volume(2);
```
result1 =

side_length = 2

❸ About to return to the caller

result1 =

```
double volume = side_length * side_length * side_length;
return volume;
```
side_length = 2

volume = 8

❹ After function call

```
double result1 = cube_volume(2);
```
result1 = 8

Figure 3 Parameter Passing

> **Progressive figures** trace code segments to help students visualize the program flow. Color is used consistently to make variables and other elements easily recognizable.

❶ Initialize counter

counter = 1

```
for (counter = 1; counter <= 10; counter++)
{
    cout << counter << endl;
}
```

❷ Check condition

counter = 1

```
for (counter = 1; counter <= 10; counter++)
{
    cout << counter << endl;
}
```

❸ Execute loop body

counter = 1

```
for (counter = 1; counter <= 10; counter++)
{
    cout << counter << endl;
}
```

❹ Update counter

counter = 2

```
for (counter = 1; counter <= 10; counter++)
{
    cout << counter << endl;
}
```

❺ Check condition again

counter = 2

```
for (counter = 1; counter <= 10; counter++)
{
    cout << counter << endl;
}
```

Figure 3 Execution of a for Loop

> Optional **engineering exercises** engage students with applications from technical fields.

Engineering P7.12 Write a program that simulates the control software for a "people mover" system, a set of driverless trains that move in two concentric circular tracks. A set of switches allows trains to switch tracks.

In your program, the outer and inner tracks should each be divided into ten segments. Each track segment can contain a train that moves either clockwise or counterclockwise. [A] train moves to an adjacent segment in its track or, if that segment is occupied, to [th]e adjacent segment in the other track.

[D]efine a Segment structure. Each segment has a pointer to the next and previous [se]gments in its track, a pointer to the next and previous segments in the other track,

sec02/cube.cpp

```
 1  #include <iostream>
 2
 3  using namespace std;
 4
 5  /**
 6     Computes the volume of a cube.
 7     @param side_length the side length of the cube
 8     @return the volume
 9  */
10  double cube_volume(double side_length)
11  {
12     double volume = side_length * side_length * side_length;
13     return volume;
14  }
15
16  int main()
17  {
18     double result1 = cube_volume(2);
19     double result2 = cube_volume(10);
20     cout << "A cube with side length 2 has volume " << result1 << endl;
21     cout << "A cube with side length 10 has volume " << result2 << endl;
22
23     return 0;
24  }
```

Program Run

```
A cube with side length 2 has volume 8
A cube with side length 10 has volume 1000
```

> **Program listings** are carefully designed for easy reading, going well beyond simple color coding. Functions are set off by a subtle outline.

EXAMPLE CODE   See sec04 of your companion code for another implementation of the earthquake program that you saw in Section 3.3. Note that the get_description function has multiple return statements.

> **Additional example programs** are provided with the companion code for students to read, run, and modify.

Common Errors describe the kinds of errors that students often make, with an explanation of why the errors occur, and what to do about them.

Common Error 2.1

Using Undefined Variables

You must define a variable before you use it for the first time. For example, the following sequence of statements would not be legal:

```
double can_volume = 12 * liter_per_ounce;
double liter_per_ounce = 0.0296;
```

In your program, the statements are compiled in order. When the compiler reaches the first statement, it does not know that liter_per_ounce will be defined in the next line, and it reports an error.

Programming Tip 3.6

Hand-Tracing

A very useful technique for understanding whether a program works correctly is called *hand-tracing*. You simulate the program's activity on a sheet of paper. You can use this method with pseudocode or C++ code.

Get an index card, a cocktail napkin, or whatever sheet of paper is within reach. Make a column for each variable. Have the program code ready. Use a marker, such as a paper clip, to mark the current statement. In your mind, execute statements one at a time. Every time the value of a variable changes, cross out the old value and write the new value below the old one.

For example, let's trace the tax program with the data from the program run in Section 3.4. In lines 13 and 14, tax1 and tax2 are initialized to 0.

Hand-tracing helps you understand whether a program works correctly.

Programming Tips explain good programming practices, and encourage students to be more productive with tips and techniques such as hand-tracing.

```
6  int main()
7  {
8     const double RATE1 = 0.10;
9     const double RATE2 = 0.25;
10    const double RATE1_SINGLE_LIMIT = 32000;
11    const double RATE1_MARRIED_LIMIT = 64000;
12
13    double tax1 = 0;
14    double tax2 = 0;
15
```

tax1	tax2	income	marital status
0	0		

In lines 18 and 22, income and marital_status are initialized by input statements.

```
16    double income;
17    cout << "Please enter your income: ";
18    cin >> income;
19
20    cout << "Please enter s for single, m for married: ";
21    string marital_status;
22    cin >> marital_status;
23
```

tax1	tax2	income	marital status
0	0	80000	m

Because marital_status is not "s", we move to the else branch of the outer if statement (line 36).

```
24
25
26
27
28
29
30
31
32
```

Special Topic 6.5

The Range-Based for Loop

C++11 introduces a convenient syntax for visiting all elements in a "range" or sequence of elements. This loop displays all elements in a vector:

```
vector<int> values = {1, 4, 9, 16, 25, 36};
for (int v : values)
{
   cout << v << " ";
}
```

In each iteration of the loop, v is set to an element of the vector. Note that you do not use an index variable. The value of v is the element, not the index of the element.

If you want to modify elements, declare the loop variable as a reference:

```
for (int& v : values)
{
   v++;
}
```

This loop increments all elements of the vector.

You can use the reserved word auto, which was introduced in Special Topic 2.3, for the type of the element variable:

```
for (auto v : values) { cout << v << " "; }
```

Special Topics present optional topics and provide additional explanation of others.

The range-based for loop also works for arrays:

```
int primes[] = { 2, 3, 5, 7, 11, 13 };
for (int p : primes)

   cout << p << " ";
```

range-based for loop is a convenient shortcut for visiting or updating all elements of a or or an array. This book doesn't use it because one can achieve the same result by looping index values. But if you like the more concise form, and use C++11 or later, you should ainly consider using it.

special_topic_5 of your companion code for a program that demonstrates the range-based oop.

Computing & Society 7.1   Embedded Systems

An **embedded system** is a computer system that controls a device. The device contains a processor and other hardware and is controlled by a computer program. Unlike a personal computer, which has been designed to be flexible and run many different computer programs, the hardware and software of an embedded system are tailored to a specific device. Computer controlled devices are becoming increasingly common, ranging from washing machines to medical equipment, cell phones, automobile engines, and spacecraft.

Several challenges are specific to programming embedded systems. Most importantly, a much higher standard of quality control applies. Vendors are often unconcerned about bugs in personal computer software, because they can always make you install a patch or upgrade to the next version. But in an embedded device, that is not an option. Few consumers

would feel comfortable upgrading the software in their washing machines or automobile engines. If you ever handed in a programming assignment that you believed to be correct, only to have the instructor or grader find bugs in it, then you know how hard it is to write software that can reliably do its task for many years without a chance of changing it. Quality standards are especially important in devices whose failure would destroy property or endanger human life. Many personal computer purchasers buy computers that are fast and have a lot of storage, because the investment is paid back over time when many programs are run on the same equipment. But the hardware for an embedded device is not shared—it is dedicated to one device. A separate processor, memory, and so on, are built for every copy of the device. If it is possible to shave a few pennies off the manufacturing cost of every unit, the savings can add up quickly for devices that are pro-

duced in large volumes. Thus, the programmer of an embedded system has a much larger economic incentive to conserve resources than the desktop software programmer. Unfortunately, trying to conserve resources usually makes it harder to write programs that work correctly.

C and C++ are commonly used languages for developing embedded systems.

© Courtesy of Professor Prabal Dutta.

The Controller of an Embedded System

Computing & Society presents social and historical topics on computing—for interest and to fulfill the "historical and social context" requirements of the ACM/IEEE curriculum guidelines.

Interactive activities in the E-Text
engage students in active reading as they...

Trace through a code segment

1. In this activity, trace through the code by clicking on the line that will be executed next. Observe the inputs as they appear in the table below. They denote hours in "military time" between 0 and 23. For each input, click on the line inside the if statement that will be executed when the hour variable has that value.

Please click on the next line.

```
cin >> hour;
if (hour < 12)
{
    greeting = "Good morning";
}
else
{
    greeting = "Good afternoon";
}
cout << greeting << endl;
```

hour	greeting
11	Good morning
13	

2 correct, 0 errors

Start over

2. Consider the following statement:

```
if (hour < 21)
{
    response = "Goodbye";
}
else
{
    response = "Goodnight";
}
```

Build an example table

Determine the value of response when hour has the values given in the table below.

Complete the second column. Press Enter to submit each entry.

hour	response	Explanation
20	"Goodbye"	20 < 21, and the first branch of the statement executes.
	"Goodnight"	It is not true that 22 < 21, so the else clause executes.

Play with the following activity to learn how to find the largest value in an array. You visit each element in turn, incrementing the position i. When you find an element that is larger than the largest one that you have seen so far, store it as the largest. When you have visited all elements, you have found the largest value.

Press the Start button to see the array. Press the Start over button to try the activity again with different values.

Select the next action.

Explore common algorithms

```
     i
a:  20  30  34  60  21  55  78
```

largest:

Increment i   Store as largest   Done

1. Assume that weekdays are coded as 0 = Monday, 1 = Tuesday, ..., 4 = Friday, 5 = Saturday, 6 = Sunday. Rearrange the lines of code so that weekday is set to the next working day (Monday through Friday). Not all lines are useful.

Order the statements by dragging them into the left window. Use the guidelines for proper indenting.

```
if (weekday < 4)

{

    weekday++;

}

else

{

}
```

```
weekday = 5;

weekday = 0;

weekday = 1;

if (weekday <= 5)
```

Arrange code to fulfill a task

Complete a program and
get immediate feedback

2. What happens when the following code is executed?

```
BankAccount* p = new BankAccount(2000);
BankAccount* q = new BankAccount(1000);
q->withdraw(500);  ①
p = q;  ②
p->withdraw(200);  ③
```

Create a memory diagram

② Update the p variable.
Draw the arrow.

0 correct, 0 errors

2. Write a program that reads a word and prints whether

- it is short (fewer than 5 letters).
- it is long (at least 10 letters).
- it ends with the letter y.
- has the same first and last character.

▶ Show Code to be Completed

Complete the code in your IDE or go to [CODE CHECK] to complete the code and evaluate your

```
p =                                    BankAccount
                                       balance =  2000
q =                    BankAccount
                       balance =  500
```

One correct, 0 errors

Start over

Acknowledgments

Many thanks to Don Fowley, Graig Donini, Dan Sayre, Ryann Dannelly, David Dietz, Laura Abrams, and Billy Ray at John Wiley & Sons for their help with this project. An especially deep acknowledgment and thanks goes to Cindy Johnson for her hard work, sound judgment, and amazing attention to detail.

I am grateful to Mark Atkins, *Ivy Technical College*, Katie Livsie, *Gaston College*, Larry Morell, *Arkansas Tech University*, and Rama Olson, *Gaston College*, for their contributions to the supplemental material. Special thanks to Stephen Gilbert, *Orange Coast Community College*, for his help with the interactive exercises.

Every new edition builds on the suggestions and experiences of new and prior reviewers, contributors, and users. We are very grateful to the individuals who provided feedback, reviewed the manuscript, made valuable suggestions and contributions, and brought errors and omissions to my attention. They include:

Charles D. Allison, *Utah Valley State College*
Fred Annexstein, *University of Cincinnati*
Mark Atkins, *Ivy Technical College*
Stefano Basagni, *Northeastern University*
Noah D. Barnette, *Virginia Tech*
Susan Bickford, *Tallahassee Community College*
Ronald D. Bowman, *University of Alabama, Huntsville*
Robert Burton, *Brigham Young University*
Peter Breznay, *University of Wisconsin, Green Bay*
Richard Cacace, *Pensacola Junior College, Pensacola*
Kuang-Nan Chang, *Eastern Kentucky University*
Joseph DeLibero, *Arizona State University*
Subramaniam Dharmarajan, *Arizona State University*
Mary Dorf, *University of Michigan*
Marty Dulberg, *North Carolina State University*
William E. Duncan, *Louisiana State University*
John Estell, *Ohio Northern University*
Waleed Farag, *Indiana University of Pennsylvania*
Evan Gallagher, *Polytechnic Institute of New York University*
Stephen Gilbert, *Orange Coast Community College*
Kenneth Gitlitz, *New Hampshire Technical Institute*
Daniel Grigoletti, *DeVry Institute of Technology, Tinley Park*
Barbara Guillott, *Louisiana State University*
Charles Halsey, *Richland College*
Jon Hanrath, *Illinois Institute of Technology*
Neil Harrison, *Utah Valley University*
Jurgen Hecht, *University of Ontario*
Steve Hodges, *Cabrillo College*

Jackie Jarboe, *Boise State University*

Debbie Kaneko, *Old Dominion University*

Mir Behrad Khamesee, *University of Waterloo*

Sung-Sik Kwon, *North Carolina Central University*

Lorrie Lehman, *University of North Carolina, Charlotte*

Cynthia Lester, *Tuskegee University*

Yanjun Li, *Fordham University*

W. James MacLean, *University of Toronto*

LindaLee Massoud, *Mott Community College*

Adelaida Medlock, *Drexel University*

Charles W. Mellard, *DeVry Institute of Technology, Irving*

Larry Morell, *Arkansas Tech University*

Ethan V. Munson, *University of Wisconsin, Milwaukee*

Arun Ravindran, *University of North Carolina at Charlotte*

Philip Regalbuto, *Trident Technical College*

Don Retzlaff, *University of North Texas*

Jeff Ringenberg, *University of Michigan, Ann Arbor*

John P. Russo, *Wentworth Institute of Technology*

Kurt Schmidt, *Drexel University*

Brent Seales, *University of Kentucky*

William Shay, *University of Wisconsin, Green Bay*

Michele A. Starkey, *Mount Saint Mary College*

William Stockwell, *University of Central Oklahoma*

Jonathan Tolstedt, *North Dakota State University*

Boyd Trolinger, *Butte College*

Muharrem Uyar, *City College of New York*

Mahendra Velauthapillai, *Georgetown University*

Kerstin Voigt, *California State University, San Bernardino*

David P. Voorhees, *Le Moyne College*

Salih Yurttas, *Texas A&M University*

A special thank you to all of our class testers:

Pani Chakrapani and the students of the University of Redlands

Jim Mackowiak and the students of Long Beach City College, LAC

Suresh Muknahallipatna and the students of the University of Wyoming

Murlidharan Nair and the students of the Indiana University of South Bend

Harriette Roadman and the students of New River Community College

David Topham and the students of Ohlone College

Dennie Van Tassel and the students of Gavilan College

CONTENTS

ALPHABETICAL LIST OF SYNTAX BOXES

Programming Tips	Special Topics	Computing & Society

CHAPTER	Common Errors	How Tos and Worked Examples
6 Arrays and Vectors	Bounds Errors 184 Omitting the Column Size of a Two-Dimensional Array Parameter 212	Working with Arrays 200 Rolling the Dice 203 A World Population Table 213
7 Pointers and Structures	Confusing Pointers with the Data to Which They Point 228 Returning a Pointer to a Local Variable 234 Dangling Pointers 242 Memory Leaks 243	Working with Pointers 248 Producing a Mass Mailing 249
8 Streams	Mixing >> and getline Input 268	Processing Text Files 278 Looking for for Duplicates 281
9 Classes	Forgetting a Semicolon 296 Trying to Call a Constructor 306	Implementing a Class 310 Implementing a Bank Account Class 314
10 Inheritance	Private Inheritance 341 Replicating Base-Class Members 341 Forgetting the Base-Class Name 345 Slicing an Object 352 Failing to Override a Virtual Function 353	Developing an Inheritance Hierarchy 354 Implementing an Employee Hierarchy for Payroll Processing 359

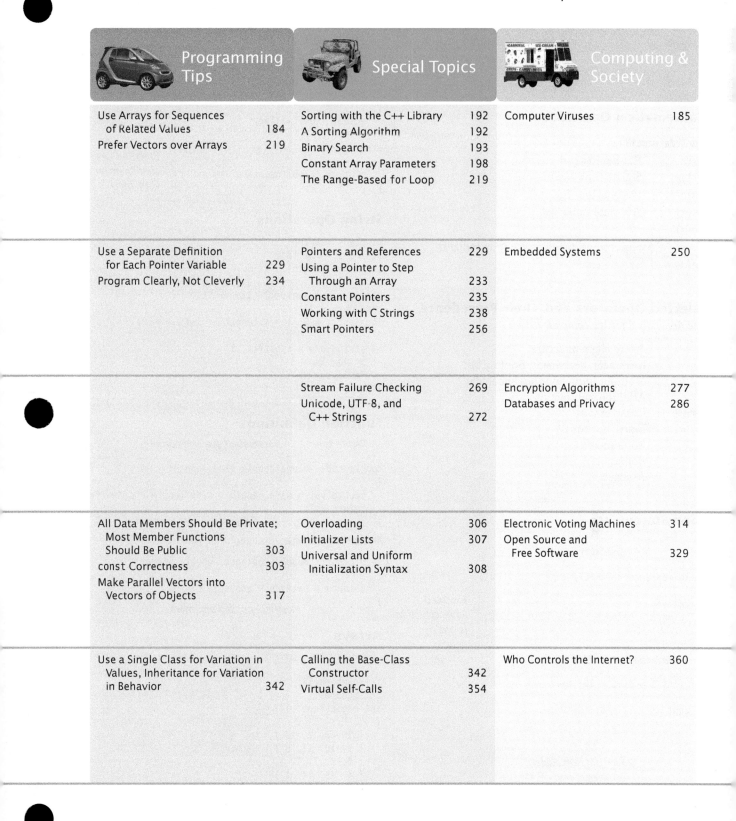

Variable and Constant Definitions

```
  Type    Name      Initial value
  /        /          /
int cans_per_pack = 6;

const double CAN_VOLUME = 0.335;
```

Mathematical Operations

```
#include <cmath>
```

pow(x, y)	Raising to a power x^y
sqrt(x)	Square root $\sqrt{x}$
log10(x)	Decimal log $\log_{10}(x)$
abs(x)	Absolute value $\lvert x\rvert$
sin(x)	
cos(x)	Sine, cosine, tangent of x (x in radians)
tan(x)	

Selected Operators and Their Precedence

(See Appendix B for the complete list.)

[]	Array element access
++ -- !	Increment, decrement, Boolean *not*
* / %	Multiplication, division, remainder
+ -	Addition, subtraction
< <= > >=	Comparisons
== !=	Equal, not equal
&&	Boolean *and*
||	Boolean *or*
=	Assignment

Loop Statements

```
             Condition
              /
while (balance < TARGET)
{
    year++;
    balance = balance * (1 + rate / 100);
}
```
Executed while condition is true

```
   Initialization  Condition  Update
     /              /          /
for (int i = 0; i < 10; i++)
{
    cout << i << endl;
}
```

Loop body executed at least once

```
do
{
    cout << "Enter a positive integer: ";
    cin >> input;
}
while (input <= 0);
```

Conditional Statement

```
           Condition
            /
if (floor >= 13)
{
    actual_floor = floor - 1;     Executed when
}                                 condition is true
else if (floor >= 0)     Second condition (optional)
{
    actual_floor = floor;
}
else
{                                 Executed when all
    cout << "Floor negative" << endl;   conditions are false
}                                       (optional)
```

String Operations

```
#include <string>
string s = "Hello";
int n = s.length(); // 5
string t = s.substr(1, 3); // "ell"
string c = s.substr(2, 1); // "l"
char ch = s[2]; // 'l'
for (int i = 0; i < s.length(); i++)
{
    string c = s.substr(i, 1);
    or char ch = s[i];
    Process c or ch
}
```

Function Definitions

```
   Return type      Parameter type and name
    /                /              /
double cube_volume(double side_length)
{
    double vol = side_length * side_length * side_length;
    return vol;            Exits function and returns result.
}
```

```
Reference parameter
                      /
void deposit(double& balance, double amount)
{
    balance = balance + amount;
}             Modifies supplied argument
```

Arrays

```
 Element type    Length
   /              /
int numbers[5];
int squares[] = { 0, 1, 4, 9, 16 };
int magic_square[4][4] =
{
    { 16, 3, 2, 13 },
    { 5, 10, 11, 8 },
    { 9, 6, 7, 12 },
    { 4, 15, 14, 1 }
};

for (int i = 0; i < size; i++)
{
    Process numbers[i]
}
```

Vectors

```cpp
#include <vector>
```
Element type — Initial values (C++ 11)
```cpp
vector<int> values = { 0, 1, 4, 9, 16 };
```
Initially empty
```cpp
vector<string> names;
```
Add elements to the end
```cpp
names.push_back("Ann");
names.push_back("Cindy"); // names.size() is now 2

names.pop_back(); // Removes last element

names[0] = "Beth"; // Use [] for element access
```

Pointers

```cpp
int n = 10;
int* p = &n; // p set to address of n
*p = 11; // n is now 11
```

Memory address

```cpp
int a[5] = { 0, 1, 4, 9, 16 };
p = a; // p points to start of a
*p = 11; // a[0] is now 11
p++; // p points to a[1]
p[2] = 11; // a[3] is now 11
```

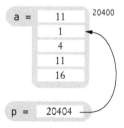

Input and Output

```cpp
#include <iostream>
cin >> x; // x can be int, double, string
cout << x;

while (cin >> x) { Process x }
if (cin.fail()) // Previous input failed
```

```cpp
#include <fstream>
string filename = ...;
ifstream in(filename);
ofstream out("output.txt");

string line; getline(in, line);
char ch; in.get(ch);
```

Range-based for Loop

An array, vector, or other container (C++ 11)
```cpp
for (int v : values)
{
    cout << v << endl;
}
```

Output Manipulators

```cpp
#include <iomanip>
```

endl	Output new line
fixed	Fixed format for floating-point
setprecision(n)	Number of digits after decimal point for fixed format
setw(n)	Field width for the next item
left	Left alignment (use for strings)
right	Right alignment (default)
setfill(ch)	Fill character (default: space)

Class Definition

```cpp
class BankAccount
{
public:
    BankAccount(double amount); // Constructor declaration
    void deposit(double amount); // Member function declaration
    double get_balance() const; // Accessor member function
    ...
private: // Data member
    double balance;
};

void BankAccount::deposit(double amount) ⎤ Member function
{                                          ⎬ definition
    balance = balance + amount;            ⎦
}
```

Inheritance

Derived class — Base class
```cpp
class CheckingAccount : public BankAccount
{
public:                    // Member function
    void deposit(double amount); // overrides base class
private:
    int transactions; // Added data member
};                    //    in derived class

void CheckingAccount::deposit(double amount)
{                                    // Calls base class
    BankAccount::deposit(amount); // member function
    transactions++;
}
```

CHAPTER 1

INTRODUCTION

© JanPietruszka/iStockphoto.

CHAPTER GOALS

To learn about the architecture of computers

To learn about machine languages and higher-level programming languages

To become familiar with your compiler

To compile and run your first C++ program

To recognize compile-time and run-time errors

To describe an algorithm with pseudocode

To understand the activity of programming

CHAPTER CONTENTS

Just as you gather tools, study a project, and make a plan for tackling it, in this chapter you will gather up the basics you need to start learning to program. After a brief introduction to computer hardware, software, and programming in general, you will learn how to write and run your first C++ program. You will also learn how to diagnose and fix programming errors, and how to use pseudocode to describe an algorithm—a step-by-step description of how to solve a problem—as you plan your programs.

1.1 What Is Programming?

Computers execute very basic instructions in rapid succession.

You have probably used a computer for work or fun. Many people use computers for everyday tasks such as electronic banking or writing a term paper. Computers are good for such tasks. They can handle repetitive chores, such as totaling up numbers or placing words on a page, without getting bored or exhausted.

The flexibility of a computer is quite an amazing phenomenon. The same machine can balance your checkbook, print your term paper, and play a game. In contrast, other machines carry out a much narrower range of tasks; a car drives and a toaster toasts. Computers can carry out a wide range of tasks because they execute different programs, each of which directs the computer to work on a specific task.

A computer program is a sequence of instructions and decisions.

The computer itself is a machine that stores data (numbers, words, pictures), interacts with devices (the monitor, the sound system, the printer), and executes programs. A **computer program** tells a computer, in minute detail, the sequence of steps that are needed to fulfill a task. The physical computer and peripheral devices are collectively called the **hardware**. The programs the computer executes are called the **software**.

Today's computer programs are so sophisticated that it is hard to believe that they are composed of extremely primitive operations. A typical operation may be one of the following:

- Put a red dot at this screen position.
- Add up these two numbers.
- If this value is negative, continue the program at a certain instruction.

The computer user has the illusion of smooth interaction because a program contains a huge number of such operations, and because the computer can execute them at great speed.

Programming is the act of designing and implementing computer programs.

The act of designing and implementing computer programs is called *programming*. In this book, you will learn how to program a computer—that is, how to direct the computer to execute tasks.

To write a computer game with motion and sound effects or a word processor that supports fancy fonts and pictures is a complex task that requires a team of many highly skilled programmers. Your first programming efforts will be more mundane. The concepts and skills you learn in this book form an important foundation, and you should not be disappointed if your first programs do not rival the sophisticated software that is familiar to you. Actually, you will find that there is an immense thrill even in simple programming tasks. It is an amazing experience to see the computer precisely and quickly carry out a task that would take you hours of drudgery, to make small changes in a program that lead to immediate improvements, and to see the computer become an extension of your mental powers.

1.2 The Anatomy of a Computer

To understand the programming process, you need to have a rudimentary understanding of the building blocks that make up a computer. We will look at a personal computer. Larger computers have faster, larger, or more powerful components, but they have fundamentally the same design.

At the heart of the computer lies the **central processing unit** (CPU) (see Figure 1). It consists of a single *chip*, or a small number of chips. A computer chip (integrated circuit) is a component with a plastic or metal housing, metal connectors, and inside wiring made principally from silicon. For a CPU chip, the inside wiring is enormously complicated. For example, the Pentium chip (a popular CPU for personal computers at the time of this writing) is composed of several million structural elements, called *transistors*.

> The central processing unit (CPU) performs program control and data processing.

The CPU performs program control and data processing. That is, the CPU locates and executes the program instructions; it carries out arithmetic operations such as addition, subtraction, multiplication, and division; it fetches data from external memory or devices and stores data back.

> Storage devices include memory and secondary storage.

There are two kinds of storage. Primary storage, or memory, is made from electronic circuits that can store data, provided they are supplied with electric power. **Secondary storage**, usually a **hard disk** (see Figure 2) or a solid-state drive, provides slower and less expensive storage that persists without electricity. A hard disk consists of rotating platters, which are coated with a magnetic material. A solid-state drive uses electronic components that can retain information without power, and without moving parts.

© Amorphis/iStockphoto.

Figure 1   Central Processing Unit

Figure 2
A Hard Disk   © PhotoDisc, Inc./Getty Images.

Programs and data are typically stored on the hard disk and loaded into memory when the program starts. The program then updates the data in memory and writes the modified data back to the hard disk.

To interact with a human user, a computer requires peripheral devices. The computer transmits information (called *output*) to the user through a display screen, speakers, and printers. The user can enter information (called *input*) by using a keyboard or a pointing device such as a mouse.

Some computers are self-contained units, whereas others are interconnected through *networks*. Through the network cabling, the computer can read data and programs from central storage locations or send data to other computers. For the user of a networked computer it may not even be obvious which data reside on the computer itself and which are transmitted through the network.

Figure 3 gives a schematic overview of the architecture of a personal computer. Program instructions and data (such as text, numbers, audio, or video) reside in secondary storage or elsewhere on the network. When a program is started, its instructions are brought into memory, where the CPU can read them. The CPU reads and executes one instruction at a time. As directed by these instructions, the CPU reads data, modifies it, and writes it back to memory or secondary storage. Some program instructions will cause the CPU to place dots on the display screen or printer or to vibrate the speaker. As these actions happen many times over and at great speed, the human user will perceive images and sound. Some program instructions read user input from the keyboard, mouse, touch sensor, or microphone. The program analyzes the nature of these inputs and then executes the next appropriate instruction.

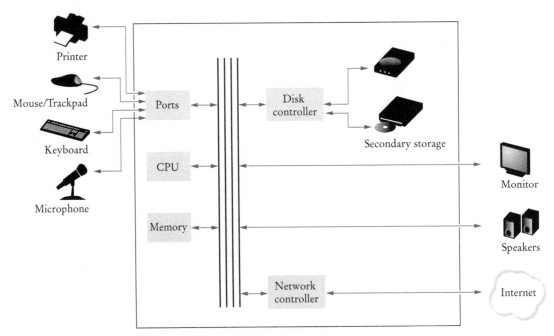

Figure 3 Schematic Design of a Personal Computer

Computing & Society 1.1   Computers Are Everywhere

When computers were first invented in the 1940s, a computer filled an entire room. Figure 4 shows the ENIAC (electronic numerical integrator and computer), completed in 1946 at the University of Pennsylvania. The ENIAC was used by the military to compute the trajectories of projectiles. Nowadays, computing facilities of search engines, Internet shops, and social networks fill huge buildings called data centers. At the other end of the spectrum, computers are all around us. Your cell phone has a computer inside, as do many credit cards and fare cards for public transit. A modern car has several computers—to control the engine, brakes, lights, and radio.

The advent of ubiquitous computing changed many aspects of our lives. Factories used to employ people to do repetitive assembly tasks that are today carried out by computer-controlled robots, operated by a few people who know how to work with those computers. Books, music, and movies nowadays are often consumed on computers, and computers are almost always involved in their production. The book that you are reading right now could not have

© Maurice Savage/Alamy Stock Photo.

This transit card contains a computer.

been written without computers.

Knowing about computers and how to program them has become an essential skill in many careers. Engineers design computer-controlled cars and medical equipment that preserve lives. Computer scientists develop programs that help people come together to support social causes. For example, activists used social networks to share videos showing abuse by repressive regimes, and this information was instrumental in changing public opinion.

As computers, large and small, become ever more embedded in our everyday lives, it is increasingly important for everyone to understand how they work, and how to work with them. As you use this book to learn how to program a computer, you will develop a good understanding of computing fundamentals that will make you a more informed citizen and, perhaps, a computing professional.

© UPPA/Photoshot.

Figure 4   The ENIAC

1.3 Machine Code and Programming Languages

On the most basic level, computer instructions are extremely primitive. The processor executes *machine instructions*. A typical sequence of machine instructions is

1. Move the contents of memory location 40000 into the CPU.
2. If that value is greater than 100, continue with the instruction that is stored in memory location 11280.

Actually, machine instructions are encoded as numbers so that they can be stored in memory. On a Pentium processor, this sequence of instruction is encoded as the sequence of numbers

Computer programs are stored as machine instructions in a code that depends on the processor type.

$$161 \; 40000 \; 45 \; 100 \; 127 \; 11280$$

On a processor from a different manufacturer, the encoding would be different. When this kind of processor fetches this sequence of numbers, it decodes them and executes the associated sequence of commands.

How can we communicate the command sequence to the computer? The simplest method is to place the actual numbers into the computer memory. This is, in fact, how the very earliest computers worked. However, a long program is composed of thousands of individual commands, and it is a tedious and error-prone affair to look up the numeric codes for all commands and place the codes manually into memory. As already mentioned, computers are really good at automating tedious and error-prone activities. It did not take long for computer scientists to realize that the computers themselves could be harnessed to help in the programming process.

Computer scientists devised **high-level programming languages** that allow programmers to describe tasks, using a **syntax** that is more closely related to the problems to be solved. In this book, we will use the C++ programming language, which was developed by Bjarne Stroustrup in the 1980s.

C++ is a general-purpose language that is in widespread use for systems and embedded programming.

Over the years, C++ has grown by the addition of many features. A standardization process culminated in the publication of the international C++ standard in 1998. A minor update to the standard was issued in 2003. A major revision came to fruition in 2011, followed by updates in 2014 and 2017. At this time, C++ is the most commonly used language for developing system software such as databases and operating systems. Just as importantly, C++ is commonly used for programming "embedded systems", computers that control devices such as automobile engines or robots.

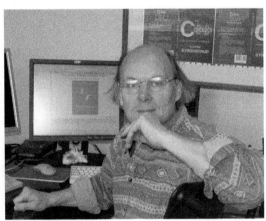

© Courtesy of Bjarne Stroustrup.

Bjarne Stroustrup

Here is a typical statement in C++:

```
if (int_rate > 100) { cout << "Interest rate error"; }
```

High-level programming languages are independent of the processor.

This means, "If the interest rate is over 100, display an error message". A special computer program, a **compiler**, translates this high-level description into machine instructions for a particular processor.

High-level languages are independent of the underlying hardware. C++ instructions work equally well on an Intel Pentium and a processor in a cell phone. Of course, the compiler-generated machine instructions are different, but the programmer who uses the compiler need not worry about these differences.

1.4 Becoming Familiar with Your Programming Environment

Set aside some time to become familiar with the programming environment that you will use for your class work.

Many students find that the tools they need as programmers are very different from the software with which they are familiar. You should spend some time making yourself familiar with your programming environment. Because computer systems vary widely, this book can give only an outline of the steps you need to follow. It is a good idea to participate in a hands-on lab, or to ask a knowledgeable friend to give you a tour.

Step 1 Start the C++ development environment.

Computer systems differ greatly in this regard. On many computers there is an **integrated development environment** in which you can write and test your programs. On other computers you first launch an **editor**, a program that functions like a word processor, in which you can enter your C++ instructions; then open a *console window* and type commands to execute your program. Other programming environments are online. In such an environment, you write programs in a web browser. The programs are then executed on a remote machine, and the results are displayed in the web browser window. You need to find out how to get started with your environment.

Step 2 Write a simple program.

The traditional choice for the very first program in a new programming language is a program that displays a simple greeting: "Hello, World!". Let us follow that tradition. Here is the "Hello, World!" program in C++:

```cpp
#include <iostream>

using namespace std;

int main()
{
```

```
        cout << "Hello, World!" << endl;
        return 0;
    }
```

We will examine this program in the next section.

No matter which programming environment you use, you begin your activity by typing the program statements into an editor window.

An editor is a program for entering and modifying text, such as a C++ program.

Create a new file and call it `hello.cpp`, using the steps that are appropriate for your environment. (If your environment requires that you supply a project name in addition to the file name, use the name `hello` for the project.) Enter the program instructions *exactly* as they are given above. Alternatively, locate an electronic copy of the program in the source files for this book and paste it into your editor. (You can download the full set of files for this book from its companion site at `wiley.com/go/bclo3`.)

C++ is case sensitive. You must be careful about distinguishing between upper- and lowercase letters.

As you write this program, pay careful attention to the various symbols, and keep in mind that C++ is **case sensitive**. You must enter upper- and lowercase letters exactly as they appear in the program listing. You cannot type `MAIN` or `Endl`. If you are not careful, you will run into problems—see Common Error 1.2.

Step 3   Compile and run the program.

The compiler translates C++ programs into machine code.

The process for building and running a C++ program depends greatly on your programming environment. In some integrated development environments, you simply push a button. In other environments, you may have to type commands. When you run the test program, the message

```
Hello, World!
```

will appear somewhere on the screen (see Figures 5 and 6).

Figure 5   Running the `hello` Program in an Integrated Development Environment

```
Terminal                                              _□X
File  Edit  View  Terminal  Help
~$ cd cs1/bookcode/ch01
~/cs1/bookcode/ch01$ g++ -o hello hello.cpp
~/cs1/bookcode/ch01$ ./hello
Hello, World!
~/cs1/bookcode/ch01$ ▯
```

Figure 6   Compiling and Running the hello Program in a Console Window

> The linker combines machine code with library code into an executable program.

It is useful to know what goes on behind the scenes when your program gets built. First, the compiler translates the C++ **source code** (that is, the statements that you wrote) into machine instructions. The **machine code** contains only the translation of the code that you wrote. That is not enough to actually run the program. To display a string on a window, quite a bit of low-level activity is necessary. The implementors of your C++ development environment provided a library that includes the definition of cout and its functionality. A **library** is a collection of code that has been programmed and translated by someone else, ready for you to use in your program. (More complicated programs are built from more than one machine code file and more than one library.) A program called the **linker** takes your machine code and the necessary parts from the C++ library and builds an **executable file**. (Figure 7 gives an overview of these steps.) The executable file is usually called hello.exe or hello, depending on your computer system. You can run the executable program even after you exit the C++ development environment.

Step 4   Organize your work.

As a programmer, you write programs, try them out, and improve them. You store your programs in *files*. Files have names, and the rules for legal names differ from one system to another. Some systems allow spaces in file names; others don't. Some distinguish between upper- and lowercase letters; others don't. Most C++ compilers require that C++ files end in an **extension** .cpp, .cxx, .cc, or .C; for example, demo.cpp.

Editor   Compiler   Machine code   Linker   Executable Program

Source File   Library files

Figure 7   From Source Code to Executable Program

Files are stored in **folders** or **directories**. A folder can contain files as well as other folders, which themselves can contain more files and folders (see Figure 8). This hierarchy can be quite large, and you need not be concerned with all of its branches.

However, you should create folders for organizing your work. It is a good idea to make a separate folder for your programming class. Inside that folder, make a separate folder for each assignment.

Some programming environments place your programs into a default location if you don't specify a folder yourself. In that case, you need to find out where those files are located.

Be sure that you understand where your files are located in the folder hierarchy. This information is essential when you submit files for grading, and for making *backup copies*.

You will spend many hours creating and improving C++ programs. It is easy to delete a file by accident, and occasionally files are lost because of a computer malfunction. To avoid the frustration of recreating lost files, get in the habit of making backup copies of your work on a memory stick or on another computer.

> Develop a strategy for keeping backup copies of your work before disaster strikes.

```
home
  cay
    cs1
      homework1
        face.cpp
      textbook
        ch01
          sec04
            hello
            hello.cpp
        ch02
          how_to_1
            vending.cpp
```

Figure 8   A Folder Hierarchy

Programming Tip 1.1

Backup Copies

Backing up files on a memory stick is an easy and convenient storage method for many people. Another increasingly popular form of backup is Internet file storage. Here are a few pointers to keep in mind.

© Tatiana Popova/iStockphoto.

- *Back up often.* Backing up a file takes only a few seconds, and you will hate yourself if you have to spend many hours recreating work that you could have saved easily. I recommend that you back up your work once every thirty minutes.

- *Rotate backups.* Use more than one directory for backups, and rotate them. That is, first back up to the first directory. Then back up to the second directory. Then use the third, and then go back to the first. That way you always have three recent backups. If your recent changes made matters worse, you can then go back to the older version.

- *Pay attention to the backup direction.* Backing up involves copying files from one place to another. It is important that you do this right—that is, copy from your work location to the backup location. If you do it the wrong way, you will overwrite a newer file with an older version.

- *Check your backups once in a while.* Double-check that your backups are where you think they are. There is nothing more frustrating than to find out that the backups are not there when you need them.

- *Relax, then restore.* When you lose a file and need to restore it from backup, you are likely to be in an unhappy, nervous state. Take a deep breath and think through the recovery process before you start. It is not uncommon for an agitated computer user to wipe out the last backup when trying to restore a damaged file.

1.5 Analyzing Your First Program

In this section, we will analyze the first C++ program in detail. Here again is the source code:

sec05/hello.cpp

```
1  #include <iostream>
2
3  using namespace std;
4
5  int main()
6  {
7     cout << "Hello, World!" << endl;
8     return 0;
9  }
```

The first line,

```
#include <iostream>
```

tells the compiler to include a service for "stream input/output". You will learn in Chapter 8 what a stream is. For now, you should simply remember to add this line into all programs that perform input or output.

The next line,

```
using namespace std;
```

tells the compiler to use the "standard namespace". Namcspaces are a mechanism for avoiding naming conflicts in large programs. You need not be concerned about namespaces. For the programs that you will be writing in this book, you will always use the standard namespace. Simply add `using namespace std;` at the top of every program that you write, just below the `#include` directives.

The construction

```
int main()
{
   . . .
   return 0;
}
```

defines a *function* called `main` that "returns" an "integer" (that is, a whole number without a fractional part, called `int` in C++) with value 0. This value indicates that the program finished successfully. A **function** is a collection of programming instructions that carry out a particular task. Every C++ program must have a `main` function. Most C++ programs contain other functions besides `main`, but it will take us until Chapter 5 to discuss functions and return values.

Every C++ program contains a function called main.

For now, it is a good idea to consider all these parts as the "plumbing" that is necessary to write a simple program. Simply place the code that you want to execute inside the braces of the `main` function. (The basic structure of a C++ program is shown in Syntax 1.1.)

Syntax 1.1   C++ Program

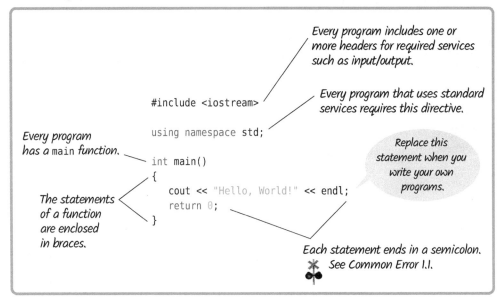

Every program includes one or more headers for required services such as input/output.

Every program that uses standard services requires this directive.

```
#include <iostream>

using namespace std;

int main()
{
    cout << "Hello, World!" << endl;
    return 0;
}
```

Every program has a main function.

The statements of a function are enclosed in braces.

Replace this statement when you write your own programs.

Each statement ends in a semicolon. ✳ See Common Error 1.1.

**Use cout and the <<
operator to display
values on the screen.**

To display values on the screen, you use an entity called cout and the << operator (sometimes called the *insertion* operator). For example, the statement

```
cout << 39 + 3;
```

displays the number 42.

The statement

**Enclose text strings
in quotation marks.**

```
cout << "Hello";
```

displays the **string** Hello. A string is a sequence of characters. You must enclose the contents of a string inside quotation marks so that the compiler knows you literally mean the text "Hello" and not a function with the same name.

**Use + to add two
numbers and *
to multiply two
numbers.**

You can send more than one item to cout. Use a << before each one of them. For example,

```
cout << "The answer is " << 6 * 7;
```

displays The answer is 42 (in C++, the * denotes multiplication).

**Send endl to cout
to end a line of
displayed output.**

The endl symbol denotes an *end of line* marker. When this marker is sent to cout, the cursor is moved to the first column in the next screen row. If you don't use an end of line marker, then the next displayed item will simply follow the current string on the same line. In this program we only printed one item, but in general we will want to print multiple items, and it is a good habit to end all lines of output with an end of line marker.

**End each statement
with a semicolon.**

Finally, note that the output and return statements end in a semicolon, just as every English sentence ends in a period.

Syntax 1.2   Output Statement

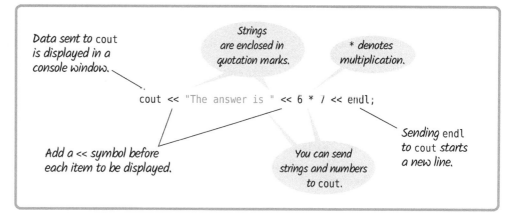

Data sent to cout is displayed in a console window.

Strings are enclosed in quotation marks.

* denotes multiplication.

```
cout << "The answer is " << 6 * 7 << endl;
```

Add a << symbol before each item to be displayed.

You can send strings and numbers to cout.

Sending endl to cout starts a new line.

Common Error 1.1

Omitting Semicolons

In C++, statements such as output or return statements end in a semicolon. Forgetting to type a semicolon is a common error. It confuses the compiler because the compiler uses the semicolon to find where one statement ends and the next one starts. The compiler does not use line ends or closing braces to recognize the ends of statements. For example, the compiler considers

```
cout << "Hello, World!" << endl
return 0;
```

a single statement, as if you had written

```
cout << "Hello, World!" << endl return 0;
```

and then it doesn't understand that statement, because it does not expect the word return in the middle of an output command. The remedy is simple. Just scan every statement for a terminating semicolon, just as you would check that every English sentence ends in a period.

Sometimes, the error message that flags the missing semicolon is displayed in the following line. When you see such a message, be sure to check the preceding line as well.

Special Topic 1.1

Escape Sequences

How can you display a string containing quotation marks, such as

```
Hello, "World"
```

You can't use

```
cout << "Hello, "World"";
```

As soon as the compiler reads "Hello, ", it thinks the string is finished, and then it gets all confused about World. Compilers have a one-track mind, and if a simple analysis of the input doesn't make sense to them, they just refuse to go on, and they report an error. In contrast, a human would probably realize that the second and third quotation marks were supposed to be part of the string.

Well, how do we then display quotation marks on the screen? The designers of C++ provided an escape hatch. Mark each quotation mark with a backslash character (\), like this:

```
cout << "Hello, \"World\"";
```

The sequence \" denotes a literal quote, not the end of a string. Such a sequence is called an **escape sequence**.

There are a few other escape sequences. If you actually want to show a backslash on the display, you use the escape sequence \\. The statement

```
cout << "Hello\\World";
```

prints

```
Hello\World
```

Finally, the escape sequence \n denotes a **newline** character that starts a new line on the screen. The command

```
cout << "Hello, World!\n";
```

has the same effect as

```
cout << "Hello, World!" << endl;
```

1.6 Errors

Programming languages follow very strict conventions. When you talk to another person, and you scramble or omit a word or two, your conversation partner will usually still understand what you have to say. But when you make an error in a C++ program, the compiler will not try to guess what you meant. (This is actually a good thing. If the compiler were to guess wrongly, the resulting program would do the wrong thing—quite possibly with disastrous effects.) In this section, you will learn how to cope with errors in your program.

Experiment a little with the `hello.cpp` program. What happens if you make a typing error such as

© Martin Carlsson/iStockphoto.

Programmers spend a fair amount of time fixing compile-time and run-time errors.

```
cot << "Hello, World!" << endl;
cout << "Hello, World! << endl;
cout << "Hollo, World!" << endl;
```

A compile-time error
is a violation of
the programming
language rules that
is detected by
the compiler.

In the first case, the compiler will complain that it has no clue what you mean by cot. The exact wording of the error message is dependent on the compiler, but it might be something like "Undefined symbol cot". This is a **compile-time error** or **syntax error**. Something is wrong according to the language rules, and the compiler finds it. When the compiler finds one or more errors, it will not translate the program to machine code, and as a consequence there is no program to run. You must fix the error and compile again. It is common to go through several rounds of fixing compile-time errors before compilation succeeds for the first time.

If the compiler finds an error, it will not simply stop and give up. It will try to report as many errors as it can find, so you can fix them all at once. Sometimes, however, one error throws it off track. This is likely to happen with the error in the second line. Because the programmer forgot the closing quote, the compiler will keep looking for the end of the string. In such cases, it is common for the compiler to emit bogus error reports for neighboring lines. You should fix only those error messages that make sense to you and then recompile.

The error in the third line is of a different kind. The program will compile and run, but its output will be wrong. It will print

```
Hollo, World!
```

A run-time error causes a program to take an action that the programmer did not intend.

This is a **run-time error**. The program is syntactically correct and does something, but it doesn't do what it is supposed to do. The compiler cannot find the error, and it must be flushed out when the program runs, by testing it and carefully looking at its output. Because run-time errors are caused by logical flaws in the program, they are often called **logic errors**. Some kinds of run-time errors are so severe that they generate an **exception**: a signal from the processor that aborts the program with an error message. For example, if your program includes the statement `cout << 1 / 0;` your program may terminate with a "divide by zero" exception.

During program development, errors are unavoidable. Once a program is longer than a few lines, it requires superhuman concentration to enter it correctly without slipping up once. You will find yourself omitting semicolons or quotes more often than you would like, but the compiler will track down these problems for you.

The programmer is responsible for inspecting and testing the program to guard against run-time errors.

Run-time errors are more troublesome. The compiler will not find them—in fact, the compiler will cheerfully translate any program as long as its syntax is correct— but the resulting program will do something wrong. It is the responsibility of the program author to test the program and find any run-time errors. Program testing is an important topic that you will encounter many times in this book.

Common Error 1.2

Misspelling Words

If you accidentally misspell a word, strange things may happen, and it may not always be completely obvious from the error messages what went wrong. Here is a good example of how simple spelling errors can cause trouble:

```
#include <iostream>

using namespace std;

int Main()
{
   cout << "Hello, World!" << endl;
   return 0;
}
```

This code defines a function called Main. The compiler will not consider this to be the same as the main function, because Main starts with an uppercase letter and the C++ language is **case sensitive**. Upper- and lowercase letters are considered to be completely different from each other, and to the compiler Main is no better match for main than rain. The compiler will compile your Main function, but when the linker is ready to build the executable file, it will complain about the missing main function and refuse to link the program. Of course, the message "missing main function" should give you a clue where to look for the error.

If you get an error message that seems to indicate that the compiler is on the wrong track, it is a good idea to check for spelling and capitalization. In C++, most names use only lowercase letters. If you misspell the name of a symbol (for example out instead of cout), the compiler will complain about an "undefined symbol" (or, on some systems, an "undeclared identifier" or "not declared in this scope"). This error message is usually a good clue that you made a spelling error.

1.7 Problem Solving: Algorithm Design

You will soon learn how to program calculations and decision making in C++. But before we look at the mechanics of implementing computations in the next chapter, let's consider how you can describe the steps that are necessary for finding the solution to a problem.

1.7.1 The Algorithm Concept

You may have run across advertisements that encourage you to pay for a computerized service that matches you up with a love partner. Think how this might work. You fill out a form and send it in. Others do the same. The data are processed by a computer program. Is it reasonable to assume that the computer can perform the task of finding the best match for you? Suppose your younger brother, not the computer, had all the forms on his desk. What instructions could you give him? You can't say, "Find the best-looking person who likes inline skating and browsing the Internet". There is no objective standard for good looks, and your brother's opinion (or that

© mammamaart/iStockphoto.

Finding the perfect partner is not a problem that a computer can solve.

of a computer program analyzing the photos of prospective partners) will likely be different from yours. If you can't give written instructions for someone to solve the problem, there is no way the computer can magically find the right solution. The computer can only do what you tell it to do. It just does it faster, without getting bored or exhausted.

For that reason, a computerized match-making service cannot guarantee to find the optimal match for you. Instead, you may be presented with a set of potential partners who share common interests with you. That is a task that a computer program can solve.

In order for a computer program to provide an answer to a problem that computes an answer, it must follow a sequence of steps that is

- Unambiguous
- Executable
- Terminating

An algorithm for solving a problem is a sequence of steps that is unambiguous, executable, and terminating.

The step sequence is *unambiguous* when there are precise instructions for what to do at each step and where to go next. There is no room for guesswork or personal opinion. A step is *executable* when it can be carried out in practice. For example, a computer can list all people that share your hobbies, but it can't predict who will be your life-long partner. Finally, a sequence of steps is *terminating* if it will eventually come to an end. A program that keeps working without delivering an answer is clearly not useful.

A sequence of steps that is unambiguous, executable, and terminating is called an **algorithm**. Although there is no algorithm for finding a partner, many problems do have algorithms for solving them. The next section gives an example.

© Claudiad/iStockphoto.

An algorithm is a recipe for finding a solution.

1.7.2 An Algorithm for Solving an Investment Problem

Consider the following investment problem:

> You put $10,000 into an account that earns 5 percent interest per year. How many years does it take for the account balance to be double the original?

Could you solve this problem by hand? Sure, you could. You figure out the balance as follows:

year	interest	balance
0		10000
1	10000.00 x 0.05 = 500.00	10000.00 + 500.00 = 10500.00
2	10500.00 x 0.05 = 525.00	10500.00 + 525.00 = 11025.00
3	11025.00 x 0.05 = 551.25	11025.00 + 551.25 = 11576.25
4	11576.25 x 0.05 = 578.81	11576.25 + 578.81 = 12155.06

You keep going until the balance is at least $20,000. Then the last number in the year column is the answer.

Of course, carrying out this computation is intensely boring to you or your younger brother. But computers are very good at carrying out repetitive calculations quickly and flawlessly. What is important to the computer is a description of the steps for finding the solution. Each step must be clear and unambiguous, requiring no guesswork. Here is such a description:

Set year to 0, balance to 10000.

year	interest	balance
0		10000

> *While the balance is less than $20,000*
>   *Add 1 to the year.*
>   *Set the interest to balance x 0.05 (i.e., 5 percent interest).*
>   *Add the interest to the balance.*

year	interest	balance
0		10000
1	500.00	10500.00
14	942.82	19799.32
(15)	989.96	20789.28

> *Report year as the answer.*

These steps are not yet in a language that a computer can understand, but you will soon learn how to formulate them in C++. This informal description is called **pseudocode**. We examine the rules for writing pseudocode in the next section.

1.7.3 Pseudocode

Pseudocode is an informal description of a sequence of steps for solving a problem.

There are no strict requirements for pseudocode because it is read by human readers, not a computer program. Here are the kinds of pseudocode statements and how we will use them in this book:

- Use statements such as the following to describe how a value is set or changed:

  > *total cost = purchase price + operating cost*
  > *Multiply the balance value by 1.05.*
  > *Remove the first and last character from the word.*

- Describe decisions and repetitions as follows:

  > *If total cost 1 < total cost 2*
  > *While the balance is less than $20,000*
  > *For each picture in the sequence*

  Use indentation to indicate which statements should be selected or repeated:

  > *For each car*
  >   *operating cost = 10 x annual fuel cost*
  >   *total cost = purchase price + operating cost*

  Here, the indentation indicates that both statements should be executed for each car.

- Indicate results with statements such as:

  > *Choose car2.*
  > *Report year as the answer.*

1.7.4 From Algorithms to Programs

In Section 1.7.2, we developed pseudocode for finding how long it takes to double an investment. Let's double-check that the pseudocode represents an algorithm; that is, that it is unambiguous, executable, and terminating.

Our pseudocode is unambiguous. It simply tells how to update values in each step. The pseudocode is executable because we use a fixed interest rate. Had we said to use the actual interest rate that will be charged in years to come, and not a fixed rate of 5 percent per year, the instructions would not have been executable. There is no way for anyone to know what the interest rate will be in the future. It requires a bit of thought to see that the steps are terminating: With every step, the balance goes up by at least $500, so eventually it must reach $20,000.

Therefore, we have found an algorithm to solve our investment problem, and we know we can find the solution by programming a computer. The existence of an algorithm is an essential prerequisite for programming a task. You need to first discover and describe an algorithm for the task before you start programming (see Figure 9). In the chapters that follow, you will learn how to express algorithms in the C++ language.

Understand the problem

Develop and describe an algorithm

Test the algorithm with simple inputs

Translate the algorithm into C++

Compile and test your program

Figure 9 The Software Development Process

HOW TO 1.1

Describing an Algorithm with Pseudocode

This is the first of many "How To" sections in this book that give you step-by-step procedures for carrying out important tasks in developing computer programs.

Before you are ready to write a program in C++, you need to develop an algorithm—a method for arriving at a solution for a particular problem. Describe the algorithm in pseudocode—a sequence of precise steps formulated in English. To illustrate, we'll devise an algorithm for this problem:

Problem Statement You have the choice of buying one of two cars. One is more fuel efficient than the other, but also more expensive. You know the price and fuel efficiency (in miles per gallon, mpg) of both cars. You plan to keep the car for ten years. Assume a price of $4 per gallon of gas and usage of 15,000 miles per year. You will pay cash for the car and not worry about financing costs. Which car is the better deal?

© dlewis33/Getty Images.

Step 1 Determine the inputs and outputs.

In our sample problem, we have these inputs:

- *purchase price1* and *fuel efficiency1*, the price and fuel efficiency (in mpg) of the first car
- *purchase price2* and *fuel efficiency2*, the price and fuel efficiency of the second car

We simply want to know which car is the better buy. That is the desired output.

Step 2   Break down the problem into smaller tasks.

For each car, we need to know the total cost of driving it. Let's do this computation separately for each car. Once we have the total cost for each car, we can decide which car is the better deal.

The total cost for each car is *purchase price + operating cost*.

We assume a constant usage and gas price for ten years, so the operating cost depends on the cost of driving the car for one year.

The operating cost is *10 x annual fuel cost*.

The annual fuel cost is *price per gallon x annual fuel consumed*.

The annual fuel consumed is *annual miles driven / fuel efficiency*. For example, if you drive the car for 15,000 miles and the fuel efficiency is 15 miles/gallon, the car consumes 1,000 gallons.

Step 3   Describe each subtask in pseudocode.

In your description, arrange the steps so that any intermediate values are computed before they are needed in other computations. For example, list the step

total cost = purchase price + operating cost

after you have computed *operating cost*.

Here is the algorithm for deciding which car to buy:

```
For each car, compute the total cost as follows:
    annual fuel consumed = annual miles driven / fuel efficiency
    annual fuel cost = price per gallon x annual fuel consumed
    operating cost = 10 x annual fuel cost
    total cost = purchase price + operating cost
If total cost of car1 < total cost of car2
    Choose car1.
Else
    Choose car2.
```

Step 4   Test your pseudocode by working a problem.

We will use these sample values:

Car 1: $25,000, 50 miles/gallon
Car 2: $20,000, 30 miles/gallon

Here is the calculation for the cost of the first car:

```
annual fuel consumed = annual miles driven / fuel efficiency = 15000 / 50 = 300
annual fuel cost = price per gallon x annual fuel consumed = 4 x 300 = 1200
operating cost = 10 x annual fuel cost = 10 x 1200 = 12000
total cost = purchase price + operating cost = 25000 + 12000 = 37000
```

Similarly, the total cost for the second car is $40,000. Therefore, the output of the algorithm is to choose car 1.

The following Worked Example demonstrates how to use the concepts in this chapter and the steps in the How To to solve another problem. In this case, you will see how to develop an algorithm for laying tile in an alternating pattern of colors. You should read the Worked Example to review what you have learned, and for help in tackling another problem.

In future chapters, Worked Examples are indicated by a brief description of the problem tackled in the example, plus a reminder to view it in your eText or download it from the book's companion Web site at wiley.com/go/bclo3. You will find any code related to the Worked Example included with the book's companion code for the chapter. When you see the Worked Example description, go to the example and view the code to learn how the problem was solved.

WORKED EXAMPLE 1.1

Writing an Algorithm for Tiling a Floor

Problem Statement   Your task is to tile a rectangular bathroom floor with alternating black and white tiles measuring 4 × 4 inches. The floor dimensions, measured in inches, are multiples of 4.

Step 1   Determine the inputs and outputs.

The inputs are the floor dimensions (length × width), measured in inches. The output is a tiled floor.

Step 2   Break down the problem into smaller tasks.

A natural subtask is to lay one row of tiles. If you can solve that task, then you can solve the problem by laying one row next to the other, starting from a wall, until you reach the opposite wall.

How do you lay a row? Start with a tile at one wall. If it is white, put a black one next to it. If it is black, put a white one next to it. Keep going until you reach the opposite wall. The row will contain *width / 4* tiles.

© rban/iStockphoto.

Step 3   Describe each subtask in pseudocode.

In the pseudocode, you want to be more precise about exactly where the tiles are placed.

> *Place a black tile in the northwest corner.*
> *While the floor is not yet filled, repeat the following steps:*
> > *Repeat this step width / 4 – 1 times:*
> > > *If the previously placed tile was white*
> > > > *Pick a black tile.*
> > > *Else*
> > > > *Pick a white tile.*
> > > *Place the picked tile east of the previously placed tile.*
> > *Locate the tile at the beginning of the row that you just placed. If there is space to the south, place a tile of the opposite color below it.*

Step 4   Test your pseudocode by working a problem.

Suppose you want to tile an area measuring 20 × 12 inches.
   The first step is to place a black tile in the northwest corner.

Next, alternate four tiles until reaching the east wall. *(width / 4 − 1 = 20 / 4 − 1 = 4)*

There is room to the south. Locate the tile at the beginning of the completed row. It is black. Place a white tile south of it.

1	2	3	4	5
6				

Complete the row.

1	2	3	4	5
6	7	8	9	10

There is still room to the south. Locate the tile at the beginning of the completed row. It is white. Place a black tile south of it.

Complete the row.

1	2	3	4	5
6	7	8	9	10
11	12	13	14	15

Now the entire floor is filled, and you are done.

CHAPTER SUMMARY

Define "computer program" and programming.

- Computers execute very basic instructions in rapid succession.
- A computer program is a sequence of instructions and decisions.
- Programming is the act of designing and implementing computer programs.

Describe the components of a computer.

- The central processing unit (CPU) performs program control and data processing.
- Storage devices include memory and secondary storage.

Describe the process of translating high-level languages to machine code.

- Computer programs are stored as machine instructions in a code that depends on the processor type.
- C++ is a general-purpose language that is in widespread use for systems and embedded programming.
- High-level programming languages are independent of the processor.

Become familiar with your C++ programming environment.

- Set aside some time to become familiar with the programming environment that you will use for your class work.
- An editor is a program for entering and modifying text, such as a C++ program.
- C++ is case sensitive. You must be careful about distinguishing between upper- and lowercase letters.
- The compiler translates C++ programs into machine code.
- The linker combines machine code with library code into an executable program.

- Develop a strategy for keeping backup copies of your work before disaster strikes.

Describe the building blocks of a simple program.

- Every C++ program contains a function called main.
- Use cout and the << operator to display values on the screen.
- Enclose text strings in quotation marks.
- Use + to add two numbers and * to multiply two numbers.
- Send endl to cout to end a line of displayed output.
- End each statement with a semicolon.

Classify program errors as compile-time and run-time errors.

- A compile-time error is a violation of the programming language rules that is detected by the compiler.
- A run-time error causes a program to take an action that the programmer did not intend.
- The programmer is responsible for inspecting and testing the program to guard against run-time errors.

Write pseudocode for simple algorithms.

- An algorithm for solving a problem is a sequence of steps that is unambiguous, executable, and terminating.
- Pseudocode is an informal description of a sequence of steps for solving a problem.

REVIEW EXERCISES

■ **R1.1** Explain the difference between using a computer program and programming a computer.

■ **R1.2** Which parts of a computer can store program code? Which can store user data?

■ **R1.3** Which parts of a computer serve to give information to the user? Which parts take user input?

■■ **R1.4** A toaster is a single-function device, but a computer can be programmed to carry out different tasks. Is your cell phone a single-function device, or is it a programmable computer?

■■ **R1.5** Explain two benefits of using C++ over machine code.

■■ **R1.6** On your own computer or on your lab computer, find the exact location (folder or directory name) of

     a. The sample file hello.cpp (after you saved it in your development environment).

     b. The standard header file <iostream>.

■■ **R1.7** What does this program print?

```
#include <iostream>
using namespace std;
int main()
{
   cout << "6 * 7 = " << 6 * 7 << endl;
   return 0;
}
```

■■ **R1.8** What does this program print? Pay close attention to spaces.

```
#include <iostream>
using namespace std;
int main()
{
   cout << "Hello" << "World" << endl;
   return 0;
}
```

■■ **R1.9** What does this program print?

```
#include <iostream>
using namespace std;
int main()
{
   cout << "Hello" << endl << "World" << endl;
   return 0;
}
```

■■ **R1.10** Write three versions of the hello.cpp program that have different compile-time errors. Write a version that has a run-time error.

■ **R1.11** How do you discover compile-time errors? How do you discover run-time errors?

■■ **R1.12** Write an algorithm to settle the following question: A bank account starts out with $10,000. Interest is compounded monthly at 6 percent per year (0.5 percent per month). Every month, $500 is withdrawn to meet college expenses. After how many years is the account depleted?

■■■ **R1.13** Consider the question in Exercise R1.12. Suppose the numbers ($10,000, 6 percent, $500) were user selectable. Are there values for which the algorithm you developed would not terminate? If so, change the algorithm to make sure it always terminates.

■■■ **R1.14** In order to estimate the cost of painting a house, a painter needs to know the surface area of the exterior. Develop an algorithm for computing that value. Your inputs are the width, length, and height of the house, the number of windows and doors, and their dimensions. (Assume the windows and doors have a uniform size.)

■■ **R1.15** You want to decide whether you should drive your car to work or take the train. You know the one-way distance from your home to your place of work, and the fuel efficiency of your car (in miles per gallon). You also know the one-way price of a train ticket. You assume the cost of gas at $4 per gallon, and car maintenance at 5 cents per mile. Write an algorithm to decide which commute is cheaper.

■■ **R1.16** Suppose you put your younger brother in charge of backing up your work. Write a set of detailed instructions for carrying out his task. Explain how often he should do it, and what files he needs to copy from which folder to which location. Explain how he should verify that the backup was carried out correctly.

■■■ **R1.17** The cafeteria offers a discount card for sale that entitles you, during a certain period, to a free meal whenever you have bought a given number of meals at the regular price. The exact details of the offer change from time to time. Describe an algorithm that lets you determine whether a particular offer is a good buy. What other inputs do you need?

■ **R1.18** Write pseudocode for an algorithm that describes how to prepare Sunday breakfast in your household.

■■ **R1.19** The ancient Babylonians had an algorithm for determining the square root of a number *a*. Start with an initial guess of *a* / 2. Then find the average of your guess *g* and *a* / *g*. That's your next guess. Repeat until two consecutive guesses are close enough. Write pseudocode for this algorithm.

■■ **R1.20** Write an algorithm to create a tile pattern composed of black and white tiles, with a fringe of black tiles all around and two or three black tiles in the center, equally spaced from the boundary. The inputs to your algorithm are the total number of rows and columns in the pattern.

■■■ **R1.21** Write an algorithm to create a tile pattern composed of alternating black and white squares, like this:

■■■ **R1.22** Write an algorithm that allows a robot to mow a rectangular lawn, provided it has been placed in a corner, like this:

The robot (marked as R) can:

- Move forward by one unit.
- Turn left or right.
- Sense the color of the ground one unit in front of it.

■■■ **R1.23** Consider a robot that is placed in a room. The robot can:

- Move forward by one unit.
- Turn left or right.
- Sense what is in front of it: a wall, a window, or neither.

Write an algorithm that enables the robot, placed anywhere in the room, to count the number of windows. For example, in the room at right, the robot (marked as R) should find that it has two windows.

■■■ **R1.24** Consider a robot that has been placed in a maze. The right-hand rule tells you how to escape from a maze: Always have the right hand next to a wall, and eventually you will find an exit. The robot can:

- Move forward by one unit.
- Turn left or right.
- Sense what is in front of it: a wall, an exit, or neither.

Write an algorithm that lets the robot escape the maze. You may assume that there is an exit that is reachable by the right-hand rule. Your challenge is to deal with situations in which the path turns. The robot can't see turns. It can only see what is directly in front of it.

© Skip ODonnell/iStockphoto.

■■■ **Business R1.25** Suppose you received a loyalty promotion that lets you purchase one item, valued up to $100, from an online catalog. You want to make the best of the offer. You have a list of all items for sale, some of which are less than $100, some more. Write an algorithm to produce the item that is closest to $100. If there is more than one such item, list them all. Remember that a computer will inspect one item at a time—it can't just glance at a list and find the best one.

■■ **Engineering R1.26** A television manufacturer advertises that a television set has a certain size, measured diagonally. You wonder how the set will fit into your living room. Write an algorithm that yields the horizontal and vertical size of the television. Your inputs are the diagonal size and the aspect ratio (the ratio of width to height, usually 16 : 9 for television sets).

© Don Bayley/iStockPhoto.

■■■ **Engineering R1.27** Cameras today can correct "red eye" problems caused when the photo flash makes eyes look red. Write pseudocode for an algorithm that can detect red eyes. Your input is a pattern of colors, such as that below.

You are given the number of rows and columns. For any row or column number, you can query the color, which will be red, black, or something else. If you find that the center of the black pixels coincides with the center of the red pixels, you have found a red eye, and your output should be "yes". Otherwise, your output is "no".

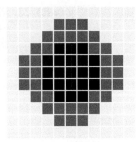

■■ Engineering R1.28 The San Francisco taxi commission set the following rates for 2017:

- First 1/5th of a mile: $3.50
- Each additional 1/5th of a mile or fraction thereof: $0.55
- Each minute of waiting or traffic delay: $0.55

The charge for "waiting or traffic delay" applies instead of the mileage charge for each minute in which the speed is slower than the break-even point. The break-even point is the speed at which 1/5th of a mile is traversed in one minute.

Develop an algorithm that yields the fare for traveling a given distance in a given amount of time, assuming that the taxi moves at a constant speed.

© Mark Massel/iStockphoto.

■■ Engineering R1.29 Suppose you know how long it takes a car to accelerate from 0 to 60 miles per hour. Develop an algorithm for computing the time required to travel a given distance (for example 5 miles), assuming that the car is initially at rest, accelerates to a given speed (for example 25 miles per hour), and drives at that speed until the distance is covered. *Hint:* An object that starts at rest and accelerates at a constant rate a for t seconds travels a distance of $s = 1/2at^2$.

■■ Engineering R1.30 Taxi meters measure the distance traveled by counting the number of revolutions of an axle. The meter is initialized by driving a known distance. A disreputable taxi driver tricks his customers into paying more per trip. He does this by slightly deflating his taxi's tires after the meter has been initialized, so that they have a smaller radius. This way, the tire will have a greater number of revolutions per trip, making each trip appear to be a greater number of miles.

Develop an algorithm for computing what the deflated tire radius must be if the taxi driver would like a short x-mile taxi ride to appear to be a longer y-mile taxi ride. Inputs are the proper tire radius R and the distances x and y.

PRACTICE EXERCISES

■ E1.1 Write a program that prints a greeting of your choice, perhaps in a language other than English.

■■ E1.2 Write a program that prints the sum of the first ten positive integers, $1 + 2 + \cdots + 10$.

■■ E1.3 Write a program that prints the product of the first ten positive integers, $1 \times 2 \times \cdots \times 10$. (Use * to indicate multiplication in C++.)

■■ E1.4 Write a program that prints the balance of an account after the first, second, and third year. The account has an initial balance of $1,000 and earns 5 percent interest per year.

■ **E1.5** Write a program that displays your name inside a box on the screen, like this: ☐ Dave ☐
Do your best to approximate lines with characters such as | - +.

■■ **E1.6** Write a program that prints your name in Morse code, like this:

.... .- .-. .-. -.--

Use a separate output statement for each letter.

■ **E1.7** Write a program that prints three items, such as the names of your three best friends or favorite movies, on three separate lines.

■ **E1.8** Write a program that prints a poem of your choice. If you don't have a favorite poem, search the Internet for "Emily Dickinson" or "e e cummings".

■ **Business E1.9** Write a program that prints a two-column list of your friends' birthdays. In the first column, print the names of your best friends; in the second, print their birthdays.

■ **Business E1.10** In the United States there is no federal sales tax, so every state may impose its own sales taxes. Look on the Internet for the sales tax charged in five U.S. states, then write a program that prints the tax rate for five states of your choice.

```
Sales Tax Rates
---------------
Alaska:     0%
Hawaii:     4%
  . . .
```

■ **Business E1.11** To speak more than one language is a valuable skill in the labor market today. One of the basic skills is learning to greet people. Write a program that prints a two-column list with the greeting phrases shown in the table. In the first column, print the phrase in English, in the second column, print the phrase in a language of your choice. If you don't speak a language other than English, use an online translator or ask a friend.

List of Phrases to Translate
Good morning.
It is a pleasure to meet you.
Please call me tomorrow.
Have a nice day!

■■ **Engineering E1.12** Write a program that prints out the following English/metric conversions:

1 kilogram = 2.21 pounds
1 pound = 0.454 kilograms
1 foot = 0.305 meters
1 meter = 3.28 feet
1 mile = 1.61 kilometers
1 kilometer = 0.621 miles

PROGRAMMING PROJECTS

• P1.1 Write a program that prints the message, "Hello, my name is Hal!" Then, on a new line, the program should print the message "What would you like me to do?" Then it's the user's turn to type in an input. You haven't yet learned how to do it—just use the following lines of code:

```
string user_input;
getline(cin, user_input);
```

Finally, the program should ignore the user input and print the message "I am sorry, I cannot do that."

This program uses the string data type. To access this feature, you must place the line

```
#include <string>
```

before the main function.

Here is a typical program run. The user input is printed in color.

```
Hello, my name is Hal!
What would you like me to do?
Clean up my room
I am sorry, I cannot do that.
```

When running the program, remember to press the Enter key after typing the last word of the input line.

•• P1.2 Write a program that prints out a message "Hello, my name is Hal!" Then, on a new line, the program should print the message "What is your name?" As in Exercise P1.1, just use the following lines of code:

```
string user_name;
getline(cin, user_name);
```

Finally, the program should print the message "Hello, *user name*. I am glad to meet you!" To print the user name, simply use

```
cout << user_name;
```

As in Exercise P1.1, you must place the line

```
#include <string>
```

before the main function.

Here is a typical program run. The user input is printed in color.

```
Hello, my name is Hal!
What is your name?
Dave
Hello, Dave. I am glad to meet you!
```

••• P1.3 Write a program that prints your name in large letters, such as

```
*   *   **    ****   ****   *   *
*   *  *  *  *    *  *    *  *  *
*****  *    *  ****   ****    * *
*   *  ******  *    *  *    *    *
*   *  *    *  *    *  *    *    *
```

P1.4 Write a program that prints a face similar to (but different from) the following:

```
/////
+-----+
(| o o |)
|   ^  |
|  '_' |
+-----+
```

P1.5 Write a program that prints a house that looks exactly like the following:

```
  /\
 /  \
+----+
| .-.|
|| ||
+-+-++
```

P1.6 Write a program that prints an animal speaking a greeting, similar to (but different from) the following:

```
/\_/\      -----
( ' ' )  / Hello \
(  -  ) <  Junior |
| | |   \ Coder!/
(_|_)      -----
```

P1.7 Write a program that prints an imitation of a Piet Mondrian painting. (Search the Internet if you are not familiar with his paintings.) Use character sequences such as @@@ or ::: to indicate different colors, and use - and | to form lines.

P1.8 Write a program that prints the United States flag, using * and = characters.

Engineering P1.9 The atmospheres of the gas giant planets (Jupiter, Saturn, Uranus, and Neptune) are mostly comprised of hydrogen (H_2) followed by helium (He). The atmospheres of the terrestrial planets are mostly comprised of carbon dioxide (CO_2) followed by nitrogen (N_2) for Venus and Mars, and for Earth, mostly Nitrogen (N_2) followed by Oxygen (O_2). Write a program that outputs this information in a chart with four columns for the type of planet, the name of the planet, its primary atmospheric gas, and its secondary atmospheric gas.

© Courtesy NASA/JPL-Caltech.

Engineering P1.10 Write a program that displays the following image, using characters such as / \ - | + for the lines. Write Ω as "Ohm".

FUNDAMENTAL DATA TYPES

705	Taipei		
549	Osaka/Kansai	29	Final Call
11	Taipei	1	inal Call
82	Manila	23	inal Call
683	Toronto	502	Final Call
250	Nanjing	2	Final Call
852	Bangkok/D	17	Final Call
165	Harbin	62	inal Call
904	Kuala Lumpur		Cancelled
21	Jinjiang	21	Boarding
820	Nanjing	503	
677		506	Gate Char
206	Kaohsiung		
683	Singapore	49	Boarding
69	Shanghai/P	40	Boarding
	Singap	46	

© samxmeg/iStockphoto.

CHAPTER GOALS

To be able to define and initialize variables and constants

To understand the properties and limitations of integer and floating-point numbers

To write arithmetic expressions and assignment statements in C++

To appreciate the importance of comments and good code layout

To create programs that read and process input, and display the results

To process strings, using the standard C++ string type

CHAPTER CONTENTS

Jiang
Nanjing
503
506 Gate Chang

Kaohsiung
Singapore   49 Boarding
Shanghai/P   40 Boarding
Singapore   46
Taipei   512
                   25 Est 11
JieyangChaost   510

Numbers and character strings (such as the ones on this display board) are important data types in any C++ program. In this chapter, you will learn how to work with numbers and text, and how to write simple programs that perform useful tasks with them.

2.1 Variables

When your program carries out computations, you will want to store values so that you can use them later. In a C++ program, you use *variables* to store values. In this section, you will learn how to define and use variables.

To illustrate the use of variables, we will develop a program that solves the following problem. Soft drinks are sold in cans and bottles. A store offers a six-pack of 12-ounce cans for the same price as a two-liter bottle. Which should you buy? (Twelve fluid ounces equal approximately 0.355 liters.)

In our program, we will define variables for the number of cans per pack and for the volume of each can. Then we will compute the volume of a six-pack in liters and print out the answer.

cans: © blackred/iStockphoto. bottle: © travismanley/iStockphoto.

What contains more soda? A six-pack of 12-ounce cans or a two-liter bottle?

2.1.1 Variable Definitions

The following statement defines a variable named cans_per_pack:

```
int cans_per_pack = 6;
```

A **variable** is a storage location in a computer program. Each variable has a name and holds a value.

A variable is similar to a parking space in a parking garage. The parking space has an identifier (such as "J053"), and it can hold a vehicle. A variable has a name (such as cans_per_pack), and it can hold a value (such as 6).

> A variable is a storage location with a name.

Like a variable in a computer program, a parking space has an identifier and contents.

Javier Larrea/Age Fotostock.

When defining a
variable, you usually
specify an initial
value.

When defining a variable, you usually want to **initialize** it. That is, you specify the value that should be stored in the variable. Consider again this variable definition:

```
int cans_per_pack = 6;
```

The variable cans_per_pack is initialized with the value 6.

When defining a
variable, you also
specify the type of
its values.

Like a parking space that is restricted to a certain type of vehicle (such as a compact car, motorcycle, or electric vehicle), a variable in C++ stores data of a specific **type**. C++ supports quite a few data types: numbers, text strings, files, dates, and many others. You must specify the type whenever you define a variable (see Syntax 2.1).

Syntax 2.1   Variable Definition

Types introduced in this chapter are the number types int *and* double *(see Table 2) and the* string *type (see Section 2.5).*

See Table 3 for rules and examples of valid names.

```
int cans_per_pack = 6;
```

A variable definition ends with a semicolon.

Use a descriptive variable name. See Programming Tip 2.1.

Supplying an initial value is optional, but it is usually a good idea. See Common Error 2.2.

The cans_per_pack variable is an **integer**, a whole number without a fractional part. In C++, this type is called int. (See the next section for more information about number types in C++.)

Note that the type comes *before* the variable name:

```
int cans_per_pack = 6;
```

Each parking space is suitable for a particular type of vehicle, just as each variable holds a value of a particular type.

© Ingenui/iStockphoto.

Table 1 shows variations of variable definitions.

Table 1 Variable Definitions in C++

Variable Name	Comment
`int cans = 6;`	Defines an integer variable and initializes it with 6.
`int total = cans + bottles;`	The initial value need not be a **constant**. (Of course, cans and bottles must have been previously defined.)
🚫 `int bottles = "10";`	**Error:** You cannot initialize a number with a string.
`int bottles;`	Defines an integer variable without initializing it. This can be a cause for errors—see Common Error 2.2.
`int cans, bottles;`	Defines two integer variables in a single statement. In this book, we will define each variable in a separate statement.
⚠ `bottles = 1;`	**Caution:** The type is missing. This statement is not a definition but an assignment of a new value to an existing variable—see Section 2.1.4.

2.1.2 Number Types

Use the int type for numbers that cannot have a fractional part.

In C++, there are several different types of numbers. You use the *integer* number type, called `int` in C++, to denote a whole number without a fractional part. For example, there must be an integer number of cans in any pack of cans—you cannot have a fraction of a can.

Use the double type for floating-point numbers.

When a fractional part is required (such as in the number 0.355), we use **floating-point numbers**. The most commonly used type for floating-point numbers in C++ is called `double`. (If you want to know the reason, read Special Topic 2.1.) Here is the definition of a floating-point variable:

```
double can_volume = 0.355;
```

When a value such as 6 or 0.355 occurs in a C++ program, it is called a number **literal**. Table 2 shows how to write integer and floating-point literals in C++.

Table 2 Number Literals in C++

Number	Type	Comment
6	int	An integer has no fractional part.
-6	int	Integers can be negative.
0	int	Zero is an integer.
0.5	double	A number with a fractional part has type `double`.
1.0	double	An integer with a fractional part .0 has type `double`.
1E6 or 1e6	double	A number in exponential notation: 1×10^6 or 1000000. Numbers in exponential notation always have type `double`.

Table 2 Number Literals in C++

Number	Type	Comment
2.96E-2	double	Negative exponent: $2.96 \times 10^{-2} = 2.96\ /\ 100 = 0.0296$
🚫 100,000		**Error:** Do not use a comma as a decimal separator.
🚫 3 1/2		**Error:** Do not use fractions; use decimal notation: 3.5.

2.1.3 Variable Names

By convention, variable names should start with a lowercase letter.

When you define a variable, you should pick a name that explains its purpose. For example, it is better to use a descriptive name, such as can_volume, than a terse name, such as cv.

In C++, there are a few simple rules for variable names:

1. Variable names must start with a letter or the underscore (_) character, and the remaining characters must be letters, numbers, or underscores.
2. You cannot use other symbols such as $ or %. Spaces are not permitted inside names either. You can use an underscore instead, as in can_volume.
3. Variable names are **case sensitive**, that is, Can_volume and can_volume are different names. For that reason, it is a good idea to use only lowercase letters in variable names. It is also a convention among many C++ programmers that variable names should start with a lowercase letter.
4. You cannot use **reserved words** such as double or return as names; these words are reserved exclusively for their special C++ meanings. (See Appendix A.)

Table 3 shows examples of legal and illegal variable names in C++.

Table 3 Variable Names in C++

Variable Name	Comment
can_volume1	Variable names consist of letters, numbers, and the underscore character.
x	In mathematics, you use short variable names such as x or y. This is legal in C++, but not very common, because it can make programs harder to understand (see Programming Tip 2.1).
⚠ Can_volume	**Caution:** Variable names are case sensitive. This variable name is different from can_volume.
🚫 6pack	**Error:** Variable names cannot start with a number.
🚫 can volume	**Error:** Variable names cannot contain spaces.
🚫 double	**Error:** You cannot use a reserved word as a variable name.
🚫 ltr/fl.oz	**Error:** You cannot use symbols such as . or /

2.1.4 The Assignment Statement

An assignment statement stores a new value in a variable, replacing the previously stored value.

You use the **assignment statement** to place a new value into a variable. Here is an example:

```
cans_per_pack = 8;
```

The left-hand side of an assignment statement consists of a variable. The right-hand side is an expression that has a value. That value is stored in the variable, overwriting its previous contents.

There is an important difference between a variable definition and an assignment statement:

```
int cans_per_pack = 6; // Variable definition
. . .
cans_per_pack = 8; // Assignment statement
```

The first statement is the *definition* of cans_per_pack. It is an instruction to create a new variable of type int, to give it the name cans_per_pack, and to initialize it with 6. The second statement is an *assignment statement:* an instruction to replace the contents of the *existing* variable cans_per_pack with another value.

Syntax 2.2   Assignment

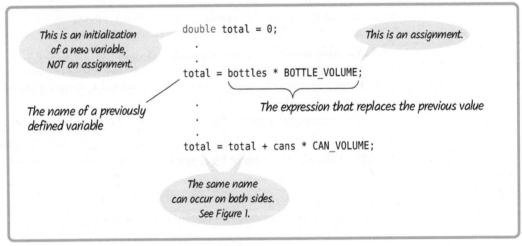

The assignment operator = does *not* denote mathematical equality.

The = sign doesn't mean that the left-hand side is *equal* to the right-hand side. The expression on the right is evaluated, and its value is placed into the variable on the left.

Do not confuse this *assignment operation* with the = used in algebra to denote *equality*. The assignment operator is an instruction to do something, namely place a value into a variable. The mathematical equality states the fact that two values are equal.

For example, in C++, it is perfectly legal to write

```
total_volume = total_volume + 2;
```

It means to look up the value stored in the variable total_volume, add 2 to it, and place the result back into total_volume. (See Figure 1.) The net effect of executing this statement is to increment total_volume by 2. For example, if total_volume was 2.13 before execution of the statement, it is set to 4.13 afterwards. Of course, in mathematics it would make no sense to write that $x = x + 2$. No value can equal itself plus 2.

Figure 1 Executing the Assignment total_volume = total_volume + 2

2.1.5 Constants

When a variable is defined with the reserved word const, its value can never change. Constants are commonly written using capital letters to distinguish them visually from regular variables:

```
const double BOTTLE_VOLUME = 2;
```

It is good programming style to use named constants in your program to explain the meanings of numeric values. For example, compare the statements

```
double total_volume = bottles * 2;
```

and

```
double total_volume = bottles * BOTTLE_VOLUME;
```

A programmer reading the first statement may not understand the significance of the number 2. The second statement, with a named constant, makes the computation much clearer.

You cannot change the value of a variable that is defined as const.

2.1.6 Comments

As your programs get more complex, you should add **comments**, explanations for human readers of your code. Here is an example:

```
const double CAN_VOLUME = 0.355; // Liters in a 12-ounce can
```

This comment explains the significance of the value 0.355 to a human reader. The compiler does not process comments at all. It ignores everything from a // **delimiter** to the end of the line.

Use comments to add explanations for humans who read your code. The compiler ignores comments.

Just as a television commentator explains the news, you use comments in your program to explain its behavior.

© jgroup/iStockphoto.

You use the // syntax for single-line comments. If you have a comment that spans multiple lines, enclose it between /* and */ delimiters. The compiler ignores these delimiters and everything in between.

Here is a typical example, a long comment at the beginning of a program, to explain the program's purpose:

```
/*
    This program computes the volume (in liters) of a six-pack of soda cans
    and the total volume of a six-pack and a two-liter bottle.
*/
```

We are now ready to finish our program. The following program shows the use of variables, constants, and the assignment statement. The program displays the volume of a six-pack of cans and the total volume of the six-pack and a two-liter bottle. We use constants for the can and bottle volumes. The total_volume variable is initialized with the volume of the cans. Using an assignment statement, we add the bottle volume.

sec01/volume1.cpp

```cpp
1  #include <iostream>
2
3  using namespace std;
4
5  /*
6      This program computes the volume (in liters) of a six-pack of soda
7      cans and the total volume of a six-pack and a two-liter bottle.
8  */
9  int main()
10 {
11    int cans_per_pack = 6;
12    const double CAN_VOLUME = 0.355; // Liters in a 12-ounce can
13    double total_volume = cans_per_pack * CAN_VOLUME;
14
15    cout << "A six-pack of 12-ounce cans contains "
16       << total_volume << " liters." << endl;
17
18    const double BOTTLE_VOLUME = 2; // Two-liter bottle
19
20    total_volume = total_volume + BOTTLE_VOLUME;
21
22    cout << "A six-pack and a two-liter bottle contain "
23       << total_volume << " liters." << endl;
24
25    return 0;
26 }
```

Program Run

```
A six-pack of 12-ounce cans contains 2.13 liters.
A six-pack and a two-liter bottle contain 4.13 liters.
```

Common Error 2.1

Using Undefined Variables

You must define a variable before you use it for the first time. For example, the following sequence of statements would not be legal:

```
double can_volume = 12 * liter_per_ounce;
double liter_per_ounce = 0.0296;
```

In your program, the statements are compiled in order. When the compiler reaches the first statement, it does not know that liter_per_ounce will be defined in the next line, and it reports an error.

Common Error 2.2

Using Uninitialized Variables

If you define a variable but leave it uninitialized, then your program can act unpredictably. To understand why, consider what happens when you define a variable. Just enough space is set aside in memory to hold values of the type you specify. For example, with the definition

```
int bottles;
```

a block of memory big enough to hold integers is reserved. There is already *some* value in that memory. After all, you don't get freshly minted transistors—just an area of memory that has previously been used, filled with flotsam left over from prior computations. (In this regard, a variable differs from a parking space. A parking space can be empty, containing no vehicle. But a variable always holds some value.)

If you use the variable without initializing it, then that prior value will be used, yielding unpredictable results. For example, consider the program segment

```
int bottles; // Forgot to initialize
int bottle_volume = bottles * 2; // Result is unpredictable
```

There is no way of knowing what value will be computed. If you are unlucky, a plausible value will happen to appear when you run the program at home, and an entirely different result will occur when the program is graded.

Programming Tip 2.1

Choose Descriptive Variable Names

We could have saved ourselves a lot of typing by using shorter variable names, as in

```
double cv = 0.355;
```

Compare this definition with the one that we actually used, though. Which one is easier to read? There is no comparison. Just reading can_volume is a lot less trouble than reading cv and then *figuring out* it must mean "can volume".

In practical programming, this is particularly important when programs are written by more than one person. It may be obvious to *you* that cv stands for can volume and not current velocity, but will it be obvious to the person who needs to update your code years later? For that matter, will you remember yourself what cv means when you look at the code three months from now?

Programming Tip 2.2
Do Not Use Magic Numbers

A **magic number** is a numeric constant that appears in your code without explanation. For example,

```
total_volume = bottles * 2;
```

Why 2? Are bottles twice as voluminous as cans? No, the reason is that every bottle contains 2 liters. Use a named constant to make the code self-documenting:

```
const double BOTTLE_VOLUME = 2;
total_volume = bottles * BOTTLE_VOLUME;
```

© FinnBrandt/iStockphoto.

There is another reason for using named constants. Suppose circumstances change, and the bottle volume is now 1.5 liters. If you used a named constant, you make a single change, and you are done. Otherwise, you have to look at every value of 2 in your program and ponder whether it means a bottle volume, or something else. In a program that is more than a few pages long, that is incredibly tedious and error-prone.

Even the most reasonable cosmic constant is going to change one day. You think there are 365 days per year? Your customers on Mars are going to be pretty unhappy about your silly prejudice. Make a constant

```
const int DAYS_PER_YEAR = 365;
```

Special Topic 2.1
Numeric Types in C++

In addition to the int and double types, C++ has several other numeric types.

C++ has two floating-point types. The float type uses half the storage of the double type that we use in this book, but it can only store 6–7 digits. Many years ago, when computers had far less memory than they have today, float was the standard type for floating-point computations, and programmers would indulge in the luxury of "double precision" only when they needed the additional digits. Today, the float type is rarely used.

By the way, these numbers are called "floating-point" because of their internal representation in the computer. Consider numbers 29600, 2.96, and 0.0296. They can be represented in a very similar way: namely, as a sequence of the significant digits—296—and an indication of the position of the decimal point. When the values are multiplied or divided by 10, only the position of the decimal point changes; it "floats". Computers use base 2, not base 10, but the principle is the same.

In addition to the int type, C++ has integer types short, long, and long long. For each integer type, there is an unsigned equivalent. For example, the short type typically has a range from −32,768 to 32,767, whereas unsigned short has a range from 0 to 65,535. These strange-looking limits are the result of the use of binary numbers in computers. A short value uses 16 binary digits, which can encode $2^{16} = 65,536$ values. Keep in mind that the ranges for integer types are not standardized, and they differ among compilers. Table 4 contains typical values.

Table 4 Number Types

Type	Typical Range	Typical Size
int	−2,147,483,648 … 2,147,483,647 (about 2 billion)	4 bytes
unsigned	0 … 4,294,967,295	4 bytes

Table 4 **Number Types**

Type	Typical Range	Typical Size
short	−32,768 ... 32,767	2 bytes
unsigned short	0 ... 65,535	2 bytes
long long	−9,223,372,036,854,775,808 ... 9,223,372,036,854,775,807	8 bytes
long	Depending on the compiler, the same as int or long long	4 or 8 bytes
double	The double-precision floating-point type, with a range of about $\pm 10^{308}$ and about 15 significant decimal digits	8 bytes
float	The single-precision floating-point type, with a range of about $\pm 10^{38}$ and about 7 significant decimal digits	4 bytes

Special Topic 2.2

Numeric Ranges and Precisions

Because numbers are represented in the computer with a limited number of digits, they cannot represent arbitrary integer or floating-point numbers.

The int type has a *limited range:* On most platforms, it can represent numbers up to a little more than two billion. For many applications, this is not a problem, but you cannot use an int to represent the world population.

If a computation yields a value that is outside the int range, the result *overflows*. No error is displayed. Instead, the result is truncated to fit into an int, yielding a useless value. For example,

```
int one_billion = 1000000000;
cout << 3 * one_billion << endl;
```

displays −1294967296.

In situations such as this, you can switch to double values. However, read Common Error 2.6 for more information about a related issue: roundoff errors.

Special Topic 2.3

Defining Variables with auto

Instead of providing a type for a variable, you can use the reserved word auto. Then the type is automatically deduced from the type of the initial value. For example,

```
auto cans = 6; // This variable has type int
const auto CAN_VOLUME = 0.355; // This constant has type double
```

For simple types such as int or double, it is better to use the explicit type in the variable definition. The auto reserved word is useful to avoid complex types that can be automatically determined.

2.2 Arithmetic

In the following sections, you will learn how to carry out arithmetic and mathematical calculations in C++.

2.2.1 Arithmetic Operators

© hocus-focus/iStockphoto.

C++ supports the same four basic arithmetic operations as a calculator—addition, subtraction, multiplication, and division—but it uses different symbols for multiplication and division.

You must write a * b to denote multiplication. Unlike in mathematics, you cannot write a b, a · b, or a × b. Similarly, division is always indicated with a /, never a ÷ or a fraction bar.

For example, $\frac{a+b}{2}$ becomes (a + h) / 2.

Parentheses are used just as in algebra: to indicate in which order the subexpressions should be computed. For example, in the expression (a + b) / 2, the sum a + b is computed first, and then the sum is divided by 2. In contrast, in the expression

    a + b / 2

Use * for multiplication and / for division.

only b is divided by 2, and then the sum of a and b / 2 is formed. Just as in regular algebraic notation, multiplication and division have a *higher precedence* than addition and subtraction. For example, in the expression a + b / 2, the / is carried out first, even though the + operation occurs further to the left. If both arguments of an arithmetic operation are integers, the result is an integer. If one or both arguments are floating-point numbers, the result is a floating-point number. For example, 4 * 0.5 is 2.0.

2.2.2 Increment and Decrement

The ++ operator adds 1 to a variable; the -- operator subtracts 1.

Changing a variable by adding or subtracting 1 is so common that there is a special shorthand for it, namely

    counter++;
    counter--;

The ++ increment operator gave the C++ programming language its name. C++ is the incremental improvement of the C language.

2.2.3 Integer Division and Remainder

If both arguments of / are integers, the remainder is discarded.

Division works as you would expect, as long as at least one of the numbers involved is a floating-point number. That is, 7.0 / 4.0, 7 / 4.0, and 7.0 / 4 all yield 1.75. However, if *both* numbers are integers, then the result of the division is always an integer, with the remainder discarded. That is,

    7 / 4

evaluates to 1 because 7 divided by 4 is 1 with a remainder of 3 (which is discarded). This can be a source of subtle programming errors—see Common Error 2.3.

If you are interested in the remainder only, use the % operator:

```
7 % 4
```

is 3, the remainder of the **integer division** of 7 by 4. The % symbol has no analog in algebra. It was chosen because it looks similar to /, and the remainder operation is related to division. The operator is called **modulus**. (Some people call it *modulo* or *mod*.) It has no relationship with the percent operation that you find on some calculators.

Here is a typical use for the integer / and % operations. Suppose you have an amount of pennies in a piggybank:

```
int pennies = 1729;
```

You want to determine the value in dollars and cents. You obtain the dollars through an integer division by 100.

```
int dollars = pennies / 100;  // Sets dollars to 17
```

The integer division discards the remainder. To obtain the remainder, use the % operator:

```
int cents = pennies % 100;  // Sets cents to 29
```

© Michael Flippo/iStockphoto.

Another common use of the % operator is to check whether a number is even or odd. If a number n is even, then n % 2 is zero.

Integer division and the % operator yield the dollar and cent values of a piggybank full of pennies.

Table 5 Integer Division and Remainder

Expression (where n = 1729)	Value	Comment
n % 10	9	n % 10 is always the last digit of n.
n / 10	172	This is always n without the last digit.
n % 100	29	The last two digits of n.
n / 10.0	172.9	Because 10.0 is a floating-point number, the fractional part is not discarded.
-n % 10	-9	Because the first argument is negative, the remainder is also negative.
n % 2	1	n % 2 is 0 if n is even, 1 or −1 if n is odd.

2.2.4 Converting Floating-Point Numbers to Integers

When a floating-point value is assigned to an integer variable, the fractional part is discarded:

```
double price = 2.55;
int dollars = price; // Sets dollars to 2
```

Discarding the fractional part is not always what you want. Often, you want to round to the *nearest* integer. To round a positive floating-point value to the nearest integer, add 0.5 and then convert to an integer:

```
int dollars = price + 0.5; // Rounds to the nearest integer
```

In our example, adding 0.5 turns all values above 2.5 into values above 3. In particular, 2.55 is turned into 3.05, which is then truncated to 3. (For a negative floating-point value, you subtract 0.5.)

Because truncation is a potential cause for errors, your compiler may issue a warning that assigning a floating-point value to an integer variable is unsafe. See Special Topic 2.4 on how to avoid this warning.

> Assigning a floating-point variable to an integer drops the fractional part.

2.2.5 Powers and Roots

In C++, there are no symbols for powers and roots. To compute them, you must call **functions**. To take the square root of a number, you use the sqrt function. For example, $\sqrt{x}$ is written as sqrt(x). To compute x^n, you write pow(x, n).

To use the sqrt and pow functions, you must place the line #include <cmath> at the top of your program file. The header file <cmath> is a standard C++ header that is available with all C++ systems, as is <iostream>.

> The C++ library defines many mathematical functions such as sqrt (square root) and pow (raising to a power).

As you can see, the effect of the /, sqrt, and pow operations is to flatten out mathematical terms. In algebra, you use fractions, exponents, and roots to arrange expressions in a compact two-dimensional form. In C++, you have to write all expressions in a linear arrangement. For example, the mathematical expression

$$b \times \left(1 + \frac{r}{100}\right)^n$$

becomes

```
b * pow(1 + r / 100, n)
```

Figure 2 shows how to analyze such an expression.

Figure 2   Analyzing an Expression

Table 6 Arithmetic Expressions

Mathematical Expression	C++ Expression	Comments
$\dfrac{x + y}{2}$	`(x + y) / 2`	The parentheses are required; x + y / 2 computes $x + \frac{y}{2}$.
$\dfrac{xy}{2}$	`x * y / 2`	Parentheses are not required; operators with the same precedence are evaluated left to right.
$\left(1 + \dfrac{r}{100}\right)^n$	`pow(1 + r / 100, n)`	Remember to add `#include <cmath>` to the top of your program.
$\sqrt{a^2 + b^2}$	`sqrt(a * a + b * b)`	`a * a` is simpler than `pow(a, 2)`.
$\dfrac{i + j + k}{3}$	`(i + j + k) / 3.0`	If i, j, and k are integers, using a denominator of 3.0 forces floating-point division.

Table 7 shows additional functions that are declared in the `<cmath>` header. Inputs and outputs are floating-point numbers.

Table 7 Other Mathematical Functions

Function	Description
`sin(x)`	sine of x (x in radians)
`cos(x)`	cosine of x
`tan(x)`	tangent of x
`log(x)`	(natural log) $\ln(x), x > 0$
`log10(x)`	(decimal log) $\log_{10}(x), x > 0$
`abs(x)`	absolute value $|x|$

EXAMPLE CODE   See sec02 of your companion code for a program that gives examples of working with numbers in C++.

Common Error 2.3

Unintended Integer Division

It is unfortunate that C++ uses the same symbol, namely /, for both integer and floating-point division. These are really quite different operations. It is a common error to use integer division by accident. Consider this segment that computes the average of three integers:

```
cout << "Please enter your last three test scores: ";
int s1;
int s2;
int s3;
cin >> s1 >> s2 >> s3;
```

```
double average = (s1 + s2 + s3) / 3; // Error
cout << "Your average score is " << average << endl;
```

What could be wrong with that? Of course, the average of s1, s2, and s3 is

$$\frac{s1+s2+s3}{3}$$

Here, however, the / does not mean division in the mathematical sense. It denotes integer division because both s1 + s2 + s3 and 3 are integers. For example, if the scores add up to 14, the average is computed to be 4, the result of the integer division of 14 by 3. That integer 4 is then moved into the floating-point variable average. The remedy is to make the numerator or denominator into a floating-point number:

```
double total = s1 + s2 + s3;
double average = total / 3;
```

or

```
double average = (s1 + s2 + s3) / 3.0;
```

Common Error 2.4

Unbalanced Parentheses

Consider the expression

```
(-(b * b - 4 * a * c) / (2 * a)
```

What is wrong with it? Count the parentheses. There are three (and two). The parentheses are *unbalanced*. This kind of typing error is very common with complicated expressions. Now consider this expression.

© Croko/iStockphoto.

```
-(b * b - (4 * a * c))) / (2 * a
```

This expression has three (and three), but it still is not correct. In the middle of the expression,

```
-(b * b - (4 * a * c))) / (2 * a
                      ↑
```

there are only two (but three), which is an error. In the middle of an expression, the count of (must be greater than or equal to the count of), and at the end of the expression the two counts must be the same.

Here is a simple trick to make the counting easier without using pencil and paper. It is difficult for the brain to keep two counts simultaneously. Keep only one count when scanning the expression. Start with 1 at the first opening parenthesis, add 1 whenever you see an opening parenthesis, and subtract one whenever you see a closing parenthesis. Say the numbers aloud as you scan the expression. If the count ever drops below zero, or is not zero at the end, the parentheses are unbalanced. For example, when scanning the previous expression, you would mutter

```
-(b * b - (4 * a * c ) ) ) / (2 * a
 1         2           1 0 −1
```

and you would find the error.

Common Error 2.5

Forgetting Header Files

Every program that carries out input or output needs the <iostream> header. If you use mathematical functions such as sqrt, you need to include <cmath>. If you forget to include the appropriate header file, the compiler will not know symbols such as cout or sqrt. If the compiler complains about an undefined function or symbol, check your header files.

Sometimes you may not know which header file to include. Suppose you want to compute the absolute value of an integer using the abs function. As it happens, this version of abs is not defined in the <cmath> header but in <cstdlib>. How can you find the correct header file? You need to locate the documentation of the abs function, preferably using the online help of your development environment or a reference site on the Internet such as http://cplusplus.com (see Figure 3). The documentation includes a short description of the function and the name of the header file that you must include.

Figure 3 Online Documentation

Common Error 2.6

Roundoff Errors

Roundoff errors are a fact of life when calculating with floating-point numbers. You probably have encountered that phenomenon yourself with manual calculations. If you calculate 1/3 to two decimal places, you get 0.33. Multiplying again by 3, you obtain 0.99, not 1.00.

In the processor hardware, numbers are represented in the binary number system, not in decimal. You still get roundoff errors when binary digits are lost. They just may crop up at different places than you might expect. Here is an example.

```cpp
#include <iostream>

using namespace std;

int main()
{
   double price = 4.35;
   int cents = 100 * price; // Should be 100 * 4.35 = 435
   cout << cents << endl; // Prints 434!
```

```
        return 0;
    }
```

Of course, one hundred times 4.35 is 435, but the program prints 434.

Most computers represent numbers in the binary system. In the binary system, there is no exact representation for 4.35, just as there is no exact representation for 1/3 in the decimal system. The representation used by the computer is just a little less than 4.35, so 100 times that value is just a little less than 435. When a floating-point value is converted to an integer, the entire fractional part, which is almost 1, is thrown away, and the integer 434 is stored in cents. The remedy is to add 0.5 in order to round to the nearest integer:

```
int cents = 100 * price + 0.5;
```

Programming Tip 2.3

Spaces in Expressions

It is easier to read

```
x1 = (-b + sqrt(b * b - 4 * a * c)) / (2 * a);
```

than

```
x1=(-b+sqrt(b*b-4*a*c))/(2*a);
```

Simply put spaces around all operators + - * / % =. However, don't put a space after a *unary* minus: a – used to negate a single quantity, such as -b. That way, it can be easily distinguished from a *binary* minus, as in a - b.

It is customary not to put a space after a function name. That is, write sqrt(x) and not sqrt (x).

Special Topic 2.4

Casts

Occasionally, you need to store a value into a variable of a different type. Whenever there is the risk of *information loss*, the compiler issues a warning. For example, if you store a double value into an int variable, you can lose information in two ways:

- The fractional part is lost.
- The magnitude may be too large.

For example,

```
int n = 1.0E100; // NO
```

is not likely to work, because 10^{100} is larger than the largest representable integer.

Nevertheless, sometimes you do want to convert a floating-point value into an integer value. If you are prepared to lose the fractional part and you know that this particular floating-point number is not larger than the largest possible integer, then you can turn off the warning by using a **cast**. A cast is a conversion from one type (such as double) to another type (such as int) that is not safe in general, but that you know to be safe in a particular circumstance. You express a cast in C++ as follows:

```
int cents = static_cast<int>(100 * price + 0.5);
```

Special Topic 2.5

Combining Assignment and Arithmetic

In C++, you can combine arithmetic and assignment. For example, the instruction

```
total += cans * CAN_VOLUME;
```

is a shortcut for

```
total = total + cans * CAN_VOLUME;
```

Similarly,

```
total *= 2;
```

is another way of writing

```
total = total * 2;
```

Many programmers find this a convenient shortcut. If you like it, go ahead and use it in your own code. For simplicity, we won't use it in this book, though.

Computing & Society 2.1   **The Pentium Floating-Point Bug**

In 1994, Intel Corporation released what was then its most powerful processor, the Pentium. Unlike previous generations of its processors, it had a very fast floating-point unit. Intel's goal was to compete aggressively with the makers of higher-end processors for engineering workstations. The Pentium was a huge success immediately.

In the summer of 1994, Dr. Thomas Nicely of Lynchburg College, Virginia, ran an extensive set of computations to analyze the sums of reciprocals of certain sequences of prime numbers. The results were not always what his theory predicted, even after he took into account the inevitable roundoff errors. Then Dr. Nicely noted that the same program did produce the correct results when running on the slower 486 processor that preceded the Pentium in Intel's lineup. This should not have happened. The optimal round-off behavior of floating-point calculations were standardized by the Institute for Electrical and Electronic Engineers (IEEE) and Intel claimed to adhere to the IEEE standard in both the 486 and the Pentium processors. Upon further checking, Dr. Nicely discovered that there was a very small set of numbers for which the product of two numbers was computed differently on the two processors. For example,

$$4{,}195{,}835 - \left(\left(4{,}195{,}835/3{,}145{,}727\right) \times 3{,}145{,}727\right)$$

is mathematically equal to 0, and it did compute as 0 on a 486 processor. On his Pentium processor the result was 256.

As it turned out, Intel had independently discovered the bug in its testing and had started to produce chips that fixed it. The bug was caused by an error in a table that was used to speed up the processor's floating-point multiplication algorithm. Intel determined that the problem was exceedingly rare. They claimed that under normal use, a typical consumer would only notice the problem once every 27,000 years. Unfortunately for Intel, Dr. Nicely had not been a normal user.

Now Intel had a real problem on its hands. It figured that the cost of replacing all Pentium processors that it had sold so far would cost a great deal of money. Intel already had more orders for the chip than it could produce, and it would be particularly galling to have to give out the scarce chips as free replacements instead of selling them. Intel's management decided to punt and initially offered to replace the processors only for those customers who could prove that their work required absolute precision in mathematical calculations. Naturally, that did not go over well with the hundreds of thousands of customers who had paid retail prices of $700 and more for a Pentium chip and did not want to live with the nagging feeling that perhaps, one day, their income tax program would produce a faulty return. Ultimately, Intel caved in to public demand and replaced all defective chips, at a cost of about 475 million dollars.

This graph shows a set of numbers for which the original Pentium processor obtained the wrong quotient.

Courtesy of Larry Hoyle, Institute for Policy & Social Research, University of Kansas.

2.3 Input and Output

In the following sections, you will see how to read user input and how to control the appearance of the output that your programs produce.

2.3.1 Input

In this section, you will see how to place user input into a variable. Consider for example the volume1.cpp program in Section 2.1.6. Rather than assuming that the price for the two-liter bottle and the six-pack of cans are identical, we can ask the program user for the prices.

When a program asks for user input, it should first print a message that tells the user which input is expected. Such a message is called a **prompt**.

```
cout << "Please enter the number of bottles: "; // Display prompt
```

Do not add an endl after the prompt. You want the input to appear after the colon, not on the following line.

Next, the program issues a command to read the input. The cin object reads input from the console window. You use the >> operator (sometimes called the *extraction* operator) to place an input value into a variable, like this:

Use the >> operator to read a value and place it in a variable.

```
int bottles;
cin >> bottles;
```

When the program executes the input statement, it waits for the user to provide input. The user also needs to press the Enter key so that the program accepts the input. After the user supplies the input, the number is placed into the bottles variable, and the program continues.

Note that in this code segment, there was no need to initialize the bottles variable because it is being filled by the very next statement. As a rule of thumb, you should initialize a variable when you declare it *unless* it is filled in an input statement that follows immediately.

You can read more than one value in a single input statement:

```
cout << "Please enter the number of bottles and cans: ";
cin >> bottles >> cans;
```

The user can supply both inputs on the same line:

```
Please enter the number of bottles and cans: 2 6
```

Syntax 2.3   Input Statement

Display a prompt in the console window.
```
cout << "Enter the number of bottles: ";
```
Define a variable to hold the input value. — `int bottles;`
`cin >> bottles;`

Don't use endl *here.*

The program waits for user input, then places the input into the variable.

Alternatively, the user can press the Enter key after each input:

```
Please enter the number of bottles and cans: 2
6
```

2.3.2 Formatted Output

When you print the result of a computation, you often want some control over its appearance. For example, when you print an amount in dollars and cents, you usually want it to be rounded to two significant digits. That is, you want the output to look like

```
Price per ounce: 0.04
```

instead of

```
Price per ounce: 0.0409722
```

You use manipulators to specify how values should be formatted.

The following command instructs cout to use two digits after the decimal point for all floating-point numbers:

```
cout << fixed << setprecision(2);
```

This command does not produce any output; it just manipulates cout so that it will change the output format. The values fixed and setprecision are called *manipulators*. We will discuss manipulators in detail in Chapter 8. For now, just remember to include the statement given above whenever you want currency values displayed neatly.

To use manipulators, you must include the <iomanip> header in your program:

```
#include <iomanip>
```

You can combine the manipulators and the values to be displayed into a single statement:

```
cout << fixed << setprecision(2)
    << "Price per ounce: "
    << price_per_ounce << endl;
```

There is another manipulator that is sometimes handy. When you display several rows of data, you usually want the columns to line up.

You use the setw manipulator to set the *width* of the next output field. The width is the total number of characters used for showing the value, including digits, the

You use manipulators to line up your output in neat columns.

© Koele/iStockphoto.

decimal point, and spaces. Controlling the width is important when you want columns of numbers to line up.

For example, if you want a number to be printed in a column that is eight characters wide, you use

```
cout << setw(8) << price_per_ounce;
```

This command prints the value price_per_ounce in a field of width 8, for example

$$\boxed{}\boxed{}\boxed{}\boxed{}\boxed{0}\boxed{.}\boxed{0}\boxed{4}$$

(where each ▢ represents a space).

There is a notable difference between the setprecision and setw manipulators. Once you set the precision, that value is used for all floating-point numbers in that statement. But the width affects only the *next* value. Subsequent values are formatted without added spaces.

Our next example program will prompt for the price of a six-pack and the volume of each can, then print out the price per ounce. The program puts to work what you just learned about reading input and formatting output.

sec03/volume2.cpp

```cpp
 1  #include <iostream>
 2  #include <iomanip>
 3
 4  using namespace std;
 5
 6  int main()
 7  {
 8     // Read price per pack
 9
10     cout << "Please enter the price for a six-pack: ";
11     double pack_price;
12     cin >> pack_price;
13
14     // Read can volume
15
16     cout << "Please enter the volume for each can (in ounces): ";
17     double can_volume;
18     cin >> can_volume;
19
20     // Compute pack volume
21
22     const double CANS_PER_PACK = 6;
23     double pack_volume = can_volume * CANS_PER_PACK;
24
25     // Compute and print price per ounce
26
27     double price_per_ounce = pack_price / pack_volume;
28
29     cout << fixed << setprecision(2);
30     cout << "Price per ounce: " << price_per_ounce << endl;
31
32     return 0;
33  }
```

Program Run

```
Please enter the price for a six-pack: 2.95
Please enter the volume for each can (in ounces): 12
Price per ounce: 0.04
```

Table 8 Formatting Output

Output Statement	Output	Comment
`cout << 12.345678;`	12.3457	By default, a number is printed with 6 significant digits.

`cout << fixed`
`    << setprecision(2)`
`    << 12.3;`
	12.30	Use the `fixed` and `setprecision` manipulators to control the number of digits after the decimal point.

`cout << ":" << setw(6)` `    << 12;`	: 12	Four spaces are printed before the number, for a total width of 6 characters.
`cout << ":" << setw(2)` `    << 123;`	:123	If the width not sufficient, it is ignored.
`cout << setw(6)` `    << ":" << 12;`	:12	The width only refers to the next item. Here, the : is preceded by five spaces.

2.4 Problem Solving: First Do It By Hand

A very important step for developing an algorithm is to first carry out the computations *by hand*. If you can't compute a solution yourself, it's unlikely that you'll be able to write a program that automates the computation.

To illustrate the use of hand calculations, consider the following problem.

A row of black and white tiles needs to be placed along a wall. For aesthetic reasons, the architect has specified that the first and last tile shall be black.

Your task is to compute the number of tiles needed and the gap at each end, given the space available and the width of each tile.

To make the problem more concrete, let's assume the following dimensions:

- Total width: 100 inches
- Tile width: 5 inches

The obvious solution would be to fill the space with 20 tiles, but that would not work—the last tile would be white.

Pick concrete values for a typical situation to use in a hand calculation.

Instead, look at the problem this way: The first tile must always be black, and then we add some number of white/black pairs:

The first tile takes up 5 inches, leaving 95 inches to be covered by pairs. Each pair is 10 inches wide. Therefore the number of pairs is 95 / 10 = 9.5. However, we need to discard the fractional part because we can't have fractions of tile pairs.

Therefore, we will use 9 tile pairs or 18 tiles, together with the initial black tile. Altogether, we require 19 tiles.

The tiles span $19 \times 5 = 95$ inches, leaving a total gap of $100 - 19 \times 5 = 5$ inches. The gap should be evenly distributed at both ends. At each end, the gap is $(100 - 19 \times 5) / 2 = 2.5$ inches.

This computation gives us enough information to devise an algorithm with arbitrary values for the total width and tile width.

number of pairs = integer part of (total width - tile width) / (2 x tile width)
number of tiles = 1 + 2 x number of pairs
gap at each end = (total width - number of tiles x tile width) / 2

As you can see, doing a hand calculation gives enough insight into the problem that it becomes easy to develop an algorithm.

EXAMPLE CODE   See sec04 of your companion code for a program that implements this algorithm.

WORKED EXAMPLE 2.1
Computing Travel Time

Learn how to develop a hand calculation to compute the time that a robot requires to retrieve an item from rocky terrain. See your E-Text or visit wiley.com/go/bclo3.

Courtesy of NASA.

HOW TO 2.1
Carrying out Computations

Many programming problems require that you carry out arithmetic computations. This How To shows you how to turn a problem statement into pseudocode and, ultimately, a C++ program.

Problem Statement   Suppose you are asked to write a program that simulates a vending machine. A customer selects an item for purchase and inserts a bill into the vending machine. The vending machine dispenses the purchased item and gives change. We will assume that all item prices are multiples of 25 cents, and the machine gives all change in dollar coins and quarters. Your task is to compute how many coins of each type to return.

Step 1   Understand the problem: What are the inputs? What are the desired outputs?

In this problem, there are two inputs:
* The denomination of the bill that the customer inserts
* The price of the purchased item

There are two desired outputs:

- The number of dollar coins that the machine returns
- The number of quarters that the machine returns

Step 2   Work out examples by hand.

Let's assume that a customer purchased an item that cost $2.25 and inserted a $5 bill. The customer is due $2.75, or two dollar coins and three quarters.

That is easy for you to see, but how can a C++ program come to the same conclusion? The computation is simpler if you work in pennies, not dollars. The change due the customer is 275 pennies. Dividing by 100 yields 2, the number of dollars. Dividing the remainder (75) by 25 yields 3, the number of quarters.

Step 3   Write pseudocode for computing the answers.

In the previous step, you worked out a specific instance of the problem. You now need to come up with a method that works in general.

Given an arbitrary item price and payment, how can you compute the change due in coins? First, compute the change due in pennies:

change due = 100 x bill value - item price in pennies

To get the dollars, divide by 100 and discard the remainder:

dollar coins = change due / 100 (without remainder)

The remaining amount due can be computed in two ways. If you are familiar with the modulus operator, you can simply compute

change due = change due % 100

Alternatively, subtract the penny value of the dollar coins from the change due:

change due = change due - 100 x dollar coins

To get the quarters due, divide by 25:

quarters = change due / 25

Step 4   Define the variables and constants that you need, and specify their types.

Here, we have five variables:

- `bill_value`
- `item_price`
- `change_due`
- `dollar_coins`
- `quarters`

A vending machine takes bills and gives change in coins.

Jupiter Images/Getty Images.

Should we introduce constants to explain 100 and 25 as PENNIES_PER_DOLLAR and PENNIES_PER_QUARTER? Doing so will make it easier to convert the program to international markets, so we will take this step.

It is very important that change_due and PENNIES_PER_DOLLAR are of type int because the computation of dollar_coins uses integer division. Similarly, the other variables are integers.

Step 5   Turn the pseudocode into C++ statements.

If you did a thorough job with the pseudocode, this step should be easy. Of course, you have to know how to express mathematical operations (such as powers or integer division) in C++.

```
change_due = PENNIES_PER_DOLLAR * bill_value - item_price;
dollar_coins = change_due / PENNIES_PER_DOLLAR;
change_due = change_due % PENNIES_PER_DOLLAR;
quarters = change_due / PENNIES_PER_QUARTER;
```

Step 6   Provide input and output.

Before starting the computation, we prompt the user for the bill value and item price:

```
cout << "Enter bill value (1 = $1 bill, 5 = $5 bill, etc.): ";
cin >> bill_value;
cout << "Enter item price in pennies: ";
cin >> item_price;
```

When the computation is finished, we display the result. For extra credit, we use the setw manipulator to make sure that the output lines up neatly.

```
cout << "Dollar coins: " << setw(6) << dollar_coins << endl
     << "Quarters:     " << setw(6) << quarters << endl;
```

Step 7   Include the required headers and provide a main function.

We need the <iostream> header for all input and output. Because we use the setw manipulator, we also require <iomanip>. This program does not use any special mathematical functions. Therefore, we do not include the <cmath> header.

In the main function, you need to define constants and variables (Step 4), carry out computations (Step 5), and provide input and output (Step 6). Clearly, you will want to first get the input, then do the computations, and finally show the output. Define the constants at the beginning of the function, and define each variable just before it is needed.

Here is the complete program:

how_to_1/vending.cpp

```
 1  #include <iostream>
 2  #include <iomanip>
 3
 4  using namespace std;
 5
 6  int main()
 7  {
 8     const int PENNIES_PER_DOLLAR = 100;
 9     const int PENNIES_PER_QUARTER = 25;
10
11     cout << "Enter bill value (1 = $1 bill, 5 = $5 bill, etc.): ";
12     int bill_value;
13     cin >> bill_value;
14     cout << "Enter item price in pennies: ";
15     int item_price;
16     cin >> item_price;
17
18     int change_due = PENNIES_PER_DOLLAR * bill_value - item_price;
19     int dollar_coins = change_due / PENNIES_PER_DOLLAR;
```

```
20    change_due = change_due % PENNIES_PER_DOLLAR;
21    int quarters = change_due / PENNIES_PER_QUARTER;
22
23    cout << "Dollar coins: " << setw(6) << dollar_coins << endl
24      << "Quarters:      " << setw(6) << quarters << endl;
25
26    return 0;
27 }
```

Program Run

```
Enter bill value (1 = $1 bill, 5 = $5 bill, etc.): 5
Enter item price in pennies: 225
Dollar coins:      2
Quarters:          3
```

WORKED EXAMPLE 2.2

Computing the Cost of Stamps

Learn how to use arithmetic functions to simulate a stamp vending machine. See your E-Text or visit wiley.com/go/bclo3.

2.5 Strings

Strings are sequences of characters.

Many programs process text, not numbers. Text consists of **characters**: letters, numbers, punctuation, spaces, and so on. A **string** is a sequence of characters. For example, the string "Harry" is a sequence of five characters.

© essxboy/iStockphoto.

2.5.1 The string Type

You can define variables that hold strings.

```
string name = "Harry";
```

The string type is a part of the C++ standard. To use it, simply include the header file, <string>:

```
#include <string>
```

We distinguish between string *variables* (such as the variable name defined above) and string *literals* (character sequences enclosed in quotes, such as "Harry"). The string stored in a string variable can change. A string literal denotes a particular string, just as a number literal (such as 2) denotes a particular number.

Unlike number variables, string variables are guaranteed to be initialized even if you do not supply an initial value. By default, a string variable is set to an empty string: a string containing no characters. An empty string literal is written as "". The definition

```
string response;
```

has the same effect as

```
string response = "";
```

2.5.2 Concatenation

Use the + operator to *concatenate* strings; that is, to put them together to yield a longer string.

Given two strings, such as "Harry" and "Morgan", you can **concatenate** them to one long string. The result consists of all characters in the first string, followed by all characters in the second string. In C++, you use the + operator to concatenate two strings. For example,

```
string fname = "Harry";
string lname = "Morgan";
string name = fname + lname;
```

results in the string

```
"HarryMorgan"
```

What if you'd like the first and last name separated by a space? No problem:

```
string name = fname + " " + lname;
```

This statement concatenates three strings: fname, the string literal " ", and lname. The result is

```
"Harry Morgan"
```

2.5.3 String Input

You can read a string from the console:

```
cout << "Please enter your name: ";
string name;
cin >> name;
```

When a string is read with the >> operator, only one word is placed into the string variable. For example, suppose the user types

```
Harry Morgan
```

as the response to the prompt. This input consists of two words. After the call cin >> name, the string "Harry" is placed into the variable name. Use another input statement to read the second word.

2.5.4 String Functions

The length member function yields the number of characters in a string.

The number of characters in a string is called the *length* of the string. For example, the length of "Harry" is 5. You can compute the length of a string with the length function. Unlike the sqrt or pow function, the length function is invoked with the **dot notation**.

That is, you write the string whose length you want, then a period, then the name of the function, followed by parentheses:

```
int n = name.length();
```

Many C++ functions require you to use this dot notation, and you must memorize (or look up) which do and which don't. These functions are called **member functions**. We say that the member function length is *invoked on* the variable name.

Once you have a string, you can extract substrings by using the substr member function. The member function call

```
s.substr(start, length)
```

returns a string that is made from the characters in the string s, starting at character start, and containing length characters. Here is an example:

```
string greeting = "Hello, World!";
string sub = greeting.substr(0, 5);
// sub is "Hello"
```

The substr operation makes a string that consists of five characters taken from the string greeting. Indeed, "Hello" is a string of length 5 that occurs inside greeting. A curious aspect of the substr operation is the starting position. Starting position 0 means "start at the beginning of the string". The first position in a string is labeled 0, the second one 1, and so on. For example, here are the position numbers in the greeting string:

```
H  e  l  l  o  ,     W  o  r  l  d  !
0  1  2  3  4  5  6  7  8  9  10 11 12
```

The position number of the last character (12) is always one less than the length of the string.

Let's figure out how to extract the substring "World". Count characters starting at 0, not 1. You find that W, the 8th character, has position number 7. The string you want is 5 characters long. Therefore, the appropriate substring command is

```
string w = greeting.substr(7, 5);
```

```
                        5
                   ⌜‾‾‾‾‾‾‾‾⌝
H  e  l  l  o  ,     W  o  r  l  d  !
0  1  2  3  4  5  6 ↑7  8  9  10 11↑12
```

If you omit the length, you get all characters from the given position to the end of the string. For example,

```
greeting.substr(7)
```

is the string "World!" (including the exclamation point).

In a string that contains characters other than the English alphabet, digits, and punctuation marks, a character may take up more than a single char value. We will discuss this issue further in Chapter 8.

Here is a simple program that puts these concepts to work. The program asks for your name and that of your significant other. It then prints out your initials.

The operation `first.substr(0, 1)` makes a string consisting of one character, taken from the start of `first`. The program does the same for `second`. Then it concatenates the resulting one-character strings with the string literal `"&"` to get a string of length 3, the `initials` string. (See Figure 4.)

© Rich Legg/iStockphoto.

Initials are formed from the first letter of each name.

```
first =  R  o  d  o  l  f  o
         0  1  2  3  4  5  6

second = S  a  l  l  y
         0  1  2  3  4

initials = R  &  S
           0  1  2
```

Figure 4 Building the `initials` String

sec05/initials.cpp

```cpp
1   #include <iostream>
2   #include <string>
3
4   using namespace std;
5
6   int main()
7   {
8      cout << "Enter your first name: ";
9      string first;
10     cin >> first;
11     cout << "Enter your significant other's first name: ";
12     string second;
13     cin >> second;
14     string initials = first.substr(0, 1)
15        + "&" + second.substr(0, 1);
16     cout << initials << endl;
17
18     return 0;
19  }
```

Program Run

```
Enter your first name: Rodolfo
Enter your significant other's first name: Sally
R&S
```

Table 9 String Operations

Statement	Result	Comment
`string str = "C";` `str = str + "++";`	str is set to "C++"	When applied to strings, + denotes concatenation.
🚫 `string str = "C" + "++";`	**Error**	**Error:** You cannot concatenate two string literals.

`cout << "Enter name: ";`
`cin >> name;`
(User input: Harry Morgan)
	name contains "Harry"	The >> operator places the next word into the string variable.

`cout << "Enter name: ";`
`cin >> name >> last_name;`
(User input: Harry Morgan)
	name contains "Harry", last_name contains "Morgan"	Use multiple >> operators to read more than one word.

`string greeting = "H & S";` `int n = greeting.length();`	n is set to 5	Each space counts as one character.
`string str = "Sally";` `string str2 = str.substr(1, 3);`	str2 is set to "all"	Extracts the substring of length 3 starting at position 1. (The initial position is 0.)
`string str = "Sally";` `string str2 = str.substr(1);`	str2 is set to "ally"	If you omit the length, all characters from the position until the end are included.
`string a = str.substr(0, 1);`	a is set to the initial letter in str	Extracts the substring of length 1 starting at position 0.
`string b = str.substr(str.length() - 1);`	b is set to the last letter in str	The last letter has position `str.length() - 1`. We need not specify the length.

Computing & Society 2.2 **International Alphabets and Unicode**

The English alphabet is pretty simple: upper- and lowercase *a* to *z*. Other European languages have accent marks and special characters. For example, German has three so-called *umlaut* characters, ä, ö, ü, and a *double-s* character ß. These are not optional frills; you couldn't write a page of German text without using these characters a few times. German keyboards have keys for these characters.

This poses a problem for computer users and designers. The American standard character encoding (called ASCII, for American Standard Code for Information Interchange) specifies 128 codes: 52 upper- and lowercase characters, 10 digits, 32 typographical symbols, and 34 control characters (such as space, newline, and 32 others for controlling printers and other devices). The umlaut and double-s are

The German Keyboard Layout

not among them. Some German data processing systems replace seldom-used ASCII characters with German letters: [\ ] { | } ~ are replaced with Ä Ö Ü ä ö ü ß. While most people can live without these characters, C++ programmers definitely cannot. Other encoding schemes take advantage of the fact that one byte can encode 256 different characters, of which only 128 are standardized by ASCII. Unfortunately, there are multiple incompatible standards for such encodings, resulting in a certain amount of aggravation among European computer users.

Many countries don't use the Roman script at all. Russian, Greek, Hebrew, Arabic, and Thai letters, to name just a few, have completely different shapes. To complicate matters, Hebrew and Arabic are typed from right to left. Each of these alphabets has between 30 and 100 letters, and the countries using them have established encoding standards for them.

The situation is much more dramatic in languages that use the Chinese script: the Chinese dialects, Japanese, and Korean. The Chinese script is not alphabetic but *ideographic*. A character represents an idea or thing. Most words are made up of one, two, or three of these ideographic characters. (Over 50,000 ideographs are known, of which about 20,000 are in active use.) Therefore, two bytes are needed to encode them. China, Taiwan, Japan, and Korea have incompatible encoding standards for them. (Japanese and Korean writing uses a mixture of native syllabic and Chinese ideographic characters.)

The inconsistencies among character encodings have been a major nuisance for international electronic communication and for software manufacturers vying for a global market. Starting in 1988, a consortium of hardware and software manufacturers developed a uniform 21-**bit** encoding scheme called **Unicode** that is capable of encoding text in essentially all written languages of the world. About 100,000 characters have been given codes, including more than 70,000 Chinese, Japanese, and Korean ideographs. Even extinct languages, such as Egyptian hieroglyphs, have been included in Unicode.

© Joel Carillet/iStockphoto.

Hebrew, Arabic, and English

© Saipg/iStockphoto.

The Chinese Script

CHAPTER SUMMARY

Write variable definitions in C++.

- A variable is a storage location with a name.
- When defining a variable, you usually specify an initial value.
- When defining a variable, you also specify the type of its values.
- Use the `int` type for numbers that cannot have a fractional part.
- Use the `double` type for floating-point numbers.
- By convention, variable names should start with a lowercase letter.
- An assignment statement stores a new value in a variable, replacing the previously stored value.
- The assignment operator = does *not* denote mathematical equality.

- You cannot change the value of a variable that is defined as const.
- Use comments to add explanations for humans who read your code. The compiler ignores comments.

Use the arithmetic operations in C++.

- Use * for multiplication and / for division.
- The ++ operator adds 1 to a variable; the -- operator subtracts 1.
- If both arguments of / are integers, the remainder is discarded.
- The % operator computes the remainder of an integer division.
- A common use of the % operator is to check whether a number is even or odd.
- Assigning a floating-point variable to an integer drops the fractional part.
- The C++ library defines many mathematical functions such as sqrt (square root) and pow (raising to a power).

Write programs that read user input and write formatted output.

- Use the >> operator to read a value and place it in a variable.
- You use manipulators to specify how values should be formatted.

Carry out hand calculations when developing an algorithm.

- Pick concrete values for a typical situation to use in a hand calculation.

Write programs that process strings.

- Strings are sequences of characters.
- Use the + operator to *concatenate* strings; that is, put them together to yield a longer string.
- The length member function yields the number of characters in a string.
- A member function is invoked using the dot notation.
- Use the substr member function to extract a substring of a string.

REVIEW EXERCISES

- **R2.1** Write declarations for storing the following quantities. Choose between integers and floating-point numbers. Declare constants when appropriate.
    - **a.** The number of days per week
    - **b.** The number of days until the end of the semester
    - **c.** The number of centimeters in an inch
    - **d.** The height of the tallest person in your class, in centimeters

- **R2.2** What is the value of mystery after this sequence of statements?

```
int mystery = 1;
mystery = 1 - 2 * mystery;
mystery = mystery + 1;
```

- **R2.3** What is wrong with the following sequence of statements?

```
int mystery = 1;
mystery = mystery + 1;
int mystery = 1 - 2 * mystery;
```

- ■■ **R2.4** Write the following mathematical expressions in C++.

$$s = s_0 + v_0 t + \frac{1}{2} g t^2 \qquad\qquad FV = PV \cdot \left(1 + \frac{INT}{100}\right)^{YRS}$$

$$G = 4\pi^2 \frac{a^3}{p^2(m_1 + m_2)} \qquad\qquad c = \sqrt{a^2 + b^2 - 2ab\cos\gamma}$$

- ■■ **R2.5** Write the following C++ expressions in mathematical notation.
    - **a.** `dm = m * (sqrt(1 + v / c) / sqrt(1 - v / c) - 1);`
    - **b.** `volume = PI * r * r * h;`
    - **c.** `volume = 4 * PI * pow(r, 3) / 3;`
    - **d.** `z = sqrt(x * x + y * y);`

- ■■ **R2.6** What are the values of the following expressions? In each line, assume that

```
double x = 2.5;
double y = -1.5;
int m = 18;
int n = 4;
```

- **a.** `x + n * y - (x + n) * y`
- **b.** `m / n + m % n`
- **c.** `5 * x - n / 5`
- **d.** `1 - (1 - (1 - (1 - (1 - n))))`
- **e.** `sqrt(sqrt(n))`

- **R2.7** What are the values of the following expressions? In each line, assume that

```
string s = "Hello";
string t = "World";
```

- **a.** `s.length() + t.length()`
- **b.** `s.substr(1, 2)`

       c. s.substr(s.length() / 2, 1)

       d. s + t

       e. t + s

▪ **R2.8** Find at least five *compile-time* errors in the following program.

```
#include iostream

int main();
{
   cout << "Please enter two numbers:"
   cin << x, y;
   cout << "The sum of << x << "and" << y
      << "is: " x + y << endl;
   return;
}
```

▪▪ **R2.9** Find at least four *run-time* errors in the following program.

```
#include <iostream>

using namespace std;

int main()
{
   int total;
   int x1;
   cout << "Please enter a number: ";
   cin >> x1;
   total = total + x1;
   cout << "Please enter another number: ";
   int x2;
   cin >> x2;
   total = total + x1;
   double average = total / 2;
   cout << "The average of the two numbers is "
      << average << "endl";
   return 0;
}
```

▪ **R2.10** Explain the differences between 2, 2.0, "2", and "2.0".

▪ **R2.11** Explain what each of the following program segments computes.

       a. int x = 2;
          int y = x + x;

       b. string s = "2";
          string t = s + s;

▪▪ **R2.12** Write pseudocode for a program that reads a word and then prints the first character, the last character, and the characters in the middle. For example, if the input is Harry, the program prints H y arr.

▪▪ **R2.13** Write pseudocode for a program that reads a name (such as Harold James Morgan) and then prints a monogram consisting of the initial letters of the first, middle, and last names (such as HJM).

▪▪▪ **R2.14** Write pseudocode for a program that computes the first and last digits of a number. For example, if the input is 23456, the program should print out 2 and 6. *Hint:* %, log10.

■ **R2.15** Modify the pseudocode for the program in How To 2.1 so that the program gives change in quarters, dimes, and nickels. You can assume that the price is a multiple of 5 cents. To develop your pseudocode, first work with a couple of specific values.

■■ **R2.16** A cocktail shaker is composed of three cone sections.

The volume of a cone section with height h and top and bottom radius r_1 and r_2 is $V = \pi \dfrac{\left(r_1^2 + r_1 r_2 + r_2^2\right)h}{3}$. Compute the total volume by

hand for one set of realistic values for the radii and heights. Then develop an algorithm that works for arbitrary dimensions.

■■■ **R2.17** You are cutting off a piece of pie like this, where c is the length of the straight part (called the chord length) and h is the height of the piece.

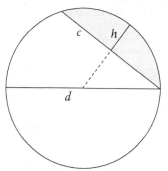

There is an approximate formula for the area: $A \approx \dfrac{2}{3}ch + \dfrac{h^3}{2c}$

However, h is not so easy to measure, whereas the diameter d of a pie is usually well-known. Calculate the area where the diameter of the pie is 12 inches and the chord length of the segment is 10 inches. Generalize to an algorithm that yields the area for any diameter and chord length.

■■ **R2.18** The following pseudocode describes how to obtain the name of a day, given the day number (0 = Sunday, 1 = Monday, and so on.)

Define a string called names containing "SunMonTueWedThuFriSat".
Compute the starting position as 3 x the day number.
Extract the substring of names at the starting position with length 3.

Check this pseudocode, using the day number 4. Draw a diagram of the string that is being computed, similar to Figure 4.

■■■ **R2.19** The following pseudocode describes how to swap two letters in a word.

We are given a string str and two positions i and j. (i comes before j)
Set first to the substring from the start of the string to the last position before i.
Set middle to the substring from positions i + 1 to j – 1.
Set last to the substring from position j + 1 to the end of the string.
Concatenate the following five strings: first, the string containing just the character at position j,
*   middle, the string containing just the character at position i, and last.*

Check this pseudocode, using the string "Gateway" and positions 2 and 4. Draw a diagram of the string that is being computed, similar to Figure 4.

■■ **R2.20** Run the following program, and explain the output you get.

```
#include <iostream>

using namespace std;

int main()
{
   int total;
   cout << "Please enter a number: ";
   double x1;
   cin >> x1;
   total = total + x1;
   cout << "total: " << total << endl;
   cout << "Please enter a number: ";
   double x2;
   cin >> x2;
   total = total + x2;
   cout << "total: " << total << endl;
   total = total / 2;
   cout << "total: " << total << endl;
   cout << "The average is " << total << endl;
   return 0;
}
```

Note the **trace messages** (in blue) that are inserted to show the current contents of the total variable. How do you fix the program? (The program has two separate errors.)

■■ **R2.21** How do you get the first character of a string? The last character? How do you remove the first character? The last character?

■■ **R2.22** For each of the following computations in C++, determine whether the result is exact, an overflow, or a roundoff error.

    a. 2.0 - 1.1
    b. 1.0E6 * 1.0E6
    c. 65536 * 65536
    d. 1000000 * 1000000

■■■ **R2.23** Write a program that prints the values

```
3 * 1000 * 1000 * 1000
3.0 * 1000 * 1000 * 1000
```

Explain the results.

■ **R2.24** This chapter contains a number of recommendations regarding variables and constants that make programs easier to read and maintain. Briefly summarize these recommendations.

PRACTICE EXERCISES

■ **E2.1** Write a program that displays the dimensions of a letter-size (8.5 × 11 inches) sheet of paper in millimeters. There are 25.4 millimeters per inch. Use constants and comments in your program.

■ **E2.2** Write a program that computes and displays the circumference of a letter-size (8.5 × 11 inches) sheet of paper and the length of its diagonal.

■ **E2.3** Write a program that reads a number and displays the square, cube, and fourth power. Use the pow function only for the fourth power.

■ **E2.4** Write a program that prompts the user for two integers and then prints
- The sum
- The difference
- The product
- The average

■■ **E2.5** Write a program that prompts the user for two integers and then prints
- The distance (absolute value of the difference)
- The maximum (the larger of the two)
- The minimum (the smaller of the two)

Hint: The max and min functions are defined in the <algorithm> header.

■■ **E2.6** Write a program that prompts the user for a measurement in meters and then converts it to miles, feet, and inches.

■ **E2.7** Write a program that prompts the user for a radius and then prints
- The area and circumference of a circle with that radius
- The volume and surface area of a sphere with that radius

■■ **E2.8** Write a program that asks the user for the lengths of the sides of a rectangle and then prints
- The area and perimeter of the rectangle
- The length of the diagonal (use the Pythagorean theorem)

■ **E2.9** Improve the program discussed in How To 2.1 to allow input of quarters in addition to bills.

■■ **E2.10** Write a program that asks the user to input
- The number of gallons of gas in the tank
- The fuel efficiency in miles per gallon
- The price of gas per gallon

Then print the cost per 100 miles and how far the car can go with the gas in the tank.

■ **E2.11** *File names and extensions.* Write a program that prompts the user for the drive letter (C), the path (\Windows\System), the file name (Readme), and the extension (txt). Then print the complete file name C:\Windows\System\Readme.txt. (If you use UNIX or a Macintosh, skip the drive name and use / instead of \ to separate directories.)

■■ **E2.12** Write a program that reads a number between 1,000 and 999,999 from the user and prints it *with a comma separating the thousands.* Here is a sample dialog; the user input is in color:

```
Please enter an integer between 1000 and 999999: 23456
23,456
```

■■■ **E2.13** Write a program that reads a number between 1,000 and 999,999 from the user, where the user enters a comma in the input. Then print the number without a comma. Here is a sample dialog; the user input is in color:

```
Please enter an integer between 1,000 and 999,999: 23,456
23456
```

Hint: Read the input as a string. Measure the length of the string. Suppose it contains n characters. Then extract substrings consisting of the first $n - 4$ characters and the last three characters.

■ **E2.14** *Printing a grid.* Write a program that prints the following grid to play tic-tac-toe.

```
+--+--+--+
|  |  |  |
+--+--+--+
|  |  |  |
+--+--+--+
|  |  |  |
+--+--+--+
```

Of course, you could simply write seven statements of the form

```
cout << "+--+--+--+";
```

You should do it the smart way, though. Define string variables to hold two kinds of patterns: a comb-shaped pattern

```
+--+--+--+
|  |  |  |
```

and the bottom line. Print the comb three times and the bottom line once.

■■ **E2.15** Write a program that reads an integer and breaks it into a sequence of individual digits. For example, the input 16384 is displayed as

```
1 6 3 8 4
```

You may assume that the input has no more than five digits and is not negative.

■■ **E2.16** Write a program that reads two times in military format (0900, 1730) and prints the number of hours and minutes between the two times. Here is a sample run. User input is in color.

```
Please enter the first time: 0900
Please enter the second time: 1730
8 hours 30 minutes
```

Extra credit if you can deal with the case where the first time is later than the second:

```
Please enter the first time: 1730
Please enter the second time: 0900
15 hours 30 minutes
```

■■■ **E2.17** *Writing large letters.* A large letter H can be produced like this:

```
*   *
*   *
*****
*   *
*   *
```

It can be defined as a string constant like this:

```
const string LETTER_H =
   "*   *\n*   *\n*****\n*   *\n*   *\n";
```

(The \n character is explained in Special Topic 1.1.) Do the same for the letters E, L, and O. Then write the message

```
H
E
L
L
O
```

in large letters.

■ ■ **E2.18** Write a program that transforms numbers 1, 2, 3, ..., 12 into the corresponding month names January, February, March, ..., December. *Hint:* Make a very long string "January February March ...", in which you add spaces such that each month name has *the same length*. Then use substr to extract the month you want.

© José Luis Gutiérrez/iStockphoto.

PROGRAMMING PROJECTS

■ ■ **P2.1** Easter Sunday is the first Sunday after the first full moon of spring. To compute the date, you can use this algorithm, invented by the mathematician Carl Friedrich Gauss in 1800:

1. Let y be the year (such as 1800 or 2001).

2. Divide y by 19 and call the remainder a. Ignore the quotient.

3. Divide y by 100 to get a quotient b and a remainder c.

4. Divide b by 4 to get a quotient d and a remainder e.

5. Divide 8 * b + 13 by 25 to get a quotient g. Ignore the remainder.

6. Divide 19 * a + b - d - g + 15 by 30 to get a remainder h. Ignore the quotient.

7. Divide c by 4 to get a quotient j and a remainder k.

8. Divide a + 11 * h by 319 to get a quotient m. Ignore the remainder.

9. Divide 2 * e + 2 * j - k - h + m + 32 by 7 to get a remainder r. Ignore the quotient.

10. Divide h - m + r + 90 by 25 to get a quotient n. Ignore the remainder.

11. Divide h - m + r + n + 19 by 32 to get a remainder p. Ignore the quotient.

Then Easter falls on day p of month n. For example, if y is 2001:

```
a = 6           g = 6          m = 0     n = 4
b = 20, c = 1   h = 18         r = 6     p = 15
d = 5, e = 0    j = 0, k = 1
```

Therefore, in 2001, Easter Sunday fell on April 15. Write a program that prompts the user for a year and prints out the month and day of Easter Sunday.

■ ■ ■ **P2.2** In this project, you will perform calculations with triangles. A triangle is defined by the *x*- and *y*-coordinates of its three corner points.

Your job is to compute the following properties of a given triangle:

- the lengths of all sides
- the angles at all corners
- the perimeter
- the area

Supply a program that prompts a user for the corner point coordinates and produces a nicely formatted table of the triangle properties.

■ Business P2.3 A video club wants to reward its best members with a discount based on the member's number of movie rentals and the number of new members referred by the member. The discount is in percent and is equal to the sum of the rentals and the referrals, but it cannot exceed 75 percent. (*Hint:* The min function in the `<algorithm>` header.) Write a program to calculate the value of the discount.

Here is a sample run:

```
Enter the number of movie rentals: 56
Enter the number of members referred to the video club: 3
The discount is equal to:     59.00 percent.
```

■■■ P2.4 Write a program that helps a person decide whether to buy a hybrid car. Your program's inputs should be:

- The cost of a new car
- The estimated miles driven per year
- The estimated gas price
- The estimated resale value after 5 years

Compute the total cost of owning the car for 5 years. (For simplicity, we will not take the cost of financing into account.) Obtain realistic prices for a new and used hybrid and a comparable car from the Web. Run your program twice, using today's gas price and 15,000 miles per year. Include pseudocode and the program runs with your assignment.

© asiseeit/iStockphoto.

■■ Business P2.5 The following pseudocode describes how a bookstore computes the price of an order from the total price and the number of the books that were ordered.

> *Read the total book price and the number of books.*
> *Compute the tax (7.5% of the total book price).*
> *Compute the shipping charge ($2 per book).*
> *The price of the order is the sum of the total book price, the tax, and the shipping charge.*

Print the price of the order. Translate this pseudocode into a C++ program.

■■ Business P2.6 The following pseudocode describes how to turn a string containing a ten-digit phone number (such as `"4155551212"`) into a more readable string with parentheses and dashes, like this: `"(415) 555-1212"`.

> *Take the substring consisting of the first three characters and surround it with "(" and ")". This is the area code.*
> *Concatenate the area code, the substring consisting of the next three characters, a hyphen, and the substring consisting of the last four characters. This is the formatted number.*

Translate this pseudocode into a C++ program that reads a telephone number into a string variable, computes the formatted number, and prints it.

■■ Business P2.7 The following pseudocode describes how to extract the dollars and cents from a price given as a floating-point value. For example, a price of 2.95 yields values 2 and 95 for the dollars and cents.

Assign the price to an integer variable dollars.
Multiply the difference price - dollars by 100 and add 0.5.
Assign the result to an integer variable cents.

Translate this pseudocode into a C++ program. Read a price and print the dollars and cents. Test your program with inputs 2.95 and 4.35.

■■ **Business P2.8** *Giving change.* Implement a program that directs a cashier how to give change. The program has two inputs: the amount due and the amount received from the customer. Display the dollars, quarters, dimes, nickels, and pennies that the customer should receive in return.

■ **Engineering P2.9** Consider the following circuit.

© Captainflash/iStockphoto.

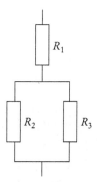

Write a program that reads the resistances of the three resistors and computes the total resistance, using the rules for series and parallel resistors that are derived from Ohm's law.

■■ **Engineering P2.10** The dew point temperature T_d can be calculated (approximately) from the relative humidity RH and the actual temperature T by

$$T_d = \frac{b \cdot f(T,RH)}{a - f(T,RH)}$$

$$f(T,RH) = \frac{a \cdot T}{b + T} + \ln(RH)$$

where $a = 17.27$ and $b = 237.7°$ C.

Write a program that reads the relative humidity (between 0 and 1) and the temperature (in degrees C) and prints the dew point value. Use the C++ log function to compute the natural logarithm.

■■■ **Engineering P2.11** The pipe clip temperature sensors shown here are robust sensors that can be clipped directly onto copper pipes to measure the temperature of the liquids in the pipes.

Each sensor contains a device called a *thermistor*. Thermistors are semiconductor devices that exhibit a temperature-dependent resistance described by:

$$R = R_0\, e^{\beta\left(\frac{1}{T} - \frac{1}{T_0}\right)}$$

where R is the resistance (in Ω) at the temperature T (in $^\circ$K), and R_0 is the resistance (in Ω) at the temperature T_0 (in $^\circ$K). β is a constant that depends on the material used to make the thermistor. Thermistors are specified by providing values for R_0, T_0, and β.

The thermistors used to make the pipe clip temperature sensors have $R_0 = 1075\ \Omega$ at $T_0 = 85\ ^\circ$C, and $\beta = 3969\ ^\circ$K. (Notice that β has units of $^\circ$K. Recall that the temperature in $^\circ$K is obtained by adding 273 to the temperature in $^\circ$C.) The liquid temperature, in $^\circ$C, is determined from the resistance R, in Ω, using

$$T = \frac{\beta T_0}{T_0 \ln\left(\dfrac{R}{R_0}\right) + \beta} - 273$$

Write a C++ program that prompts the user for the thermistor resistance R and prints a message giving the liquid temperature in $^\circ$C.

■■■ **Engineering P2.12** The circuit shown below illustrates some important aspects of the connection between a power company and one of its customers. The customer is represented by three parameters, V_t, P, and pf. V_t is the voltage accessed by plugging into a wall outlet. Customers depend on having a dependable value of V_t in order for their appliances to work properly. Accordingly, the power company regulates the value of V_t carefully. P describes the amount of power used by the customer and is the primary factor in determining the customer's

© TebNad/iStockphoto.

electric bill. The power factor, pf, is less familiar. (The power factor is calculated as the cosine of an angle so that its value will always be between zero and one.) In this problem you will be asked to write a C++ program to investigate the significance of the power factor.

In the figure, the power lines are represented, somewhat simplistically, as resistances in Ohms. The power company is represented as an AC voltage source. The source voltage, V_s, required to provide the customer with power P at voltage V_t can be determined using the formula

$$V_s = \sqrt{\left(V_t + \frac{2RP}{V_t}\right)^2 + \left(\frac{2RP}{pf\,V_t}\right)^2 (1 - pf^2)}$$

(V_s has units of Vrms.) This formula indicates that the value of V_s depends on the value of pf. Write a C++ program that prompts the user for a power factor value and then prints a message giving the corresponding value of V_s, using the values for P, R, and V_t shown in the figure above.

■■■ **Engineering P2.13** Consider the following tuning circuit connected to an antenna, where C is a variable capacitor whose capacitance ranges from C_{min} to C_{max}.

The tuning circuit selects the frequency $f = \dfrac{1}{2\pi\sqrt{LC}}$. To design this circuit for a given frequency, take $C = \sqrt{C_{min}\,C_{max}}$ and calculate the required inductance L from f and C. Now the circuit can be tuned to any frequency in the range

$$f_{min} = \frac{1}{2\pi\sqrt{LC_{max}}} \text{ to } f_{max} = \frac{1}{2\pi\sqrt{LC_{min}}}.$$

Write a C++ program to design a tuning circuit for a given frequency, using a variable capacitor with given values for C_{min} and C_{max}. (A typical input is $f = 16.7$ MHz, $C_{min} = 14$ pF, and $C_{max} = 365$ pF.) The program should read in f (in Hz), C_{min} and C_{max} (in F), and print the required inductance value and the range of frequencies to which the circuit can be tuned by varying the capacitance.

■ **Engineering P2.14** According to the Coulomb force law, the electric force between two charged particles of charge Q_1 and Q_2 Coulombs, that are a distance r meters apart, is

$$F = \frac{Q_1 Q_2}{4\pi\varepsilon r^2} \text{ Newtons, where } \varepsilon = 8.854 \times 10^{-12} \text{ Farads/meter. Write a program that}$$

calculates the force on a pair of charged particles, based on the user input of Q_1 Coulombs, Q_2 Coulombs, and r meters, and then computes and displays the electric force.

■■ **Engineering P2.15** According to Newton's law of gravitation, the gravitational force between two masses M_1 and M_2 (in kilograms), that are a distance r meters apart, is $F = GM_1M_2/r^2$, where $G = 6.67 \times 10^{-11} N(m/kg)^2$. Write a program that calculates the force on a pair of masses, based on the user input of M_1, M_2, and r.

■■ **Engineering P2.16**   The relationship between angles measured in units of degrees and units of radians is π radians $= 180°$. Write a program that converts angles in degrees to angles in radians. The input is a positive integer.

Note: Make sure that numerical output is not greater than 2π radians or $360°$. For example, $370° = 0.174533$ radian.

■■ **Engineering P2.17**   The equation for the distance traveled by a freely falling object is $y = 1/2gt^2$, where t is time in seconds and g is the acceleration of gravity near the surface of the Earth, $g = 9.8$ m/s^2. Notice that this equation is independent of the mass of the object.

Create a program that outputs a sentence expressing the distance traveled in the given time. For example, an input of 10 seconds should have the output sentence "After the first 10 seconds, the object has fallen 490 meters."

CHAPTER 3

DECISIONS

© zennie/iStockphoto.

One of the essential features of computer programs is their ability to make decisions. Like a train that changes tracks depending on how the switches are set, a program can take different actions, depending on inputs and other circumstances.

In this chapter, you will learn how to program simple and complex decisions. You will apply what you learn to the task of checking user input.

3.1 The if Statement

The if statement allows a program to carry out different actions depending on the nature of the data to be processed.

The if statement is used to implement a decision. When a condition is fulfilled, one set of statements is executed. Otherwise, another set of statements is executed (see Syntax 3.1).

Here is an example using the if statement. In many countries, the number 13 is considered unlucky. Rather than offending superstitious tenants, building owners sometimes skip the thirteenth floor; floor 12 is immediately followed by floor 14. Of course, floor 13 is not usually left empty or, as some conspiracy theorists believe, filled with secret offices and research labs. It is simply called floor 14. The computer that controls the building elevators needs to compensate for this foible and adjust all floor numbers above 13.

Let's simulate this process in C++. We will ask the user to type in the desired floor number and then compute the actual floor. When the input is above 13, then we need to decrement the input to obtain the actual floor.

© DrGrounds/iStockphoto.

This elevator panel "skips" the thirteenth floor. The floor is not actually missing—the computer that controls the elevator adjusts the floor numbers above 13.

An if *statement is like a fork in the road. Depending upon a decision, different parts of the program are executed.*

© Media Bakery.

For example, if the user provides an input of 20, the program determines the actual floor as 19. Otherwise, we simply use the supplied floor number.

```
int actual_floor;

if (floor > 13)
{
   actual_floor = floor - 1;
}
else
{
   actual_floor = floor;
}
```

The flowchart in Figure 1 shows the branching behavior.

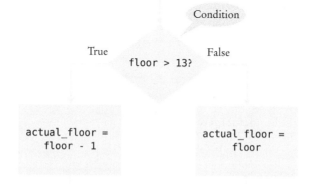

Figure 1   Flowchart for if Statement

Syntax 3.1   if Statement

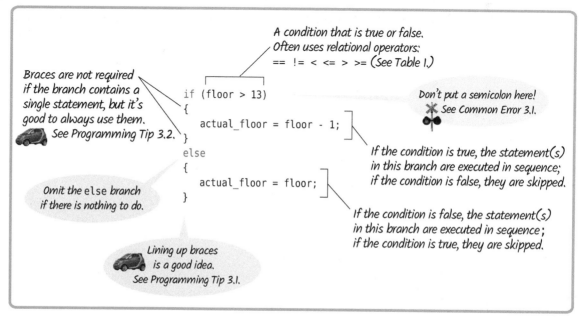

In our example, each branch of the if statement contains a single statement. You can include as many statements in each branch as you like. Sometimes, it happens that there is nothing to do in the else branch of the statement. In that case, you can omit it entirely, such as in this example:

```
int actual_floor = floor;

if (floor > 13)
{
   actual_floor--;
} // No else needed
```

See Figure 2 for the flowchart.

Figure 2   Flowchart for if Statement with No else Branch

The following program puts the if statement to work. This program asks for the desired floor and then prints out the actual floor.

sec01/elevator1.cpp

```cpp
1  #include <iostream>
2
3  using namespace std;
4
5  int main()
6  {
7     int floor;
8     cout << "Floor: ";
9     cin >> floor;
10    int actual_floor;
11    if (floor > 13)
12    {
13       actual_floor = floor - 1;
14    }
15    else
16    {
17       actual_floor = floor;
18    }
19
20    cout << "The elevator will travel to the actual floor "
21       << actual_floor << endl;
```

```
22
23      return 0;
24  }
```

Program Run

```
Floor: 20
The elevator will travel to the actual floor 19
```

Common Error 3.1

A Semicolon After the `if` Condition

The following code fragment has an unfortunate error:

```
if (floor > 13) ; // ERROR
{
    floor--;
}
```

There should be no semicolon after the `if` condition. The compiler interprets this statement as follows: If `floor` is greater than 13, execute the statement that is denoted by a single semicolon, that is, the do-nothing statement. The statement enclosed in braces is no longer a part of the `if` statement. It is always executed. Even if the value of `floor` is not above 13, it is decremented.

Placing a semicolon after the `else` reserved word is also wrong:

```
if (floor > 13)
{
    actual_floor = floor - 1;
}
else ;
{
    actual_floor = floor;
}
```

In this case, the do-nothing statement is executed if `floor > 13` is not fulfilled. This is the end of the `if` statement. The next statement, enclosed in braces, is executed in both cases; that is, `actual_floor` is always set to `floor`.

Programming Tip 3.1

Brace Layout

Programmers vary in how they align braces in their code. In this book, we follow the simple rule of making { and } line up.

```
if (floor > 13)
{
    floor--;
}
```

This style makes it easy to spot matching braces.

Some programmers put the opening brace on the same line as the `if`:

```
if (floor > 13) {
    floor--;
}
```

© Timothy Large/iStockphoto.

Properly lining up your code makes your programs easier to read.

This style makes it harder to match the braces, but it saves a line of code, allowing you to view more code on the screen without scrolling. There are passionate advocates of both styles.

It is important that you pick a layout style and stick with it consistently within a given programming project. Which style you choose may depend on your personal preference or a coding style guide that you need to follow.

Programming Tip 3.2
Always Use Braces

When a branch of an `if` statement consists of a single statement, you need not use braces. For example, the following is legal:

```
if (floor > 13)
    floor--;
```

However, it is a good idea to always include the braces:

```
if (floor > 13)
{
    floor--;
}
```

The braces makes your code easier to read, and you are less likely to make errors such as the one described in Common Error 3.1.

Programming Tip 3.3
Tabs

Block-structured code has the property that nested statements are indented by one or more levels:

```
int main()
{
|   int floor;
|   . . .
|   if (floor > 13)
|   {
|   |   floor--;
|   } |
|   . . .
|   return 0;
} | |
0   1   2   Indentation level
```

How do you move the cursor from the leftmost column to the appropriate indentation level? A perfectly reasonable strategy is to hit the space bar a sufficient number of times. However, many programmers use the Tab key instead. A tab moves the cursor to the next indentation level.

While the Tab *key* is nice, some editors use *tab characters* for alignment, which is not so nice. Tab characters can lead to problems when you send your file to another person or a printer. There is no universal agreement on the width of a tab character, and some software will ignore tabs altogether. It is therefore best to save your files with spaces instead of tabs. Most editors have a setting to automatically convert all tabs to spaces. Look at the documentation of your development environment to find out how to activate this useful setting.

© Vincent LaRussa/John Wiley & Sons, Inc.

You use the Tab key to move the cursor to the next indentation level.

Programming Tip 3.4

Avoid Duplication in Branches

Look to see whether you *duplicate code* in each branch. If so, move it out of the `if` statement. Here is an example of such duplication:

```cpp
if (floor > 13)
{
   actual_floor = floor - 1;
   cout << "Actual floor: " << actual_floor << endl;
}
else
{
   actual_floor = floor;
   cout << "Actual floor: " << actual_floor << endl;
}
```

The output statement is exactly the same in both branches. This is not an error—the program will run correctly. However, you can simplify the program by moving the duplicated statement, like this:

```cpp
if (floor > 13)
{
   actual_floor = floor - 1;
}
else
{
   actual_floor = floor;
}
cout << "Actual floor: " << actual_floor << endl;
```

Removing duplication is particularly important when programs are maintained for a long time. When there are two sets of statements with the same effect, it can easily happen that a programmer modifies one set but not the other.

Special Topic 3.1

The Conditional Operator

C++ has a *conditional operator* of the form

    condition ? *value*$_1$: *value*$_2$

The value of that expression is either *value*$_1$ if the test passes or *value*$_2$ if it fails. For example, we can compute the actual floor number as

```cpp
actual_floor = floor > 13 ? floor - 1 : floor;
```

which is equivalent to

```cpp
if (floor > 13)
{
   actual_floor =  floor - 1;
}
else
{
   actual_floor = floor;
}
```

You can use the conditional operator anywhere that a value is expected, for example:

```cpp
cout << "Actual floor: " << (floor > 13 ? floor - 1 : floor);
```

We don't use the conditional operator in this book, but it is a convenient construct that you will find in many C++ programs.

3.2 Comparing Numbers and Strings

Relational operators (< <= > >= == !=) are used to compare numbers and strings.

Every `if` statement contains a *condition*. In many cases, the condition involves comparing two values. For example, in the previous examples we tested `floor > 13`. The comparison `>` is called a **relational operator**. C++ has six relational operators (see Table 1).

As you can see, only two C++ relational operators (`>` and `<`) look as you would expect from the mathematical notation. Computer keyboards do not have keys for ≥, ≤, or ≠, but the `>=`, `<=`, and `!=` operators are easy to remember because they look similar. The `==` operator is initially confusing to most newcomers to C++. In C++, `=` already has a meaning, namely assignment.

© arturbo/iStockphoto.

In C++, you use a relational operator to check whether one value is greater than another.

The `==` operator denotes equality testing:

```
floor = 13;  // Assign 13 to floor
if (floor == 13)  // Test whether floor equals 13
```

You must remember to use `==` inside tests and to use `=` outside tests. (See Common Error 3.2 for more information.)

Table 1 Relational Operators

C++	Math Notation	Description
>	>	Greater than
>=	≥	Greater than or equal
<	<	Less than
<=	≤	Less than or equal
==	=	Equal
!=	≠	Not equal

You can compare strings as well:

```
if (input == "Quit") . . .
```

Use `!=` to check whether two strings are different. In C++, letter case matters. For example, `"Quit"` and `"quit"` are not the same string.

Syntax 3.2 Comparisons

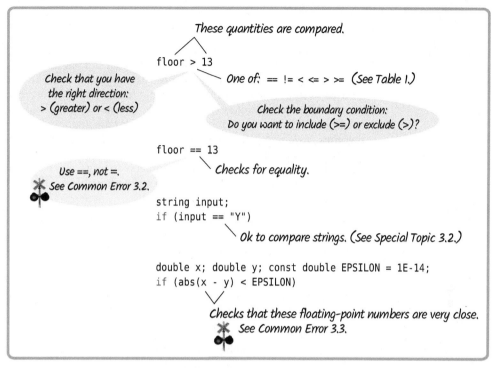

EXAMPLE CODE See sec02 of your companion code for a program that compares numbers and strings.

Table 2 summarizes how to use relational operators in C++.

Table 2 **Relational Operator Examples**

Expression	Value	Comment
3 <= 4	true	3 is less than 4; <= tests for "less than or equal".
⃠ 3 =< 4	**Error**	The "less than or equal" operator is <=, not =<. The "less than" symbol comes first.
3 > 4	false	> is the opposite of <=.
4 < 4	false	The left-hand side must be strictly smaller than the right-hand side.
4 <= 4	true	Both sides are equal; <= tests for "less than or equal".
3 == 5 - 2	true	== tests for equality.
3 != 5 - 1	true	!= tests for inequality. It is true that 3 is not 5 – 1.
⃠ 3 = 6 / 2	**Error**	Use == to test for equality.
1.0 / 3.0 == 0.333333333	false	Although the values are very close to one another, they are not exactly equal. See Common Error 3.3.
⃠ "10" > 5	**Error**	You cannot compare a string to a number.

Common Error 3.2

Confusing = and ==

The rule for the correct usage of = and == is very simple: In tests, always use == and never use =. If it is so simple, why can't the compiler be helpful and flag any errors?

Actually, the C++ language allows the use of = inside tests. To understand this, we have to go back in time. The creators of C, the predecessor to C++, were very frugal. They did not want to have special values true and false. Instead, they allowed any numeric value inside a condition, with the convention that 0 denotes false and any non-0 value denotes true. Furthermore, in C and C++ assignments have values. For example, the value of the assignment expression floor = 13 is 13.

These two features—namely that numbers can be used as truth values and that assignments are expressions with values—conspire to make a horrible pitfall. The test

```
if (floor = 13) // ERROR
```

is legal C++, but it does not test whether floor and 13 are equal. Instead, the code sets floor to 13, and because that value is not zero, the condition of the if statement is always fulfilled.

Fortunately, most compilers issue a warning when they encounter such a statement. You should take such warnings seriously. (See Programming Tip 3.5 for more advice about compiler warnings.)

Some shell-shocked programmers are so nervous about using = that they use == even when they want to make an assignment:

```
floor == floor - 1; // ERROR
```

This statement tests whether floor equals floor - 1. It doesn't do anything with the outcome of the test, but that is not an error. Some compilers will warn that "the code has no effect", but others will quietly accept the code.

Common Error 3.3

Exact Comparison of Floating-Point Numbers

Floating-point numbers have only a limited precision, and calculations can introduce roundoff errors. You must take these inevitable roundoffs into account when comparing floating-point numbers. For example, the following code multiplies the square root of 2 by itself. Ideally, we expect to get the answer 2:

© caracterdesign/iStockphoto.

Take limited precision into account when comparing floating-point numbers.

```
double r = sqrt(2.0);
if (r * r == 2)
{
   cout << "sqrt(2) squared is 2" << endl;
}
else
{
   cout << "sqrt(2) squared is not 2 but "
      << setprecision(18) << r * r << endl;
}
```

This program displays

```
sqrt(2) squared is not 2 but 2.00000000000000044
```

It does not make sense in most circumstances to compare floating-point numbers exactly. Instead, we should test whether they are *close enough*. That is, the magnitude of their difference should be less than some threshold. Mathematically, we would write that x and y are close enough if

$$|x - y| < \varepsilon$$

for a very small number, ε. ε is the Greek letter epsilon, a letter used to denote a very small quantity. It is common to set ε to 10^{-14} when comparing `double` numbers:

```
const double EPSILON = 1E-14;
double r = sqrt(2.0);
if (abs(r * r - 2) < EPSILON)
{
    cout << "sqrt(2) squared is approximately 2";
}
```

Include the `<cmath>` header when you use the abs function.

Programming Tip 3.5
Compile with Zero Warnings

There are two kinds of messages that the compiler gives you: *errors* and *warnings*. Error messages are fatal; the compiler will not translate a program with one or more errors. Warning messages are advisory; the compiler will translate the program, but there is a good chance that the program will not do what you expect it to do.

It is a good idea to learn how to activate warnings with your compiler, and to write code that emits no warnings at all. For example, consider the test

```
if (floor = 13)
```

One C++ compiler emits a curious warning message: "Suggest parentheses around assignment used as truth value". Sadly, the message is misleading because it was not written for students. Nevertheless, such a warning gives you another chance to look at the offending statement and fix it, in this case, by replacing the = with an ==.

In order to make warnings more visible, many compilers require you to take some special action. This might involve clicking a checkbox in an integrated environment or supplying a special option on the command line. Ask your instructor or lab assistant how to turn on warnings for your compiler.

Special Topic 3.2
Lexicographic Ordering of Strings

If you compare strings using < <= > >=, they are compared in "lexicographic" order. This ordering is very similar to the way in which words are sorted in a dictionary.

For example, consider this code fragment.

```
string name = "Tom";
if (name < "Dick") . . .
```

The condition is not fulfilled, because in the dictionary Dick comes before Tom. There are a few differences between the ordering in a dictionary and in C++. In C++:

Corbis Digital Stock.

To see which of two terms comes first in the dictionary, consider the first letter in which they differ.

- All uppercase letters come before the lowercase letters. For example, "Z" comes before "a".
- The space character comes before all printable characters.

- Numbers come before letters.
- For the ordering of punctuation marks, see Appendix C.

Lexicographic order is used to compare strings.

When comparing two strings, the first letters of each word are compared, then the second letters, and so on, until one of the strings ends or a letter pair doesn't match.

If one of the strings ends, the longer string is considered the "larger" one. For example, compare "car" with "cart". The first three letters match, and we reach the end of the first string. Therefore "car" comes before "cart" in lexicographic ordering.

When you reach a mismatch, the string containing the "larger" character is considered "larger". For example, let's compare "cat" with "cart". The first two letters match. Since t comes after r, the string "cat" comes after "cart" in the lexicographic ordering.

c	a	r

c	a	r	t

c	a	t

Letters   r comes
match   before t

Lexicographic Ordering

HOW TO 3.1

Implementing an if Statement

This How To walks you through the process of implementing an if statement. We will illustrate the steps with the following example problem:

Problem Statement   The university bookstore has a Kilobyte Day sale every October 24, giving an 8 percent discount on all computer accessory purchases if the price is less than $128, and a 16 percent discount if the price is at least $128. Write a program that asks the cashier for the original price and then prints the discounted price.

Step 1   Decide upon the branching condition.

In our sample problem, the obvious choice for the condition is:

original price < 128?

That is just fine, and we will use that condition in our solution.

But you could equally well come up with a correct solution if you chose the opposite condition: Is the original price at least (≥) $128? You might choose this condition if you put yourself into the position of a shopper who wants to know when the bigger discount applies.

© MikePanic/iStockphoto.

Sales discounts are often higher for expensive products. Use the if statement to implement such a decision.

Step 2   Give pseudocode for the work that needs to be done when the condition is true.

In this step, you list the action or actions that are taken in the "positive" branch. The details depend on your problem. You may want to print a message, compute values, or even exit the program.

In our example, we need to apply an 8 percent discount:

discounted price = 0.92 x original price

Step 3   Give pseudocode for the work (if any) that needs to be done when the condition is *not* true.

What do you want to do in the case that the condition of Step 1 is not fulfilled? Sometimes, you want to do nothing at all. In that case, use an if statement without an else branch.

In our example, the condition tested whether the price was less than $128. If that condition is *not* true, the price is at least $128, so the higher discount of 16 percent applies to the sale:

discounted price = 0.84 x original price

Step 4 Double-check relational operators.

First, be sure that the test goes in the right *direction*. It is a common error to confuse > and <. Next, consider whether you should use the < operator or its close cousin, the <= operator.

What should happen if the original price is exactly $128? Reading the problem carefully, we find that the lower discount applies if the original price is *less than* $128, and the higher discount applies when it is *at least* $128. A price of $128 should therefore *not* fulfill our condition, and we must use <, not <=.

Step 5 Remove duplication.

Check which actions are common to both branches, and move them outside. (See Programming Tip 3.4.)

In our example, we have two statements of the form

discounted price = ___ x original price

They only differ in the discount rate. It is best to just set the rate in the branches, and to do the computation afterwards:

If original price < 128
    discount rate = 0.92
Else
    discount rate = 0.84
discounted price = discount rate x original price

Step 6 Test both branches.

Formulate two test cases, one that fulfills the condition of the if statement, and one that does not. Ask yourself what should happen in each case. Then follow the pseudocode and act each of them out.

In our example, let us consider two scenarios for the original price: $100 and $200. We expect that the first price is discounted by $8, the second by $32.

When the original price is 100, then the condition 100 < 128 is true, and we get

discount rate = 0.92
discounted price = 0.92 x 100 = 92

When the original price is 200, then the condition 200 < 128 is false, and

discount rate = 0.84
discounted price = 0.84 x 200 = 168

In both cases, we get the expected answer.

Step 7 Assemble the if statement in C++.

Type the skeleton

```
if ()
{
}
else
{
}
```

and fill it in, as shown in Syntax 3.1. Omit the else branch if it is not needed.

In our example, the completed statement is

```
if (original_price < 128)
{
    discount_rate = 0.92;
}
else
{
    discount_rate = 0.84;
}

discounted_price = discount_rate * original_price;
```

EXAMPLE CODE   See how_to_1 of your companion code for a program that calculates a discounted price.

WORKED EXAMPLE 3.1

Extracting the Middle

Learn how to extract the middle character from a string, or the two middle characters if the length of the string is even. See your E-Text or visit wiley.com/go/bclo3.

c	r	a	t	e
0	1	2	3	4

Computing & Society 3.1   **Dysfunctional Computerized Systems**

Making decisions is an essential part of any computer program. Nowhere is this more obvious than in a computer system that helps sort luggage at an airport. After scanning the luggage identification codes, the system sorts the items and routes them to different conveyor belts. Human operators then place the items onto trucks. When the city of Denver built a huge airport to replace an outdated and congested facility, the luggage system contractor went a step further. The new system was designed to replace the human operators with robotic carts. Unfortunately, the system plainly did not work. It was plagued by mechanical problems, such as luggage falling onto the tracks and jamming carts. Equally frustrating were the software glitches. Carts would uselessly accumulate at some locations when they were needed elsewhere.

The airport had been scheduled to open in 1993, but without a functioning luggage system, the opening was delayed for over a year while the contractor tried to fix the problems. The contractor never succeeded, and ultimately a manual system was installed. The delay cost the city and airlines close to a billion dollars, and the contractor, once the leading luggage systems vendor in the United States, went bankrupt.

Clearly, it is very risky to build a large system based on a technology that has never been tried on a smaller scale. In 2013, the rollout of universal healthcare in the United States was put in jeopardy by a dysfunctional web site for selecting insurance plans. The system promised an insurance shopping experience similar to booking airline flights. But, the HealthCare.gov site didn't simply present the available insurance plans. It also had to check the income level of each applicant and use that information to determine the subsidy level. That task turned out to be quite a bit harder than checking whether a credit card had sufficient credit to pay for an airline ticket. The Obama administration would have been well advised to design a signup process that did not rely on an untested computer program.

Lyn Alweis/Contributor/Getty Images.

The Denver airport originally had a fully automatic system for moving luggage, replacing human operators with robotic carts. Unfortunately, the system never worked and was dismantled before the airport was opened.

3.3 Multiple Alternatives

Multiple alternatives are required for decisions that have more than two cases.

In Section 3.1, you saw how to program a two-way branch with an `if` statement. In many situations, there are more than two cases. In this section, you will see how to implement a decision with multiple alternatives. For example, consider a program that displays the effect of an earthquake, as measured by the Richter scale (see Table 3).

Value	Effect
Table 3 **Richter Scale**	
8	Most structures fall
7	Many buildings destroyed
6	Many buildings considerably damaged, some collapse
4.5	Damage to poorly constructed buildings

The Richter scale is a measurement of the strength of an earthquake. Every step in the scale, for example from 6.0 to 7.0, signifies a tenfold increase in the strength of the quake.

In this case, there are five branches: one each for the four descriptions of damage, and one for no destruction.

You use multiple `if` statements to implement multiple alternatives, like this:

```
if (richter >= 8.0)
{
   cout << "Most structures fall";
}
else if (richter >= 7.0)
{
   cout << "Many buildings destroyed";
}
else if (richter >= 6.0)
{
   cout << "Many buildings considerably damaged, "
      << "some collapse";
}
else if (richter >= 4.5)
{
   cout << "Damage to poorly constructed buildings";
}
else
{
   cout << "No destruction of buildings";
}
```

© kevinruss/iStockphoto.

The 1989 Loma Prieta earthquake that damaged the Bay Bridge in San Francisco and destroyed many buildings measured 7.1 on the Richter scale.

As soon as one of the four tests succeeds, the effect is displayed, and no further tests are attempted. If none of the four cases applies, the final `else` clause applies, and a default message is printed. Figure 3 shows the flowchart for this multiple-branch statement.

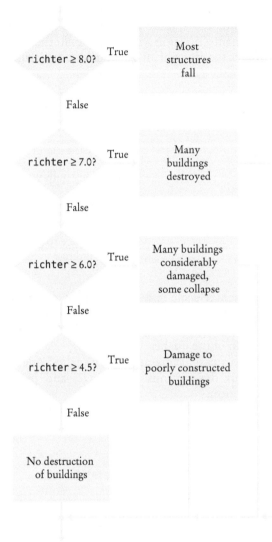

Figure 3 Multiple Alternatives

Here you must sort the conditions and test against the largest cutoff first. Suppose we reverse the order of tests:

```
if (richter >= 4.5) // Tests in wrong order
{
   cout << "Damage to poorly constructed buildings";
}
else if (richter >= 6.0)
{
   cout << "Many buildings considerably damaged, some collapse";
}
else if (richter >= 7.0)
{
```

```
        cout << "Many buildings destroyed";
    }
    else if (richter >= 8.0)
    {
        cout << "Most structures fall";
    }
```

This does not work. Suppose the value of richter is 7.1. That value is at least 4.5, matching the first case. The other tests will never be attempted.

When using multiple if statements, pay attention to the order of the conditions.

In this example, it is also important that we use a sequence of else if clauses, not just multiple independent if statements. Consider this sequence of independent tests:

```
if (richter >= 8.0) // Didn't use else
{
    cout << "Most structures fall";
}
if (richter >= 7.0)
{
    cout << "Many buildings destroyed";
}
if (richter >= 6.0)
{
    cout << "Many buildings considerably damaged, some collapse";
}
if (richter >= 4.5)
{
    cout << "Damage to poorly constructed buildings";
}
```

Now the alternatives are no longer exclusive. If richter is 7.1, then the last *three* tests all match, and three messages are printed.

EXAMPLE CODE   See sec03 of your companion code for the full program that prints earthquake descriptions.

Special Topic 3.3

The switch **Statement**

A sequence of if statements that compares a *single integer value* against several *constant* alternatives can be implemented as a switch statement. For example,

```
int digit;
. . .
switch (digit)
{
    case 1: digit_name = "one"; break;
    case 2: digit_name = "two"; break;
    case 3: digit_name = "three"; break;
    case 4: digit_name = "four"; break;
    case 5: digit_name = "five"; break;
    case 6: digit_name = "six"; break;
    case 7: digit_name = "seven"; break;
    case 8: digit_name = "eight"; break;
    case 9: digit_name = "nine"; break;
    default: digit_name = ""; break;
}
```

© travelpixpro/iStockphoto.

The switch *statement lets you choose from a fixed set of alternatives.*

This is a shortcut for

```
int digit;
if (digit == 1) { digit_name = "one"; }
else if (digit == 2) { digit_name = "two"; }
else if (digit == 3) { digit_name = "three"; }
else if (digit == 4) { digit_name = "four"; }
else if (digit == 5) { digit_name = "five"; }
else if (digit == 6) { digit_name = "six"; }
else if (digit == 7) { digit_name = "seven"; }
else if (digit == 8) { digit_name = "eight"; }
else if (digit == 9) { digit_name = "nine"; }
else { digit_name = ""; }
```

Well, it isn't much of a shortcut, but it has one advantage—it is obvious that all branches test the *same* value, namely digit.

It is possible to have multiple case clauses for a branch, such as

```
case 1: case 3: case 5: case 7: case 9:
   odd = true; break;
```

The default branch is chosen if none of the case clauses match.

Every branch of the switch must be terminated by a break instruction. If the break is missing, execution *falls through* to the next branch, and so on, until finally a break or the end of the switch is reached. In practice, this fall-through behavior is rarely useful, but it is a common cause of errors. If you accidentally forget the break statement, your program compiles but executes unwanted code. Many programmers consider the switch statement somewhat dangerous and prefer the if statement.

We leave it to you to use the switch statement for your own code or not. At any rate, you need to have a reading knowledge of switch in case you find it in other programmers' code.

3.4 Nested Branches

When a decision statement is contained inside the branch of another decision statement, the statements are *nested*.

It is often necessary to include an if statement inside another. Such an arrangement is called a *nested* set of statements. Here is a typical example.

In the United States, different tax rates are used depending on the taxpayer's marital status. There are different tax schedules for single and for married taxpayers. Married taxpayers add their income together and pay taxes on the total. Table 4 gives the tax rate computations, using a simplified version of the tax rate schedule. A different tax rate applies to each "bracket". In this schedule, the income at the first bracket is

Computing income taxes requires multiple levels of decisions.

© ericsphotography/iStockphoto.

taxed at 10 percent, and the income at the second bracket is taxed at 25 percent. The income limits for each bracket depend on the marital status.

Table 4 Federal Tax Rate Schedule		
If your status is Single and if the taxable income is	the tax is	of the amount over
at most $32,000	10%	$0
over $32,000	$3,200 + 25%	$32,000
If your status is Married and if the taxable income is	the tax is	of the amount over
at most $64,000	10%	$0
over $64,000	$6,400 + 25%	$64,000

Now compute the taxes due, given a filing status and an income figure. The key point is that there are two *levels* of decision making. First, you must branch on the marital status. Then, for each filing status, you must have another branch on income level. The two-level decision process is reflected in two levels of if statements in the program at the end of this section. (See Figure 4 for a flowchart.)

In theory, nesting can go deeper than two levels. A three-level decision process (first by state, then by filing status, then by income level) requires three nesting levels.

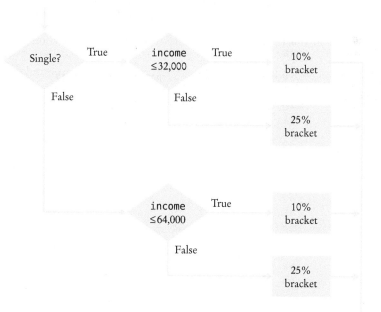

Figure 4   Income Tax Computation

sec04/tax.cpp

```cpp
1  #include <iostream>
2  #include <string>
3
4  using namespace std;
5
6  int main()
7  {
8     const double RATE1 = 0.10;
9     const double RATE2 = 0.25;
10    const double RATE1_SINGLE_LIMIT = 32000;
11    const double RATE1_MARRIED_LIMIT = 64000;
12
13    double tax1 = 0;
14    double tax2 = 0;
15
16    double income;
17    cout << "Please enter your income: ";
18    cin >> income;
19
20    cout << "Please enter s for single, m for married: ";
21    string marital_status;
22    cin >> marital_status;
23
24    if (marital_status == "s")
25    {
26       if (income <= RATE1_SINGLE_LIMIT)
27       {
28          tax1 = RATE1 * income;
29       }
30       else
31       {
32          tax1 = RATE1 * RATE1_SINGLE_LIMIT;
33          tax2 = RATE2 * (income - RATE1_SINGLE_LIMIT);
34       }
35    }
36    else
37    {
38       if (income <= RATE1_MARRIED_LIMIT)
39       {
40          tax1 = RATE1 * income;
41       }
42       else
43       {
44          tax1 = RATE1 * RATE1_MARRIED_LIMIT;
45          tax2 = RATE2 * (income - RATE1_MARRIED_LIMIT);
46       }
47    }
48
49    double total_tax = tax1 + tax2;
50
51    cout << "The tax is $" << total_tax << endl;
52    return 0;
53 }
```

Program Run

```
Please enter your income: 80000
Please enter s for single, m for married: m
The tax is $10400
```

Common Error 3.4

The Dangling else Problem

When an if statement is nested inside another if statement, the following error may occur.

```
double shipping_charge = 5.00; // $5 inside continental U.S.
if (country == "USA")
   if (state == "HI")
      shipping_charge = 10.00; // Hawaii is more expensive
else // Pitfall!
   shipping_charge = 20.00; // As are foreign shipments
```

The indentation level seems to suggest that the else is grouped with the test country == "USA". Unfortunately, that is not the case. The compiler ignores all indentation and matches the else with the preceding if. That is, the code is actually

```
double shipping_charge = 5.00; // $5 inside continental U.S.
if (country == "USA")
   if (state == "HI")
      shipping_charge = 10.00; // Hawaii is more expensive
   else // Pitfall!
      shipping_charge = 20.00; // As are foreign shipments
```

That isn't what you want. You want to group the else with the first if.

The ambiguous else is called a *dangling* else. You can avoid this pitfall if you *always use braces,* as recommended in Programming Tip 3.2:

```
double shipping_charge = 5.00; // $5 inside continental U.S.
if (country == "USA")
{
   if (state == "HI")
   {
      shipping_charge = 10.00; // Hawaii is more expensive
   }
}
else
{
   shipping_charge = 20.00; // As are foreign shipments
}
```

Programming Tip 3.6

Hand-Tracing

A very useful technique for understanding whether a program works correctly is called *hand-tracing*. You simulate the program's activity on a sheet of paper. You can use this method with pseudocode or C++ code.

Get an index card, a cocktail napkin, or whatever sheet of paper is within reach. Make a column for each variable. Have the program code ready. Use a marker, such as a paper clip, to mark the current statement. In your mind, execute statements one at a time. Every time the value of a variable changes, cross out the old value and write the new value below the old one.

For example, let's trace the tax program with the data from the program run in Section 3.4.

© thomasd007/iStockphoto.

Hand-tracing helps you understand whether a program works correctly.

In lines 13 and 14, tax1 and tax2 are initialized to 0.

```
6 int main()
7 {
8    const double RATE1 = 0.10;
9    const double RATE2 = 0.25;
10   const double RATE1_SINGLE_LIMIT = 32000;
11   const double RATE1_MARRIED_LIMIT = 64000;
12
13   double tax1 = 0;
14   double tax2 = 0;
15
```

tax1	tax2	income	marital status
0	0		

In lines 18 and 22, income and marital_status are initialized by input statements.

```
16   double income;
17   cout << "Please enter your income: ";
18   cin >> income;
19
20   cout << "Please enter s for single, m for married: ";
21   string marital_status;
22   cin >> marital_status;
23
```

tax1	tax2	income	marital status
0	0	80000	m

Because marital_status is not "s", we move to the else branch of the outer if statement (line 36).

```
24   if (marital_status == "s")
25   {
26      if (income <= RATE1_SINGLE_LIMIT)
27      {
28         tax1 = RATE1 * income;
29      }
30      else
31      {
32         tax1 = RATE1 * RATE1_SINGLE_LIMIT;
33         tax2 = RATE2 * (income - RATE1_SINGLE_LIMIT);
34      }
35   }
36   else
37   {
```

Because income is not <= 64000, we move to the else branch of the inner if statement (line 42).

```
38      if (income <= RATE1_MARRIED_LIMIT)
39      {
40         tax1 = RATE1 * income;
41      }
42      else
43      {
44         tax1 = RATE1 * RATE1_MARRIED_LIMIT;
45         tax2 = RATE2 * (income - RATE1_MARRIED_LIMIT);
46      }
```

The values of tax1 and tax2 are updated.

```
43      {
44         tax1 = RATE1 * RATE1_MARRIED_LIMIT;
45         tax2 = RATE2 * (income - RATE1_MARRIED_LIMIT);
46      }
47   }
```

tax1	tax2	income	marital status
0̸	0̸	80000	m
6400	4000		

Their sum total_tax is computed and printed. Then the program ends.

```
48
49   double total_tax = tax1 + tax2;
50
51   cout << "The tax is $" << total_tax << endl;
52   return 0;
53 }
```

tax1	tax2	income	marital status	total tax
0̸	0̸	80000	m	
6400	4000			10400

Because the program trace shows the expected output ($10,400), it successfully demonstrated that this test case works correctly.

3.5 Problem Solving: Flowcharts

Flowcharts are made up of elements for tasks, input/outputs, and decisions.

You have seen examples of flowcharts earlier in this chapter. A flowchart shows the structure of decisions and tasks that are required to solve a problem. When you have to solve a complex problem, it is a good idea to draw a flowchart to visualize the flow of control.

The basic flowchart elements are shown in Figure 5.

Simple task   Input/output   Condition   True

                                                                     False

Figure 5
Flowchart Elements

Each branch of a decision can contain tasks and further decisions.

The basic idea is simple enough. Link tasks and input/output boxes in the sequence in which they should be executed. Whenever you need to make a decision, draw a diamond with two outcomes (see Figure 6).

Each branch can contain a sequence of tasks and even additional decisions. If there are multiple choices for a value, lay them out as in Figure 7.

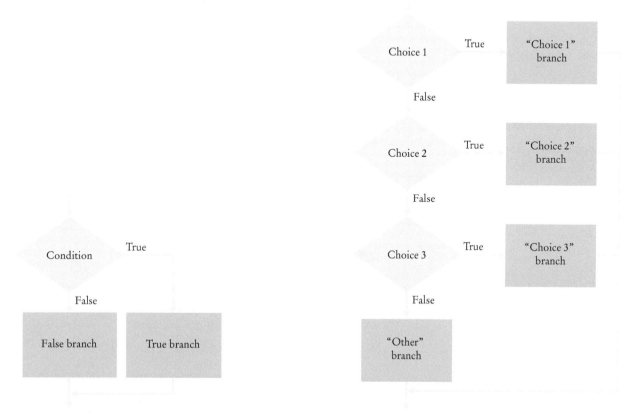

Figure 6 Flowchart with Two Outcomes

Figure 7 Flowchart with Multiple Choices

There is one issue that you need to be aware of when drawing flowcharts. Unconstrained branching and merging can lead to "spaghetti code", a messy network of possible pathways through a program.

There is a simple rule for avoiding spaghetti code: Never point an arrow *inside another branch*.

To understand the rule, consider this example: Shipping costs are $5 inside the United States, except that to Hawaii and Alaska they are $10. International shipping costs are also $10. You might start out with a flowchart like the following:

Spaghetti code has so many pathways that it becomes impossible to understand.

> **Never point an arrow inside another branch.**

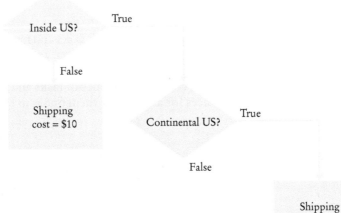

Now you may be tempted to reuse the "shipping cost = $10" task:

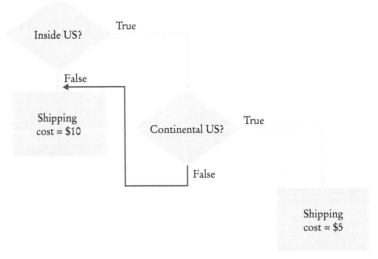

Don't do that! The red arrow points inside a different branch. Instead, add another task that sets the shipping cost to $10, like this:

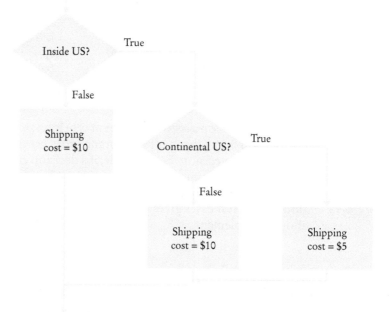

Not only do you avoid spaghetti code, but it is also a better design. In the future it may well happen that the cost for international shipments is different from that to Alaska and Hawaii.

Flowcharts can be very useful for getting an intuitive understanding of the flow of an algorithm. However, they get large rather quickly when you add more details. At that point, it makes sense to switch from flowcharts to pseudocode.

EXAMPLE CODE   See sec05 of your companion code for a program that computes shipping costs.

3.6 Problem Solving: Test Cases

> Each branch of your program should be covered by a test case.

Consider how to test the tax computation program from Section 3.4. Of course, you cannot try out all possible inputs of filing status and income level. Even if you could, there would be no point in trying them all. If the program correctly computes one or two tax amounts in a given bracket, then we have a good reason to believe that all amounts will be correct.

You want to aim for complete *coverage* of all decision points. Here is a plan for obtaining a comprehensive set of test cases:

- There are two possibilities for the filing status and two tax brackets for each status, yielding four test cases.
- Test a handful of *boundary* conditions, such as an income that is at the boundary between two brackets, and a zero income.
- If you are responsible for error checking (which is discussed in Section 3.8), also test an invalid input, such as a negative income.

Make a list of the test cases and the expected outputs:

Test Case		Expected Output	Comment
30,000	s	3,000	10% bracket
72,000	s	13,200	3,200 + 25% of 40,000
50,000	m	5,000	10% bracket
104,000	m	16,400	6,400 + 25% of 40,000
32,000	s	3,200	boundary case
0		0	boundary case

When you develop a set of test cases, it is helpful to have a flowchart of your program (see Section 3.5). Check off each branch that has a test case. Include **boundary test cases** for each decision. For example, if a decision checks whether an input is less than 100, test with an input of 100.

It is always a good idea to design test cases *before* starting to code. Working through the test cases gives you a better understanding of the algorithm that you are about to implement.

It is a good idea to design test cases before implementing a program.

Programming Tip 3.7
Make a Schedule and Make Time for Unexpected Problems

Commercial software is notorious for being delivered later than promised. For example, Microsoft originally promised that its Windows Vista operating system would be available late in 2003, then in 2005, then in March 2006; it finally was released in January 2007. Some of the early promises might not have been realistic. It was in Microsoft's interest to let prospective customers expect the imminent availability of the product. Had customers known the actual delivery date, they might have switched to a different product in the meantime. Undeniably, though, Microsoft had not anticipated the full complexity of the tasks it had set itself to solve.

Microsoft can delay the delivery of its product, but it is likely that you cannot. As a student or a programmer, you are expected to manage your time wisely and to finish your assignments on time. You can probably do simple programming exercises the night before the due date, but an assignment that looks twice as hard may well take four times as long, because more things can go wrong. You should therefore make a schedule whenever you start a programming project.

First, estimate realistically how much time it will take you to:

- Design the program logic.
- Develop test cases.
- Type in the program and fix syntax errors.
- Test and debug the program.

For example, for the income tax program I might estimate an hour for the design; 30 minutes for developing test cases; an hour for data entry and fixing syntax errors; and an hour for testing and debugging. That is a total of 3.5 hours. If I work two hours a day on this project, it will take me almost two days.

Then think of things that can go wrong. Your computer might break down. You might be stumped by a problem with the computer system.

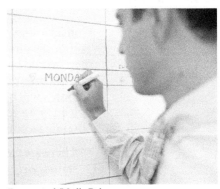

Bananastock/Media Bakery.

Make a schedule for your programming work and build in time for problems.

(That is a particularly important concern for beginners. It is *very* common to lose a day over a trivial problem just because it takes time to track down a person who knows the magic command to overcome it.) As a rule of thumb, *double* the time of your estimate. That is, you should start four days, not two days, before the due date. If nothing went wrong, great; you have the program done two days early. When the inevitable problem occurs, you have a cushion of time that protects you from embarrassment and failure.

3.7 Boolean Variables and Operators

Sometimes, you need to evaluate a logical condition in one part of a program and use it elsewhere. To store a condition that can be true or false, you use a *Boolean variable*. Boolean variables are named after the mathematician George Boole (1815–1864), a pioneer in the study of logic.

The Boolean type bool has two values, false and true.

Jon Patton/E+/iStockphoto.

A Boolean variable is also called a flag because it can be either up (true) or down (false).

In C++, the `bool` data type represents the Boolean type. Variables of type `bool` can hold exactly two values, denoted `false` and `true`. These values are not strings or integers; they are special values, just for Boolean variables.

Here is a definition of a Boolean variable:

```
bool failed = true;
```

You can use the value later in your program to make a decision:

```
if (failed) // Only executed if failed has been set to true
{
    . . .
}
```

When you make complex decisions, you often need to combine Boolean values. An operator that combines Boolean conditions is called a **Boolean operator**. In C++, the `&&` operator (called *and*) yields `true` only when *both* conditions are true. The `||` operator (called *or*) yields the result `true` if *at least one* of the conditions is true.

Suppose you write a program that processes temperature values, and you want to test whether a given temperature corresponds to liquid water. (At sea level, water freezes at 0 degrees Celsius and boils at 100 degrees.) Water is liquid if the temperature is greater than zero *and* less than 100:

```
if (temp > 0 && temp < 100) { cout << "Liquid"; }
```

At this geyser in Iceland, you can see ice, liquid water, and steam.

© toos/iStockphoto.

C++ has two Boolean operators that combine conditions: && (*and*) and || (*or*).

The condition of the test has two parts, joined by the && operator. (As shown in Table 5 and Appendix B, the > and < operators have higher precedence than the && operator.)

Table 5 Selected Operators and Their Precedence

Operator	Description
++ -- + (unary) – (unary) !	Increment, decrement, positive, negative, Boolean *not*
* / %	Multiplication, division, remainder
+ -	Addition, subtraction
< <= > >=	Comparisons
== !=	Equal, not equal
&&	Boolean *and*
||	Boolean *or*

Each part is a Boolean value that can be true or false. The combined expression is true if both individual expressions are true. If either one of the expressions is false, then the result is also false (see Figure 8).

A	B	A && B
true	true	true
true	false	false
false	true	false
false	false	false

A	B	A || B
true	true	true
true	false	true
false	true	true
false	false	false

A	!A
true	false
false	true

Figure 8   Boolean Truth Tables

Conversely, let's test whether water is *not* liquid at a given temperature. That is the case when the temperature is at most 0 *or* at least 100. Use the || (*or*) operator to combine the expressions:

```
if (temp <= 0 || temp >= 100) { cout << "Not liquid"; }
```

Figure 9 shows flowcharts for these examples.

EXAMPLE CODE   See sec07 of your companion code for a program that compares numbers using Boolean expressions.

To invert a condition, use the ! (*not*) operator.

Sometimes you need to *invert* a condition with the *not* logical operator. The ! operator takes a single condition and evaluates to true if that condition is false and to false if the condition is true. In this example, output occurs if the value of the Boolean variable frozen is false:

```
if (!frozen)
{
    cout << "Not frozen";
}
```

Figure 9   Flowcharts for *and* and *or* Combinations

Table 6 illustrates additional examples of evaluating Boolean operators.

Table 6 Boolean Operators

Expression	Value	Comment
`0 < 200 && 200 < 100`	false	Only the first condition is true. Note that the < operator has a higher precedence than the && operator.
`0 < 200 || 200 < 100`	true	The first condition is true.
`0 < 200 || 100 < 200`	true	The || is not a test for "either-or". If both conditions are true, the result is true.
⊘ `0 < 200 < 100`	true	**Error:** The expression 0 < 200 is true, which is converted to 1. The expression 1 < 100 is true. You never want to write such an expression; see Common Error 3.5.
⊘ `-10 && 10 > 0`	true	**Error:** –10 is not zero. It is converted to true. You never want to write such an expression; see Common Error 3.5.
`0 < x && x < 100 || x == -1`	`(0 < x && x < 100) || x == -1`	The && operator has a higher precedence than the || operator.
`!(0 < 200)`	false	0 < 200 is true, therefore its negation is false.
`frozen == true`	frozen	There is no need to compare a Boolean variable with true.
`frozen == false`	!frozen	It is clearer to use ! than to compare with false.

Common Error 3.5

Combining Multiple Relational Operators

Consider the expression

```
if (0 <= temp <= 100) // Error
```

This looks just like the mathematical test $0 \leq temp \leq 100$. Unfortunately, it is not.

Let us dissect the expression `0 <= temp <= 100`. The first half, `0 <= temp`, is a test with outcome `true` or `false`, depending on the value of `temp`. The outcome of that test (`true` or `false`) is then compared against 100. Can one compare truth values and floating-point numbers? Is `true` larger than 100 or not? Unfortunately, to stay compatible with the C language, C++ converts `false` to 0 and `true` to 1. Therefore, the expression will always evaluate to true.

You must be careful not to mix logical and arithmetic expressions in your programs. Instead, use *and* to combine two separate tests:

```
if (0 <= temp && temp <= 100) . . .
```

Another common error, along the same lines, is to write

```
if (x && y > 0) . . . // Error
```

instead of

```
if (x > 0 && y > 0) . . .
```

Unfortunately, the compiler will not issue an error message. Instead, it converts `x` to `true` or `false`. Zero is converted to `false`, and any nonzero value is converted to `true`. If `x` is not zero, then it tests whether `y` is greater than 0, and finally it computes the *and* of these two truth values. Naturally, that computation makes no sense.

Common Error 3.6

Confusing && and || Conditions

It is a surprisingly common error to confuse *and* and *or* conditions. A value lies between 0 and 100 if it is at least 0 *and* at most 100. It lies outside that range if it is less than 0 *or* greater than 100. There is no golden rule; you just have to think carefully.

Often the *and* or *or* is clearly stated, and then it isn't too hard to implement it. But sometimes the wording isn't as explicit. It is quite common that the individual conditions are nicely set apart in a bulleted list, but with little indication of how they should be combined. Consider these instructions for filing a tax return. You can claim single filing status if any one of the following is true:

- You were never married.
- You were legally separated or divorced on the last day of the tax year.
- You were widowed, and did not remarry.

Because the test passes if *any one* of the conditions is true, you must combine the conditions with *or*. Elsewhere, the same instructions state that you may use the more advantageous status of married filing jointly if all five of the following conditions are true:

- Your spouse died less than two years ago and you did not remarry.
- You have a child whom you can claim as dependent.
- That child lived in your home for all of the tax year.
- You paid over half the cost of keeping up your home for this child.
- You filed a joint return with your spouse the year he or she died.

Because *all* of the conditions must be true for the test to pass, you must combine them with an *and*.

Special Topic 3.4

Short-Circuit Evaluation of Boolean Operators

When the && and || operators are computed, evaluation stops as soon as the truth value is determined. When an && is evaluated and the first condition is false, the second condition is not evaluated, because it does not matter what the outcome of the second test is.

For example, consider the expression

```
quantity > 0 && price / quantity < 10
```

The && and || operators are computed using *short-circuit evaluation:* As soon as the truth value is determined, no further conditions are evaluated.

Suppose the value of quantity is zero. Then the test quantity > 0 fails, and the second test is not attempted. That is just as well, because it is illegal to divide by zero.

Similarly, when the first condition of an || expression is true, then the remainder is not evaluated since the result must be true.

This process is called **short-circuit evaluation**.

In a short circuit, electricity travels along the path of least resistance. Similarly, short-circuit evaluation takes the fastest path for computing the result of a Boolean expression.

© YouraPechkin/iStockphoto.

Special Topic 3.5

De Morgan's Law

Humans generally have a hard time comprehending logical conditions with *not* operators applied to *and/or* expressions. **De Morgan's Law**, named after the logician Augustus De Morgan (1806–1871), can be used to simplify these Boolean expressions.

Suppose we want to charge a higher shipping rate if we don't ship within the continental United States.

```
if (!(country == "USA"
        && state != "AK"
        && state != "HI"))
    shipping_charge = 20.00;
```

This test is a little bit complicated, and you have to think carefully through the logic. When it is *not* true that the country is USA *and* the state is not Alaska *and* the state is not Hawaii, then charge $20.00. Huh? It is not true that some people won't be confused by this code.

The computer doesn't care, but it takes human programmers to write and maintain the code. Therefore, it is useful to know how to simplify such a condition.

De Morgan's Law has two forms: one for the negation of an *and* expression and one for the negation of an *or* expression:

!(A && B)   is the same as   !A || !B
!(A || B)   is the same as   !A && !B

De Morgan's Law tells you how to negate && and || conditions.

Pay particular attention to the fact that the *and* and *or* operators are *reversed* by moving the *not* inward. For example, the negation of "the state is Alaska *or* it is Hawaii",

```
!(state == "AK" || state == "HI")
```

is "the state is not Alaska *and* it is not Hawaii":

```
!(state == "AK") && !(state == "HI")
```

That is, of course, the same as

```
state != "AK" && state != "HI"
```

Now apply the law to our shipping charge computation:

```
!(country == "USA"
    && state != "AK"
    && state != "HI")
```

is equivalent to

```
!(country == "USA")
    || !(state != "AK")
    || !(state != "HI")
```

That yields the simpler test

```
country != "USA"
    || state == "AK"
    || state == "HI"
```

To simplify conditions with negations of *and* or *or* expressions, it is usually a good idea to apply De Morgan's Law to move the negations to the innermost level.

3.8 Application: Input Validation

An important application for the if statement is *input validation*. Whenever your program accepts user input, you need to make sure that the user-supplied values are valid before you use them in your computations.

Consider our elevator program. Assume that the elevator panel has buttons labeled 1 through 20 (but not 13). The following are illegal inputs:

- The number 13
- Zero or a negative number
- A number larger than 20
- An input that is not a sequence of digits, such as five

In each of these cases, we will want to give an error message and exit the program.

Like a quality control worker, you want to make sure that user input is correct before processing it.   Tetra Images/Media Bakery.

It is simple to guard against an input of 13:

```
if (floor == 13)
{
   cout << "Error: There is no thirteenth floor." << endl;
   return 1;
}
```

The statement

```
return 1;
```

immediately exits the main function and therefore terminates the program. It is a convention to return with the value 0 if the program completed normally, and with a non-zero value when an error was encountered.

When reading a value, check that it is within the required range.

Here is how you ensure that the user doesn't enter a number outside the valid range:

```
if (floor <= 0 || floor > 20)
{
   cout << "Error: The floor must be between 1 and 20." << endl;
   return 1;
}
```

However, dealing with an input that is not a valid integer is a more serious problem. When the statement

```
cin >> floor;
```

is executed, and the user types in an input that is not an integer (such as five), then the integer variable floor is not set. Instead, the input stream cin is set to a failed state. You call the fail member function to test for that failed state.

```
if (cin.fail())
{
   cout << "Error: Not an integer." << endl;
   return 1;
}
```

Use the fail function to test whether the input stream has failed.

The order of the if statements is important. You must *first* test for cin.fail(). After all, if the input failed, no value has been assigned to floor, and it makes no sense to compare it against other values.

Input failure is quite serious in C++. Once input has failed, all subsequent attempts at input will fail as well. Special Topic 4.1 shows how to write programs that are more tolerant of bad input. For now, our goal is simply to detect bad input and to exit the program when it occurs.

Here is the complete elevator program with input validation.

sec08/elevator2.cpp

```
 1  #include <iostream>
 2
 3  using namespace std;
 4
 5  int main()
 6  {
 7     int floor;
 8     cout << "Floor: ";
 9     cin >> floor;
10
11     // The following statements check various input errors
```

```
12    if (cin.fail())
13    {
14        cout << "Error: Not an integer." << endl;
15        return 1;
16    }
17    if (floor == 13)
18    {
19        cout << "Error: There is no thirteenth floor." << endl;
20        return 1;
21    }
22    if (floor <= 0 || floor > 20)
23    {
24        cout << "Error: The floor must be between 1 and 20." << endl;
25        return 1;
26    }
27
28    // Now we know that the input is valid
29    int actual_floor;
30    if (floor > 13)
31    {
32        actual_floor = floor - 1;
33    }
34    else
35    {
36        actual_floor = floor;
37    }
38
39    cout << "The elevator will travel to the actual floor "
40        << actual_floor << endl;
41
42    return 0;
43 }
```

Program Run

```
Floor: 13
Error: There is no thirteenth floor.
```

Computing & Society 3.2   Artificial Intelligence

When one uses a sophisticated computer program such as a tax preparation package, one is bound to attribute some intelligence to the computer. The computer asks sensible questions and makes computations that we find a mental challenge. After all, if doing one's taxes were easy, we wouldn't need a computer to do it for us.

As programmers, however, we know that all this apparent intelligence is an illusion. Human programmers have carefully "coached" the software in all possible scenarios, and it simply replays the actions and decisions that were programmed into it.

Would it be possible to write computer programs that are genuinely intelligent in some sense? From the earliest days of computing, there was a sense that the human brain might be nothing but an immense computer, and that it might well be feasible to program computers to imitate some processes of human thought. Serious research into *artificial intelligence* began in the mid-1950s, and the first twenty years brought some impressive successes. Programs that play chess—surely an activity that appears to require remarkable intellectual powers—have become so good that they now routinely beat all but the best

human players. As far back as 1975, an *expert-system* program called Mycin gained fame for being better in diagnosing meningitis in patients than the average physician.

From the very outset, one of the stated goals of the AI community was to produce software that could translate text from one language to another, for example from English to Russian. That undertaking proved to be enormously complicated. Human language appears to be much more subtle and interwoven with the human experience than had originally been thought. Systems such as Apple's Siri can answer common questions about the weather, appointments, and traffic. However, beyond a narrow range, they are more entertaining than useful.

In some areas, artificial intelligence technology has seen substantial advances. One of the most astounding examples is the rapid development of self-driving car technology. Starting in 2004, the Defense Advanced Research Projects Agency (DARPA) organized a series of competitions in which computer-controlled vehicles had to complete an obstacle course without a human driver or remote control. The first event was a disappointment, with none of the entrants finishing the route. In 2005, five vehicles completed a grueling 212 km course in the Mojave desert. Stanford's Stanley came in first, with an average speed of 30 km/h. In 2007, DARPA moved the competition to an "urban" environ-ment, an abandoned air force base. Vehicles had to be able to interact with each other, follow-ing California traffic laws. Self-driving cars are now tested on public roads in several states, and it is expected that they will become commercially available within a decade.

When a system with artificial intelligence replaces a human in an activity such as giving medical advice or driving a vehicle, an important question arises. Who is responsible for mistakes? We accept that human doctors and drivers occa-sionally make mistakes with lethal consequences.

Will we do the same for medical expert systems and self-driving cars?

Vaughn Youtz/Zuma Press.

Winner of the 2007 DARPA Urban Challenge

CHAPTER SUMMARY

Use the `if` statement to implement a decision.

- The `if` statement allows a program to carry out different actions depending on the nature of the data to be processed.

Implement comparisons of numbers and objects.

- Relational operators (< <= > >= == !=) are used to compare numbers and strings.
- Lexicographic order is used to compare strings.

Implement complex decisions that require multiple `if` statements.

- Multiple alternatives are required for decisions that have more than two cases.
- When using multiple `if` statements, pay attention to the order of the conditions.

Implement decisions whose branches require further decisions.

- When a decision statement is contained inside the branch of another decision statement, the statements are *nested*.
- Nested decisions are required for problems that have two levels of decision making.

Draw flowcharts for visualizing the control flow of a program.

- Flowcharts are made up of elements for tasks, input/outputs, and decisions.
- Each branch of a decision can contain tasks and further decisions.
- Never point an arrow inside another branch.

Design test cases for your programs.

- Each branch of your program should be covered by a test case.
- It is a good idea to design test cases before implementing a program.

Use the Boolean data type to store and combine conditions that can be true or false.

- The Boolean type `bool` has two values, `false` and `true`.
- C++ has two Boolean operators that combine conditions: `&&` (*and*) and `||` (*or*).
- To invert a condition, use the `!` (*not*) operator.
- The `&&` and `||` operators are computed using *short-circuit evaluation*: As soon as the truth value is determined, no further conditions are evaluated.
- De Morgan's Law tells you how to negate `&&` and `||` conditions.

Apply `if` statements to detect whether user input is valid.

- When reading a value, check that it is within the required range.
- Use the `fail` function to test whether the input stream has failed.

■ **R3.1** What is the value of each variable after the `if` statement?

```
a. int n = 1; int k = 2; int r = n;
   if (k < n) { r = k; }
b. int n = 1; int k = 2; int r;
   if (n < k) { r = k; }
   else { r = k + n; }
c. int n = 1; int k = 2; int r = k;
   if (r < k) { n = r; }
   else { k = n; }
d. int n = 1; int k = 2; int r = 3;
   if (r < n + k) { r = 2 * n; }
   else { k = 2 * r; }
```

■■ **R3.2** Explain the difference between

```
s = 0;
if (x > 0) { s++; }
if (y > 0) { s++; }
```

and

```
s = 0;
if (x > 0) { s++; }
else if (y > 0) { s++; }
```

■■ **R3.3** Find the errors in the following `if` statements.

```
a. if x > 0 then cout << x;
b. if (x > 0) ; { y = 1; } else ; { y = -1; }
c. if (1 + x > pow(x, sqrt(2)) { y = y + x; }
d. if (x = 1) { y++; }
e. cin >> x; if (cin.fail()) { y = y + x; }
```

■ **R3.4** What do these code fragments print?

```
a. int n = 1; int m = -1;
   if (n < -m) { cout << n; } else { cout << m; }
b. int n = 1; int m = -1;
   if (-n >= m) { cout << n; } else { cout << m; }
c. double x = 0; double y = 1;
   if (abs(x - y) < 1) { cout << x; } else { cout << y; }
d. double x = sqrt(2); double y = 2;
   if (x * x == y) { cout << x; } else { cout << y; }
```

■■ **R3.5** Suppose x and y are variables of type `double`. Write a code fragment that sets y to x if x is positive and to 0 otherwise.

■■ **R3.6** Suppose x and y are variables of type `double`. Write a code fragment that sets y to the absolute value of x without calling the `abs` function. Use an `if` statement.

■■ **R3.7** Explain why it is more difficult to compare floating-point numbers than integers. Write C++ code to test whether an integer n equals 10 and whether a floating-point number x equals 10.

■ **R3.8** Common Error 3.2 explains that a C++ compiler will not report an error when you use an assignment operator instead of a test for equality, but it may issue a warning. Write a test program containing a statement

```
if (floor = 13)
```

What does your compiler do when you compile the program?

■■ **R3.9** Given two pixels on a computer screen with integer coordinates (x_1, y_1) and (x_2, y_2), write conditions to test whether they are

    a. The same pixel.

    b. Very close together (with distance < 5).

■ **R3.10** It is easy to confuse the = and == operators. Write a test program containing the statement

```
if (floor = 13)
```

What error message do you get? Write another test program containing the statement

```
count == 0;
```

What does your compiler do when you compile the program?

■■ **R3.11** Each square on a chess board can be described by a letter and number, such as g5 in this example:

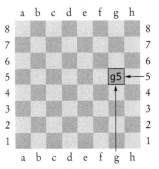

The following pseudocode describes an algorithm that determines whether a square with a given letter and number is dark (black) or light (white).

    If the letter is an a, c, e, or g
        If the number is odd
            color = "black"
        Else
            color = "white"
    Else
        If the number is even
            color = "black"
        Else
            color = "white"

Using the procedure in Programming Tip 3.6, trace this pseudocode with input g5.

■■ **R3.12** Give a set of four test cases for the algorithm of Exercise R3.11 that covers all branches.

R3.13 In a scheduling program, we want to check whether two appointments overlap. For simplicity, appointments start at a full hour, and we use military time (with hours 0–23). The following pseudocode describes an algorithm that determines whether the appointment with start time *start1* and end time *end1* overlaps with the appointment with start time *start2* and end time *end2*.

> *If start1 > start2*
>   *s = start1*
> *Else*
>   *s = start2*
> *If end1 < end2*
>   *e = end1*
> *Else*
>   *e = end2*
> *If s < e*
>   *The appointments overlap.*
> *Else*
>   *The appointments don't overlap.*

Trace this algorithm with an appointment from 10–12 and one from 11–13, then with an appointment from 10–11 and one from 12–13.

R3.14 Draw a flowchart for the algorithm in Exercise R3.13.

R3.15 Draw a flowchart for the algorithm in Exercise E3.13.

R3.16 Draw a flowchart for the algorithm in Exercise E3.14.

R3.17 Develop a set of test cases for the algorithm in Exercise R3.13.

R3.18 Develop a set of test cases for the algorithm in Exercise E3.14.

R3.19 Write pseudocode for a program that prompts the user for a month and day and prints out whether it is one of the following four holidays:

- New Year's Day (January 1)
- Independence Day (July 4)
- Veterans Day (November 11)
- Christmas Day (December 25)

R3.20 Write pseudocode for a program that assigns letter grades for a quiz, according to the following table:

Score	Grade
90-100	A
80-89	B
70-79	C
60-69	D
< 60	F

R3.21 Explain how the lexicographic ordering of strings in C++ differs from the ordering of words in a dictionary or telephone book. *Hint:* Consider strings such as IBM, wiley.com, Century 21, and While-U-Wait.

R3.22 Of the following pairs of strings, which comes first in lexicographic order?

  a. "Tom", "Dick"
  b. "Tom", "Tomato"

    c. "church", "Churchill"

    d. "car manufacturer", "carburetor"

    e. "Harry", "hairy"

    f. "C++", " Car"

    g. "Tom", "Tom"

    h. "Car", "Carl"

    i. "car", "bar"

- **R3.23** Explain the difference between a sequence of else if clauses and nested if statements. Give an example for each.

- - **R3.24** Give an example of a sequence of else if clauses where the order of the tests does not matter. Give an example where the order of the tests matters.

- **R3.25** Rewrite the condition in Section 3.3 to use < operators instead of >= operators. What is the impact on the order of the comparisons?

- - **R3.26** Give a set of test cases for the tax program in Exercise P3.8. Manually compute the expected results.

- **R3.27** Make up another C++ code example that shows the dangling else problem, using the following statement. A student with a GPA of at least 1.5, but less than 2, is on probation. With less than 1.5, the student is failing.

- - - **R3.28** Complete the following truth table by finding the truth values of the Boolean expressions for all combinations of the Boolean inputs p, q, and r.

p	q	r	(p && q) || !r	!(p && (q || !r))
false	false	false		
false	false	true		
false	true	false		
...				
5 more combinations				
...				

- - - **R3.29** True or false? *A* && *B* is the same as *B* && *A* for any Boolean conditions *A* and *B*.

- **R3.30** The "advanced search" feature of many search engines allows you to use Boolean operators for complex queries, such as "(cats OR dogs) AND NOT pets". Contrast these search operators with the Boolean operators in C++.

- - **R3.31** Suppose the value of b is false and the value of x is 0. What is the value of each of the following expressions?

    a. b && x == 0

    b. b || x == 0

    c. !b && x == 0

d. !b || x == 0
e. b && x != 0
f. b || x != 0
g. !b && x != 0
h. !b || x != 0

■■ **R3.32** Simplify the following expressions. Here, b is a variable of type bool.

a. b == true
b. b == false
c. b != true
d. b != false

■■■ **R3.33** Simplify the following statements. Here, b is a variable of type bool and n is a variable of type int.

a. if (n == 0) { b = true; } else { b = false; }

   (*Hint:* What is the value of n == 0?)

b. if (n == 0) { b = false; } else { b = true; }
c. b = false; if (n > 1) { if (n < 2) { b = true; } }
d. if (n < 1) { b = true; } else { b = n > 2; }

■ **R3.34** What is wrong with the following program?

```
cout << "Enter the number of quarters: ";
cin >> quarters;
total = total + quarters * 0.25;
cout << "Total: " << total << endl;
if (cin.fail()) { cout << "Input error."; }
```

■■■ **R3.35** Reading numbers is surprisingly difficult because a C++ input stream looks at the input one character at a time. First, white space is skipped. Then the stream consumes those input characters that can be a part of a number. Once the stream has recognized a number, it stops reading if it finds a character that cannot be a part of a number. However, if the first non-white space character is not a digit or a sign, or if the first character is a sign and the second one is not a digit, then the stream fails.

Consider a program reading an integer:

```
cout << "Enter the number of quarters: ";
int quarters;
cin >> quarters;
```

For each of the following user inputs, circle how many characters have been read and whether the stream is in the failed state or not.

a. 15.9
b. 15 9
c. +159
d. -15A9
e. Fifteen
f. -Fifteen
g. + 15
h. 1.5E3
i. +1+5

PRACTICE EXERCISES

- **E3.1** Write a program that reads an integer and prints whether it is negative, zero, or positive.

- **E3.2** Write a program that reads a floating-point number and prints "zero" if the number is zero. Otherwise, print "positive" or "negative". Add "small" if the absolute value of the number is less than 1, or "large" if it exceeds 1,000,000.

- **E3.3** Write a program that reads an integer and prints how many digits the number has, by checking whether the number is ≥ 10, ≥ 100, and so on. (Assume that all integers are less than ten billion.) If the number is negative, first multiply it with –1.

- **E3.4** Write a program that reads three numbers and prints "all the same" if they are all the same, "all different" if they are all different, and "neither" otherwise.

- **E3.5** Write a program that reads three numbers and prints "increasing" if they are in increasing order, "decreasing" if they are in decreasing order, and "neither" otherwise. Here, "increasing" means "strictly increasing", with each value larger than its predecessor. The sequence 3 4 4 would not be considered increasing.

- **E3.6** Repeat Exercise E3.5, but before reading the numbers, ask the user whether increasing/decreasing should be "strict" or "lenient". In lenient mode, the sequence 3 4 4 is increasing and the sequence 4 4 4 is both increasing and decreasing.

- **E3.7** Write a program that reads in three integers and prints "in order" if they are sorted in ascending *or* descending order, or "not in order" otherwise. For example,

  ```
  1 2 5    in order
  1 5 2    not in order
  5 2 1    in order
  1 2 2    in order
  ```

- **E3.8** Write a program that reads four integers and prints "two pairs" if the input consists of two matching pairs (in some order) and "not two pairs" otherwise. For example,

  ```
  1 2 2 1    two pairs
  1 2 2 3    not two pairs
  2 2 2 2    two pairs
  ```

- **E3.9** A compass needle points a given number of degrees away from North, measured clockwise. Write a program that reads the angle and prints out the nearest compass direction; one of N, NE, E, SE, S, SW, W, NW. In the case of a tie, prefer the nearest principal direction (N, E, S, or W).

- **E3.10** Write a program that reads a temperature value and the letter C for Celsius or F for Fahrenheit. Print whether water is liquid, solid, or gaseous at the given temperature at sea level.

- **E3.11** The boiling point of water drops by about one degree centigrade for every 300 meters (or 1,000 feet) of altitude. Improve the program of Exercise E3.10 to allow the user to supply the altitude in meters or feet.

- **E3.12** Add error handling to Exercise E3.11. If the user does not enter a number when expected, or provides an invalid unit for the altitude, print an error message and end the program.

E3.13 When two points in time are compared, each given as hours (in military time, ranging from 0 and 23) and minutes, the following pseudocode determines which comes first.

> *If hour1 < hour2*
> *time1 comes first.*
> *Else if hour1 and hour2 are the same*
> *If minute1 < minute2*
>   *time1 comes first.*
> *Else if minute1 and minute2 are the same*
>   *time1 and time2 are the same.*
> *Else*
>   *time2 comes first.*
> *Else*
> *time2 comes first.*

Write a program that prompts the user for two points in time and prints the time that comes first, then the other time.

E3.14 The following algorithm yields the season (Spring, Summer, Fall, or Winter) for a given month and day.

> *If month is 1, 2, or 3, season = "Winter"*
> *Else if month is 4, 5, or 6, season = "Spring"*
> *Else if month is 7, 8, or 9, season = "Summer"*
> *Else if month is 10, 11, or 12, season = "Fall"*
> *If month is divisible by 3 and day >= 21*
> *If season is "Winter", season = "Spring"*
> *Else if season is "Spring", season = "Summer"*
> *Else if season is "Summer", season = "Fall"*
> *Else season = "Winter"*

Write a program that prompts the user for a month and day and then prints the season, as determined by this algorithm.

© rotofrank/iStockphoto.

E3.15 Write a program that reads in two floating-point numbers and tests whether they are the same up to two decimal places. Here are two sample runs.

```
Enter two floating-point numbers: 2.0 1.99998
They are the same up to two decimal places.
Enter two floating-point numbers: 2.0 1.98999
They are different.
```

E3.16 *Unit conversion.* Write a unit conversion program that asks the users from which unit they want to convert (fl. oz, gal, oz, lb, in, ft, mi) and to which unit they want to convert (ml, l, g, kg, mm, cm, m, km). Reject incompatible conversions (such as gal → km). Ask for the value to be converted, then display the result:

```
Convert from? gal
Convert to? ml
Value? 2.5
2.5 gal = 9462.5 ml
```

E3.17 Write a program that prompts the user to provide a single character from the alphabet. Print Vowel or Consonant, depending on the user input. If the user input is not a letter (between a and z or A and Z), or is a string of length > 1, print an error message.

■■ **E3.18** Write a program that asks the user to enter a month (1 for January, 2 for February, and so on) and then prints the number of days in the month. For February, print "28 or 29 days".

```
Enter a month: 5
30 days
```

Do not use a separate if/else branch for each month. Use Boolean operators.

PROGRAMMING PROJECTS

■■ **P3.1** Write a program that translates a letter grade into a number grade. Letter grades are A, B, C, D, and F, possibly followed by + or –. Their numeric values are 4, 3, 2, 1, and 0. There is no F+ or F–. A + increases the numeric value by 0.3, a – decreases it by 0.3. However, an A+ has value 4.0.

```
Enter a letter grade: B-
The numeric value is 2.7.
```

■■ **P3.2** Write a program that translates a number between 0 and 4 into the closest letter grade. For example, the number 2.8 (which might have been the average of several grades) would be converted to B–. Break ties in favor of the better grade; for example 2.85 should be a B.

■■ **P3.3** Write a program that takes user input describing a playing card in the following shorthand notation:

A	Ace
2 ... 10	Card values
J	Jack
Q	Queen
K	King
D	Diamonds
H	Hearts
S	Spades
C	Clubs

Your program should print the full description of the card. For example,

```
Enter the card notation: QS
Queen of Spades
```

■■ **P3.4** Write a program that reads in three floating-point numbers and prints the largest of the three inputs. For example:

```
Please enter three numbers: 4 9 2.5
The largest number is 9.
```

■■ **P3.5** Write a program that reads in three strings and sorts them lexicographically.

```
Enter three strings: Charlie Able Baker
Able
Baker
Charlie
```

■■ **P3.6** Write a program that prompts for the day and month of the user's birthday and then prints a horoscope. Make up fortunes for programmers, like this:

```
Please enter your birthday (month and day): 6 16
Gemini are experts at figuring out the behavior of complicated programs.
You feel where bugs are coming from and then stay one step ahead.
Tonight, your style wins approval from a tough critic.
```

Each fortune should contain the name of the astrological sign. (You will find the names and date ranges of the signs at a distressingly large number of sites on the Internet.)

© lillisphotography/iStockphoto.

■■ P3.7 The original U.S. income tax of 1913 was quite simple. The tax was

- 1 percent on the first $50,000.
- 2 percent on the amount over $50,000 up to $75,000.
- 3 percent on the amount over $75,000 up to $100,000.
- 4 percent on the amount over $100,000 up to $250,000.
- 5 percent on the amount over $250,000 up to $500,000.
- 6 percent on the amount over $500,000.

There was no separate schedule for single or married taxpayers. Write a program that computes the income tax according to this schedule.

■■■ P3.8 Write a program that computes taxes for the following schedule:

If your status is Single and if the taxable income is over	but not over	the tax is	of the amount over
$0	$8,000	10%	$0
$8,000	$32,000	$800 + 15%	$8,000
$32,000		$4,400 + 25%	$32,000

If your status is Married and if the taxable income is over	but not over	the tax is	of the amount over
$0	$16,000	10%	$0
$16,000	$64,000	$1,600 + 15%	$16,000
$64,000		$8,800 + 25%	$64,000

■■■ P3.9 The tax.cpp program uses a simplified version of the 2008 U.S. income tax schedule. Look up the tax brackets and rates for the current year, for both single and married filers, and implement a program that computes the actual income tax.

- **P3.10** Write a program that reads in the x- and y-coordinates of two corner points of a rectangle and then prints out whether the rectangle is a square, or is in "portrait" or "landscape" orientation.

- - **P3.11** Write a program that reads in the x- and y-coordinates of three corner points of a triangle and prints out whether it has an obtuse angle, a right angle, or only acute angles.

- - - **P3.12** Write a program that reads in the x- and y-coordinates of four corner points of a quadrilateral and prints out whether it is a square, a rectangle, a trapezoid, a rhombus, or none of those shapes.

- - - **P3.13** *Roman numbers.* Write a program that converts a positive integer into the Roman number system. The Roman number system has digits

I	1
V	5
X	10
L	50
C	100
D	500
M	1,000

© Straitshooter/iStockphoto.

Numbers are formed according to the following rules.

  a. Only numbers up to 3,999 are represented.

  b. As in the decimal system, the thousands, hundreds, tens, and ones are expressed separately.

  c. The numbers 1 to 9 are expressed as

I	1
II	2
III	3
IV	4
V	5
VI	6
VII	7
VIII	8
IX	9

  As you can see, an I preceding a V or X is subtracted from the value, and you can never have more than three I's in a row.

  d. Tens and hundreds are done the same way, except that the letters X, L, C and C, D, M are used instead of I, V, X, respectively.

Your program should take an input, such as 1978, and convert it to Roman numerals, MCMLXXVIII.

■■■ **P3.14** A year with 366 days is called a leap year. Leap years are necessary to keep the calendar synchronized with the sun because the earth revolves around the sun once every 365.25 days. Actually, that figure is not entirely precise, and for all dates after 1582 the *Gregorian correction* applies. Usually years that are divisible by 4 are leap years, for example 1996. However, years that are divisible by 100 (for example, 1900) are not leap years, but years that are divisible by 400 are leap years (for example, 2000). Write a program that asks the user for a year and computes whether that year is a leap year. Use a single `if` statement and Boolean operators.

■■■ **P3.15** French country names are feminine when they end with the letter e, masculine otherwise, except for the following which are masculine even though they end with e:

- le Belize
- le Cambodge
- le Mexique
- le Mozambique
- le Zaïre
- le Zimbabwe

Write a program that reads the French name of a country and adds the article: le for masculine or la for feminine, such as le Canada or la Belgique.

However, if the country name starts with a vowel, use l'; for example, l'Afghanistan.

For the following plural country names, use les:

- les Etats-Unis
- les Pays-Bas

■■■ **Business P3.16** Write a program to simulate a bank transaction. There are two bank accounts: checking and savings. First, ask for the initial balances of the bank accounts; reject negative balances. Then ask for the transactions; options are deposit, withdrawal, and transfer. Then ask for the account; options are checking and savings. Then ask for the amount; reject transactions that overdraw an account. At the end, print the balances of both accounts.

■■ **Business P3.17** Write a program that reads in the name and salary of an employee. Here the salary will denote an *hourly* wage, such as $9.25. Then ask how many hours the employee worked in the past week. Be sure to accept fractional hours. Compute the pay. Any overtime work (over 40 hours per week) is paid at 150 percent of the regular wage. Print a paycheck for the employee.

■■ **Business P3.18** When you use an automated teller machine (ATM) with your bank card, you need to use a personal identification number (PIN) to access your account. If a user fails more than three times when entering the PIN, the machine will block the card. Assume that the user's PIN is "1234" and write a program that asks the user for the PIN no more than three times, and does the following:

- If the user enters the right number, print a message saying, "Your PIN is correct", and end the program.
- If the user enters a wrong number, print a message saying, "Your PIN is incorrect" and, if you have asked for the PIN less than three times, ask for it again.
- If the user enters a wrong number three times, print a message saying "Your bank card is blocked" and end the program.

© Mark Evans/iStockphoto.

■ **Business P3.19** Calculating the tip when you go to a restaurant is not difficult, but your restaurant wants to suggest a tip according to the service diners receive. Write a program that calculates a tip according to the diner's satisfaction as follows:

- Ask for the diners' satisfaction level using these ratings: 1 = Totally satisfied, 2 = Satisfied, 3 = Dissatisfied.
- If the diner is totally satisfied, calculate a 20 percent tip.
- If the diner is satisfied, calculate a 15 percent tip.
- If the diner is dissatisfied, calculate a 10 percent tip.
- Report the satisfaction level and tip in dollars and cents.

■ **Business P3.20** A supermarket awards coupons depending on how much a customer spends on groceries. For example, if you spend $50, you will get a coupon worth eight percent of that amount. The following table shows the percent used to calculate the coupon awarded for different amounts spent. Write a program that calculates and prints the value of the coupon a person can receive based on groceries purchased.

Here is a sample run:

```
Please enter the cost of your groceries: 14
You win a discount coupon of $ 1.12. (8% of your purchase)
```

Money Spent	Coupon Percentage
Less than $10	No coupon
From $10 to $60	8%
More than $60 to $150	10%
More than $150 to $210	12%
More than $210	14%

■ **Engineering P3.21** Write a program that prompts the user for a wavelength value and prints a description of the corresponding part of the electromagnetic spectrum, as given in Table 7.

© drxy/iStockphoto.

Table 7 Electromagnetic Spectrum		
Type	Wavelength (m)	Frequency (Hz)
Radio Waves	$> 10^{-1}$	$< 3 \times 10^9$
Microwaves	10^{-3} to 10^{-1}	3×10^9 to 3×10^{11}
Infrared	7×10^{-7} to 10^{-3}	3×10^{11} to 4×10^{14}
Visible light	4×10^{-7} to 7×10^{-7}	4×10^{14} to 7.5×10^{14}
Ultraviolet	10^{-8} to 4×10^{-7}	7.5×10^{14} to 3×10^{16}
X-rays	10^{-11} to 10^{-8}	3×10^{16} to 3×10^{19}
Gamma rays	$< 10^{-11}$	$> 3 \times 10^{19}$

■ **Engineering P3.22** Repeat Exercise P3.21, modifying the program so that it prompts for the frequency instead.

■■ **Engineering P3.23** Repeat Exercise P3.21, modifying the program so that it first asks the user whether the input will be a wavelength or a frequency.

■■■ **Engineering P3.24** A minivan has two sliding doors. Each door can be opened by either a dashboard switch, its inside handle, or its outside handle. However, the inside handles do not work if a child lock switch is activated. In order for the sliding doors to open, the gear shift must be in park, *and* the master unlock switch must be activated. (This book's author is the long-suffering owner of just such a vehicle.)

© nano/iStockphoto.

Your task is to simulate a portion of the control software for the vehicle. The input is a sequence of values for the switches and the gear shift, in the following order:

- Dashboard switches for left and right sliding door, child lock, and master unlock (0 for off or 1 for activated)
- Inside and outside handles on the left and right sliding doors (0 or 1)
- The gear shift setting (one of P N D 1 2 3 R).

A typical input would be 0 0 0 1 0 1 0 0 P.

Print "left door opens" and/or "right door opens" as appropriate. If neither door opens, print "both doors stay closed".

■ **Engineering P3.25** Sound level L in units of decibel (dB) is determined by

$$L = 20 \log_{10}(p/p_0)$$

where p is the sound pressure of the sound (in Pascals, abbreviated Pa), and p_0 is a reference sound pressure equal to 20×10^{-6} Pa (where L is 0 dB). The following table gives descriptions for certain sound levels.

Threshold of pain	130 dB
Possible hearing damage	120 dB
Jack hammer at 1 m	100 dB
Traffic on a busy roadway at 10 m	90 dB
Normal conversation	60 dB
Calm library	30 dB
Light leaf rustling	0 dB

© Photobuff/iStockphoto.

Write a program that reads a value and a unit, either dB or Pa, and then prints the closest description from the list above.

■■ **Engineering P3.26** The electric circuit shown below is designed to measure the temperature of the gas in a chamber.

$R_s = 75\ \Omega$

11.43 V

Voltmeter

$V_s = 20\ V$

R V_m

The resistor R represents a temperature sensor enclosed in the chamber. The resistance R, in Ω, is related to the temperature T, in $°C$, by the equation

$$R = R_0 + kT$$

In this device, assume $R_0 = 100\ \Omega$ and $k = 0.5$. The voltmeter displays the value of the voltage, V_m, across the sensor. This voltage V_m indicates the temperature, T, of the gas according to the equation

$$T = \frac{R}{k} - \frac{R_0}{k} = \frac{R_s}{k} \frac{V_m}{V_s - V_m} - \frac{R_0}{k}$$

Suppose the voltmeter voltage is constrained to the range $V_{min} = 12$ volts $\leq V_m \leq V_{max} = 18$ volts. Write a program that accepts a value of V_m and checks that it's between 12 and 18. The program should return the gas temperature in degrees Celsius when V_m is between 12 and 18 and an error message when it isn't.

■■■ **Engineering P3.27** Crop damage due to frost is one of the many risks confronting farmers. The figure below shows a simple alarm circuit designed to warn of frost. The alarm circuit uses a device called a thermistor to sound a buzzer when the temperature drops below freezing. Thermistors are semiconductor devices that exhibit a temperature dependent resistance described by the equation

$$R = R_0 e^{\beta\left(\frac{1}{T} - \frac{1}{T_0}\right)}$$

where R is the resistance, in Ω, at the temperature T, in $°K$, and R_0 is the resistance, in Ω, at the temperature T_0, in $°K$. β is a constant that depends on the material used to make the thermistor.

9 V

9 V

Thermistor R R_3

Buzzer

R_2 R_4

Comparator

The circuit is designed so that the alarm will sound when

$$\frac{R_2}{R + R_2} < \frac{R_4}{R_3 + R_4}$$

The thermistor used in the alarm circuit has $R_0 = 33{,}192\ \Omega$ at $T_0 = 40\ °C$, and $\beta = 3{,}310\ °K$. (Notice that β has units of $°K$. Recall that the temperature in $°K$ is obtained by adding $273°$ to the temperature in $°C$.) The resistors R_2, R_3, and R_4 have a resistance of $156.3\ k\Omega = 156{,}300\ \Omega$.

Write a C++ program that prompts the user for a temperature in $°F$ and prints a message indicating whether or not the alarm will sound at that temperature.

■ **Engineering P3.28** A mass $m = 2$ kilograms is attached to the end of a rope of length $r = 3$ meters. The mass is whirled around at high speed. The rope can withstand a maximum tension of $T = 60$ Newtons. Write a program that accepts a rotation speed v and determines if such a speed will cause the rope to break. *Hint:* $T = mv^2/r$.

■■ **Engineering P3.29** A mass m is attached to the end of a rope of length $r = 3$ meters. The rope can only be whirled around at speeds of 1, 10, 20, or 40 meters per second. The rope can withstand a maximum tension of $T = 60$ Newtons. Write a program where the user enters the value of the mass m, and the program determines the greatest speed at which it can be whirled without breaking the rope. *Hint:* $T = mv^2/r$.

■■ **Engineering P3.30** The average person can jump off the ground with a velocity of 7 mph without fear of leaving the planet. However, if an astronaut jumps with this velocity while standing on Halley's Comet, will the astronaut ever come back down? Create a program that allows the user to input a launch velocity (in mph) from the surface of Halley's Comet and determine whether a jumper will return to the surface. If not, the program should calculate how much more massive the comet must be in order to return the jumper to the surface.

Courtesy NASA/JPL-Caltech.

Hint: Escape velocity is $v_{escape} = \sqrt{2\dfrac{GM}{R}}$, where $G = 6.67 \times 10^{-11} N\ m^2/kg^2$ is the gravitational constant, $M = 1.3 \times 10^{22}\ kg$ is the mass of Halley's comet, and $R = 1.153 \times 10^6\ m$ is its radius.

CHAPTER 4

LOOPS

© photo75/iStockphoto.

To implement while, for, and do loops

To avoid infinite loops and off-by-one errors

To understand nested loops

To implement programs that read and process data sets

To use a computer for simulations

In a loop, a part of a program is repeated over and over, until a specific goal is reached. Loops are important for calculations that require repeated steps and for processing input consisting of many data items. In this chapter you will learn about loop statements in C++, as well as techniques for writing programs that process input and simulate activities in the real world.

4.1 The while Loop

In this section, you will learn how to repeatedly execute statements until a goal has been reached.

Recall the investment problem from Chapter 1. You put $10,000 into a bank account that earns 5 percent interest per year. How many years does it take for the account balance to be double the original investment?

© AlterYourReality/iStockphoto.

Because the interest earned also earns interest, a bank balance grows exponentially.

In Chapter 1 we developed the following algorithm for this problem:

Start with a year value of 0, a column for the interest, and a balance of $10,000.

year	interest	balance
0		$10,000

Repeat the following steps while the balance is less than $20,000
  Add 1 to the year value.
  Compute the interest as balance x 0.05 (i.e., 5 percent interest).
  Add the interest to the balance.
Report the final year value as the answer.

You now know how to define and update the variables in C++. What you don't yet know is how to carry out "Repeat steps while the balance is less than $20,000".

In a particle accelerator, subatomic particles traverse a loop-shaped tunnel multiple times, gaining the speed required for physical experiments. Similarly, in computer science, statements in a loop are executed while a condition is true.

© mmac72/iStockphoto.

Syntax 4.1   while Statement

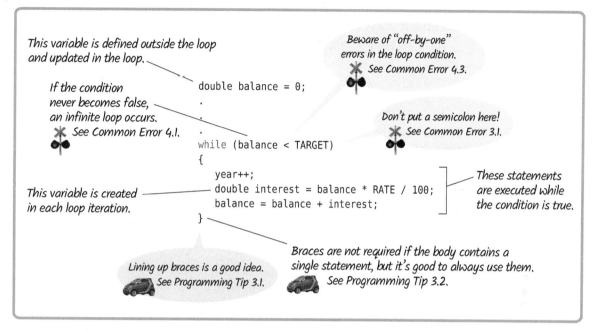

This variable is defined outside the loop and updated in the loop.

If the condition never becomes false, an infinite loop occurs.
※ See Common Error 4.1.

This variable is created in each loop iteration.

Beware of "off-by-one" errors in the loop condition.
※ See Common Error 4.3.

Don't put a semicolon here!
※ See Common Error 3.1.

```
double balance = 0;
   .
   .
   .
while (balance < TARGET)
{
    year++;
    double interest = balance * RATE / 100;
    balance = balance + interest;
}
```

These statements are executed while the condition is true.

Lining up braces is a good idea. See Programming Tip 3.1.

Braces are not required if the body contains a single statement, but it's good to always use them. See Programming Tip 3.2.

Loops execute a block of code repeatedly while a condition remains true.

In C++, the while statement implements such a repetition (see Syntax 4.1). The code

```
while (condition)
{
    statements
}
```

keeps executing the statements while the condition is true. In our case, we want to increment the year counter and add interest while the balance is less than the target balance of $20,000:

```
while (balance < TARGET)
{
    year++;
    double interest = balance * RATE / 100;
    balance = balance + interest;
}
```

A while statement is an example of a **loop**. If you draw a flowchart, the flow of execution loops again to the point where the condition is tested (see Figure 1).

balance < TARGET?   False

True

Increment year

Add interest to balance

Figure 1   Flowchart of a while Loop

When you define a variable *inside* the loop body, the variable is created for each iteration of the loop and removed after the end of each iteration. For example, consider the interest variable in this loop:

```
while (balance < TARGET)
{
   year++;
   double interest = balance * RATE / 100;
   balance = balance + interest;
} // interest no longer defined here
```

A new interest variable is created in each iteration.

In contrast, the balance and years variables were defined *outside* the loop body. That way, the same variable is used for all iterations of the loop.

Here is the program that solves the investment problem. Figure 2 illustrates the program's execution.

sec01/doublinv.cpp

```
 1  #include <iostream>
 2
 3  using namespace std;
 4
 5  int main()
 6  {
 7     const double RATE = 5;
 8     const double INITIAL_BALANCE = 10000;
 9     const double TARGET = 2 * INITIAL_BALANCE;
10
11     double balance = INITIAL_BALANCE;
12     int year = 0;
13
14     while (balance < TARGET)
15     {
16        year++;
17        double interest = balance * RATE / 100;
18        balance = balance + interest;
19     }
20
21     cout << "The investment doubled after "
22        << year << " years." << endl;
23
24     return 0;
25  }
```

Program Run

```
The investment doubled after 15 years.
```

① Check the loop condition

        The condition is true

```
while (balance < TARGET)
{
   year++;
   double interest = balance * RATE / 100;
   balance = balance + interest;
}
```

balance =   10000

  year =   0

Figure 2 Execution of the doublinv Loop

Figure 2 (continued)
Execution of the
doublinv Loop

2 Execute the statements in the loop

```
balance =   10500

year =      1

interest =  500
```

```
while (balance < TARGET)
{
    year++;
    double interest = balance * RATE / 100;
    balance = balance + interest;
}
```

3 Check the loop condition again   The condition is still true

```
balance =   10500

year =      1
```

```
while (balance < TARGET)
{
    year++;
    double interest = balance * RATE / 100;
    balance = balance + interest;
}
```

4 After 15 iterations   The condition is
                                                         no longer true

```
balance =   20789.28

year =      15
```

```
while (balance < TARGET)
{
    year++;
    double interest = balance * RATE / 100;
    balance = balance + interest;
}
```

5 Execute the statement following the loop

```
balance =   20789.28

year =      15
```

```
while (balance < TARGET)
{
    year++;
    double interest = balance * RATE / 100;
    balance = balance + interest;
}
cout << year << endl;
```

Table 1 while Loop Examples

Loop	Output	Explanation

`i = 5;`
`while (i > 0)`
`{`
`   cout << i << " ";`
`   i--;`
`}`
	5 4 3 2 1	When i is 0, the loop condition is false, and the loop ends.

`i = 5;`
`while (i > 0)`
`{`
`   cout << i << " ";`
`   i++;`
`}`
	5 6 7 8 9 10 11 ...	The i++ statement is an error causing an "infinite loop" (see Common Error 4.1).

Table 1 while Loop Examples

Loop	Output	Explanation

<pre>i = 5;
while (i > 5)
{
   cout << i << " ";
   i--;
}</pre>
	(No output)	The statement i > 5 is false, and the loop is never executed.

<pre>i = 5;
while (i < 0)
{
   cout << i << " ";
   i--;
}</pre>
	(No output)	The programmer probably thought, "Stop when i is less than 0". However, the loop condition controls when the loop is executed, not when it ends (see Common Error 4.2).

<pre>i = 5;
while (i > 0) ;
{
   cout << i << " ";
   i--;
}</pre>
	(No output, program does not terminate)	Note the semicolon before the {. This loop has an empty body. It runs forever, checking whether i > 0 and doing nothing in the body.

Common Error 4.1

Infinite Loops

A very annoying loop error is an *infinite loop:* a loop that runs forever and can be stopped only by killing the program or restarting the computer. If there are output statements in the program, then line after line of output flashes by on the screen. Otherwise, the program just sits there and *hangs*, seeming to do nothing. On some systems, you can terminate a hanging program by hitting Ctrl + C. On others, you can close the window in which the program runs.

A common reason for infinite loops is forgetting to update the variable that controls the loop:

```
year = 1;
while (year <= 20)
{
   balance = balance * (1 + RATE / 100);
}
```

© ohiophoto/iStockphoto.

Like this hamster who can't stop running in the treadmill, an infinite loop never ends.

Here the programmer forgot to add a year++ command in the loop. As a result, the year always stays at 1, and the loop never comes to an end.

Another common reason for an infinite loop is accidentally incrementing a counter that should be decremented (or vice versa). Consider this example:

```
year = 20;
while (year > 0)
{
```

```
      balance = balance * (1 + RATE / 100);
      year++;
   }
```

The year variable really should have been decremented, not incremented. This is a common error because incrementing counters is so much more common than decrementing that your fingers may type the ++ on autopilot. As a consequence, year is always larger than 0, and the loop never ends. (Actually, year may eventually exceed the largest representable positive integer and *wrap around* to a negative number. Then the loop ends—of course, with a completely wrong result.)

Common Error 4.2

Don't Think "Are We There Yet?"

When doing something repetitive, most of us want to know when we are done. For example, you may think, "I want to get at least $20,000," and set the loop condition to

```
balance >= TARGET
```

But the while loop thinks the opposite: How long am I allowed to keep going? The correct loop condition is

```
while (balance < TARGET)
```

In other words: "Keep at it while the balance is less than the target."

When writing a loop condition, don't ask, "Are we there yet?" The condition determines how long the loop will keep going. © MsSponge/iStockphoto.

Common Error 4.3

Off-by-One Errors

Consider our computation of the number of years that are required to double an investment:

```
int year = 0;
while (balance < TARGET)
{
   year++;
   double interest = balance * RATE / 100;
   balance = balance + interest;
}
cout << "The investment doubled after " << year << " years." << endl;
```

Should year start at 0 or at 1? Should you test for balance < TARGET or for balance <= TARGET? It is easy to be *off by one* in these expressions.

Some people try to solve **off-by-one errors** by randomly inserting +1 or -1 until the program seems to work—a terrible strategy. It can take a long time to compile and test all the various possibilities. Expending a small amount of mental effort is a real time saver.

Fortunately, off-by-one errors are easy to avoid, simply by working through a couple of test cases and using the information from the test cases to come up with a rationale for your decisions.

Should year start at 0 or at 1? Look at a scenario with simple values: an initial balance of $100 and an interest rate of 50 percent. After year 1, the balance is $150, and after year 2 it is

An off-by-one error is a common error when programming loops. Think through simple test cases to avoid this type of error.

$225, or over $200. So the investment doubled after 2 years. The loop executed two times, incrementing year each time. Hence year must start at 0, not at 1.

year	balance
0	$100
1	$150
2	$225

In other words, the balance variable denotes the balance after the end of the year. At the outset, the balance variable contains the balance after year 0 and not after year 1.

Next, should you use a < or <= comparison in the test? If you want to settle this question with an example, you need to find a scenario in which the final balance is exactly twice the initial balance. This happens when the interest is 100 percent. The loop executes once. Now year is 1, and balance is exactly equal to 2 * INITIAL_BALANCE. Has the investment doubled after one year? It has. Therefore, the loop should not execute again. If the test condition is balance < TARGET, the loop stops, as it should. If the test condition had been balance <= TARGET, the loop would have executed once more.

In other words, you keep adding interest while the balance *has not yet doubled*.

Computing & Society 4.1   The First Bug

According to legend, the first bug was found in the Mark II, a huge electrome-chanical computer at Harvard University. It really was caused by a bug—a moth was trapped in a relay switch.

Actually, from the note that the operator left in the log book next to the moth (see the photo), it appears as if the term "bug" had already been in active use at the time.

The pioneering computer scientist Maurice Wilkes wrote, "Somehow, at the Moore School and afterwards, one had always assumed there would be no particular difficulty in getting pro- grams right. I can remember the exact instant in time at which it dawned on me that a great part of my future life would be spent finding mistakes in my own programs."

Courtesy of the Naval Surface Warfare Center, Dahlgren, VA., 1988. NHHC Collection.

The First Bug

4.2 Problem Solving: Hand-Tracing

Hand-tracing is a simulation of code execution in which you step through instructions and track the values of the variables.

In Programming Tip 3.6, you learned about the method of hand-tracing. When you hand-trace code or pseudocode, you write the names of the variables on a sheet of paper, mentally execute each step of the code and update the variables.

It is best to have the code written or printed on a sheet of paper. Use a marker, such as a paper clip, to mark the current line. Whenever a variable changes, cross out the old value and write the new value below. When a program produces output, also write down the output in another column.

Consider this example. What value is displayed?

```
int n = 1729;
int sum = 0;
while (n > 0)
{
   int digit = n % 10;
   sum = sum + digit;
   n = n / 10;
}
cout << sum << endl;
```

There are three variables: n, sum, and digit.

n	sum	digit

The first two variables are initialized with 1729 and 0 before the loop is entered.

```
   int n = 1729;
⊂⊃ int sum = 0;
   while (n > 0)
   {
      int digit = n % 10;
      sum = sum + digit;
      n = n / 10;
   }
   cout << sum << endl;
```

n	sum	digit
1729	0	

Because n is greater than zero, enter the loop. The variable digit is set to 9 (the remainder of dividing 1729 by 10). The variable sum is set to 0 + 9 = 9.

```
   int n = 1729;
   int sum = 0;
   while (n > 0)
   {
      int digit = n % 10;
⊂⊃    sum = sum + digit;
      n = n / 10;
   }
   cout << sum << endl;
```

n	sum	digit
1729	0̷	
	9	9

Finally, n becomes 172. (Recall that the remainder in the division 1729/10 is discarded because both arguments are integers.)

Cross out the old values and write the new ones under the old ones.

```
int n = 1729;
int sum = 0;
while (n > 0)
{
    int digit = n % 10;
    sum = sum + digit;
    n = n / 10;
}
cout << sum << endl;
```

n	sum	digit
~~1729~~	~~0~~	
172	9	9

Now check the loop condition again.

```
int n = 1729;
int sum = 0;
while (n > 0)
{
    int digit = n % 10;
    sum = sum + digit;
    n = n / 10;
}
cout << sum << endl;
```

Because n is still greater than zero, repeat the loop. Now digit becomes 2, sum is set to $9 + 2 = 11$, and n is set to 17.

n	sum	digit
~~1729~~	~~0~~	
~~172~~	~~9~~	~~9~~
17	11	2

Repeat the loop once again, setting digit to 7, sum to $11 + 7 = 18$, and n to 1.

n	sum	digit
~~1729~~	~~0~~	
~~172~~	~~9~~	~~9~~
~~17~~	~~11~~	~~2~~
1	18	7

Enter the loop for one last time. Now digit is set to 1, sum to 19, and n becomes zero.

n	sum	digit
~~1729~~	~~0~~	
~~172~~	~~9~~	~~9~~
~~17~~	~~11~~	~~2~~
~~1~~	~~18~~	~~7~~
0	19	1

```
int n = 1729;
int sum = 0;
while (n > 0)
{
    int digit = n % 10;
    sum = sum + digit;
    n = n / 10;
}
cout << sum << endl;
```

Because n equals zero, this condition is not true.

The condition n > 0 is now false. Continue with the statement after the loop.

```
int n = 1729;
int sum = 0;
while (n > 0)
{
    int digit = n % 10;
    sum = sum + digit;
    n = n / 10;
}
cout << sum << endl;
```

n	sum	digit	output
1729	0		
172	9	9	
17	11	2	
1	18	7	
0	19	1	19

This statement is an output statement. The value that is output is the value of sum, which is 19.

Of course, you can get the same answer by just running the code. However, hand-tracing can give you an *insight* that you would not get if you simply ran the code. Consider again what happens in each iteration:

- We extract the last digit of n.
- We add that digit to sum.
- We strip the digit off n.

In other words, the loop forms the sum of the digits in n. You now know what the loop does for any value of n, not just the one in the example. (Why would anyone want to form the sum of the digits? Operations of this kind are useful for checking the validity of credit card numbers and other forms of ID numbers—see Exercise P4.21.)

Hand-tracing does not just help you understand code that works correctly. It is a powerful technique for finding errors in your code. When a program behaves in a way that you don't expect, get out a sheet of paper and track the values of the variables as you mentally step through the code.

You don't need a working program to do hand-tracing. You can hand-trace pseudocode. In fact, it is an excellent idea to hand-trace your pseudocode before you go to the trouble of translating it into actual code, to confirm that it works correctly.

Hand-tracing can help you understand how an unfamiliar algorithm works.

Hand-tracing can show errors in code or pseudocode.

4.3 The for Loop

The for loop is used when a value runs from a starting point to an ending point with a constant increment or decrement.

It often happens that you want to execute a sequence of statements a given number of times. You can use a while loop that is controlled by a counter, as in the following example:

```
counter = 1; // Initialize the counter
while (counter <= 10) // Check the counter
{
    cout << counter << endl;
    counter++; // Update the counter
}
```

Because this loop type is so common, there is a special form for it, called the for loop (see Syntax 4.2).

```
for (counter = 1; counter <= 10; counter++)
{
    cout << counter << endl;
}
```

© Enrico Fianchini/iStockphoto.

You can visualize the for *loop as an orderly sequence of steps.*

Some people call this loop *count-controlled*. In contrast, the while loop of the preceding section can be called an *event-controlled* loop because it executes until an event occurs (for example, when the balance reaches the target). Another commonly-used term for a count-controlled loop is *definite*. You know from the outset that the loop body will be executed a definite number of times—ten times in our example. In contrast, you do not know how many iterations it takes to accumulate a target balance. Such a loop is called *indefinite*.

Syntax 4.2   for **Statement**

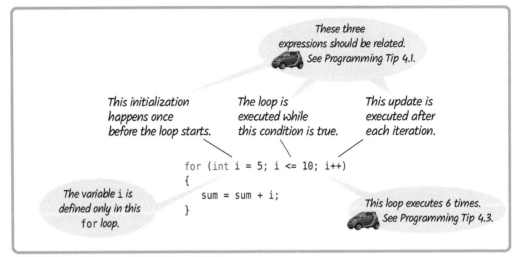

The for loop neatly groups the initialization, condition, and update expressions together. However, it is important to realize that these expressions are *not* executed together (see Figure 3).

❶ Initialize counter

```
                                        for (counter = 1; counter <= 10; counter++)
                                        {
     counter =       1                       cout << counter << endl;
                                        }
```

❷ Check condition

```
                                        for (counter = 1; counter <= 10; counter++)
                                        {
     counter =       1                       cout << counter << endl;
                                        }
```

❸ Execute loop body

```
                                        for (counter = 1; counter <= 10; counter++)
                                        {
     counter =       1                       cout << counter << endl;
                                        }
```

❹ Update counter

```
                                        for (counter = 1; counter <= 10; counter++)
                                        {
     counter =       2                       cout << counter << endl;
                                        }
```

❺ Check condition again

```
                                        for (counter = 1; counter <= 10; counter++)
                                        {
     counter =       2                       cout << counter << endl;
                                        }
```

Figure 3   Execution of a for Loop

- The initialization is executed once, before the loop is entered. **❶**
- The condition is checked before each iteration. **❷** **❺**
- The update is executed after each iteration. **❹**

A for loop can count down instead of up:

```
for (counter = 10; counter >= 0; counter--) . . .
```

The increment or decrement need not be in steps of 1:

```
for (counter = 0; counter <= 10; counter = counter + 2) . . .
```

So far, we assumed that the counter variable had already been defined before the for loop. Alternatively, you can define a variable in the loop initialization. Such a variable is defined *only* in the loop:

```
for (int counter = 1; counter <= 10; counter++)
{
   . . .
} // counter no longer defined here
```

See Table 2 for additional variations.

Table 2 for Loop Examples

Loop	Values of i	Comment
`for (i = 0; i <= 5; i++)`	0 1 2 3 4 5	Note that the loop is executed 6 times. (See Programming Tip 4.3.)
`for (i = 5; i >= 0; i--)`	5 4 3 2 1 0	Use i-- for decreasing values.
`for (i = 0; i < 9; i = i + 2)`	0 2 4 6 8	Use i = i + 2 for a step size of 2.
`for (i = 0; i != 9; i = i + 2)`	0 2 4 6 8 10 12 14 ... (infinite loop)	You can use < or <= instead of != to avoid this problem.
`for (i = 1; i <= 20; i = i * 2)`	1 2 4 8 16	You can specify any rule for modifying i, such as doubling it in every step.
`for (i = 0; i < str.length(); i++)`	0 1 2 ... until the last valid index of the string str	In the loop body, use the expression `str.substr(i, 1)` to get a string containing the ith character.

Here is a typical use of the for loop. We want to print the balance of our savings account over a period of years, as shown in this table:

Year	Balance
1	10500.00
2	11025.00
3	11576.25
4	12155.06
5	12762.82

The for loop pattern applies because the variable year starts at 1 and then moves in constant increments until it reaches the target:

```
for (int year = 1; year <= nyears; year++)
{
    Update balance.
    Print year and balance.
}
```

Here is the complete program. Figure 4 shows the corresponding flowchart.

Figure 4   Flowchart of a for Loop

sec03/invtable.cpp

```cpp
1   #include <iostream>
2   #include <iomanip>
3
4   using namespace std;
5
6   int main()
7   {
8      const double RATE = 5;
9      const double INITIAL_BALANCE = 10000;
10     double balance = INITIAL_BALANCE;
11     int nyears;
12     cout << "Enter number of years: ";
13     cin >> nyears;
14
15     cout << fixed << setprecision(2);
16     for (int year = 1; year <= nyears; year++)
17     {
18        balance = balance * (1 + RATE / 100);
19        cout << setw(4) << year << setw(10) << balance << endl;
20     }
21
22     return 0;
23  }
```

Program Run

```
Enter number of years: 10
    1   10500.00
    2   11025.00
    3   11576.25
    4   12155.06
    5   12762.82
    6   13400.96
    7   14071.00
    8   14774.55
    9   15513.28
   10   16288.95
```

Programming Tip 4.1

Use for Loops for Their Intended Purpose Only

A for loop is an *idiom* for a loop of a particular form. A value runs from the start to the end, with a constant increment or decrement.

The compiler won't check whether the initialization, condition, and update expressions are related. For example, the following loop is legal:

```cpp
// Confusing—unrelated expressions
for (cout << "Inputs: "; cin >> x; sum = sum + x)
{
   count++;
}
```

However, programmers reading such a for loop will be confused because it does not match their expectations. Use a while loop for iterations that do not follow the for idiom.

Programming Tip 4.2
Choose Loop Bounds That Match Your Task

Suppose you want to print line numbers that go from 1 to 10. Of course, you will want to use a loop

```
for (int i = 1; i <= 10; i++)
```

The values for i are bounded by the relation $1 \leq i \leq 10$. Because there are $\leq$ on both bounds, the bounds are called **symmetric**.

When traversing the characters in a string, it is more natural to use the bounds

```
for (int i = 0; i < str.length(); i++)
```

In this loop, i traverses all valid positions in the string. You can access the ith character as str.substr(i, 1). The values for i are bounded by $0 \leq i < $ str.length(), with a $\leq$ to the left and a $<$ to the right. That is appropriate, because str.length() is not a valid position. Such bounds are called **asymmetric**.

In this case, it is not a good idea to use symmetric bounds:

```
for (int i = 0; i <= str.length() - 1; i++) // Use < instead
```

The asymmetric form is easier to understand.

Programming Tip 4.3
Count Iterations

Finding the correct lower and upper bounds for an iteration can be confusing. Should you start at 0 or at 1? Should you use <= or < in the termination condition?

Counting the number of iterations is a very useful device for better understanding a loop. Counting is easier for loops with asymmetric bounds. The loop

```
for (int i = a; i < b; i++)
```

is executed b - a times. For example, the loop

```
for (int i = 0; i < 10; i++)
```

runs ten times, with values 0, 1, 2, 3, 4, 5, 6, 7, 8, and 9.

The loop with symmetric bounds,

```
for (int i = a; i <= b; i++)
```

is executed b - a + 1 times. That "+1" is the source of many programming errors.

For example,

```
for (int i = 0; i <= 10; i++)
```

runs 11 times. Maybe that is what you want; if not, start at 1 or use < 10.

One way to visualize this "+1" error is by looking at a fence. Each section has one fence post to the left, and there is a final post on the right of the last section. Forgetting to count the last value is often called a "fence post error".

How many posts do you need for a fence with four sections? It is easy to be "off by one" with problems such as this one.

© akaplummer/iStockphoto.

4.4 The do Loop

Sometimes you want to execute the body of a loop at least once and perform the loop test after the body is executed. The do loop serves that purpose:

```
do
{
    statements
}
while (condition);
```

The body of the do loop is executed first, then the condition is tested.

> The do loop is appropriate when the loop body must be executed at least once.

Some people call such a loop a *post-test* loop because the condition is tested after completing the loop body. In contrast, while and for loops are *pre-test* loops. In those loop types, the condition is tested before entering the loop body.

A typical example for such a loop is input validation. Suppose you ask a user to enter a value < 100. If the user didn't pay attention and entered a larger value, you ask again, until the value is correct. Of course, you cannot test the value until the user has entered it. This is a perfect fit for the do loop (see Figure 5):

```
int value;
do
{
    cout << "Enter a value < 100: ";
    cin >> value;
}
while (value >= 100);
```

Here, we assume that the user will enter an integer. You saw in Section 3.8 how to exit the program if a user fails to enter an integer. Special Topic 4.1 shows how to recover from such an error.

Figure 5   Flowchart of a do Loop

EXAMPLE CODE   See sec04 of your companion code for a program that illustrates the use of the do loop for input validation.

Programming Tip 4.4
Flowcharts for Loops

In Section 3.5, you learned how to use flowcharts to visualize the flow of control in a program. There are two types of loops that you can include in a flowchart; they correspond to a while loop and a do loop in C++. They differ in the placement of the condition—either before or after the loop body.

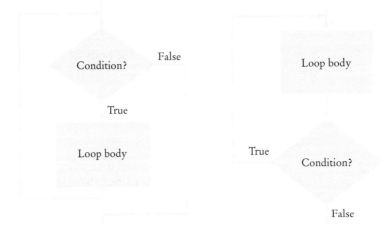

As described in Section 3.5, you want to avoid "spaghetti code" in your flowcharts. For loops, that means that you never want to have an arrow that points inside a loop body.

4.5 Processing Input

In the following sections, you will learn how to read and process a sequence of input values.

4.5.1 Sentinel Values

A sentinel value denotes the end of a data set, but it is not part of the data.

Whenever you read a sequence of inputs, you need to have some method of indicating the end of the sequence. Sometimes you are lucky and no input value can be zero. Then you can prompt the user to keep entering numbers, or 0 to finish the sequence. If zero is allowed but negative numbers are not, you can use –1 to indicate termination. A value that serves as a signal for termination is called a **sentinel**.

Let's put this technique to work in a program that computes the average of a set of salary values. In our sample program, we will use –1 as a sentinel. An employee would surely not work for a negative salary, but there may be volunteers who work for free.

Inside the loop, we read an input. If the input is not –1, we process it. In order to compute the average, we need the total sum of all salaries, and the number of inputs.

```
while (. . .)
{
   cin >> salary;
```

© Rhoberazzi/iStockphoto.

In the military, a sentinel guards a border or passage. In computer science, a sentinel value denotes the end of an input sequence or the border between input sequences.

```
      if (salary != -1)
      {
         sum = sum + salary;
         count++;
      }
   }
```

We stay in the loop while the sentinel value is not detected.

```
   while (salary != -1)
   {
      . . .
   }
```

There is just one problem: When the loop is entered for the first time, no data value has been read. Be sure to initialize salary with some value other than the sentinel:

```
   double salary = 0; // Any value other than –1 will do
```

Alternatively, use a do loop

```
   do
   {
      . . .
   }
   while (salary != -1)
```

The following program reads inputs until the user enters the sentinel, and then computes and prints the average.

sec05/sentinel.cpp

```
 1  #include <iostream>
 2
 3  using namespace std;
 4
 5  int main()
 6  {
 7     double sum = 0;
 8     int count = 0;
 9     double salary = 0;
10     cout << "Enter salaries, -1 to finish: ";
11     while (salary != -1)
12     {
13        cin >> salary;
14        if (salary != -1)
15        {
16           sum = sum + salary;
17           count++;
18        }
19     }
20     if (count > 0)
21     {
22        double average = sum / count;
23        cout << "Average salary: " << average << endl;
24     }
25     else
26     {
27        cout << "No data" << endl;
28     }
29     return 0;
30  }
```

Program Run

```
Enter salaries, -1 to finish: 10 10 40 -1
Average salary: 20
```

4.5.2 Reading Until Input Fails

Numeric sentinels only work if there is some restriction on the input. In many cases, though, there isn't. Suppose you want to compute the average of a data set that may contain 0 or negative values. Then you cannot use 0 or –1 to indicate the end of the input.

In such a situation, you can read input data until input fails. As you have seen in Section 3.8, the condition

```
cin.fail()
```

is true if the preceding input has failed. For example, suppose that the input was read with these statements:

```
double value;
cin >> value;
```

If the user enters a value that is not a number (such as Q), then the input fails.

We now encounter an additional complexity. You only know that input failed after you have entered the loop and attempted to read it. To remember the failure, use a Boolean variable:

You can use a Boolean variable to control a loop. Set the variable before entering the loop, then set it to the opposite to leave the loop.

```
cout << "Enter values, Q to quit: ";
bool done = false;
while (!done)
{
   cin >> value;
   if (cin.fail())
   {
      done = true;
   }
   else
   {
      Process value.
   }
}
```

Some programmers dislike the introduction of a Boolean variable to control a loop. Special Topic 4.2 shows an alternative mechanism for leaving a loop. However, when reading input, there is an easier way. The expression

```
cin >> value
```

can be used in a condition. It evaluates to true if cin has *not* failed after reading value. Therefore, you can read and process a set of inputs with the following loop:

```
cout << "Enter values, Q to quit: ";
while (cin >> value)
{
   Process value.
}
```

This loop is suitable for processing a single sequence of inputs. You will learn more about reading inputs in Chapter 8.

EXAMPLE CODE   See sec05 of your companion code for a program that uses a Boolean variable to control a loop.

Special Topic 4.1

Clearing the Failure State

When an input operation has failed, all further input operations also fail. Consider the doloop.cpp program in Section 4.4 in which a user is prompted to enter a value that is not negative. Suppose the user enters a value that is not an integer, such as the string zero.

Then the operation

```
cin >> value;
```

sets cin to the failed state. If you want to give the user another chance to enter a value, you need to *clear* the failed state, by calling the clear member function. You also need to read and discard the offending item:

```
cin.clear();
string item;
cin >> item;
```

Now the user can try again. Here is an improved version of the do loop:

```
do
{
   cout << "Enter a number >= 0: ";
   cin >> value;

   if (cin.fail())
   {
      // Clear the failed state
      cin.clear();
      // Read and discard the item
      string item;
      cin >> item;
      // Set to an invalid input
      value = -1;
   }
}
while (value < 0);
```

Note that we set value to an invalid input if the input was not a number, in order to enter the loop once more.

Here is another situation in which you need to clear the failed state. Suppose you read two number sequences, each of which has a letter as a sentinel. You read the first sequence:

```
cout << "Enter values, Q to quit.\n";
while (cin >> values)
{
   Process input.
}
```

Suppose the user has entered 30 10 5 Q. The input of Q has caused the failure. Because only successfully processed characters are removed from the input, the Q character is still present. Clear the stream and read the sentinel into a string variable:

```
cin.clear();
string sentinel;
cin >> sentinel;
```

Now you can go on and read more inputs.

Special Topic 4.2

The Loop-and-a-Half Problem and the break Statement

Some programmers dislike loops that are controlled by a Boolean variable, such as:

```cpp
bool done = false;
while (!done)
{
   cin >> value;
   if (cin.fail())
   {
      done = true;
   }
   else
   {
      Process value.
   }
}
```

The actual test for loop termination is in the middle of the loop, not at the top. This is called a **loop and a half** because one must go halfway into the loop before knowing whether one needs to terminate.

As an alternative, you can use the break reserved word:

```cpp
while (true)
{
   cin >> value;
   if (cin.fail()) { break; }
   Process value.
}
```

The break statement breaks out of the enclosing loop, independent of the loop condition.

In the loop-and-a-half case, break statements can be beneficial. But it is difficult to lay down clear rules as to when they are safe and when they should be avoided. We do not use the break statement in this book.

Special Topic 4.3

Redirection of Input and Output

Consider the sentinel.cpp program that computes the average value of an input sequence. If you use such a program, then it is quite likely that you already have the values in a file, and it seems a shame that you have to type them all in again. The command line interface of your operating system provides a way to link a file to the input of a program, as if all the characters in the file had actually been typed by a user. If you type

```
sentinel < numbers.txt
```

the program is executed. Its input instructions no longer expect input from the keyboard. All input commands get their input from the file numbers.txt. This process is called *input redirection*.

Input redirection is an excellent tool for testing programs. When you develop a program and fix its bugs, it is boring to keep entering the same input every time you run the program. Spend a few minutes putting the inputs into a file, and use redirection.

You can also redirect output. In this program, that is not terribly useful. If you run

```
sentinel < numbers.txt > output.txt
```

the file output.txt contains the input prompts and the output, such as

Use input redirection to read input from a file. Use output redirection to capture program output in a file.

```
Enter salaries, -1 to finish:
Average salary: 15
```

However, redirecting output is obviously useful for programs that produce lots of output. You can print the file containing the output or edit it before you turn it in for grading.

4.6 Problem Solving: Storyboards

When you design a program that interacts with a user, you need to make a plan for that interaction. What information does the user provide, and in which order? What information will your program display, and in which format? What should happen when there is an error? When does the program quit?

> A storyboard consists of annotated sketches for each step in an action sequence.

This planning is similar to the development of a movie or a computer game, where *storyboards* are used to plan action sequences. A storyboard is made up of panels that show a sketch of each step. Annotations explain what is happening and note any special situations. Storyboards are also used to develop software—see Figure 6.

> Developing a storyboard helps you understand the inputs and outputs that are required for a program.

Making a storyboard is very helpful when you begin designing a program. You need to ask yourself which information you need in order to compute the answers that the program user wants. You need to decide how to present those answers. These are important considerations that you want to settle before you design an algorithm for computing the answers.

Let's look at a simple example. We want to write a program that helps users with questions such as "How many tablespoons are in a pint?" or "How many inches are 30 centimeters?"

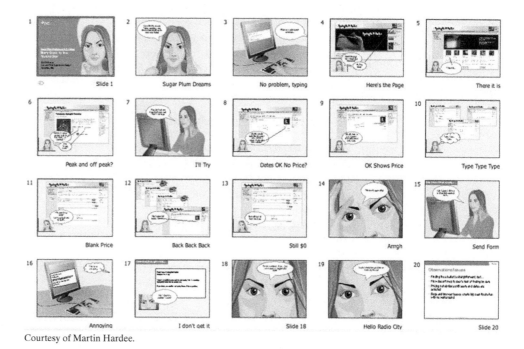

Courtesy of Martin Hardee.

Figure 6 Storyboard for the Design of a Web Application

What information does the user provide?

- The quantity and unit to convert from
- The unit to convert to

What if there is more than one quantity? A user may have a whole table of centimeter values that should be converted into inches.

What if the user enters units that our program doesn't know how to handle, such as ångström?

What if the user asks for impossible conversions, such as inches to gallons?

Let's get started with a storyboard panel. It is a good idea to write the user inputs in a different color. (Underline them if you don't have a color pen handy.)

Converting a Sequence of Values

What unit do you want to convert from? cm
What unit do you want to convert to? in
Enter values, terminated by zero ———— *Allows conversion of multiple values*
30
30 cm = 11.81 in ——
100   *Format makes clear what got converted*
100 cm = 39.37 in
0
What unit do you want to convert from?

The storyboard shows how we deal with a potential confusion. A user who wants to know how many inches are 30 centimeters may not read the first prompt carefully and specify inches. But then the output is "30 in = 76.2 cm", alerting the user to the problem.

The storyboard also raises an issue. How is the user supposed to know that "cm" and "in" are valid units? Would "centimeter" and "inches" also work? What happens when the user enters a wrong unit? Let's make another storyboard to demonstrate error handling.

Handling Unknown Units (needs improvement)

What unit do you want to convert from? cm
What unit do you want to convert to? inches
Sorry, unknown unit.
What unit do you want to convert to? inch
Sorry, unknown unit.
What unit do you want to convert to? gm

To eliminate frustration, it is better to list the units that the user can supply.

From unit (in, ft, mi, mm, cm, m, km, oz, lb, g, kg, tsp, tbsp, pint, gal): cm
To unit: in ——
                    No need to list the units again

We switched to a shorter prompt to make room for all the unit names. Exercise R4.24 explores a different alternative.

There is another issue that we haven't addressed yet. How does the user quit the program? The first storyboard gives the impression that the program will go on forever.

We can ask the user after seeing the sentinel that terminates an input sequence.

Exiting the Program

From unit (in, ft, mi, mm, cm, m, km, oz, lb, g, kg, tsp, tbsp, pint, gal): cm
To unit: in
Enter values, terminated by zero
30
30 cm = 11.81 in
0 ———————————— Sentinel triggers the prompt to exit
More conversions (y, n)? n
(Program exits)

As you can see from this case study, a storyboard is essential for developing a working program. You need to know the flow of the user interaction in order to structure your program.

4.7 Common Loop Algorithms

In the following sections, we discuss some of the most common algorithms that are implemented as loops. You can use them as starting points for your loop designs.

4.7.1 Sum and Average Value

Computing the sum of a number of inputs is a very common task. Keep a *running total:* a variable to which you add each input value. Of course, the total should be initialized with 0.

```
double total = 0;
double input;
while (cin >> input)
{
    total = total + input;
}
```

To compute an average, count how many values you have, and divide by the count. Be sure to check that the count is not zero.

To compute an average, keep a total and a count of all values.

```
double total = 0;
int count = 0;
double input;
while (cin >> input)
{
    total = total + input;
    count++;
}
double average = 0;
if (count > 0) { average = total / count; }
```

4.7.2 Counting Matches

To count values that fulfill a condition, check all values and increment a counter for each match.

You often want to know how many values fulfill a particular condition. For example, you may want to count how many spaces are in a string. Keep a counter, a variable that is initialized with 0 and incremented whenever there is a match.

```cpp
int spaces = 0;
for (int i = 0; i < str.length(); i++)
{
   string ch = str.substr(i, 1);
   if (ch == " ")
   {
      spaces++;
   }
}
```

For example, if str is the string "My Fair Lady", spaces is incremented twice (when i is 2 and 7).

Note that the spaces variable is declared outside the loop. We want the loop to update a single variable. The ch variable is declared inside the loop. A separate variable is created for each iteration and removed at the end of each loop iteration.

This loop can also be used for scanning inputs. The following loop reads text, a word at a time, and counts the number of words with at most three letters:

```cpp
int short_words = 0;
string input;
while (cin >> input)
{
   if (input.length() <= 3)
   {
      short_words++;
   }
}
```

In a loop that counts matches, a counter is incremented whenever a match is found.

© Hiob/iStockphoto.

4.7.3 Finding the First Match

If your goal is to find a match, exit the loop when the match is found

When you count the values that fulfill a condition, you need to look at all values. However, if your task is to find a match, then you can stop as soon as the condition is fulfilled.

Here is a loop that finds the first space in a string. Because we do not visit all elements in the string, a while loop is a better choice than a for loop:

```cpp
bool found = false;
int position = 0;
while (!found && position < str.length())
{
   string ch = str.substr(position, 1);
   if (ch == " ") { found = true; }
```

© drflet/iStockphoto.

When searching, you look at items until a match is found.

```
        else { position++; }
    }
```

If a match was found, then found is true and position is the index of the first match. If the loop did not find a match, then found remains false after the end of the loop.

Note that the variable position is declared *outside* the while loop because you may want to use it after the loop has finished.

4.7.4 Prompting Until a Match is Found

In the preceding example, we searched a string for a character that matches a condition. You can apply the same process for user input. Suppose you are asking a user to enter a positive value < 100. Keep asking until the user provides a correct input:

```
bool valid = false;
double input;
while (!valid)
{
    cout << "Please enter a positive value < 100: ";
    cin >> input;
    if (0 < input && input < 100) { valid = true; }
    else { cout << "Invalid input." << endl; }
}
```

Note that the variable input is declared *outside* the while loop because you will want to use the input after the loop has finished. If it had been declared inside the loop body, you would not be able to use it outside the loop.

4.7.5 Maximum and Minimum

To find the largest value, update the largest value seen so far whenever you see a larger one.

To compute the largest value in a sequence, keep a variable that stores the largest element that you have encountered, and update it when you find a larger one:

```
double largest;
cin >> largest;
double input;
while (cin >> input)
{
    if (input > largest)
    {
        largest = input;
    }
}
```

© CEFutcher/iStockphoto.

To find the height of the tallest bus rider, remember the largest value so far, and update it whenever you see a taller one.

This algorithm requires that there is at least one input.

To compute the smallest value, simply reverse the comparison:

```
double smallest;
cin >> smallest;
double input;
while (cin >> input)
{
```

```
    if (input < smallest)
    {
        smallest = input;
    }
}
```

4.7.6 Comparing Adjacent Values

When processing a sequence of values in a loop, you sometimes need to compare a value with the value that just preceded it. For example, suppose you want to check whether a sequence of inputs contains adjacent duplicates such as 1 7 2 9 9 4 9.

Now you face a challenge. Consider the typical loop for reading a value:

```
double input;
while (cin >> input)
{
    // Now input contains the current input
    . . .
}
```

To compare adjacent inputs, store the preceding input in a variable.

How can you compare the current input with the preceding one? At any time, input contains the current input, overwriting the previous one.

The answer is to store the previous input, like this:

```
double input;
double previous;
while (cin >> input)
{
    if (input == previous) { cout << "Duplicate input" << endl; }
    previous = input;
}
```

One problem remains. When the loop is entered for the first time, previous has not yet been set. You can solve this problem with an initial input operation outside the loop:

```
double input;
double previous;
cin >> previous;
while (cin >> input)
{
    if (input == previous) { cout << "Duplicate input" << endl; }
    previous = input;
}
```

When comparing adjacent values, store the previous value in a variable.   © tingberg/iStockphoto.

EXAMPLE CODE   See sec07 of your companion code for a program that demonstrates common loop algorithms.

HOW TO 4.1

Writing a Loop

This How To walks you through the process of implementing a loop statement. We will illustrate the steps with the following example problem:

Problem Statement Read twelve temperature values (one for each month), and display the number of the month with the highest temperature. For example, according to http://worldclimate.com, the average maximum temperatures for Death Valley are (in order by month):

© Stevegeer/iStockphoto.

18.2 22.6 26.4 31.1 36.6 42.2
45.7 44.5 40.2 33.1 24.2 17.6

In this case, the month with the highest temperature (45.7 degrees Celsius) is July, and the program should display 7.

Step 1 Decide what work must be done *inside* the loop.

Every loop needs to do some kind of repetitive work, such as

- Reading another item.
- Updating a value (such as a bank balance or total).
- Incrementing a counter.

If you can't figure out what needs to go inside the loop, start by writing down the steps that you would take if you solved the problem by hand. For example, with the temperature reading problem, you might write

> *Read the first value.*
> *Read the second value.*
> *If the second value is higher than the first value*
> *Set highest temperature to the second value.*
> *Set highest month to 2.*
> *Read the next value.*
> *If the value is higher than the first and second values*
> *Set highest temperature to the value.*
> *Set highest month to 3.*
> *Read the next value.*
> *If the value is higher than the highest temperature seen so far*
> *Set highest temperature to the value.*
> *Set highest month to 4.*
> ` . . .`

Now look at these steps and reduce them to a set of *uniform* actions that can be placed into the loop body. The first action is easy:

> *Read the next value.*

The next action is trickier. In our description, we used tests "higher than the first", "higher than the first and second", "higher than the highest temperature seen so far". We need to settle on one test that works for all iterations. The last formulation is the most general.

Similarly, we must find a general way of setting the highest month. We need a variable that stores the current month, running from 1 to 12. Then we can formulate the second loop action:

If the value is higher than the highest temperature
  Set highest temperature to the value.
  Set highest month to current month.

Altogether our loop is

While . . .
  Read the next value.
  If the value is higher than the highest temperature
    Set the highest temperature to the value.
    Set highest month to current month.
  Increment current month.

Step 2   Specify the loop condition.

What goal do you want to reach in your loop? Typical examples are:

- Has the counter reached the final value?
- Have you read the last input value?
- Has a value reached a given threshold?

In our example, we simply want the current month to reach 12.

Step 3   Determine the loop type.

We distinguish between two major loop types. A *count-controlled* loop is executed a definite number of times. In an *event-controlled* loop, the number of iterations is not known in advance—the loop is executed until some event happens.

Count-controlled loops can be implemented as `for` statements. For other loops, consider the loop condition. Do you need to complete one iteration of the loop body before you can tell when to terminate the loop? In that case, choose a `do` loop. Otherwise, use a `while` loop.

Sometimes, the condition for terminating a loop changes in the middle of the loop body. In that case, you can use a Boolean variable that specifies when you are ready to leave the loop. Such a variable is called a **flag**. Follow this pattern:

```
bool done = false;
while (!done)
{
   Do some work.
   If all work has been completed
   {
      done = true;
   }
   else
   {
      Do more work.
   }
}
```

In summary,

- If you know in advance how many times a loop is repeated, use a `for` loop.
- If the loop body must be executed at least once, use a `do` loop.
- Otherwise, use a `while` loop.

In our example, we read 12 temperature values. Therefore, we choose a `for` loop.

Step 4 Set up variables for entering the loop for the first time.

List all variables that are used and updated in the loop, and determine how to initialize them. Commonly, counters are initialized with 0 or 1, totals with 0.

In our example, the variables are

current month
highest value
highest month

We need to be careful how we set up the highest temperature value. We can't simply set it to 0. After all, our program needs to work with temperature values from Antarctica, all of which may be negative.

A good option is to set the highest temperature value to the first input value. Of course, then we need to remember to only read in another 11 values, with the current month starting at 2.

We also need to initialize the highest month with 1. After all, in an Australian city, we may never find a month that is warmer than January.

Step 5 Process the result after the loop has finished.

In many cases, the desired result is simply a variable that was updated in the loop body. For example, in our temperature program, the result is the highest month. Sometimes, the loop computes values that contribute to the final result. For example, suppose you are asked to average the temperatures. Then the loop should compute the sum, not the average. After the loop has completed, you are ready to compute the average: divide the sum by the number of inputs.

Here is our complete loop:

Read value.
highest temperature = value
highest month = 1
For current month from 2 to 12
  Read next value.
  If the value is higher than the highest temperature
    Set highest temperature to the value.
    Set highest month to current month.

Step 6 Trace the loop with typical examples.

Hand-trace your loop code, as described in Section 4.2. Choose example values that are not too complex—executing the loop 3–5 times is enough to check for the most common errors. Pay special attention when entering the loop for the first and last time.

Sometimes, you want to make a slight modification to make tracing feasible. For example, when hand-tracing the investment doubling problem, use an interest rate of 20 percent rather than 5 percent. When hand-tracing the temperature loop, use 4 data values, not 12.

Let's say the data are 22.6 36.6 44.5 24.2. Here is the walkthrough:

current month	current value	highest month	highest value
		~~1~~	22.6
~~2~~	36.6	~~2~~	36.6
~~3~~	44.5	3	44.5
4	24.2		

The trace demonstrates that *highest month* and *highest value* are properly set.

Step 7   Implement the loop in C++.

Here's the loop for our example. Exercise E4.4 asks you to complete the program.

```cpp
double highest_value;
cin >> highest_value;
int highest_month = 1;
for (int current_month = 2; current_month <= 12; current_month++)
{
   double next_value;
   cin >> next_value;
   if (next_value > highest_value)
   {
      highest_value = next_value;
      highest_month = current_month;
   }
}
cout << highest_month << endl;
```

WORKED EXAMPLE 4.1

Credit Card Processing

Learn how to use a loop to remove spaces from a credit card number. See your E-Text or visit wiley.com/go/bclo3.

© MorePixels/iStockphoto.

4.8 Nested Loops

When the body of a loop contains another loop, the loops are nested. A typical use of nested loops is printing a table with rows and columns.

In Section 3.4, you saw how to nest two `if` statements. Similarly, complex iterations sometimes require a **nested loop**: a loop inside another loop statement. When processing tables, nested loops occur naturally. An outer loop iterates over all rows of the table. An inner loop deals with the columns in the current row.

In this section you will see how to print a table. For simplicity, we will simply print powers x^n, as in the table below.

Here is the pseudocode for printing the table:

Print table header.
For x from 1 to 10
   Print table row.
   Print endl.

x^1	x^2	x^3	x^4
1	1	1	1
2	4	8	16
3	9	27	81
...	...	...	...
10	100	1000	10000

How do you print a table row? You need to print a value for each exponent. This requires a second loop:

For n from 1 to 4
   Print x^n.

This loop must be placed inside the preceding loop.

The hour and minute displays in a digital clock are an example of nested loops. The hours loop 12 times, and for each hour, the minutes loop 60 times.

© davejkahn/iStockphoto.

We say that the inner loop is *nested* inside the outer loop (see Figure 7).

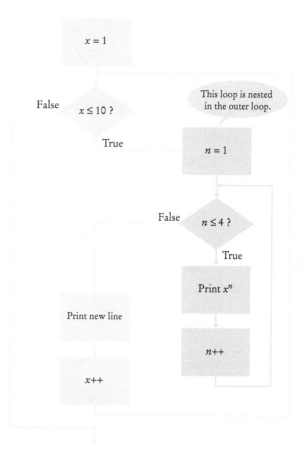

Figure 7   Flowchart of a Nested Loop

There are 10 rows in the outer loop. For each x, the program prints four columns in the inner loop. Thus, a total of $10 \times 4 = 40$ values are printed.

Following is the complete program. Note that we also use loops to print the table header. However, those loops are not nested.

sec08/powtable.cpp

```cpp
1  #include <iostream>
2  #include <iomanip>
3  #include <cmath>
4
5  using namespace std;
6
7  int main()
8  {
9     const int NMAX = 4;
10    const double XMAX = 10;
11
12    // Print table header
13
14    for (int n = 1; n <= NMAX; n++)
15    {
16       cout << setw(10) << n;
17    }
18    cout << endl;
19    for (int n = 1; n <= NMAX; n++)
20    {
21       cout << setw(10) << "x ";
22    }
23    cout << endl << endl;
24
25    // Print table body
26
27    for (double x = 1; x <= XMAX; x++)
28    {
29       // Print table row
30
31       for (int n = 1; n <= NMAX; n++)
32       {
33          cout << setw(10) << pow(x, n);
34       }
35       cout << endl;
36    }
37
38    return 0;
39 }
```

Program Run

1	2	3	4
x	x	x	x
1	1	1	1
2	4	8	16
3	9	27	81
4	16	64	256
5	25	125	625
6	36	216	1296
7	49	343	2401
8	64	512	4096
9	81	729	6561
10	100	1000	10000

Table 3 Nested Loop Examples

Nested Loops	Output	Explanation
| ```cpp
for (i = 1; i <= 3; i++)
{
   for (j = 1; j <= 4; j++)  { cout << "*"; }
   cout << endl;
}
``` | ```
****
****
****
``` | Prints 3 rows of 4 asterisks each. |
| ```cpp
for (i = 1; i <= 4; i++)
{
   for (j = 1; j <= 3; j++) { cout << "*"; }
   cout << endl;
}
``` | ```
***
***
***
***
``` | Prints 4 rows of 3 asterisks each. |
| ```cpp
for (i = 1; i <= 4; i++)
{
   for (j = 1; j <= i; j++) { cout << "*"; }
   cout << endl;
}
``` | ```
*
**
***
****
``` | Prints 4 rows of lengths 1, 2, 3, and 4. |
| ```cpp
for (i = 1; i <= 3; i++)
{
   for (j = 1; j <= 5; j++)
   {
      if (j % 2 == 0) { cout << "*"; }
      else { cout << "-"; }
   }
   cout << endl;
}
``` | ```
-*-*-
-*-*-
-*-*-
``` | Prints asterisks in even columns, dashes in odd columns. |
| ```cpp
for (i = 1; i <= 3; i++)
{
   for (j = 1; j <= 5; j++)
   {
      if ((i + j) % 2 == 0) { cout << "*"; }
      else { cout << " "; }
   }
   cout << endl;
}
``` | ```
* * *
 * *
* * *
``` | Prints a checkerboard pattern. |

WORKED EXAMPLE 4.2

Manipulating the Pixels in an Image

Learn how to use nested loops for manipulating the pixels in an image. The outer loop traverses the rows of the image, and the inner loop accesses each pixel of a row. See your E-Text or visit wiley.com/go/bclo3.

Cay Horstmann.

4.9 Problem Solving: Solve a Simpler Problem First

When developing a solution to a complex problem, first solve a simpler task.

As you learn more about programming, the complexity of the tasks that you are asked to solve will increase. When you face a complex task, you should apply an important skill: simplifying the problem, and solving the simpler problem first.

This is a good strategy for several reasons. Usually, you learn something useful from solving the simpler task. Moreover, the complex problem can seem unsurmountable, and you may find it difficult to know where to get started. When you are successful with a simpler problem first, you will be much more motivated to try the harder one.

It takes practice and a certain amount of courage to break down a problem into a sequence of simpler ones. The best way to learn this strategy is to practice it. When you work on your next assignment, ask yourself what is the absolutely simplest part of the task that is helpful for the end result, and start from there. With some experience, you will be able to design a plan that builds up a complete solution as a manageable sequence of intermediate steps.

Let us look at an example. You are asked to arrange pictures, lining them up along the top edges, separating them with small gaps, and starting a new row whenever you run out of room in the current row.

National Gallery of Art (see Credits page for details.)

We use the Picture type of Worked Example 4.2. The add member function can be used to add one picture to another:

```
pic.add(pic2, x, y);
```

The second picture is added so that its top-left corner is at the given x and y position. The original picture grows to hold all pixels of the added picture. We will use this member function repeatedly in order to build up the result.

Instead of tackling the entire assignment at once, here is a plan that solves a series of simpler problems.

Make a plan consisting of a series of tasks, each a simple extension of the previous one, and ending with the original problem.

1. Draw one picture.

2. Draw two pictures next to each other.

3. Draw two pictures with a gap between them.

4. Draw all pictures in a long row.

5. Draw a row of pictures until you run out of room, then put one more picture in the next row.

Let's get started with this plan.

1. The purpose of the first step is to become familiar with the `Picture` type. As it turns out, the pictures are in files a.png ... t.png. Let's load the first one:

```
Picture pic("a.png");
pic.save("gallery.png");
```

That's enough to produce the picture.

2. Now let's put the next picture after the first. We need to position it at the rightmost x-coordinate of the preceding picture.

pic.width()

```
Picture pic("a.png");
Picture pic2("b.png");
pic.add(pic2, pic.width(), 0);
```

3. The next step is to separate the two by a small gap when the second is added:

`pic.width()`

GAP

```
const int GAP = 10;

Picture pic("a.png");
Picture pic2("b.png");
pic.add(pic2, pic.width() + GAP, 0);
```

4. Now let's put all pictures in a row. Read the pictures in a loop, and then put each picture to the right of the one that preceded it. In the loop, you need to track the *x*-coordinate at which the next image should be inserted.

x   pic2

```
const int GAP = 10;
const string names = "abcdefghijklmnopqrst";
const int PICTURES = names.length();

Picture pic("a.png");
int x = pic.width() + GAP;
for (int i = 1; i < PICTURES; i++)
{
   Picture pic2(names.substr(i, 1) + ".png");
   pic.add(pic2, x, 0);
   x = x + pic2.width() + GAP;
}
```

5. Of course, we don't want to have all pictures in a row. The right margin of a picture should not extend past MAX_WIDTH.

```
if (x + pic.width() < MAX_WIDTH)
{
   Place pic on current row.
}
else
{
   Place pic on next row.
}
```

If the image doesn't fit any more, then we need to put it on the next row, below all the pictures in the current row. We'll set a variable max_y to the maximum *y*-coordinate of all placed pictures, updating it whenever a new picture is placed:

```
if (pic2.height() > max_y)
{
   max_y = pic2.height();
}
```

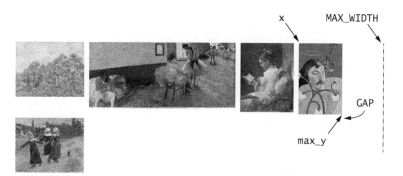

The following statement places a picture on the next row:

```
pic.add(pic2, 0, max_y + GAP);
```

Now we have written complete programs for all preliminary stages. We know how to line up the pictures, how to separate them with gaps, how to find out when to start a new row, and where to start it.

EXAMPLE CODE   See sec09 of your companion code for the preliminary stages of the gallery program.

With this knowledge, producing the final version is straightforward. Here is the program listing.

sec09/gallery6.cpp

```cpp
1  #include "picture.h"
2  #include <string>
3
4  using namespace std;
5
6  int main()
7  {
8     const int MAX_WIDTH = 720;
9     const int GAP = 10;
10    const string names = "abcdefghijklmnopqrst";
11    const int PICTURES = names.length();
12
13    // Read the first picture
14    Picture pic("a.png");
15
16    // x and y are the top-left corner of the next picture
17    int x = pic.width() + GAP;
18    int y = 0;
19
20    // max_y is the largest y encountered so far
21    int max_y = pic.height();
22    for (int i = 1; i < PICTURES; i++)
23    {
24       // Read the next picture
25       Picture pic2(names.substr(i, 1) + ".png");
26       if (x + pic2.width() >= MAX_WIDTH) // The picture doesn't fit on the row
27       {
28          // Place the picture on the next row
29          x = 0;
30          y = max_y + GAP;
31       }
```

```
32          pic.add(pic2, x, y);
33          // Update x and max_y
34          x = x + pic2.width() + GAP;
35          if (y + pic2.height() > max_y)
36          {
37             max_y = y + pic2.height();
38          }
39      }
40      pic.save("gallery.png");
41      return 0;
42 }
```

4.10 Random Numbers and Simulations

In a simulation, you use the computer to simulate an activity. You can introduce randomness by calling the random number generator.

A *simulation program* uses the computer to simulate an activity in the real world (or an imaginary one). Simulations are commonly used for predicting climate change, analyzing traffic, picking stocks, and many other applications in science and business. In the following sections, you will learn how to implement simulations that model phenomena with a degree of randomness.

4.10.1 Generating Random Numbers

Many events in the real world are difficult to predict with absolute precision, yet we can sometimes know the average behavior quite well. For example, a store may know from experience that a customer arrives every five minutes. Of course, that is an average—customers don't arrive in five minute intervals. To accurately model customer traffic, you want to take that random fluctuation into account. Now, how can you run such a simulation in the computer?

The C++ library has a *random number generator*, which produces numbers that appear to be completely random. Calling rand() yields a random integer between 0 and RAND_MAX (which is an implementation-dependent constant, typically, but not always, the largest valid int value). Call rand() again, and you get a different number. The rand function is declared in the <cstdlib> header.

The following program calls the rand function ten times.

sec10_01/random.cpp

```
 1 #include <iostream>
 2 #include <cstdlib>
 3
 4 using namespace std;
 5
 6 int main()
 7 {
 8    for (int i = 1; i <= 10; i++)
 9    {
10       int r = rand();
11       cout << r << endl;
12    }
13    return 0;
14 }
```

Program Run

```
1804289383
846930886
1681692777
1714636915
1957747793
424238335
719885386
1649760492
596516649
118964142
```

Actually, the numbers are not completely random. They are drawn from sequences of numbers that don't repeat for a long time. These sequences are actually computed from fairly simple formulas; they just behave like random numbers. For that reason, they are often called **pseudorandom numbers**.

Try running the program again. You will get the *exact same output*! This confirms that the random numbers are generated by formulas. However, when running simulations, you don't always want to get the same results. To overcome this problem, specify a *seed* for the random number sequence. Every time you use a new seed, the random number generator starts generating a new sequence. The seed is set with the srand function. A simple value to use as a seed is the current time:

```
srand(time(0));
```

Simply make this call once in your program, before generating any random numbers. Then the random numbers will be different in every program run. Also include the <ctime> header that declares the time function.

If you get a compiler warning for the call to srand, use

```
srand(static_cast<int>(time(nullptr)));
```

instead, and make sure your compiler uses C++ 11.

4.10.2 Simulating Die Tosses

In actual applications, you need to transform the output from the random number generator into different ranges. For example, to simulate the throw of a die, you need random numbers between 1 and 6.

Here is the general recipe for computing random integers between two bounds a and b. As you know from Programming Tip 4.3, there are b - a + 1 values between a and b, including the bounds themselves. First compute rand() % (b - a + 1) to obtain a random value between 0 and b - a, then add a, yielding a random value between a and b:

© ktsimage/iStockphoto.

```
int r = rand() % (b - a + 1) + a;
```

Here is a program that simulates the throw of a pair of dice.

sec10_02/dice.cpp

```
1  #include <iostream>
2  #include <string>
```

```
 3  #include <cstdlib>
 4  #include <ctime>
 5
 6  using namespace std;
 7
 8  int main()
 9  {
10     srand(time(0));
11
12     for (int i = 1; i <= 10; i++)
13     {
14        int d1 = rand() % 6 + 1;
15        int d2 = rand() % 6 + 1;
16        cout << d1 << " " << d2 << endl;
17     }
18     cout << endl;
19     return 0;
20  }
```

Program Run

```
5 1
2 1
1 2
5 1
1 2
6 4
4 4
6 1
6 3
5 2
```

4.10.3 The Monte Carlo Method

The Monte Carlo method is an ingenious method for finding approximate solutions to problems that cannot be precisely solved. (The method is named after the famous casino in Monte Carlo.) Here is a typical example: It is difficult to compute the number π, but you can approximate it quite well with the following simulation.

Simulate shooting a dart into a square surrounding a circle of radius 1. That is easy: generate random x and y coordinates between −1 and 1.

© timstarkey/iStockphoto.

If the generated point lies inside the circle, we count it as a *hit*. That is the case when $x^2 + y^2 \le 1$. Because our shots are entirely random, we expect that the ratio of *hits/tries* is approximately equal to the ratio of the areas of the circle and the square, that is, $\pi/4$. Therefore, our estimate for π is $4 \times hits/tries$. This method yields an estimate for π, using nothing but simple arithmetic.

To run the Monte Carlo simulation, you have to work a little harder with random number generation. When you throw a die, it has to come up with one of six faces. When throwing a dart, however, there are many possible outcomes. You must generate a *random floating-point number.*

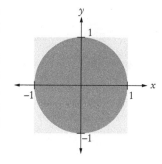

First, generate the following value:

```
double r = rand() * 1.0 / RAND_MAX; // Between 0 and 1
```

The value r is a random floating-point value between 0 and 1. (You have to multiply by 1.0 to ensure that one of the operands of the / operator is a floating-point number. The division rand() / RAND_MAX would be an integer division—see Common Error 2.3.)

To generate a random value between −1 and 1, you compute:

```
double x = -1 + 2 * r; // Between –1 and 1
```

As r ranges from 0 to 1, x ranges from $-1 + 2 \times 0 = -1$ to $-1 + 2 \times 1 = 1$.

Here is the program that carries out the simulation.

sec10_03/montecarlo.cpp

```cpp
1  #include <iostream>
2  #include <cstdlib>
3  #include <cmath>
4  #include <ctime>
5
6  using namespace std;
7
8  int main()
9  {
10     const int TRIES = 10000;
11
12     srand(time(0));
13
14     int hits = 0;
15     for (int i = 1; i <= TRIES; i++)
16     {
17        double r = rand() * 1.0 / RAND_MAX; // Between 0 and 1
18        double x = -1 + 2 * r; // Between –1 and 1
19        r = rand() * 1.0 / RAND_MAX;
20        double y = -1 + 2 * r;
21        if (x * x + y * y <= 1) { hits++; }
22     }
23     double pi_estimate = 4.0 * hits / TRIES;
24     cout << "Estimate for pi: " << pi_estimate << endl;
25     return 0;
26  }
```

Program Run

```
Estimate for pi: 3.1504
```

Computing & Society 4.2   **Digital Piracy**

As you read this, you will have written a few computer programs and experienced firsthand how much effort it takes to write even the humblest of programs. Writing a real software product, such as a financial application or a computer game, takes a lot of time and money. Few people, and fewer companies, are going to spend that kind of time and money if they don't have a reasonable chance to make more money from their effort. (Actually, some companies give away their software in the hope that users will click on advertisements or upgrade to more elaborate paid versions. Other companies give away the software that enables users to read and use files but sell the software needed to create those files. Finally, there are individuals who donate their time, out of enthusiasm, and produce programs that you can copy freely.)

When selling software, a company must rely on the honesty of its customers. It is an easy matter for an unscrupulous person to make copies of computer programs without paying for them. In most countries that is illegal. Most governments provide legal protection, such as copyright laws and patents, to encourage the development of new products. Countries that tolerate widespread piracy have found that they have an ample cheap supply of foreign software, but no local manufacturers willing to design good software for their own citizens, such as word processors in the local script or financial programs adapted to the local tax laws.

When a mass market for software first appeared, vendors were enraged by the money they lost through piracy. They tried to fight back to ensure that only the legitimate owner could use the software by using various schemes, such as *dongles*—devices that must be attached to a printer port before the software will run. Legitimate users hated these measures. They paid for the software, but they had to suffer through inconveniences, such as having multiple dongles sticking out from their computer.

Because it is so easy and inexpensive to pirate software, and the chance of being found out is minimal, you have to make a moral choice for yourself. If a package that you would really like to have is too expensive for your budget, do you steal it, or do you stay honest and get by with a more affordable product?

Of course, piracy is not limited to software. The same issues arise for other digital products as well. You may have had the opportunity to obtain copies of songs or movies without payment. Or you may have been frustrated by a copy protection device on your music player that made it difficult for you to listen to songs that you paid

for. Admittedly, it can be difficult to have a lot of sympathy for a musical ensemble whose publisher charges a lot of money for what seems to have been very little effort on their part, at least when compared to the effort that goes into designing and implementing a software package. Nevertheless, it seems only fair that artists and authors receive some compensation for their efforts.

How to pay artists, authors, and programmers fairly, without burdening honest customers, is an unsolved problem at the time of this writing, and many computer scientists are engaged in research in this area.

© RapidEye/iStockphoto.

CHAPTER SUMMARY

Explain the flow of execution in a loop.

- Loops execute a block of code repeatedly while a condition remains true.
- An off-by-one error is a common error when programming loops. Think through simple test cases to avoid this type of error.

Use the technique of hand-tracing to analyze the behavior of a program.

- Hand-tracing is a simulation of code execution in which you step through instructions and track the values of the variables.
- Hand-tracing can help you understand how an unfamiliar algorithm works.
- Hand-tracing can show errors in code or pseudocode.

Use for loops for implementing counting loops.

- The for loop is used when a value runs from a starting point to an ending point with a constant increment or decrement.

Choose between the while loop and the do loop.

- The do loop is appropriate when the loop body must be executed at least once.

Implement loops that read sequences of input data.

- A sentinel value denotes the end of a data set, but it is not part of the data.
- You can use a Boolean variable to control a loop. Set the variable before entering the loop, then set it to the opposite to leave the loop.
- Use input redirection to read input from a file. Use output redirection to capture program output in a file.

Use the technique of storyboarding for planning user interactions.

- A storyboard consists of annotated sketches for each step in an action sequence.
- Developing a storyboard helps you understand the inputs and outputs that are required for a program.

Know the most common loop algorithms.

- To compute an average, keep a total and a count of all values.
- To count values that fulfill a condition, check all values and increment a counter for each match.
- If your goal is to find a match, exit the loop when the match is found.
- To find the largest value, update the largest value seen so far whenever you see a larger one.
- To compare adjacent inputs, store the preceding input in a variable.

Use nested loops to implement multiple levels of iteration.

- When the body of a loop contains another loop, the loops are nested. A typical use of nested loops is printing a table with rows and columns.

Design programs that carry out complex tasks.

- When developing a solution to a complex problem, first solve a simpler task.
- Make a plan consisting of a series of tasks, each a simple extension of the previous one, and ending with the original problem.

Apply loops to the implementation of simulations.

- In a simulation, you use the computer to simulate an activity. You can introduce randomness by calling the random number generator.

REVIEW EXERCISES

■ R4.1 Given the variables

```
string stars = "*****";
string stripes = "=====";
```

what do these loops print?

a.
```
int i = 0;
while (i < 5)
{
   cout << stars.substr(0, i) << endl;
   i++;
}
```

b.
```
int i = 0;
while (i < 5)
{
   cout << stars.substr(0, i);
   cout << stripes.substr(i, 5 - i) << endl;
   i++;
}
```

c.
```
int i = 0;
while (i < 10)
{
   if (i % 2 == 0) { cout << stars << endl; }
   else { cout << stripes << endl; }
}
```

■ R4.2 What do these loops print?

a.
```
int i = 0; int j = 10;
while (i < j) { cout << i + " " + j << endl; i++; j--; }
```

b.
```
int i = 0; int j = 10;
while (i < j) { cout << i + j << endl; i++; j++; }
```

■ R4.3 What do these code snippets print?

a.
```
int result = 0;
for (int i = 1; i <= 10; i++) { result = result + i; }
cout << result << endl;
```

b.
```
int result = 1;
for (int i = 1; i <= 10; i++) { result = i - result; }
cout << result << endl;
```

c.
```
int result = 1;
for (int i = 5; i > 0; i--) { result = result * i; }
cout << result << endl;
```

d.
```
int result = 1;
for (int i = 1; i <= 10; i = i * 2) { result = result * i; }
cout << result << endl;
```

■ R4.4 Write a while loop that prints

a. All squares less than n. For example, if n is 100, print 0 1 4 9 16 25 36 49 64 81.

b. All positive numbers that are divisible by 10 and less than n. For example, if n is 100, print 10 20 30 40 50 60 70 80 90

c. All powers of two less than n. For example, if n is 100, print 1 2 4 8 16 32 64.

■■ **R4.5** Write a loop that computes

    a. The sum of all even numbers between 2 and 100 (inclusive).

    b. The sum of all squares between 1 and 100 (inclusive).

    c. The sum of all odd numbers between a and b (inclusive).

    d. The sum of all odd digits of n. (For example, if n is 32677, the sum would be 3 + 7 + 7 = 17.)

■ **R4.6** Provide trace tables for these loops.

    a.
```
int i = 0; int j = 10; int n = 0;
while (i < j) { i++; j--; n++; }
```

    b.
```
int i = 0; int j = 0; int n = 0;
while (i < 10) { i++; n = n + i + j; j++; }
```

    c.
```
int i = 10; int j = 0; int n = 0;
while (i > 0) { i--; j++; n = n + i - j; }
```

    d.
```
int i = 0; int j = 10; int n = 0;
while (i != j) { i = i + 2; j = j - 2; n++; }
```

■ **R4.7** What do these loops print?

    a. `for (int i = 1; i < 10; i++) { cout << i << " "; }`

    b. `for (int i = 1; i < 10; i += 2) { cout << i << " "; }`

    c. `for (int i = 10; i > 1; i--) { cout << i << " "; }`

    d. `for (int i = 0; i < 10; i++) { cout << i << " "; }`

    e. `for (int i = 1; i < 10; i = i * 2) { cout << i << " "; }`

    f. `for (int i = 1; i < 10; i++) { if (i % 2 == 0) { cout << i << " "; } }`

■ **R4.8** What is an infinite loop? On your computer, how can you terminate a program that executes an infinite loop?

■■ **R4.9** What is an "off-by-one" error? Give an example from your own programming experience.

■ **R4.10** Write a program trace for the pseudocode in Exercise E4.6, assuming the input values are 4 7 –2 –5 0.

■■ **R4.11** Is the following code legal?

```
for (int i = 0; i < 10; i++)
{
   for (int i = 0; i < 10; i++)
   {
      cout << i << " ";
   }
   cout << endl;
}
```

What does it print? Is it good coding style? If not, how would you improve it?

■ **R4.12** How many iterations do the following loops carry out? Assume that i is not changed in the loop body.

    a. `for (int i = 1; i <= 10; i++) . . .`

    b. `for (int i = 0; i < 10; i++) . . .`

    c. `for (int i = 10; i > 0; i--) . . .`

    d. `for (int i = -10; i <= 10; i++) . . .`

    e. `for (int i = 10; i >= 0; i++) . . .`

f. `for (int i = -10; i <= 10; i = i + 2) . . .`

g. `for (int i = -10; i <= 10; i = i + 3) . . .`

■■ **R4.13** Write pseudocode for a program that prints a calendar such as the following:

```
Su  M  T  W Th  F Sa
             1  2  3  4
 5  6  7  8  9 10 11
12 13 14 15 16 17 18
19 20 21 22 23 24 25
26 27 28 29 30 31
```

■ **R4.14** Write pseudocode for a program that prints a Celsius/Fahrenheit conversion table such as the following:

```
Celsius | Fahrenheit
--------+-----------
      0 |         32
     10 |         50
     20 |         68
    ...           ...
    100 |        212
```

■ **R4.15** Write pseudocode for a program that reads a student record, consisting of the student's first and last name, followed by a sequence of test scores and a sentinel of –1. The program should print the student's average score. Then provide a trace table for this sample input:

```
Harry Morgan 94 71 86 95 -1
```

■■ **R4.16** Write pseudocode for a program that reads a sequence of student records and prints the total score for each student. Each record has the student's first and last name, followed by a sequence of test scores and a sentinel of –1. The sequence is terminated by the word END. Here is a sample sequence:

```
Harry Morgan 94 71 86 95 -1
Sally Lin 99 98 100 95 90 -1
END
```

Provide a trace table for this sample input.

■ **R4.17** Rewrite the following for loop into a while loop.

```cpp
int s = 0;
for (int i = 1; i <= 10; i++)
{
   s = s + i;
}
```

■ **R4.18** Rewrite the following do/while loop into a while loop.

```cpp
int n;
cin >> n;
double x = 0;
double s;
do
{
   s = 1.0 / (1 + n * n);
   n++;
   x = x + s;
}
while (s > 0.01);
```

■ **R4.19** Provide trace tables of the following loops.

a.
```cpp
int s = 1;
int n = 1;
while (s < 10) { s = s + n; }
n++;
```

b.
```cpp
int s = 1;
for (int n = 1; n < 5; n++) { s = s + n; }
```

c.
```cpp
int s = 1;
int n = 1;
do
{
    s = s + n;
    n++;
}
while (s < 10 * n);
```

■ **R4.20** What do the following loops print? Work out the answer by tracing the code, not by using the computer.

a.
```cpp
int s = 1;
for (int n = 1; n <= 5; n++)
{
    s = s + n;
    cout << s << " ";
}
```

b.
```cpp
int s = 1;
for (int n = 1; s <= 10; cout << s << " ")
{
    n = n + 2;
    s = s + n;
}
```

c.
```cpp
int s = 1;
int n;
for (n = 1; n <= 5; n++)
{
    s = s + n;
    n++;
}
cout << s << " " << n;
```

■ **R4.21** What do the following program segments print? Find the answers by tracing the code, not by using the computer.

a.
```cpp
int n = 1;
for (int i = 2; i < 5; i++) { n = n + i; }
cout << n;
```

b.
```cpp
int i;
double n = 1 / 2;
for (i = 2; i <= 5; i++) { n = n + 1.0 / i; }
cout << i;
```

c.
```cpp
double x = 1;
double y = 1;
int i = 0;
do
{
    y = y / 2;
    x = x + y;
    i++;
```

```
        }
        while (x < 1.8);
        cout << i;
    d. double x = 1;
        double y = 1;
        int i = 0;
        while (y >= 1.5)
        {
            x = x / 2;
            y = x + y;
            i++;
        }
        cout << i;
```

■■ **R4.22** Give an example of a for loop where symmetric bounds are more natural. Give an example of a for loop where asymmetric bounds are more natural.

■ **R4.23** Add a storyboard panel for the conversion program in Section 4.6 that shows a scenario where a user enters incompatible units.

■ **R4.24** In Section 4.6, we decided to show users a list of all valid units in the prompt. If the program supports many more units, this approach is unworkable. Give a storyboard panel that illustrates an alternate approach: If the user enters an unknown unit, a list of all known units is shown.

■ **R4.25** Change the storyboards in Section 4.6 to support a menu that asks users whether they want to convert units, see program help, or quit the program. The menu should be displayed at the beginning of the program, when a sequence of values has been converted, and when an error is displayed.

■ **R4.26** Draw a flowchart for a program that carries out unit conversions as described in Section 4.6.

■■ **R4.27** In Section 4.7.5, the code for finding the largest and smallest input initializes the largest and smallest variables with an input value. Why can't you initialize them with zero?

■ **R4.28** What are nested loops? Give an example where a nested loop is typically used.

■■ **R4.29** The nested loops

```
        for (int i = 1; i <= height; i++)
        {
            for (int j = 1; j <= width; j++) { cout << "*"; }
            cout << endl;
        }
```

display a rectangle of a given width and height, such as

```
        ****
        ****
        ****
```

Write a *single* for loop that displays the same rectangle.

■■ **R4.30** Suppose you design an educational game to teach children how to read a clock. How do you generate random values for the hours and minutes?

■■■ **R4.31** In a travel simulation, Harry will visit one of his friends that are located in three states. He has ten friends in California, three in Nevada, and two in Utah. How do you produce a random number between 1 and 3, denoting the destination state, with a probability that is proportional to the number of friends in each state?

PRACTICE EXERCISES

- **E4.1** Write programs with loops that compute
    - **a.** The sum of all even numbers between 2 and 100 (inclusive).
    - **b.** The sum of all squares between 1 and 100 (inclusive).
    - **c.** All powers of 2 from 2^0 up to 2^{20}.
    - **d.** The sum of all odd numbers between a and b (inclusive), where a and b are inputs.
    - **e.** The sum of all odd digits of an input. (For example, if the input is 32677, the sum would be $3 + 7 + 7 = 17$.)

- ■ **E4.2** Write programs that read a sequence of integer inputs and print
    - **a.** The smallest and largest of the inputs.
    - **b.** The number of even and odd inputs.
    - **c.** Cumulative totals. For example, if the input is 1 7 2 9, the program should print 1 8 10 19.
    - **d.** All adjacent duplicates. For example, if the input is 1 3 3 4 5 5 6 6 2, the program should print 3 5 6.

- ■ **E4.3** Write programs that read a line of input as a string and print
    - **a.** Only the uppercase letters in the string.
    - **b.** Every second letter of the string.
    - **c.** The string, with all vowels replaced by an underscore.
    - **d.** The number of vowels in the string.
    - **e.** The positions of all vowels in the string.

- ■ **E4.4** Complete the program in How To 4.1. Your program should read twelve temperature values and print the month with the highest temperature.

- ■ **E4.5** Write a program that reads a set of floating-point values. Ask the user to enter the values, then print
    - the average of the values.
    - the smallest of the values.
    - the largest of the values.
    - the range, that is the difference between the smallest and largest.

  Of course, you may only prompt for the values once.

- ■ **E4.6** Translate the following pseudocode for finding the minimum value from a set of inputs into a C++ program.

    Set a Boolean variable "first" to true.
    While another value has been read successfully
       If first is true
          Set the minimum to the value.
          Set first to false.

Else if the value is less than the minimum
    Set the minimum to the value.
Print the minimum.

••• E4.7 Translate the following pseudocode for randomly permuting the characters in a string into a C++ program.

Read a word.
Repeat word.length() times
    Pick a random position i in the word, but not the last position.
    Pick a random position j > i in the word.
    Swap the letters at positions j and i.
Print the word.

© Anthony Rosenberg/iStockphoto.

To swap the letters, construct substrings as follows:

```
first    i    middle    j    last
```

Then replace the string with

```
first + word.substr(j, 1) + middle + word.substr(i, 1) + last
```

•• E4.8 Write a program that reads a word and prints each character of the word on a separate line. For example, if the user provides the input "Harry", the program prints

```
H
a
r
r
y
```

•• E4.9 Write a program that reads a word and prints the word in reverse. For example, if the user provides the input "Harry", the program prints

```
yrraH
```

• E4.10 Write a program that reads a word and prints the number of vowels in the word. For this exercise, assume that a e i o u y are vowels. For example, if the user provides the input "Harry", the program prints 2 vowels.

••• E4.11 Write a program that reads a word and prints the number of syllables in the word. For this exercise, assume that syllables are determined as follows: Each sequence of vowels a e i o u y, except for the last e in a word, is a vowel. However, if that algorithm yields a count of 0, change it to 1. For example,

Word	Syllables
Harry	2
hairy	2
hare	1
the	1

••• E4.12 Write a program that reads a word and prints all substrings, sorted by length. For example, if the user provides the input "rum", the program prints

```
r
u
m
ru
um
rum
```

■■■ **E4.13** Write a program that reads a string and prints the most frequently occurring letter. If there are multiple letters that occur with the same maximum frequency, print them all. For example, if the word is `mississippi`, print `is` because `i` and `s` occur four times each, and no letter occurs more frequently.

■■■ **E4.14** Write a program that reads a string and prints the longest sequence of vowels. If there are multiple sequences of the same length, print them all. For example, if the word is `oiseau`, print `eau`, and if the word is `teakwood`, print `ea` and `oo`.

■■ **E4.15** Write a program that reads a sequence of words and then prints them in a box, with each word centered, like this:

```
+----------+
|  Hello   |
|   C++    |
|programmer|
+----------+
```

■ **E4.16** Write a program that prints all powers of 2 from 2^0 up to 2^{20}.

■■ **E4.17** Write a program that reads a number and prints all of its *binary digits:* Print the remainder `number % 2`, then replace the number with `number / 2`. Keep going until the number is 0. For example, if the user provides the input 13, the output should be

```
1
0
1
1
```

■ **E4.18** Write a program that prints a multiplication table, like this:

```
 1   2   3   4   5   6   7   8   9  10
 2   4   6   8  10  12  14  16  18  20
 3   6   9  12  15  18  21  24  27  30
 ...
10  20  30  40  50  60  70  80  90 100
```

■■ **E4.19** Write a program that reads an integer and displays, using asterisks, a filled and hollow square, placed next to each other. For example if the side length is 5, the program should display

```
***** *****
***** *   *
***** *   *
***** *   *
***** *****
```

■■ **E4.20** Write a program that reads an integer and displays, using asterisks, a filled diamond of the given side length. For example, if the side length is 4, the program should display

```
   *
  ***
 *****
*******
 *****
  ***
   *
```

■■ **Media E4.21** Using the Picture type from Worked Example 4.2, write a program that reads in the file names of two pictures and superimposes them. The result is a picture whose width and height are the larger of the widths and heights of both pictures. In the area where both pictures have pixels, average the colors.

■■ **Media E4.22** Using the Picture type from Worked Example 4.2, write a program that reads in the file names of two pictures and superimposes them. The result is a picture whose width and height are the larger of the widths and heights of both pictures. In the area where both pictures have pixels, use the pixels from the first picture. However, when those pixels are green, use the pixels from the second picture.

■ **Media E4.23** Using the Picture type from Worked Example 4.2, apply a sunset effect to a picture, increasing the red value of each pixel by 30 percent (up to a maximum of 255).

■■ **Media E4.24** Using the Picture type from Worked Example 4.2, apply a "telescope" effect, turning all pixels black that are outside a circle. The center of the circle should be the image center, and the radius should be 40 percent of the width or height, whichever is smaller.

© Cay Horstmann

■ **Media E4.25** Using the Picture type from Worked Example 4.2, write a program that displays a checkerboard with 64 squares, alternating white and black.

■■ **Media E4.26** Reorganize the gallery program in Section 4.9 so that all images, starting with a.png, are added to an empty picture.

PROGRAMMING PROJECTS

■■ **P4.1** Enhance Worked Example 4.1 to check that the credit card number is valid. A valid credit card number will yield a result divisible by 10 when you:

Form the sum of all digits. Add to that sum every second digit, starting with the second digit from the right. Then add the number of digits in the second step that are greater than four. The result should be divisible by 10.

For example, consider the number 4012 8888 8888 1881. The sum of all digits is 89. The sum of the colored digits is 46. There are five colored digits larger than four, so the result is 140. 140 is divisible by 10 so the card number is valid.

■■ **P4.2** *Mean and standard deviation.* Write a program that reads a set of floating-point data values. Choose an appropriate mechanism for prompting for the end of the data set. When all values have been read, print out the count of the values, the average, and the standard deviation. The average of a data set $\{x_1, \ldots, x_n\}$ is $\bar{x} = \sum x_i / n$, where $\sum x_i = x_1 + \cdots + x_n$ is the sum of the input values. The standard deviation is

$$s = \sqrt{\frac{\sum(x_i - \bar{x})^2}{n - 1}}$$

However, this formula is not suitable for the task. By the time the program has computed $\bar{x}$, the individual x_i are long gone. Until you know how to save these values, use the numerically less stable formula

$$s = \sqrt{\frac{\sum x_i^2 - \frac{1}{n}\left(\sum x_i\right)^2}{n - 1}}$$

You can compute this quantity by keeping track of the count, the sum, and the sum of squares as you process the input values.

•• P4.3 The *Fibonacci numbers* are defined by the sequence

$f_1 = 1$

$f_2 = 1$

$f_n = f_{n-1} + f_{n-2}$

Reformulate that as

© GlobalP/iStockphoto.

```
fold1 = 1;
fold2 = 1;
fnew = fold1 + fold2;
```

Fibonacci numbers describe the growth of a rabbit population.

After that, discard `fold2`, which is no longer needed, and set `fold2` to `fold1` and `fold1` to `fnew`. Repeat `fnew` an appropriate number of times.

Implement a program that computes the Fibonacci numbers in that way.

••• P4.4 *Factoring of integers.* Write a program that asks the user for an integer and then prints out all its factors. For example, when the user enters 150, the program should print

```
2
3
5
5
```

••• P4.5 *Prime numbers.* Write a program that prompts the user for an integer and then prints out all prime numbers up to that integer. For example, when the user enters 20, the program should print

```
2
3
5
7
11
13
17
19
```

Recall that a number is a prime number if it is not divisible by any number except 1 and itself.

• P4.6 Following Section 4.9, develop a program that reads text and displays the average number of words in each sentence. Assume words are separated by spaces, and a sentence ends when a word ends in a period. Start small and just print the first word. Then print the first two words. Then print all words in the first sentence. Then print the number of words in the first sentence. Then print the number of words in the first two sentences. Then print the average number of words in the first two sentences. At this time, you should have gathered enough experience that you can complete the program.

■ **P4.7** Following Section 4.9, develop a program that reads a string and removes all duplicates. For example, if the input is Mississippi, print Misp. Start small and just print the first letter. Then print the first letter and true if the letter is not duplicated elsewhere, false otherwise. (Look for it in the remaining string.) Next, do the same for the first two letters, and print out for each letter whether or not they occur in the substring before and after the letter. Try with a string like oops. Extend to all characters in the string. Have a look at the output when the input is Mississippi. Which characters should you not report? At this time, you should have gathered enough experience that you can complete the program.

■■■ **P4.8** *The game of Nim.* This is a well-known game with a number of variants. The following variant has an interesting winning strategy. Two players alternately take marbles from a pile. In each move, a player chooses how many marbles to take. The player must take at least one but at most half of the marbles. Then the other player takes a turn. The player who takes the last marble loses.

You will write a program in which the computer plays against a human opponent. Generate a random integer between 10 and 100 to denote the initial size of the pile. Generate a random integer between 0 and 1 to decide whether the computer or the human takes the first turn. Generate a random integer between 0 and 1 to decide whether the computer plays *smart* or *stupid*. In stupid mode the computer simply takes a random legal value (between 1 and $n/2$) from the pile whenever it has a turn. In smart mode the computer takes off enough marbles to make the size of the pile a power of two minus 1—that is, 3, 7, 15, 31, or 63. That is always a legal move, except when the size of the pile is currently one less than a power of two. In that case, the computer makes a random legal move.

You will note that the computer cannot be beaten in smart mode when it has the first move, unless the pile size happens to be 15, 31, or 63. Of course, a human player who has the first turn and knows the winning strategy can win against the computer.

■■ **P4.9** *The Drunkard's Walk.* A drunkard in a grid of streets randomly picks one of four directions and stumbles to the next intersection, then again randomly picks one of four directions, and so on. You might think that on average the drunkard doesn't move very far because the choices cancel each other out, but that is actually not the case.

Represent locations as integer pairs (x, y). Implement the drunkard's walk over 100 intersections and print the beginning and ending location.

■■ **P4.10** *The Monty Hall Paradox.* Marilyn vos Savant described the following problem (loosely based on a game show hosted by Monty Hall) in a popular magazine: "Suppose you're on a game show, and you're given the choice of three doors: Behind one door is a car; behind the others, goats. You pick a door, say No. 1, and the host, who knows what's behind the doors, opens another door, say No. 3, which has a goat. He then says to you, "Do you want to pick door No. 2?" Is it to your advantage to switch your choice?"

Ms. vos Savant proved that it is to your advantage, but many of her readers, including some mathematics professors, disagreed, arguing that the probability would not change because another door was opened.

Your task is to simulate this game show. In each iteration, randomly pick a door number between 1 and 3 for placing the car. Randomly have the player pick a door. Randomly have the game show host pick a door having a goat (but not the door that the player picked). Increment a counter for strategy 1 if the player wins by switching to the host's choice, and increment a counter for strategy 2 if the player wins by sticking with the original choice. Run 1,000 iterations and print both counters.

■■ **P4.11**   *The Buffon Needle Experiment.* The following experiment was devised by Comte Georges-Louis Leclerc de Buffon (1707–1788), a French naturalist. A needle of length 1 inch is dropped onto paper that is ruled with lines 2 inches apart. If the needle drops onto a line, we count it as a *hit*. (See Figure 8.) Buffon conjectured that the quotient *tries/hits* approximates π.

For the Buffon needle experiment, you must generate two random numbers: one to describe the starting position and one to describe the angle of the needle with the x-axis. Then you need to test whether the needle touches a grid line.

Generate the *lower* point of the needle. Its x-coordinate is irrelevant, and you may assume its y-coordinate y_{low} to be any random number between 0 and 2. The angle α between the needle and the x-axis can be any value between 0 degrees and 180 degrees (π radians). The upper end of the needle has y-coordinate

$$y_{high} = y_{low} + \sin \alpha$$

The needle is a hit if y_{high} is at least 2, as shown in Figure 9.

Stop after 10,000 tries and print the quotient tries/hits. (This program is not suitable for computing the value of π. You need π in the computation of the angle.)

Figure 8   The Buffon Needle Experiment   **Figure 9**   A Hit in the Buffon Needle Experiment

■ **P4.12**   A simple random generator is obtained by the formula

$$r_{new} = (a \cdot r_{old} + b) \% m$$

and then setting r_{old} to r_{new}. If m is chosen as 2^{32}, then you can compute

$$r_{new} = a \cdot r_{old} + b$$

because the truncation of an overflowing result to the int type is equivalent to computing the remainder.

Write a program that asks the user to enter a value for r_{old}. (Such a value is often called a *seed*). Then print the first 100 random integers generated by this formula, using $a = 32310901$ and $b = 1729$.

■■ **P4.13** In the 17th century, the discipline of probability theory got its start when a gambler asked a mathematician friend to explain some observations about dice games. Why did he, on average, win a bet that at least one six would appear when rolling a die four times? And why did he seem to lose a similar bet, getting at least one double-six when rolling a pair of dice 24 times?

Nowadays, it seems astounding that any person would roll a pair of dice 24 times in a row, and then repeat that many times over. Let's do that experiment on a computer instead. Simulate each game a million times and print out the wins and losses, assuming each bet was for $1.

■■ **P4.14** Write a program that reads an integer n and a digit d between 0 and 9. Use one or more loops to count how many of the integers between 1 and n

- start with the digit d.
- end with the digit d.
- contain the digit d.

■ **Business P4.15** Write a program that reads an initial investment balance and an interest rate, then prints the number of years it takes for the investment to reach one million dollars.

■■ **Business P4.16** *Currency conversion.* Write a program that first asks the user to type today's exchange rate between U.S. dollars and Japanese yen, then reads U.S. dollar values and converts each to yen. Use 0 as a sentinel.

■■ **Business P4.17** Write a program that first asks the user to type in today's exchange rate between U.S. dollars and Japanese yen, then reads U.S. dollar values and converts each to Japanese yen. Use 0 as the sentinel value to denote the end of dollar inputs. Then the program reads a sequence of yen amounts and converts them to dollars. The second sequence is terminated by another zero value.

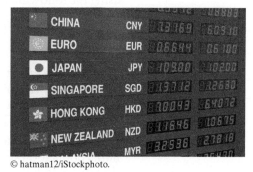
© hatman12/iStockphoto.

■■ **Business P4.18** Your company has shares of stock it would like to sell when their value exceeds a certain target price. Write a program that reads the target price and then reads the current stock price until it is at least the target price. Your program should use a Scanner to read a sequence of double values from standard input. Once the minimum is reached, the program should report that the stock price exceeds the target price.

■■ **Business P4.19** Write an application to pre-sell a limited number of cinema tickets. Each buyer can buy as many as 4 tickets. No more than 100 tickets can be sold. Implement a program called ticket_seller that prompts the user for the desired number of tickets and then displays the number of remaining tickets. Repeat until all tickets have been sold, and then display the total number of buyers.

▪▪ Business P4.20   You need to control the number of people who can be in an oyster bar at the same time. Groups of people can always leave the bar, but a group cannot enter the bar if they would make the number of people in the bar exceed the maximum of 100 occupants. Write a program that reads the sizes of the groups that arrive or depart. Use negative numbers for departures. After each input, display the current number of occupants. As soon as the bar holds the maximum number of people, report that the bar is full and exit the program.

▪▪▪ Business P4.21   *Credit Card Number Check.* The last digit of a credit card number is the *check digit*, which protects against transcription errors such as an error in a single digit or switching two digits. The following method is used to verify actual credit card numbers but, for simplicity, we will describe it for numbers with 8 digits instead of 16:

- Starting from the rightmost digit, form the sum of every other digit. For example, if the credit card number is 43589795, then you form the sum $5 + 7 + 8 + 3 = 23$.
- Double each of the digits that were not included in the preceding step. Add all digits of the resulting numbers. For example, with the number given above, doubling the digits, starting with the next-to-last one, yields 18 18 10 8. Adding all digits in these values yields $1 + 8 + 1 + 8 + 1 + 0 + 8 = 27$.
- Add the sums of the two preceding steps. If the last digit of the result is 0, the number is valid. In our case, $23 + 27 = 50$, so the number is valid.

Write a program that implements this algorithm. The user should supply an 8-digit number, and you should print out whether the number is valid or not. If it is not valid, you should print out the value of the check digit that would make the number valid.

▪▪ Engineering P4.22   In a predator-prey simulation, you compute the populations of predators and prey, using the following equations:

$$prey_{n+1} = prey_n \times (1 + A - B \times pred_n)$$
$$pred_{n+1} = pred_n \times (1 - C + D \times prey_n)$$

Here, A is the rate at which prey birth exceeds natural death, B is the rate of predation, C is the rate at which predator deaths exceed births without food, and D represents predator increase in the presence of food.

© Charles Gibson/iStockphoto.

Write a program that prompts users for these rates, the initial population sizes, and the number of periods. Then print the populations for the given number of periods. As inputs, try $A = 0.1$, $B = C = 0.01$, and $D = 0.00002$ with initial prey and predator populations of 1,000 and 20.

▪▪ Engineering P4.23   *Projectile flight.* Suppose a cannonball is propelled straight into the air with a starting velocity v_0. Any calculus book will state that the position of the ball after t seconds is $s(t) = -1/2gt^2 + v_0t$, where $g = 9.81$ m/s^2 is the gravitational force of the earth. No calculus book ever mentions why someone would want to carry out such an obviously dangerous experiment, so we will do it in the safety of the computer.

In fact, we will confirm the theorem from calculus by a simulation. In our simulation, we will consider how the ball moves in very short time intervals Δt. In a short time interval the velocity v is nearly constant, and we can compute the distance the ball moves as $\Delta s = v\Delta t$. In our program, we will simply set

```
const double DELTA_T = 0.01;
```
and update the position by
```
s = s + v * DELTA_T;
```
The velocity changes constantly—in fact, it is reduced by the gravitational force of the earth. In a short time interval, $\Delta v = -g\Delta t$, we must keep the velocity updated as
```
v = v - g * DELTA_T;
```
In the next iteration the new velocity is used to update the distance.

Now run the simulation until the cannonball falls back to the earth. Get the initial velocity as an input (100 m/sec is a good value). Update the position and velocity 100 times per second, but print out the position only every full second. Also printout the values from the exact formula $s(t) = -1/2gt^2 + v_0t$ for comparison.

Note: You may wonder whether there is a benefit to this simulation when an exact formula is available. Well, the formula from the calculus book is *not* exact. Actually, the gravitational force diminishes the farther the cannonball is away from the surface of the earth. This complicates the algebra sufficiently that it is not possible to give an exact formula for the actual motion, but the computer simulation can simply be extended to apply a variable gravitational force. For

© MOF/iStockphoto.

cannonballs, the calculus-book formula is actually good enough, but computers are necessary to compute accurate trajectories for higher-flying objects such as ballistic missiles.

■■■ **Engineering P4.24** A simple model for the hull of a ship is given by

$$|y| = \frac{B}{2}\left[1 - \left(\frac{2x}{L}\right)^2\right]\left[1 - \left(\frac{z}{T}\right)^2\right]$$

where B is the beam, L is the length, and T is the draft.

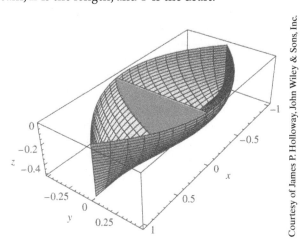

Courtesy of James P. Holloway, John Wiley & Sons, Inc.

(*Note:* There are two values of y for each x and z because the hull is symmetric from starboard to port.)

The cross-sectional area at a point x is called the "section" in nautical parlance. To compute it, let z go from 0 to $-T$ in n increments, each of size T/n. For each value of z, compute the value for y. Then sum the areas of trapezoidal strips. At right are the strips where $n = 4$.

Write a program that reads in values for B, L, T, x, and n and then prints out the cross-sectional area at x.

Courtesy of James P. Holloway, John Wiley & Sons, Inc.

■ **Engineering P4.25**   Radioactive decay of radioactive materials can be modeled by the equation $A = A_0 e^{-t(\log 2/h)}$, where A is the amount of the material at time t, A_0 is the amount at time 0, and h is the half-life.

Technetium-99 is a radioisotope that is used in imaging of the brain. It has a half-life of 6 hours. Your program should display the relative amount A/A_0 in a patient body every hour for 24 hours after receiving a dose.

© Snowleopard1/iStockphoto.

■■■ **Engineering P4.26**   The photo at left shows an electric device called a "transformer". Transformers are often constructed by wrapping coils of wire around a ferrite core. The figure below illustrates a situation that occurs in various audio devices such as cell phones and music players. In this circuit, a transformer is used to connect a speaker to the output of an audio amplifier.

© zig4photo/iStockphoto.

$R_0 = 20\ \Omega$ 1 : n

$V_s = 40\ \text{V}$ $R_s = 8\ \Omega$

Amplifier   Transformer   Speaker

The symbol used to represent the transformer is intended to suggest two coils of wire. The parameter n of the transformer is called the "turns ratio" of the transformer. (The number of times that a wire is wrapped around the core to form a coil is called the number of turns in the coil. The turns ratio is literally the ratio of the number of turns in the two coils of wire.)

When designing the circuit, we are concerned primarily with the value of the power delivered to the speakers—that power causes the speakers to produce the sounds we want to hear. Suppose we were to connect the speakers directly to the amplifier without using the transformer. Some fraction of the power available from the amplifier would get to the speakers. The rest of the available power would be lost in the amplifier itself. The transformer is added to the circuit to increase the fraction of the amplifier power that is delivered to the speakers.

The power, P_s, delivered to the speakers is calculated using the formula

$$P_s = R_s \left(\frac{nV_s}{n^2 R_0 + R_s} \right)^2$$

Write a C++ program that models the circuit shown and varies the turns ratio from 0.01 to 2 in 0.01 increments, then determines the value of the turns ratio that maximizes the power delivered to the speakers.

■■ **Media P4.27** Using the `Picture` type of Worked Example 4.2, it is easy to draw mathematical curves. Simply make a white picture and color pixels $(x, f(x))$ black. Draw the curve $f(x) = 0.00005x^3 - 0.03x^2 + 4x + 200$, where x ranges from 0 to 400.

■■■ **Media P4.28** Draw a picture of the "four-leaved rose" whose equation in polar coordinates is $r = \cos(2\theta)$. Let θ go from 0 to 2π in 1,000 steps. Each time, compute r and then compute the (x, y) coordinates from the polar coordinates by using the formula

$$x = 200r \cdot \cos(\theta) + 200, \; y = 200r \cdot \sin(\theta) + 200$$

■■■ **Media P4.29** Write a program that makes a picture of a spiral, such as the following:

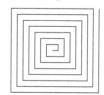

■■■ **Media P4.30** Write a program that adds a frame to a given `.png` image, like this:

Cay Horstmann.

Add the image and a slightly larger white picture to a black picture.

FUNCTIONS

© attator/iStockphoto.

CHAPTER CONTENTS

Functions are a fundamental building block of C++ programs. A function packages a computation into a form that can be easily understood and reused. (The person in the photo is executing the function "make two cups of espresso".) In this chapter, you will learn how to design and implement your own functions. Using the process of stepwise refinement, you will be able to break up complex tasks into sets of cooperating functions.

5.1 Functions as Black Boxes

A function is a named sequence of instructions.

A **function** is a sequence of instructions with a name. You have already encountered several functions. For example, the function named pow, which was introduced in Chapter 2, contains instructions to compute a power x^y. Moreover, every C++ program has a function called main.

You *call* a function in order to execute its instructions. For example, consider the following program:

```cpp
int main()
{
    double z = pow(2, 3);
    . . .
}
```

Arguments are supplied when a function is called. The return value is the result that the function computes.

By using the expression pow(2, 3), main *calls* the pow function, asking it to compute the power 2^3. The main function is temporarily suspended. The instructions of the pow function execute and compute the result. The pow function *returns* its result (that is, the value 8) back to main, and the main function resumes execution (see Figure 1).

When another function calls the pow function, it provides "inputs", such as the expressions 2 and 3 in the call pow(2, 3). These expressions are called **arguments**. This

Figure 1   Execution Flow During a Function Call

terminology avoids confusion with other inputs, such as those provided by a human user. Similarly, the "output" that the pow function computes is called the **return value**.

Functions can have multiple arguments, but they have only one return value.

Note that the return value of a function is returned to the calling function, not displayed on the screen. For example, suppose your program contains a statement

```
double z = pow(2, 3);
```

When the pow function returns its result, the return value is stored in the variable z. If you want the value to be displayed, you need to add a statement such as cout << z.

At this point, you may wonder how the pow function performs its job. For example, how does pow(2, 3) compute that 2^3 is 8? By multiplying $2 \times 2 \times 2$? With logarithms? Fortunately, as a user of the function, you *don't need to know* how the function is implemented. You just need to know the *specification* of the function: If you provide arguments x and y, the function returns x^y. Engineers use the term **black box** for a device with a given specification but unknown implementation. You can think of pow as a black box, as shown in Figure 2.

When you design your own functions, you will want to make them appear as black boxes to other programmers. Those programmers want to use your functions without knowing what goes on inside. Even if you are the only person working on a program, making each function into a black box pays off: there are fewer details that you need to keep in mind.

Figure 2
The pow Function
as a Black Box

Although a thermostat is usually white, you can think of it as a black box. The input is the desired temperature, and the output is a signal to the heater or air conditioner.

© yenwen/iStockphoto.

5.2 Implementing Functions

In this section, you will learn how to implement a function from a given specification. We will use a very simple example: a function to compute the volume of a cube with a given side length.

When writing this function, you need to

- Pick a name for the function (cube_volume).
- Declare a variable for each argument (double side_length). These variables are called **parameter variables**.
- Specify the type of the return value (double).

The cube_volume function uses a given side length to compute the volume of a cube.

© studioaraminta/iStockphoto.

Put all this information together to form the first line of the function's definition:

```
double cube_volume(double side_length)
```

Next, specify the **body** of the function: the statements that are executed when the function is called.

The volume of a cube of side length s is $s \times s \times s$. However, for greater clarity, our parameter variable has been called side_length, not s, so we need to compute side_length * side_length * side_length.

We will store this value in a variable called volume:

```
double volume = side_length * side_length * side_length;
```

In order to return the result of the function, use the return statement:

```
return volume;
```

The body of a function is enclosed in braces. Here is the complete function:

```
double cube_volume(double side_length)
{
    double volume = side_length * side_length * side_length;
    return volume;
}
```

Let's put this function to use. We'll supply a main function that calls the cube_volume function twice.

```
int main()
{
    double result1 = cube_volume(2);
    double result2 = cube_volume(10);
    cout << "A cube with side length 2 has volume " << result1 << endl;
    cout << "A cube with side length 10 has volume " << result2 << endl;

    return 0;
}
```

When the function is called with different arguments, the function returns different results. Consider the call cube_volume(2). The argument 2 corresponds to the side_length parameter variable. Therefore, in this call, side_length is 2. The function computes side_length * side_length * side_length, or 2 * 2 * 2. When the function is called with a different argument, say 10, then the function computes 10 * 10 * 10.

Now we combine both functions into a test program. Because main calls cube_volume, the cube_volume function must be known before the main function is defined. This is easily achieved by placing cube_volume first and main last in the source file. (See Special Topic 5.1 for an alternative.)

*The return statement gives the
function's result to the caller.* © princessdlaf/iStockphoto.

Syntax 5.1   Function Definition

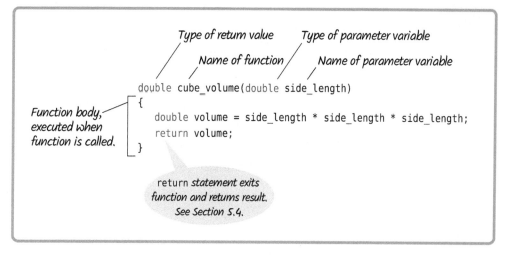

Here is the complete program. Note the comment that describes the behavior of the function. (Programming Tip 5.1 describes the format of the comment.)

sec02/cube.cpp

```cpp
1  #include <iostream>
2
3  using namespace std;
4
5  /**
6     Computes the volume of a cube.
7     @param side_length  the side length of the cube
8     @return  the volume
9  */
10 double cube_volume(double side_length)
11 {
12    double volume = side_length * side_length * side_length;
13    return volume;
14 }
15
16 int main()
17 {
18    double result1 = cube_volume(2);
19    double result2 = cube_volume(10);
20    cout << "A cube with side length 2 has volume " << result1 << endl;
21    cout << "A cube with side length 10 has volume " << result2 << endl;
22
23    return 0;
24 }
```

Program Run

```
A cube with side length 2 has volume 8
A cube with side length 10 has volume 1000
```

Programming Tip 5.1

Function Comments

Whenever you write a function, you should *comment* its behavior. Comments are for human readers, not compilers, and there is no universal standard for the layout of a function comment. In this book, we will use the following layout:

```
/**
    Computes the volume of a cube.
    @param side_length the side length of the cube
    @return the volume
*/
double cube_volume(double side_length)
{
    double volume = side_length * side_length * side_length;
    return volume;
}
```

> Function comments explain the purpose of the function, the meaning of the parameter variables and return value, as well as any special requirements.

This particular documentation style is borrowed from the Java programming language. It is widely supported by C++ tools as well, for example by the Doxygen tool (www.doxygen.org).

The comment starts with a /** delimiter. The first line of the comment describes the purpose of the function. Each @param clause describes a parameter variable and the @return clause describes the return value.

Note that the function comment does not document the implementation (*how* the function does what it does) but rather the design (*what* the function does, its inputs, and its results). The comment allows other programmers to use the function as a "black box".

5.3 Parameter Passing

> Parameter variables hold the argument values supplied in the function call.

In this section, we examine the mechanism of passing arguments into functions. When a function is called, its **parameter variables** are created (Another commonly used term for a parameter variable is *formal parameter*.) In the function call, an expression is supplied for each parameter variable, called the **argument**. (Another commonly used term for this expression is *actual parameter*.) Each parameter variable is initialized with the value of the corresponding argument.

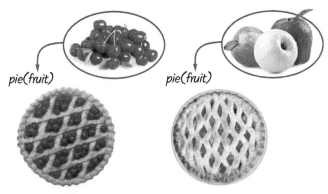

A recipe for a fruit pie may say to use any kind of fruit. Here, "fruit" is an example of a parameter variable. Apples and cherries are examples of arguments.

© DNY59/iStockphoto (cherry pie); © inhausecreative/iStockphoto (apple pie); © RedHelga/iStockphoto (cherries); © ZoneCreative/iStockphoto (apples).

Consider the function call illustrated in Figure 3:

```
double result1 = cube_volume(2);
```

- The parameter variable side_length of the cube_volume function is created. ❶
- The parameter variable is initialized with the value of the argument that was passed in the call. In our case, side_length is set to 2. ❷
- The function computes the expression side_length * side_length * side_length, which has the value 8. That value is stored in the variable volume. ❸
- The function returns. All of its variables are removed. The return value is transferred to the *caller*, that is, the function calling the cube_volume function. ❹

Figure 3 Parameter Passing

Now consider what happens in a subsequent call, cube_volume(10). A new parameter variable is created. (Recall that the previous parameter variable was removed when the first call to cube_volume returned.) It is initialized with the argument 10, and the process repeats. After the second function call is complete, its variables are again removed.

Like any other variables, parameter variables can only be set to values of compatible types. For example, the side_length parameter variable of the cube_volume function has type double. It is valid to call cube_volume(2.0) or cube_volume(2). In the latter call, the integer 2 is automatically converted to the double value 2.0. However, a call cube_volume("two") is not legal.

Programming Tip 5.2
Do Not Modify Parameter Variables

In C++, a parameter variable is just like any other variable. You *can* modify the values of the parameter variables in the body of a function. For example,

```cpp
int total_cents(int dollars, int cents)
{
   cents = dollars * 100 + cents; // Modifies parameter variable
   return cents;
}
```

However, many programmers find this practice confusing. It mixes the concept of a parameter (input to the function) with that of a variable (storage for a value). To avoid the confusion, simply introduce a separate variable:

```cpp
int total_cents(int dollars, int cents)
{
   int result = dollars * 100 + cents;
   return result;
}
```

5.4 Return Values

The return statement terminates a function call and yields the function result.

You use the return statement to specify the result of a function. When the return statement is processed, the function exits *immediately*. This behavior is convenient for handling exceptional cases at the beginning:

```cpp
double cube_volume(double side_length)
{
   if (side_length < 0) { return 0; }
   double volume = side_length * side_length * side_length;
   return volume;
}
```

If the function is called with a negative value for side_length, then the function returns 0 and the remainder of the function is not executed. (See Figure 4.)

© Tashka/iStockphoto.

Figure 4   A return Statement Exits a Function Immediately

In the preceding example, each `return` statement returned a constant or a variable. Actually, the `return` statement can return the value of any expression. Instead of saving the return value in a variable and returning the variable, it is often possible to eliminate the variable and return a more complex expression:

```
double cube_volume(double side_length)
{
   return side_length * side_length * side_length;
}
```

It is important that every branch of a function return a value. Consider the following incorrect function:

```
double cube_volume(double side_length)
{
   if (side_length >= 0)
   {
      return side_length * side_length * side_length;
   } // Error
}
```

Suppose you call `cube_volume` with a negative value for the side length. Of course, you aren't supposed to call that, but it might happen as the result of a coding error. Because the `if` condition is not true, the `return` statement is not executed. However, the function must return *something*. Depending on the circumstances, the compiler might flag this as an error, or the function might return a random value. Protect against this problem by returning some safe value:

```
double cube_volume(double side_length)
{
   if (side_length >= 0)
   {
      return side_length * side_length * side_length;
   }
   return 0;
}
```

The last statement of every function ought to be a `return` statement. This ensures that *some* value gets returned when the function reaches the end.

EXAMPLE CODE   See sec04 of your companion code for another implementation of the earthquake program that you saw in Section 3.3. Note that the `get_description` function has multiple `return` statements.

Common Error 5.1

Missing Return Value

A function always needs to return something. If the code of the function contains several branches, make sure that each one of them returns a value:

```
int sign(double x)
{
   if (x < 0) { return -1; }
   if (x > 0) { return 1; }
   // Error: missing return value if x equals 0
}
```

This function computes the sign of a number: –1 for negative numbers and +1 for positive numbers. If the argument is zero, however, no value is returned. Most compilers will issue a warning in this situation, but if you ignore the warning and the function is ever called with an argument of 0, a random quantity will be returned.

Special Topic 5.1

Function Declarations

It is a compile-time error to call a function that the compiler does not know, just as it is an error to use an undefined variable. You can avoid this error if you define all functions before they are first used. First define lower-level helper functions, then the mid-level workhorse functions, and finally main in your program.

Some programmers prefer to list the main function first in their programs. If you share that preference, you need to learn how to declare the other functions at the top of the program. A **declaration** of a function lists the return type, function name, and parameter variables, but it contains no body:

```
double cube_volume(double side_length);
```

This is an advertisement that promises that the function is implemented elsewhere. It is easy to distinguish declarations from definitions: Declarations end in a semicolon, whereas definitions are followed by a {...} block. Declarations are also called **prototypes**.

In a function prototype, the names of the parameters are optional. You could also write

```
double cube_volume(double);
```

However, it is a good idea to include parameter names in order to document the purpose of each parameter.

The declarations of common functions such as pow are contained in header files. If you have a look inside <cmath>, you will find the declaration of pow and the other math functions.

Here is an alternate organization of the cube.cpp file:

```
#include <iostream>

using namespace std;

// Declaration of cube_volume
double cube_volume(double side_length);

int main()
{
   double result1 = cube_volume(2); // Use of cube_volume
   double result2 = cube_volume(10);
   cout << "A cube with side length 2 has volume " << result1 << endl;
   cout << "A cube with side length 10 has volume " << result2 << endl;
   return 0;
}

// Definition of cube_volume
double cube_volume(double side_length)
{
   return side_length * side_length * side_length;
}
```

If you prefer this approach, go ahead and use it in your programs. You just need to be aware of one drawback. Whenever you change the name of a function or one of the parameter types, you need to fix it in both places: in the declaration and in the definition.

HOW TO 5.1

Implementing a Function

A function is a computation that can be used multiple times with different parameters, either in the same program or in different programs. Whenever a computation is needed more than once, turn it into a function.

Problem Statement To illustrate this process, suppose that you are helping archaeologists who research Egyptian pyramids. You have taken on the task of writing a function that determines the volume of a pyramid, given its height and base length.

Step 1 Describe what the function should do.

Provide a simple English description, such as "Compute the volume of a pyramid whose base is a square."

Step 2 Determine the function's "inputs".

Make a list of *all* the parameters that can vary. It is common for beginners to implement functions that are overly specific. For example, you may know that the great pyramid of Giza, the largest of the Egyptian pyramids, has a height of 146 meters and a base length of 230 meters. You should *not* use these numbers in your calculation, even if the original problem only asked about the great pyramid. It is just as easy—and far more useful—to write a function that computes the volume of *any* pyramid.

In our case, the parameters are the pyramid's height and base length. At this point, we have enough information to document the function:

© Holger Mette/iStockphoto.

```
/**
    Computes the volume of a pyramid whose base is a square.
    @param height the height of the pyramid
    @param base_length the length of one side of the pyramid's base
    @return the volume of the pyramid
*/
```

Step 3 Determine the types of the parameter variables and the return value.

The height and base length can both be floating-point numbers. Therefore, we will choose the type double for both parameter variables. The computed volume is also a floating-point number, yielding a return type of double. Therefore, the function will be defined as

```
double pyramid_volume(double height, double base_length)
```

Step 4 Write pseudocode for obtaining the desired result.

In most cases, a function needs to carry out several steps to find the desired answer. You may need to use mathematical formulas, branches, or loops. Express your function in pseudocode.
    An Internet search yields the fact that the volume of a pyramid is computed as

volume = 1/3 x height x base area

Since the base is a square, we have

base area = base length x base length

Using these two equations, we can compute the volume from the parameter variables.

Step 5   Implement the function body.

In our example, the function body is quite simple. Note the use of the `return` statement to return the result.

```
{
    double base_area = base_length * base_length;
    return height * base_area / 3;
}
```

Step 6   Test your function.

After implementing a function, you should test it in isolation. Such a test is called a **unit test**. Work out test cases by hand, and make sure that the function produces the correct results. For example, for a pyramid with height 9 and base length 10, we expect the area to be $1/3 \times 9 \times 100$ = 300. If the height is 0, we expect an area of 0.

```
int main()
{
    cout << "Volume: " << pyramid_volume(9, 10) << endl;
    cout << "Expected: 300";
    cout << "Volume: " << pyramid_volume(0, 10) << endl;
    cout << "Expected: 0";
    return 0;
}
```

The output confirms that the function worked as expected:

```
Volume: 300
Expected: 300
Volume: 0
Expected: 0
```

EXAMPLE CODE   See how_to_1 of your companion code for a program that calculates a pyramid's volume.

WORKED EXAMPLE 5.1

Generating Random Passwords

This Worked Example creates a function that generates passwords of a given length with at least one digit and one special character. See your E-Text or visit wiley.com/go/bclo3.

Enter your current password:	
Enter your new password:	
Retype your new password:	

WORKED EXAMPLE 5.2

Using a Debugger

Learn how to use a debugger to find errors in a program. See your E-Text or visit wiley.com/go/bclo3.

5.5 Functions Without Return Values

Use a return type of void to indicate that a function does not return a value.

Sometimes, you need to carry out a sequence of instructions that does not yield a value. If that instruction sequence occurs multiple times, you will want to package it into a function. In C++, you use the return type void to indicate the absence of a return value.

Here is a typical example. Your task is to print a string in a box, like this:

```
-------
!Hello!
-------
```

© jgroup/iStockphoto.

A void function returns no value, but it can produce output.

However, different strings can be substituted for Hello. A function for this task can be declared as follows:

```
void box_string(string str)
```

Now you develop the body of the function in the usual way, by formulating a general method for solving the task.

n = the length of the string
Print a line that contains the - character n + 2 times.
Print a line containing the string, surrounded with a ! to the left and right.
Print another line containing the - character n + 2 times.

Here is the function implementation:

```
/**
   Prints a string in a box.
   @param str the string to print
*/
void box_string(string str)
{
   int n = str.length();
   for (int i = 0; i < n + 2; i++) { cout << "-"; }
   cout << endl;
   cout << "!" << str << "!" << endl;
   for (int i = 0; i < n + 2; i++) { cout << "-"; }
   cout << endl;
}
```

This function doesn't compute any value. It performs some actions and then returns to the caller. Note that there is no need for a return statement.

Because there is no return value, you cannot use box_string in an expression. You can call

```
box_string("Hello");
```

but not

```
result = box_string("Hello"); // Error: box_string doesn't return a result.
```

If you want to return from a void function before reaching the end, you use a return statement without a value. For example,

```
void box_string(string str)
{
   int n = str.length();
   if (n == 0)
   {
      return; // Return immediately
   }
   . . .
}
```

EXAMPLE CODE   See sec05 of your companion code for a program that demonstrates the box_string function.

5.6 Problem Solving: Reusable Functions

Eliminate replicated code or pseudocode by defining a function.

You have used many functions from the C++ standard library. These functions have been provided as a part of standard C++ so that programmers need not recreate them. Of course, the C++ library doesn't cover every conceivable need. You will often be able to save yourself time by designing your own functions that can be used for multiple problems.

When you write nearly identical code or pseudocode multiple times, either in the same program or in separate programs, consider introducing a function. Here is a typical example of code replication:

```
int hours;
do
{
   cout << "Enter a value between 0 and 23: ";
   cin >> hours;
}
while (hours < 0 || hours > 23);

int minutes;
do
{
   cout << "Enter a value between 0 and 59: ";
   cin >> minutes;
}
while (minutes < 0 || minutes > 59);
```

This program segment reads two variables, making sure that each of them is within a certain range. It is easy to extract the common behavior into a function:

```
/**
   Prompts a user to enter a value up to a given maximum until the user
   provides a valid input.
   @param high the largest allowable input
   @return the value provided by the user (between 0 and high, inclusive)
*/
int read_int_up_to(int high)
{
   int input;
   do
   {
      cout << "Enter a value between 0 and " << high << ": ";
      cin >> input;
   }
   while (input < 0 || input > high);
```

```
        return input;
    }
```

Then use this function twice:

```
int hours = read_int_up_to(23);
int minutes = read_int_up_to(59);
```

We have now removed the replication of the loop—it only occurs once, inside the function.

Note that the function can be reused in other programs that need to read integer values. However, we should consider the possibility that the smallest value need not always be zero.

Design your functions to be reusable. Supply parameter variables for the values that can vary when the function is reused.

Here is a better alternative:

```
/**
    Prompts a user to enter a value within a given range until the user
    provides a valid input.
    @param low the smallest allowable input
    @param high the largest allowable input
    @return the value provided by the user (between low and high, inclusive)
*/
int read_int_between(int low, int high)
{
    int input;
    do
    {
        cout << "Enter a value between " << low << " and " << high << ": ";
        cin >> input;
    }
    while (input < low || input > high);
    return input;
}
```

In our program, we call

```
int hours = read_int_between(0, 23);
```

Another program can call

```
int month = read_int_between(1, 12);
```

In general, you will want to provide parameter variables for the values that vary when a function is reused.

EXAMPLE CODE   See sec06 of your companion code for a program that demonstrates the read_int_between function.

When carrying out the same task multiple times, use a function.

© Lawrence Sawyer/iStockphoto.

5.7 Problem Solving: Stepwise Refinement

Use the process of stepwise refinement to decompose complex tasks into simpler ones.

One of the most powerful strategies for problem solving is the process of **stepwise refinement**. To solve a difficult task, break it down into simpler tasks. Then keep breaking down the simpler tasks into even simpler ones, until you are left with tasks that you know how to solve.

Here is an application of this process to a problem of everyday life. You get up in the morning and simply must *get coffee*. How do you get coffee? You see whether you can get someone else, such as your mother or mate, to bring you some. If that fails, you must *make coffee*. How do you make coffee? If there is instant coffee available, you can *make instant coffee*. How do you make instant

© AdShooter/iStockphoto.

A production process is broken down into sequences of assembly steps.

coffee? Simply *boil water* and mix the boiling water with the instant coffee. How do you boil water? If there is a microwave, then you fill a cup with water, place it in the microwave and heat it for three minutes. Otherwise, you fill a kettle with water and heat it on the stove until the water comes to a boil. On the other hand, if you don't have instant coffee, you must *brew coffee*. How do you brew coffee? You add water to the coffee maker, put in a filter, *grind coffee*, put the coffee in the filter, and turn the coffee maker on. How do you grind coffee? You add coffee beans to the coffee grinder and push the button for 60 seconds.

Figure 5 shows a flowchart view of the coffee-making solution. Refinements are shown as expanding boxes. In C++, you implement a refinement as a function. For example, a function `brew_coffee` would call `grind_coffee`, and it would be called from a function `make_coffee`.

Let us apply the process of stepwise refinement to a programming problem.

When printing a check, it is customary to write the check amount both as a number ("$274.15") and as a text string ("two hundred seventy four dollars and 15 cents"). Doing so reduces the recipient's temptation to add a few digits in front of the amount.

For a human, this isn't particularly difficult, but how can a computer do this? There is no built-in function that turns 274 into `"two hundred seventy four"`. We need to program this function. Here is the description of the function we want to write:

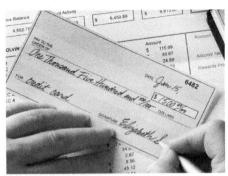

© YinYang/iStockphoto.

```
/**
   Turns a number into its English name.
   @param number a positive integer < 1,000
   @return the name of number (e.g., "two hundred seventy four")
*/
string int_name(int number)
```

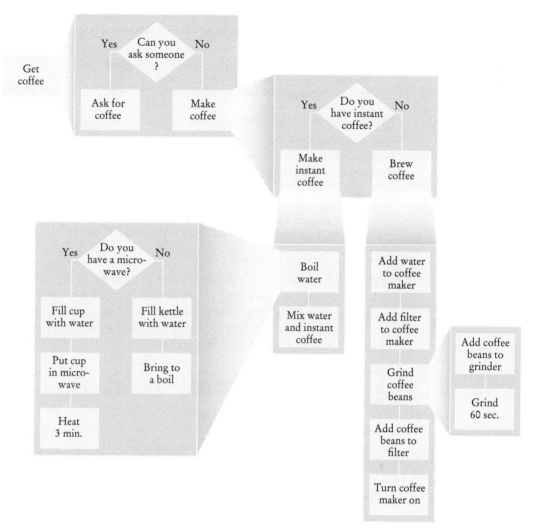

Figure 5 Flowchart of Coffee-Making Solution

When you discover that you need a function, write a description of the parameter variables and return values.

How can this function do its job? Let's look at a simple case first. If the number is between 1 and 9, we need to compute `"one"` ... `"nine"`. In fact, we need the same computation *again* for the hundreds (`two hundred`). Using the stepwise decomposition process, we design another function for this simpler task. Again, rather than implementing the function, we first write the comment:

```
/**
    Turns a digit into its English name.
    @param digit an integer between 1 and 9
    @return the name of digit ("one" ... "nine")
*/
string digit_name(int digit)
```

A function may require simpler functions to carry out its work.

This sounds simple enough to implement, using an `if` statement with nine branches. No further functions should be required for completing the `digit_name` function, so we will worry about the implementation later.

Numbers between 10 and 19 are special cases. Let's have a separate function `teen_name` that converts them into strings `"eleven"`, `"twelve"`, `"thirteen"`, and so on:

```
/**
    Turns a number between 10 and 19 into its English name.
    @param number  an integer between 10 and 19
    @return the name of the number ("ten" ... "nineteen")
*/
string teen_name(int number)
```

Next, suppose that the number is between 20 and 99. Then we show the tens as `"twenty"`, `"thirty"`, ..., `"ninety"`. For simplicity and consistency, put that computation into a separate function:

```
/**
    Gives the name of the tens part of a number between 20 and 99.
    @param number  an integer between 20 and 99
    @return the name of the tens part of the number ("twenty" ... "ninety")
*/
string tens_name(int number)
```

Now suppose the number is at least 20 and at most 99. If the number is evenly divisible by 10, we use `tens_name`, and we are done. Otherwise, we print the tens with `tens_name` and the ones with `digit_name`. If the number is between 100 and 999, then we show a digit, the word `"hundred"`, and the remainder as described previously.

Here is the pseudocode of the algorithm:

> *int_name(number)*
> *part = number // The part that still needs to be converted*
> *name = ""*
>
> *If part >= 100*
>   *name = name of hundreds in part + "hundred"*
>   *Remove hundreds from part.*
>
> *If part >= 20*
>   *Append tens_name(part) to name.*
>   *Remove tens from part.*
> *Else if part >= 10*
>   *Append teen_name(part) to name.*
>   *part = 0*
>
> *If (part > 0)*
>   *Append digit_name(part) to name.*

This pseudocode has a number of important improvements over the verbal description. It shows how to arrange the tests, starting with the comparisons against the larger numbers, and it shows how the smaller number is subsequently processed in further `if` statements.

On the other hand, this pseudocode is vague about the actual conversion of the pieces, just referring to "name of hundreds" and the like. Furthermore, we were vague about spaces. As it stands, the code would produce strings with no spaces, `twohundredseventyfour`, for example. Compared to the complexity of the main problem, one would hope that spaces are a minor issue. It is best not to muddy the pseudocode with minor details.

Now turn the pseudocode into real code. The last three cases are easy, because helper functions are already developed for them:

```cpp
if (part >= 20)
{
   name = name + " " + tens_name(part);
   part = part % 10;
}
else if (part >= 10)
{
   name = name + " " + teen_name(part);
   part = 0;
}

if (part > 0)
{
   name = name + " " + digit_name(part);
}
```

Finally, let us tackle the case of numbers between 100 and 999. Because part < 1000, part / 100 is a single digit, and we obtain its name by calling digit_name. Then we add the "hundred" suffix:

```cpp
if (part >= 100)
{
   name = digit_name(part / 100) + " hundred";
   part = part % 100;
}
```

Now you have seen all the important building blocks for the int_name function. Here is the complete program:

sec07/intname.cpp

```cpp
1  #include <iostream>
2  #include <string>
3
4  using namespace std;
5
6  /**
7     Turns a digit into its English name.
8     @param digit an integer between 1 and 9
9     @return the name of digit ("one" ... "nine")
10 */
11 string digit_name(int digit)
12 {
13    if (digit == 1) return "one";
14    if (digit == 2) return "two";
15    if (digit == 3) return "three";
16    if (digit == 4) return "four";
17    if (digit == 5) return "five";
18    if (digit == 6) return "six";
19    if (digit == 7) return "seven";
20    if (digit == 8) return "eight";
21    if (digit == 9) return "nine";
22    return "";
23 }
24
25 /**
26    Turns a number between 10 and 19 into its English name.
```

```
27        @param number an integer between 10 and 19
28        @return the name of the given number ("ten" ... "nineteen")
29   */
30   string teen_name(int number)
31   {
32      if (number == 10) return "ten";
33      if (number == 11) return "eleven";
34      if (number == 12) return "twelve";
35      if (number == 13) return "thirteen";
36      if (number == 14) return "fourteen";
37      if (number == 15) return "fifteen";
38      if (number == 16) return "sixteen";
39      if (number == 17) return "seventeen";
40      if (number == 18) return "eighteen";
41      if (number == 19) return "nineteen";
42      return "";
43   }
44
45    /**
46        Gives the name of the tens part of a number between 20 and 99.
47        @param number an integer between 20 and 99
48        @return the name of the tens part of the number ("twenty" ... "ninety")
49   */
50   string tens_name(int number)
51   {
52      if (number >= 90) return "ninety";
53      if (number >= 80) return "eighty";
54      if (number >= 70) return "seventy";
55      if (number >= 60) return "sixty";
56      if (number >= 50) return "fifty";
57      if (number >= 40) return "forty";
58      if (number >= 30) return "thirty";
59      if (number >= 20) return "twenty";
60      return "";
61   }
62
63   /**
64        Turns a number into its English name.
65        @param number a positive integer < 1,000
66        @return the name of the number (e.g. "two hundred seventy four")
67   */
68   string int_name(int number)
69   {
70      int part = number; // The part that still needs to be converted
71      string name; // The return value
72
73      if (part >= 100)
74      {
75         name = digit_name(part / 100) + " hundred";
76         part = part % 100;
77      }
78
79      if (part >= 20)
80      {
81         name = name + " " + tens_name(part);
82         part = part % 10;
83      }
84      else if (part >= 10)
85      {
```

```
86          name = name + " " + teen_name(part);
87          part = 0;
88      }
89
90      if (part > 0)
91      {
92          name = name + " " + digit_name(part);
93      }
94
95      return name;
96 }
97
98 int main()
99 {
100     cout << "Please enter a positive integer: ";
101     int input;
102     cin >> input;
103     cout << int_name(input) << endl;
104     return 0;
105 }
```

Program Run

```
Please enter a positive integer: 729
seven hundred twenty nine
```

Programming Tip 5.3

Keep Functions Short

There is a certain cost for writing a function. You need to design, code, and test the function. The function needs to be documented. You need to spend some effort to make the function reusable rather than tied to a specific context. To avoid this cost, it is always tempting just to stuff more and more code in one place rather than going through the trouble of breaking up the code into separate functions. It is quite common to see inexperienced programmers produce functions that are several hundred lines long.

As a rule of thumb, a function that is so long that its code will not fit on a single screen in your development environment should probably be broken up.

Programming Tip 5.4

Tracing Functions

When you design a complex set of functions, it is a good idea to carry out a manual **walk-through** before entrusting your program to the computer.

Take an index card, or some other piece of paper, and write down the function call that you want to study. Write the name of the function and the names and values of the parameter variables, like this:

int_name(number = 416)

Then write the names and initial values of the function variables. Write them in a table, since you will update them as you walk through the code.

int_name(number = 416)	
part	name
416	""

We enter the test part >= 100. part / 100 is 4 and part % 100 is 16. digit_name(4) is easily seen to be "four". (Had digit_name been complicated, you would have started another sheet of paper to figure out that function call. It is quite common to accumulate several sheets in this way.)

Now name has changed to name + " " + digit_name(part / 100) + " hundred", that is "four hundred", and part has changed to part % 100, or 16.

int_name(number = 416)	
part	name
~~416~~	~~""~~
16	"four hundred"

Now you enter the branch part >= 10. teen_name(16) is sixteen, so the variables now have the values

int_name(number = 416)	
part	name
~~416~~	~~""~~
~~16~~	~~"four hundred"~~
0	"four hundred sixteen"

Now it becomes clear why you need to set part to 0 in line 87. Otherwise, you would enter the next branch and the result would be "four hundred sixteen six". Tracing the code is an effective way to understand the subtle aspects of a function.

Programming Tip 5.5

Stubs

When writing a larger program, it is not always feasible to implement and test all functions at once. You often need to test a function that calls another, but the other function hasn't yet been implemented. Then you can temporarily replace the missing function with a **stub**. A stub is a function that returns a simple value that is sufficient for testing another function. Here are examples of stub functions:

```
/**
   Turns a digit into its English name.
   @param digit  an integer between 1 and 9
   @return the name of digit ("one" ... "nine")
```

```
*/
string digit_name(int digit)
{
   return "mumble";
}

/**
   Gives the name of the tens part of a number between 20 and 99.
   @param number  an integer between 20 and 99
   @return  the tens name of the number ("twenty" ... "ninety")
*/
string tens_name(int number)
{
   return "mumblety";
}
```

If you combine these stubs with the int_name function and test it with an argument of 274, you will get a result of "mumble hundred mumblety mumble", which indicates that the basic logic of the int_name function is working correctly.

Stubs are incomplete functions that can be used for testing.

© lillisphotography/iStockphoto.

WORKED EXAMPLE 5.3

Calculating a Course Grade

Learn how to use stepwise refinement to solve the problem of converting a set of letter grades into an average grade for a course. See your E-Text or visit wiley.com/go/bclo3.

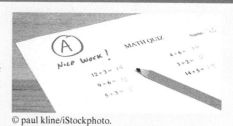

© paul kline/iStockphoto.

5.8 Variable Scope and Global Variables

The scope of a variable is the part of the program in which it is visible.

It is possible to define the same variable name more than once in a program. When the variable name is used, you need to know to which definition it belongs. In this section, we discuss the rules for dealing with multiple definitions of the same name.

A variable that is defined within a function is visible from the point at which it is defined until the end of the block in which it was defined. This area is called the **scope** of the variable.

Consider the `volume` variables in the following example:

```cpp
double cube_volume(double side_length)
{
   double volume = side_length * side_length * side_length;
   return volume;
}

int main()
{
   double volume = cube_volume(2);
   cout << volume << endl;

   return 0;
}
```

Each `volume` variable is defined in a separate function, and their scopes do not overlap.

It is not legal to define two variables with the same name in the same scope. For example, the following is *not* legal:

```cpp
int main()
{
   double volume = cube_volume(2);
   double volume = cube_volume(10);
      // ERROR: cannot define another volume variable in this scope
   . . .
}
```

However, you can define another variable with the same name in a **nested block**. Here, we define two variables called `amount`.

```cpp
double withdraw(double balance, double amount)
{
   if (. . .)
   {
      double amount = 10; // Another variable named amount
      . . .
   }
   . . .
}
```

© jchamp/iStockphoto (Railway and Main); © StevenCarrieJohnson/iStockphoto (Main and N. Putnam); © jsmith/iStockphoto (Main and South St.).

In the same way that there can be a street named "Main Street" in different cities, a C++ program can have multiple variables with the same name.

A variable in a nested block shadows a variable with the same name in an outer block.

The scope of the parameter variable amount is the entire function, *except* inside the nested block. Inside the nested block, amount refers to the variable that was defined in that block. We say that the inner variable *shadows* the variable that is defined in the outer block. You should avoid this potentially confusing situation in the functions that you write, simply by renaming one of the variables.

A local variable is defined inside a function. A global variable is defined outside a function.

Variables that are defined inside functions are called **local variables**. C++ also supports **global variables**: variables that are defined outside functions. A global variable is visible to all functions that are defined after it. For example, the <iostream> header defines global variables cin and cout.

Here is an example of a global variable:

```
int balance = 10000; // A global variable

void withdraw(double amount)
{
   if (balance >= amount)
   {
      balance = balance - amount;
   }
}

int main()
{
   withdraw(1000);
   cout << balance << endl;
   return 0;
}
```

The scope of the variable balance extends over both the withdraw and the main functions.

Avoid global variables in your programs.

Generally, global variables are not a good idea. When multiple functions update global variables, the result can be difficult to predict. Particularly in larger programs that are developed by multiple programmers, it is very important that the effect of each function be clear and easy to understand. You should avoid global variables in your programs.

Programming Tip 5.6

Avoid Global Variables

There are a few cases where global variables are required (such as cin and cout), but they are quite rare. Programs with global variables are difficult to maintain and extend because you can no longer view each function as a "black box" that simply receives arguments and returns a result. When functions modify global variables, it becomes more difficult to understand the effect of function calls. As programs get larger, this difficulty mounts quickly. Instead of using global variables, use function parameters to transfer information from one part of a program to another.

5.9 Reference Parameters

If you want to write a function that changes the value of an argument, you must use a **reference parameter** in order to allow the change. We first explain why a different parameter type is necessary, then we show you the syntax for reference parameters.

Consider a function that simulates withdrawing a given amount of money from a bank account, provided that sufficient funds are available. If the amount of money is insufficient, a $10 penalty is deducted instead. The function would be used as follows:

```
double harrys_account = 1000;
withdraw(harrys_account, 100); // Now harrys_account is 900
withdraw(harrys_account, 1000); // Insufficient funds. Now harrys_account is 890
```

Here is a first attempt:

```
void withdraw(double balance, double amount) // Does not work
{
   const double PENALTY = 10;
   if (balance >= amount)
   {
      balance = balance - amount;
   }
   else
   {
      balance = balance - PENALTY;
   }
}
```

But this doesn't work.

Let's walk through the function call `withdraw(harrys_account, 100)` — see Figure 6. As the function starts, the parameter variable `balance` is created ❶ and set to the same value as `harrys_account`, and `amount` is set to 100 ❷. Then `balance` is modified ❸. Of course, that modification has no effect on `harrys_account`, because `balance` is a separate variable. When the function returns, `balance` is forgotten, and no money was withdrawn from `harrys_account` ❹.

The parameter variable `balance` is called a **value parameter**, because it is initialized with the value of the supplied argument. All functions that we have written so far use value parameters. In this situation, though, we don't just want `balance` to have the same value as `harrys_account`. We want `balance` to refer to the actual variable `harrys_account` (or `joes_account` or whatever variable is supplied in the call). The contents of *that* variable should be updated.

You use a reference parameter when you want to update a variable that was supplied in the function call. When we make `balance` into a reference parameter, then `balance` is not a new variable but a reference to an existing variable. Any change in `balance` is actually a change in the variable to which `balance` refers in that particular call.

> Modifying a value parameter has no effect on the caller.

> A reference parameter refers to a variable that is supplied in a function call.

A reference parameter for a bank balance is like an ATM card—it allows you to change the balance. In contrast, a value parameter can only tell you the balance.

© Winston Davidian/iStockphoto.

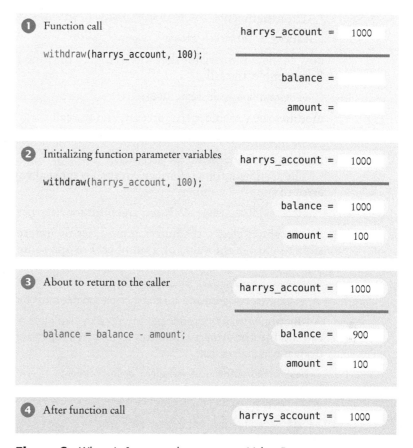

Figure 6 When balance and account are Value Parameters

Figure 7 shows the difference between value and reference parameters. To indicate a reference parameter, you place an & after the type name.

```
void withdraw(double& balance, double amount)
```

The type double& is read "a reference to a double" or, more briefly, "double ref".

The withdraw function now has two parameter variables: one of type "double ref" and the other a value parameter of type double. The body of the function is unchanged. What has changed is the meaning of the assignments to the balance variable.

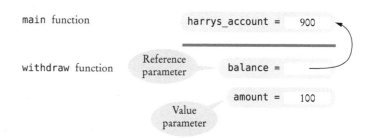

Figure 7 Reference and Value Parameters

The assignment

```
balance = balance - amount;
```

now changes the variable that was passed to the function (see Figure 8). For example, the call

```
withdraw(harrys_account, 100);
```

modifies the variable `harrys_account`, and the call

```
withdraw(sallys_account, 150);
```

modifies the variable `sallys_account`.

Modifying a reference parameter updates the variable that was supplied in the call.

The argument for a reference parameter must always be a *variable*. It would be an error to supply a number:

```
withdraw(1000, 500); // Error: argument for reference parameter must be a variable
```

The reason is clear—the function modifies the reference parameter, but it is impossible to change the value of a number. For the same reason, you cannot supply an expression:

```
withdraw(harrys_account + 150, 500);
      // Error: argument for reference parameter must be a variable
```

A function with a reference parameter can also have a return value. For example, you can modify the `withdraw` function to return a `bool` value indicating whether the withdrawal was successful:

```
bool withdraw(double& balance, double amount)
```

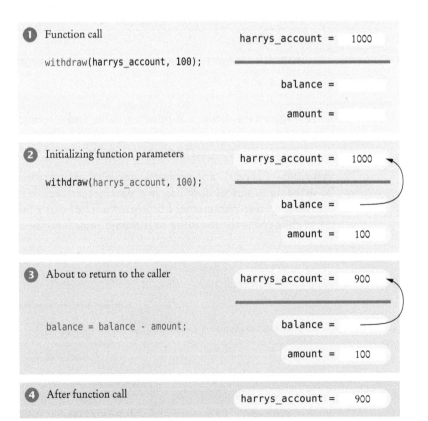

Figure 8
When balance is a
Reference Parameter

Alternatively, you can supply a second reference parameter for that purpose:

```
void withdraw(double& balance, double amount, double& success)
```

sec09/account.cpp

```cpp
1   #include <iostream>
2
3   using namespace std;
4
5   /**
6      Withdraws the amount from the given balance, or withdraws
7      a penalty if the balance is insufficient.
8      @param balance the balance from which to make the withdrawal
9      @param amount the amount to withdraw
10  */
11  void withdraw(double& balance, double amount)
12  {
13     const double PENALTY = 10;
14     if (balance >= amount)
15     {
16        balance = balance - amount;
17     }
18     else
19     {
20        balance = balance - PENALTY;
21     }
22  }
23
24  int main()
25  {
26     double harrys_account = 1000;
27     double sallys_account = 500;
28     withdraw(harrys_account, 100);
29        // Now harrys_account is 900
30     withdraw(harrys_account, 1000); // Insufficient funds
31        // Now harrys_account is 890
32     withdraw(sallys_account, 150);
33     cout << "Harry's account: " << harrys_account << endl;
34     cout << "Sally's account: " << sallys_account << endl;
35
36     return 0;
37  }
```

Program Run

```
Harry's account: 890
Sally's account: 350
```

Programming Tip 5.7

Prefer Return Values to Reference Parameters

Some programmers use reference parameters as a mechanism for setting the result of a function. For example,

```cpp
void cube_volume(double side_length, double& volume)
{
   volume = side_length * side_length * side_length;
```

```
   }
```

However, this function is less convenient than our previous cube_volume function. It cannot be used in expressions such as cout << cube_volume(2).

Use a reference parameter only when a function needs to update a variable.

Special Topic 5.2
Constant References

It is not very efficient to have a value parameter that is a large object (such as a string value). Copying the object into a parameter variable is less efficient than using a reference parameter. With a reference parameter, only the location of the variable, not its value, needs to be transmitted to the function.

You can instruct the compiler to give you the efficiency of a reference parameter and the meaning of a value parameter, by using a *constant reference* as shown below. The function

```cpp
void shout(const string& str)
{
   cout << str << "!!!" << endl;
}
```

works exactly the same as the function

```cpp
void shout(string str)
{
   cout << str << "!!!" << endl;
}
```

There is just one difference: Calls to the first function execute a bit faster.

5.10 Recursive Functions (Optional)

A **recursive function** is a function that calls itself. This is not as unusual as it sounds at first. Suppose you face the arduous task of cleaning up an entire house. You may well say to yourself, "I'll pick a room and clean it, and then I'll clean the other rooms." In other words, the cleanup task calls itself, but with a simpler input. Eventually, all the rooms will be cleaned.

In C++, a recursive function uses the same principle. Here is a typical example. We want to print triangle patterns like this:

```
[]
[][]
[][][]
[][][][]
```

Cleaning up a house can be solved recursively:
Clean one room, then clean up the rest.

© Janice Richard/iStockphoto.

Specifically, our task is to provide a function

```
void print_triangle(int side_length)
```

The triangle given above is printed by calling `print_triangle(4)`.

To see how recursion helps, consider how a triangle with side length 4 can be obtained from a triangle with side length 3.

```
[]
[][]
[][][]
[][][][]
```

Print the triangle with side length 3.
Print a line with four [].

More generally, for an arbitrary side length:

Print the triangle with side length − 1.
Print a line with side length [].

Here is the pseudocode translated to C++:

```
void print_triangle(int side_length)
{
   print_triangle(side_length - 1);
   for (int i = 0; i < side_length; i++)
   {
      cout << "[]";
   }
   cout << endl;
}
```

There is just one problem with this idea. When the side length is 1, we don't want to call `print_triangle(0)`, `print_triangle(-1)`, and so on. The solution is simply to treat this as a special case, and not to print anything when `side_length` is less than 1.

```
void print_triangle(int side_length)
{
   if (side_length < 1) { return; }
   print_triangle(side_length - 1);
   for (int i = 0; i < side_length; i++)
   {
      cout << "[]";
   }
   cout << endl;
}
```

A recursive computation solves a problem by using the solution of the same problem with simpler inputs.

Look at the `print_triangle` function one more time and notice how utterly reasonable it is. If the side length is 0, nothing needs to be printed. The next part is just as reasonable. Print the smaller triangle *and don't think about why that works*. Then print a row of []. Clearly, the result is a triangle of the desired size.

There are two key requirements to make sure that the recursion is successful:

- Every recursive call must simplify the task in some way.
- There must be special cases to handle the simplest tasks directly.

For a recursion to terminate, there must be special cases for the simplest inputs.

The `print_triangle` function calls itself again with smaller and smaller side lengths. Eventually the side length must reach 0, and the function stops calling itself.

Here is what happens when we print a triangle with side length 4.

- The call `print_triangle(4)` calls `print_triangle(3)`.
  - The call `print_triangle(3)` calls `print_triangle(2)`.
    - The call `print_triangle(2)` calls `print_triangle(1)`.
      - The call `print_triangle(1)` calls `print_triangle(0)`.
        - The call `print_triangle(0)` returns, doing nothing.
      - The call `print_triangle(1)` prints [].
    - The call `print_triangle(2)` prints [][].
  - The call `print_triangle(3)` prints [][][].
- The call `print_triangle(4)` prints [][][][].

The call pattern of a recursive function looks complicated, and the key to the successful design of a recursive function is *not to think about it*.

This set of Russian dolls looks similar to the call pattern of a recursive function.

© Nicolae Popovici/iStockphoto.

sec10/triangle.cpp

```cpp
1   #include <iostream>
2
3   using namespace std;
4
5   /**
6      Prints a triangle with a given side length.
7      @param side_length the side length (number of [] along the base)
8   */
9   void print_triangle(int side_length)
10  {
11     if (side_length < 1) { return; }
12     print_triangle(side_length - 1);
13     for (int i = 0; i < side_length; i++)
14     {
15        cout << "[]";
16     }
17     cout << endl;
18  }
19
20  int main()
21  {
22     cout << "Enter the side length: ";
23     int input;
24     cin >> input;
25     print_triangle(input);
```

```
26    return 0;
27 }
```

Program Run

```
Enter the side length: 10
[]
[][]
[][][]
[][][][]
[][][][][]
[][][][][][]
[][][][][][][]
[][][][][][][][]
[][][][][][][][][]
[][][][][][][][][][]
```

Recursion is not really necessary to print triangle shapes. You can use nested loops, like this:

```
for (int i = 0; i < side_length; i++)
{
   for (int j = 0; j < i; j++)
   {
      cout << "[]";
   }
   cout << endl;
}
```

However, this pair of loops is a bit tricky. Many people find the recursive solution simpler to understand.

HOW TO 5.2

Thinking Recursively

To solve a problem recursively requires a different mindset than to solve it by programming loops. In fact, it helps if you are, or pretend to be, a bit lazy and let others do most of the work for you. If you need to solve a complex problem, pretend that "someone else" will do most of the heavy lifting and solve the problem for all simpler inputs. Then you only need to figure out how you can turn the solutions with simpler inputs into a solution for the whole problem.

Problem Statement To illustrate the recursive thinking process, consider the problem of Section 4.2, computing the sum of the digits of a number. We want to design a function digit_sum that computes the sum of the digits of an integer n. For example, digit_sum(1729) = 1 + 7 + 2 + 9 = 19.

Step 1 Break the input into parts that can themselves be inputs to the problem.

In your mind, fix a particular input or set of inputs for the task that you want to solve, and think how you can simplify the inputs. Look for simplifications that can be solved by the same task, and whose solutions are related to the original task.

The key to finding a recursive solution is reducing the input to a simpler input for the same problem.

In the digit sum problem, consider how we can simplify an input such as n = 1729. Would it help to subtract 1? After all, digit_sum(1729) = digit_sum(1728) + 1. But consider n = 1000. There seems to be no obvious relationship between digit_sum(1000) and digit_sum(999).

A much more promising idea is to remove the last digit, that is, compute n / 10 = 172. The digit sum of 172 is directly related to the digit sum of 1729.

Step 2   Combine solutions with simpler inputs into a solution of the original problem.

In your mind, consider the solutions for the simpler inputs that you have discovered in Step 1. Don't worry *how* those solutions are obtained. Simply have faith that the solutions are readily available. Just say to yourself: These are simpler inputs, so someone else will solve the problem for me.

In the case of the digit sum task, ask yourself how you can obtain digit_sum(1729) if you know digit_sum(172). You simply add the last digit (9), and you are done. How do you get the last digit? As the remainder n % 10. The value digit_sum(n) can therefore be obtained as

```
digit_sum(n / 10) + n % 10
```

Don't worry how digit_sum(n / 10) is computed. The input is smaller, and therefore it just works.

Step 3   Find solutions to the simplest inputs.

A recursive computation keeps simplifying its inputs. To make sure that the recursion comes to a stop, you must deal with the simplest inputs separately. Come up with special solutions for them. That is usually very easy.

Look at the simplest inputs for the digit_sum test:

- A number with a single digit
- 0

A number with a single digit is its own digit sum, so you can stop the recursion when n < 10, and return n in that case. Or, if you prefer, you can be even lazier. If n has a single digit, then digit_sum(n / 10) + n % 10 equals digit_sum(0) + n. You can simply terminate the recursion when n is zero.

Step 4   Implement the solution by combining the simple cases and the reduction step.

Now you are ready to implement the solution. Make separate cases for the simple inputs that you considered in Step 3. If the input isn't one of the simplest cases, then implement the logic you discovered in Step 2.

Here is the complete digit_sum function:

```
int digit_sum(int n)
{
   // Special case for terminating the recursion
   if (n == 0) { return 0; }
   // General case
   return digit_sum(n / 10) + n % 10;
}
```

Computing & Society 5.1   **The Explosive Growth of Personal Computers**

In 1971, Marcian E. "Ted" Hoff, an engineer at Intel Corporation, was working on a chip for a manufacturer of electronic calculators. He realized that it would be a better idea to develop a *general-purpose* chip that could be *programmed* to interface with the keys and display of a calculator, rather than to do yet another custom design. Thus, the *microprocessor* was born. At the time, its primary application was as a controller for calculators, washing machines, and the like. It took years for the computer industry to notice that a genuine central processing unit was now available as a single chip.

Hobbyists were the first to catch on. In 1974 the first computer *kit*, the Altair 8800, was available from MITS Electronics for about $350. The kit consisted of the microprocessor, a circuit board, a very small amount of memory, toggle switches, and a row of display lights. Purchasers had to solder and assemble it, then program it in machine language through the toggle switches. It was not a big hit.

The first big hit was the Apple II. It was a real computer with a keyboard, a monitor, and a floppy disk drive. When it was first released, users had a $3,000 machine that could play Space Invaders, run a primitive bookkeeping program, or let users program it in BASIC. The original Apple II did not even support lowercase letters, making it worthless for word processing. The breakthrough came in 1979 with a new spreadsheet program, VisiCalc. In a spreadsheet, you enter financial data and their relationships into a grid of rows and columns (see the figure). Then you modify some of the data and watch in real time how the others change. For example, you can see how changing the mix of widgets in a manufacturing plant might affect estimated costs and profits. Corporate managers snapped up VisiCalc and the computer that was needed to run it. For them, the computer was a spreadsheet machine.

More importantly, it was a personal device. The managers were free to do the calculations that they wanted to do, not just the ones that the "high priests" in the data center provided.

Personal computers have been with us ever since, and countless users have tinkered with their hardware and software, sometimes establishing highly successful companies or creating free software for millions of users. This "freedom to tinker" is an important part of personal computing. On a personal device, you should be able to install the software that you want to install to make you more productive or creative, even if that's not the same software that most people use. You should be able to add peripheral equipment of your choice. For the first thirty years of personal computing, this freedom was largely taken for granted.

We are now entering an era where smart phones, tablets, and smart TV sets are replacing functions that were traditionally fulfilled by personal computers. While it is amazing to carry more computing power in your cell phone than in the best personal com-

Courtesy of International Business Machines Corporation, © International Business Machines Corporation.

The Visicalc Spreadsheet Running on an Apple II

puters of the 1990s, it is disturbing that we lose a degree of personal control. With some phone or tablet brands, you can install only those applications that the manufacturer publishes on the "app store". For example, Apple rejected MIT's iPad app for the educational language Scratch because it contained a virtual machine. You'd think it would be in Apple's interest to encourage the next generation to be enthusiastic about programming, but

they have a general policy of denying programmability on "their" devices, in order to thwart competitive environments such as Flash or Java.

When you select a device for making phone calls or watching movies, it is worth asking who is in control. Are you purchasing a personal device that you can use in any way you choose, or are you being tethered to a flow of data that is controlled by somebody else?

CHAPTER SUMMARY

Understand the concepts of functions, arguments, and return values.

- A function is a named sequence of instructions.
- Arguments are supplied when a function is called. The return value is the result that the function computes.

Be able to implement functions.

- When defining a function, you provide a name for the function, a variable for each argument, and a type for the result.
- Function comments explain the purpose of the function, the meaning of the parameter variables and return value, as well as any special requirements.

Describe the process of parameter passing.

- Parameter variables hold the argument values supplied in the function call.

Describe the process of returning a value from a function.

- The return statement terminates a function call and yields the function result.

Design and implement functions without return values.

- Use a return type of void to indicate that a function does not return a value.

Develop functions that can be reused for multiple problems.

- Eliminate replicated code or pseudocode by defining a function.
- Design your functions to be reusable. Supply parameter variables for the values that can vary when the function is reused.

Apply the design principle of stepwise refinement.

- Use the process of stepwise refinement to decompose complex tasks into simpler ones.
- When you discover that you need a function, write a description of the parameter variables and return values.
- A function may require simpler functions to carry out its work.

Determine the scope of variables in a program.

- The scope of a variable is the part of the program in which it is visible.
- A variable in a nested block shadows a variable with the same name in an outer block.
- A local variable is defined inside a function. A global variable is defined outside a function.
- Avoid global variables in your programs.

Describe how reference parameters work.

- Modifying a value parameter has no effect on the caller.
- A reference parameter refers to a variable that is supplied in a function call.
- Modifying a reference parameter updates the variable that was supplied in the call.

Understand recursive function calls and implement simple recursive functions.

- A recursive computation solves a problem by using the solution of the same problem with simpler inputs.
- For a recursion to terminate, there must be special cases for the simplest inputs.
- The key to finding a recursive solution is reducing the input to a simpler input for the same problem.
- When designing a recursive solution, do not worry about multiple nested calls. Simply focus on reducing a problem to a slightly simpler one.

REVIEW EXERCISES

- **R5.1** What is the difference between an argument and a return value? How many arguments can a function have? How many return values?

- **R5.2** In which sequence are the lines of the program cube.cpp in Section 5.2 executed, starting with the first line of main?

- **R5.3** Give examples of the following, either from the C++ library or from the functions discussed in this chapter:
    - **a.** A function with two double arguments and a double return value
    - **b.** A function with a double argument and a double return value
    - **c.** A function with two int arguments and an int return value
    - **d.** A function with an int argument and a string return value
    - **e.** A function with a string argument and no return value
    - **f.** A function with a reference parameter and no return value
    - **g.** A function with no arguments and an int return value

- **R5.4** True or false?
    - **a.** A function has exactly one return statement.
    - **b.** A function has at least one return statement.
    - **c.** A function has at most one return value.
    - **d.** A function with return value void never has a return statement.
    - **e.** When executing a return statement, the function exits immediately.
    - **f.** A function with return value void must print a result.
    - **g.** A function without arguments always returns the same value.

- **R5.5** Consider these functions:

```
double f(double x) { return g(x) + sqrt(h(x)); }
double g(double x) { return 4 * h(x); }
double h(double x) { return x * x + k(x) - 1; }
double k(double x) { return 2 * (x + 1); }
```

    Without actually compiling and running a program, determine the results of the following function calls:
    - **a.** double x1 = f(2);
    - **b.** double x2 = g(h(2));
    - **c.** double x3 = k(g(2) + h(2));
    - **d.** double x4 = f(0) + f(1) + f(2);
    - **e.** double x5 = f(-1) + g(-1) + h(-1) + k(-1);

- **Business R5.6** Write pseudocode for a function that translates a telephone number with letters in it (such as 1-800-FLOWERS) into the actual phone number. Use the standard letters on a phone pad.

© stacey_newman/iStockphoto.

R5.7 Design a function that prints a floating-point number as a currency value (with a $ sign and two decimal digits).

   a. Indicate how the programs ch02/sec03/volume2.cpp and ch04/sec03/invtable.cpp should change to use your function.

   b. What change is required if the programs should show a different currency, such as euro?

R5.8 For each of the variables in the following program, indicate the scope. Then determine what the program prints, without actually running the program.

```
1   int a = 0;
2   int b = 0;
3   int f(int c)
4   {
5      int n = 0;
6      a = c;
7      if (n < c)
8      {
9         n = a + b;
10     }
11     return n;
12  }
13
14  int g(int c)
15  {
16     int n = 0;
17     int a = c;
18     if (n < f(c))
19     {
20        n = a + b;
21     }
22     return n;
23  }
24
25  int main()
26  {
27     int i = 1;
28     int b = g(i);
29     cout << a + b + i << endl;
30     return 0;
31  }
```

R5.9 We have seen three kinds of variables in C++: global variables, parameter variables, and local variables. Classify the variables of Exercise R5.8 according to these categories.

R5.10 Use the process of stepwise refinement to describe the process of making scrambled eggs. Discuss what you do if you do not find eggs in the refrigerator.

R5.11 How many parameters does the following function have? How many return values does it have? *Hint:* The C++ notions of "parameter" and "return value" are not the same as the intuitive notions of "input" and "output".

```
void average(double& avg)
{
   cout << "Please enter two numbers: ";
   double x;
   double y;
```

```
        cin >> x >> y;
        avg = (x + y) / 2;
    }
```

- **R5.12** Perform a walkthrough of the int_name function with the following arguments:

    a. 5

    b. 12

    c. 21

    d. 301

    e. 324

    f. 0

    g. -2

- **R5.13** Consider the following function:

```
int f(int n)
{
    if (n <= 1) { return 1; }
    if (n % 2 == 0) // n is even
    {
        return f(n / 2);
    }
    else { return f(3 * n + 1); }
}
```

Perform traces of the computations f(1), f(2), f(3), f(4), f(5), f(6), f(7), f(8), f(9), and f(10).

- **R5.14** Eliminate the global variable in the code at the end of Section 5.8 by

    a. passing the balance to the withdraw function and returning the updated balance.

    b. passing the balance as a reference parameter to the withdraw function.

- **R5.15** Given the following functions, trace the function call print_roots(4).

```
int i;

int isqrt(int n)
{
    i = 1;
    while (i * i <= n) { i++; }
    return i - 1;
}

void print_roots(int n)
{
    for (i = 0; i <= n; i++) { cout << isqrt(i) << " "; }
}
```

How can you fix the code so that the output is as expected (that is, 0 1 1 1 2)?

- **R5.16** Consider the following function that is intended to swap the values of two integers:

```
void false_swap1(int& a, int& b)
{
    a = b;
    b = a;
}

int main()
{
```

```
    int x = 3;
    int y = 4;
    false_swap1(x, y);
    cout << x << " " << y << endl;
    return 0;
}
```

Why doesn't the function swap the contents of x and y? How can you rewrite the function to work correctly?

■■■ **R5.17** Consider the following function that is intended to swap the values of two integers:

```
void false_swap2(int a, int b)
{
    int temp = a;
    a = b;
    b = temp;
}

int main()
{
    int x = 3;
    int y = 4;
    false_swap2(x, y);
    cout << x << " " << y << endl;
    return 0;
}
```

Why doesn't the function swap the contents of x and y? How can you rewrite the function to work correctly?

■■■ **R5.18** The following function swaps two integers, without requiring a temporary variable:

```
void tricky_swap(int& a, int& b)
{
    a = a - b;
    b = a + b;
    a = b - a;
}
```

However, it fails in one important case, namely when calling tricky_swap(x, x). Explain what should happen and what actually happens.

■■■ **R5.19** In How To 5.1, it is easy enough to measure the width of a real pyramid. But how can you measure the height without climbing to the top? You need to measure the angle between the ground and the top from a point, and the distance from that point to the base. Develop a concrete plan and write pseudocode for a program that determines the volume of a pyramid from these inputs.

■■■ **R5.20** Suppose an ancient civilization had constructed circular pyramids. Write pseudocode for a program that determines the surface area from measurements that you can determine from the ground.

■■■ **R5.21** Give pseudocode for a recursive function for printing all substrings of a given string. For example, the substrings of the string "rum" are "rum" itself, "ru", "um", "r", "u", "m", and the empty string. You may assume that all letters of the string are different.

■■■ **R5.22** Give pseudocode for a recursive function that sorts all letters in a string. For example, the string "goodbye" would be sorted into "bdegooy".

PRACTICE EXERCISES

▪ **E5.1** The `max` function that is declared in the `<algorithm>` header returns the larger of its two arguments. Write a program that reads three floating-point numbers, uses the `max` function, and displays

- the larger of the first two inputs.
- the larger of the last two inputs.
- the largest of all three inputs.

▪ **E5.2** Write a function that computes the balance of a bank account with a given initial balance and interest rate, after a given number of years. Assume interest is compounded yearly.

▪ **E5.3** Write the following functions and provide a program to test them.

  a. `double smallest(double x, double y, double z)`, returning the smallest of the arguments

  b. `double average(double x, double y, double z)`, returning the average of the arguments

▪▪ **E5.4** Write the following functions and provide a program to test them:

  a. `bool all_the_same(double x, double y, double z)`, returning true if the arguments are all the same

  b. `bool all_different(double x, double y, double z)`, returning true if the arguments are all different

  c. `bool sorted(double x, double y, double z)`, returning true if the arguments are sorted, with the smallest one coming first

▪▪ **E5.5** Write the following functions:

  a. `int first_digit(int n)`, returning the first digit of the argument

  b. `int last_digit(int n)`, returning the last digit of the argument

  c. `int digits(int n)`, returning the number of digits of the argument

For example, `first_digit(1729)` is 1, `last_digit(1729)` is 9, and `digits(1729)` is 4. Provide a program that tests your functions.

▪ **E5.6** Write a function

```
string middle(string str)
```

that returns a string containing the middle character in `str` if the length of `str` is odd, or the two middle characters if the length is even. For example, `middle("middle")` returns `"dd"`.

▪ **E5.7** Write a function

```
string repeat(string str, int n)
```

that returns the string `str` repeated `n` times. For example, `repeat("ho", 3)` returns `"hohoho"`.

▪▪ **E5.8** Write a function

```
int count_vowels(string str)
```

that returns a count of all vowels in the string `str`. Vowels are the letters a, e, i, o, and u, and their uppercase variants. Use a helper function `is_vowel` that checks whether a character is a vowel.

■■ **E5.9** Write a function

```
int count_words(string str)
```

that returns a count of all words in the string str. Words are separated by spaces. For example, count_words("Mary had a little lamb") should return 5. Your function should work correctly if there are multiple spaces between words. Use helper functions to find the position of the next space following a given position, and to find the position of the next non-space character following a given position.

■■ **E5.10** Write a function that returns the average length of all words in the string str. Use the same helper functions as in Exercise E5.9.

■ **E5.11** Write functions

```
double sphere_volume(double r)
double sphere_surface(double r)
double cylinder_volume(double r, double h)
double cylinder_surface(double r, double h)
double cone_volume(double r, double h)
double cone_surface(double r, double h)
```

that compute the volume and surface area of a sphere with radius r, a cylinder with a circular base with radius r and height h, and a cone with a circular base with radius r and height h. Then write a program that prompts the user for the values of r and h, calls the six functions, and prints the results.

■■ **E5.12** Write functions

```
double distance(double x1, double x2, double y1, double y2)
void midpoint(double x1, double x2, double y1, double y2, double& xmid, double& ymid)
void slope(double x1, double x2, double y1, double y2, bool& vertical, double& s)
```

that compute the distance, midpoint, and slope of the line segment joining the points (x_1, y_1) and (x_2, y_2). The slope function should either set vertical to true and not set s, or set vertical to false and set s to the slope.

■■ **E5.13** Write a function

```
double read_double(string prompt)
```

that displays the prompt string, followed by a space, reads a floating-point number in, and returns it. Here is a typical usage:

```
salary = read_double("Please enter your salary:");
perc_raise = read_double("What percentage raise would you like?");
```

■■ **E5.14** Write a function void sort2(int& a, int& b) that swaps the values of a and b if a is greater than b and otherwise leaves a and b unchanged. For example,

```
int u = 2;
int v = 3;
int w = 4;
int x = 1;
sort2(u, v); // u is still 2, v is still 3
sort2(w, x); // w is now 1, x is now 4
```

■■ **E5.15** Write a function `sort3(int& a, int& b, int& c)` that swaps its three arguments to arrange them in sorted order. For example,

```
int v = 3;
int w = 4;
int x = 1;
sort3(v, w, x); // v is now 1, w is now 3, x is now 4
```

Hint: Use multiple calls to the `sort2` function of Exercise E5.14.

■■ **E5.16** Write a function that computes the weekday of a given date, using a formula known as *Zeller's congruence*. Let

d = the day of the month

mm = the modified month (3 = March, ..., 12 = December, 13 = January, 14 = February)

w = the weekday (0 = Monday, 1 = Tuesday, ..., 6 = Sunday)

Then

$$w = \left(d + 5 + \frac{\left(26 \times \left(mm + 1\right)\right)}{10} + \frac{5 \times \left(year \,\%\, 100\right)}{4} + \frac{21 \times \left(year/100\right)}{4} \right) \% 7$$

Here, all / denote integer division and % denotes the remainder operation.

■■ **E5.17** Write a program that prints instructions to get coffee, asking the user for input whenever a decision needs to be made. Decompose each task into a function, for example:

```
void brew_coffee()
{
    cout << "Add water to the coffee maker." << endl;
    cout << "Put a filter in the coffee maker." << endl;
    grind_coffee();
    cout << "Put the coffee in the filter." << endl;
    . . .
}
```

■■ **E5.18** Write a function that computes the Scrabble score of a word. Look up the letter values on the Internet. For example, with English letter values, the word CODE is worth 3 + 0 + 2 + 1 = 6 points.

■■ **E5.19** Write a function that tests whether a file name should come before or after another. File names are first sorted by their extension (the string after the last period) and then by the name part (the string that remains after removing the extension). For example, `before("report.doc", "notes.txt")` should return `true` and `before("report.txt", "notes.txt")` should return `false`. Provide helper functions that return the extension and name part of a file name.

■■■ **E5.20** When comparing strings, the comparison is not always satisfactory. For example, `"file10" < "file2"`, even though we would prefer it to come afterwards. Produce a `num_less` function that, when comparing two strings that are identical except for a positive integer at the end, compares the integers. For example, `num_less("file12", "file2")` should return `true`, but `num_less("file12", "file11")` and `num_less("file2", "doc12")` should return `false`. Use a helper function that returns the starting position of the number, or −1 if there is none.

■■ **E5.21** Write a recursive function

```
string reverse(string str)
```

that computes the reverse of a string. For example, reverse("flow") should return "wolf". *Hint:* Reverse the substring starting at the second character, then add the first character at the end. For example, to reverse "flow", first reverse "low" to "wol", then add the "f" at the end.

■■ **E5.22** Write a recursive function

```
bool is_palindrome(string str)
```

that returns true if str is a palindrome, that is, a word that is the same when reversed. Examples of palindrome are "deed", "rotor", or "aibohphobia". *Hint:* A word is a palindrome if the first and last letters match and the remainder is also a palindrome.

■■ **E5.23** Use recursion to implement a function bool find(string str, string match) that tests whether match is contained in str:

```
bool b = find("Mississippi", "sip"); // Sets b to true
```

Hint: If str starts with match, then you are done. If not, consider the string that you obtain by removing the first character.

■ **E5.24** Use recursion to determine the number of digits in a number n. *Hint:* If n is < 10, it has one digit. Otherwise, it has one more digit than n / 10.

PROGRAMMING PROJECTS

■■ **P5.1** It is a well-known phenomenon that most people are easily able to read a text whose words have two characters flipped, provided the first and last letter of each word are not changed. For example:

> I dn'ot gvie a dman for a man taht can olny sepll a wrod one way. (Mrak Taiwn)

Write a function string scramble(string word) that constructs a scrambled version of a given word, randomly flipping two characters other than the first and last one. Then write a program that reads words from cin and prints the scrambled words.

■■ **P5.2** Enhance the int_name function so that it works correctly for values < 1,000,000,000.

■■ **P5.3** Enhance the int_name function so that it works correctly for negative values and zero. *Caution:* Make sure the improved function doesn't print 20 as "twenty zero".

■■■ **P5.4** For some values (for example, 20), the int_name function returns a string with a leading space (" twenty"). Repair that blemish and ensure that spaces are inserted only when necessary. *Hint:* There are two ways of accomplishing this. Either ensure that leading spaces are never inserted, or remove leading spaces from the result before returning it.

■■ **P5.5** Implement the number_to_grade function of Worked Example 5.3 so that you use two sets of branches: one to determine whether the grade should be A, B, C, D, or F, and another to determine whether a + or - should be appended.

■■ **P5.6** Write a program that reads two strings containing section numbers such as "1.13.2" and "1.2.4.1" and determines which one comes first. Provide appropriate helper function.

•• **P5.7** Write a program that prompts the user for a regular English verb (such as play), the first, second, or third person, singular or plural, and present, past, or future tense. Provide these values to a function that yields the conjugated verb and prints it. For example, the input play 3 singular present should yield "he/she plays".

••• **P5.8** Write a program that reads words and arranges them in a paragraph so that all lines other than the last one are exactly forty characters long. Add spaces between words to make the last word extend to the margin. Distribute the spaces evenly. Use a helper function for that purpose. A typical output would be:

```
Four  score  and  seven  years  ago our
fathers brought forth on this continent
a new nation, conceived in liberty, and
dedicated  to  the proposition that all
men are created equal.
```

••• **P5.9** Write a program that, given a month and year, prints a calendar, such as

```
      June 2016
Su Mo Tu We Th Fr Sa
          1  2  3  4
 5  6  7  8  9 10 11
12 13 14 15 16 17 18
19 20 21 22 23 24 25
26 27 28 29 30
```

To find out the weekday of the first day of the month, call this function:

```
/**
    Computes the weekday of a given date.
    @param year the year
    @param month the month (1 = January ... 12 = December)
    @param day the day of the month
    @return the weekday (0 = Sunday ... 6 = Saturday)
*/
int day_of_week(int year, int month, int day)
{
    int y = year;
    int m = month - 1;
    if (month < 3) { y--; m = m + 4; }
    return (y + y / 4 - y / 100 + y / 400
       + 3 * m + 4 - (m - m / 8) / 2 + day) % 7;
}
```

Make a helper function to print the header and a helper function to print each row.

•• **P5.10** Write a program that reads two fractions, adds them, and prints the result so that the numerator and denominator have no common factor. For example, when adding 3/4 and 5/6, the result is 19/12. Use helper functions for obtaining the numerator and denominator of strings such as "3/4", and for computing the greatest common divisor of two integers.

••• **P5.11** Write a program that reads two positive integers and prints out the "long division". For example,

```
3640 : 15 = 242 Remainder 10
30
--
 64
 60
```

```
  --
  40
  30
  --
  10
```

Format the computation in the way that you learned in elementary school. Use helper functions to structure your program.

■■ **P5.12** Write a program that prints the decimal expansion of a fraction, marking the repeated part with an `R`. For example, 5/2 is `2.5R0`, 1/12 is `0.08R3`, and 1/7 is `0.R142857`. Use helper functions to structure your program. *Hint:* Use the long division algorithm.

■■ **P5.13** Write a program that reads a decimal expansion with a repeated part, as in Exercise P5.12, and displays the fraction that it represents. Use helper functions to structure your program.

■■ **Business P5.14** Write a program that prints a paycheck. Ask the program user for the name of the employee, the hourly rate, and the number of hours worked. If the number of hours exceeds 40, the employee is paid "time and a half", that is, 150 percent of the hourly rate on the hours exceeding 40. Your check should look similar to that in the figure below. Use fictitious names for the payer and the bank. Be sure to use stepwise refinement and break your solution into several functions. Use the `int_name` function to print the dollar amount of the check.

(WJ) **WILEY** | John Wiley & Sons, Inc.
111 River Street
Hoboken, NJ 07030-5774

Publishers' Bank Minnesota
2000 Prince Blvd
Jonesville, MN 55400

CHECK NUMBER   063331 $\frac{74\text{-}39}{311}$ 567390

Date	Amount
04/29/17	$*******274.15

PAY   4659484

TWO HUNDRED SEVENTY FOUR AND 15 / 100 **
TO THE ORDER OF:

JOHN DOE
1009 Franklin Blvd
Sunnyvale, CA 95014

⑉478108240⑉ 2006203 75⑉ 1301

■■ **P5.15** *Leap years.* Write a function

```
bool leap_year(int year)
```

that tests whether a year is a leap year: that is, a year with 366 days. Leap years are necessary to keep the calendar synchronized with the sun because the earth revolves around the sun once every 365.25 days. Actually, that figure is not entirely precise, and for all dates after 1582 the *Gregorian correction* applies. Usually years that are divisible by 4 are leap years, for example 1996. However, years that are divisible by 100 (for example, 1900) are not leap years, but years that are divisible by 400 are leap years (for example, 2000).

© mbbirdy/iStockphoto.

■■ Business P5.16 Write a program that converts a Roman number such as MCMLXXVIII to its decimal number representation. *Hint:* First write a function that yields the numeric value of each of the letters. Then use the following algorithm:

> *total = 0*
> *str = roman number string*
> *While str is not empty*
>   *If str has length 1, or value(first character of str) is at least value(second character of str)*
>   *Add value(first character of str) to total.*
>   *Remove first character from str.*
>   *Else*
>   *difference = value(second character of str) - value(first character of str)*
>   *Add difference to total.*
>   *Remove first character and second character from str.*

■■ P5.17 In Exercise P3.13 you were asked to write a program to convert a number to its representation in Roman numerals. At the time, you did not know how to eliminate duplicate code, and as a consequence the resulting program was rather long. Rewrite that program by implementing and using the following function:

© Straitshooter/iStockphoto.

```
string roman_digit(int n, string one, string five, string ten)
```

That function translates one digit, using the strings specified for the one, five, and ten values. You would call the function as follows:

```
roman_ones = roman_digit(n % 10, "I", "V", "X");
n = n / 10;
roman_tens = roman_digit(n % 10, "X", "L", "C");
. . .
```

■■ Business P5.18 *Postal bar codes.* For faster sorting of letters, the United States Postal Service encourages companies that send large volumes of mail to use a bar code denoting the zip code (see Figure 9).

The encoding scheme for a five-digit zip code is shown in Figure 10. There are full-height frame bars on each side. The five encoded digits are followed by a check digit, which is computed as follows: Add up all digits, and choose the check digit to make the sum a multiple of 10. For example, the zip code 95014 has a sum of 19, so the check digit is 1 to make the sum equal to 20.

Each digit of the zip code, and the check digit, is encoded according to the following table where 0 denotes a half bar and 1 a full bar.

```
*************  ECRLOT  **  CO57

CODE  C671RTS2
JOHN DOE                        CO57
1009 FRANKLIN BLVD
SUNNYVALE       CA  95014 - 5143
```

I|I.....I.I.I.I......I.I..I.I.I.....I.I.I..I.II.I.I.I

Figure 9   A Postal Bar Code

Frame bars

Digit 1 Digit 2 Digit 3 Digit 4 Digit 5 Check Digit

Figure 10   Encoding for Five-Digit Bar Codes

Digit	Bar 1 (weight 7)	Bar 2 (weight 4)	Bar 3 (weight 2)	Bar 4 (weight 1)	Bar 5 (weight 0)
1	0	0	0	1	1
2	0	0	1	0	1
3	0	0	1	1	0
4	0	1	0	0	1
5	0	1	0	1	0
6	0	1	1	0	0
7	1	0	0	0	1
8	1	0	0	1	0
9	1	0	1	0	0
0	1	1	0	0	0

The digit can be easily computed from the bar code using the column weights 7, 4, 2, 1, 0. For example, 01100 is $0 \times 7 + 1 \times 4 + 1 \times 2 + 0 \times 1 + 0 \times 0 = 6$. The only exception is 0, which would yield 11 according to the weight formula.

Write a program that asks the user for a zip code and prints the bar code. Use : for half bars, | for full bars. For example, 95014 becomes

||:|:::|:|:||::::::||:|::|:::|||

■■■ Business P5.19 Write a program that reads in a bar code (with : denoting half bars and | denoting full bars) and prints out the zip code it represents. Print an error message if the bar code is not correct.

■ P5.20 Use recursion to compute a^n, where n is a positive integer. *Hint:* If n is 1, then $a^n = a$. Otherwise, $a^n = a \times a^{n-1}$.

■■ Media P5.21 Write a program that reads in the width and height of a rectangle and the diameter of a circle. Then fill the rectangle with as many circles as possible, using "square circle packing":

Use the Picture class from Worked Example 4.2 and a .png file with a circle on a transparent background (supplied in the companion code). Provide a helper function to draw each row.

■■■ Media P5.22 Repeat Exercise P5.21 with "hexagonal circle packing":

•• **Engineering P5.23** The effective focal length f of a lens of thickness d that has surfaces with radii of curvature R_1 and R_2 is given by

$$\frac{1}{f} = (n-1)\left[\frac{1}{R_1} - \frac{1}{R_2} + \frac{(n-1)d}{nR_1R_2}\right]$$

where n is the refractive index of the lens medium.

Write a function that computes f in terms of the other parameters. Write a C++ program to test this function.

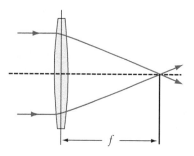

•• **Engineering P5.24** A laboratory container is shaped like the frustum of a cone:

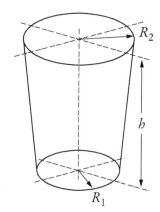

Write functions to compute the volume and surface area, using these equations:

$$V = \tfrac{1}{3}\pi h\left(R_1^2 + R_2^2 + R_1R_2\right)$$

$$S = \pi\left(R_1 + R_2\right)\sqrt{\left(R_2 - R_1\right)^2 + h^2} + \pi R_1^2$$

Write a C++ program to test these functions.

•• **Engineering P5.25** In a movie theater, the angle θ at which a viewer sees the picture on the screen depends on the distance x of the viewer from the screen. For a movie theater with the dimensions shown in the picture below, write a function that computes the angle for a given distance.

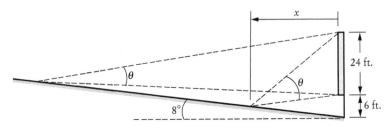

Next, provide a more general function that works for theaters with arbitrary dimensions. Write a C++ program to test these functions.

■■ **Engineering P5.26** Electric wire, like that in the photo, is a cylindrical conductor covered by an insulating material. The resistance of a piece of wire is given by the formula

$$R = \frac{\rho L}{A} = \frac{4\rho L}{\pi d^2}$$

© alacatr/iStockphoto.

where ρ is the resistivity of the conductor, and L, A, and d are the length, cross-sectional area, and diameter of the wire. The resistivity of copper is 1.678×10^{-8} Ω m. The wire diameter, d, is commonly specified by the American wire gauge (AWG), which is an integer, n. The diameter of an AWG n wire is given by the formula

$$d = 0.127 \times 92^{\frac{36-n}{39}} \text{ mm}$$

Write a C++ function

```
double diameter(int wire_gauge)
```

that accepts the wire gauge and returns the corresponding wire diameter. Write another C++ function

```
double copper_wire_resistance(double length, int wire_gauge)
```

that accepts the length and gauge of a piece of copper wire and returns the resistance of that wire. The resistivity of aluminum is 2.82×10^{-8} Ω m. Write a third C++ function

```
double aluminum_wire_resistance(double length, int wire_gauge)
```

that accepts the length and gauge of a piece of aluminum wire and returns the resistance of that wire.

Write a C++ program to test these functions.

■■ **Engineering P5.27** The drag force on a car is given by

$$F_D = \frac{1}{2}\rho v^2 A C_D$$

where ρ is the density of air (1.23 kg/m^3), v is the velocity in units of m/s, A is the projected area of the car (2.5 m^2), and C_D is the drag coefficient (0.2).

The amount of power in watts required to overcome such drag force is $P = F_D v$, and the equivalent horsepower required is Hp $= P / 746$. Write a program that accepts a car's velocity and computes the power in watts and in horsepower needed to overcome the resulting drag force. *Note:* 1 mph = 0.447 m/s.

CHAPTER 6

ARRAYS AND VECTORS

© traveler1116/iStockphoto.

CHAPTER GOALS

To become familiar with using arrays and vectors to collect values

To learn about common algorithms for processing arrays and vectors

To write functions that process arrays and vectors

To be able to use two-dimensional arrays

CHAPTER CONTENTS

In many programs, you need to collect large numbers of values. In standard C++, you use arrays and vectors for this purpose. Arrays are a fundamental structure of the C++ language. The standard C++ library provides the vector construct as a more convenient alternative when working with collections whose size is not fixed. In this chapter, you will learn about arrays, vectors, and common algorithms for processing them.

6.1 Arrays

We start this chapter by introducing the **array** data type. Arrays are the fundamental mechanism in C++ for collecting multiple values. In the following sections, you will learn how to define arrays and how to access array elements.

6.1.1 Defining Arrays

Suppose you write a program that reads a sequence of values and prints out the sequence, marking the largest value, like this:

```
32
54
67.5
29
34.5
80
115 <= largest value
44.5
100
65
```

You do not know which value to mark as the largest one until you have seen them all. After all, the last value might be the largest one. Therefore, the program must first store all values before it can print them.

Could you simply store each value in a separate variable? If you know that there are ten inputs, then you can store the values in ten variables value1, value2, value3, ..., value10. However, such a sequence of variables is not very practical to use. You would

Figure 1　An Array of Size 10

have to write quite a bit of code ten times, once for each of the variables. To solve this problem, use an array: a structure for storing a sequence of values.

Here we define an array that can hold ten values:

```
double values[10];
```

This is the definition of a variable values whose type is "array of double". That is, values stores a sequence of floating-point numbers. The [10] indicates the *size* of the array. (See Figure 1.) The array size must be a constant that is known at compile time.

When you define an array, you can specify the initial values. For example,

```
double values[] = { 32, 54, 67.5, 29, 34.5, 80, 115, 44.5, 100, 65 };
```

When you supply initial values, you don't need to specify the array size. The compiler determines the size by counting the values.

> Use an array to collect a sequence of values of the same type.

Table 1 **Defining Arrays**

`int numbers[10];`	An array of ten integers.
`const int SIZE = 10;` `int numbers[SIZE];`	It is a good idea to use a named constant for the size.
`int size = 10;` `int numbers[size];`	**Caution:** In standard C++, the size must be a constant. This array definition will not work with all compilers.
`int squares[5] = { 0, 1, 4, 9, 16 };`	An array of five integers, with initial values.
`int squares[] = { 0, 1, 4, 9, 16 };`	You can omit the array size if you supply initial values. The size is set to the number of initial values.
`int squares[5] = { 0, 1, 4 };`	If you supply fewer initial values than the size, the remaining values are set to 0. This array contains 0, 1, 4, 0, 0.
`string names[3];`	An array of three strings.

Syntax 6.1   Defining an Array

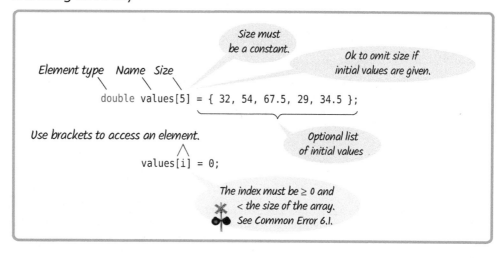

6.1.2 Accessing Array Elements

Individual elements in an array *values* are accessed by an integer index i, using the notation *values*[i].

The values stored in an array are called its **elements**. Each element has a position number, called an **index**. To access a value in the values array, you must specify which index you want to use. That is done with the [] operator:

```
values[4] = 34.5;
```

Now the element with index 4 is filled with 34.5. (See Figure 2).

```
values =                    [0]
                            [1]
                            [2]
                            [3]
                34.5        [4]
                            [5]
                            [6]
                            [7]
                            [8]
                            [9]
```

Figure 2   Filling an Array Element

You can display the contents of the element with index 4 with the following command:

```
cout << values[4] << endl;
```

An array element can be used like any variable.

As you can see, the element values[4] can be used like any variable of type double.

In C++, array positions are counted in a way that you may find surprising. If you look carefully at Figure 2, you will find that the *fifth* element was filled when we changed values[4]. In C++, the elements of arrays are numbered *starting at 0*. That is, the legal elements for the values array are

values[0], the first element

values[1], the second element

values[2], the third element

values[3], the fourth element

values[4], the fifth element

...

values[9], the tenth element

You will see in Chapter 7 why this numbering scheme was chosen in C++.

An array index must be at least zero and less than the size of the array.

You have to be careful about index values. Trying to access a element that does not exist in the array is a serious error. For example, if values has twenty elements, you are not allowed to access values[20].

Like a post office box that is identified by a box number, an array element is identified by an index.

© Luckie8/iStockphoto.

A bounds error, which occurs if you supply an invalid array index, can corrupt data or cause your program to terminate.

Attempting to access an element whose index is not within the valid index range is called a **bounds error**. The compiler does not catch this type of error. Even the running program generates *no error message*. If you make a bounds error, you silently read or overwrite another memory location. As a consequence, your program may have random errors, and it can even crash.

The most common bounds error is the following:

```cpp
double values[10];
cout << values[10];
```

There is no `values[10]` in an array with ten elements—the legal index values range from 0 to 9.

To visit all elements of an array, use a variable for the index. Suppose `values` has ten elements and the integer variable `i` takes values 0, 1, 2, and so on, up to 9. Then the expression `values[i]` yields each element in turn. For example, this loop displays all elements:

```cpp
for (int i = 0; i < 10; i++)
{
    cout << values[i] << endl;
}
```

Note that in the loop condition the index is *less than* 10 because there is no element corresponding to `values[10]`.

6.1.3 Partially Filled Arrays

An array cannot change size at run time. This is a problem when you don't know in advance how many elements you need. In that situation, you must come up with a good guess on the maximum number of elements that you need to store. We call this quantity the *capacity*. For example, we may decide that we sometimes want to store more than ten values, but never more than 100:

```cpp
const int CAPACITY = 100;
double values[CAPACITY];
```

In a typical program run, only part of the array will be occupied by actual elements. We call such an array a *partially filled array*. You must keep a *companion variable* that counts how many elements are actually used. In Figure 3 we call the companion variable `current_size`.

© Jarek Szymanski/iStockphoto.

With a partially filled array, you need to remember how many elements are filled.

Figure 3 A Partially Filled Array

The following loop collects values and fills up the `values` array.

```
int current_size = 0;
double input;
while (cin >> input)
{
   if (current_size < CAPACITY)
   {
      values[current_size] = input;
      current_size++;
   }
}
```

> With a partially filled array, keep a companion variable for the current size.

At the end of this loop, `current_size` contains the actual number of elements in the array. Note that you have to stop accepting inputs if the size of the array reaches the capacity.

To process the gathered array elements, you again use the companion variable, not the capacity. This loop prints the partially filled array:

```
for (int i = 0; i < current_size; i++)
{
   cout << values[i] << endl;
}
```

Common Error 6.1

Bounds Errors

Perhaps the most common error in using arrays is accessing a nonexistent element.

```
double values[10];
values[10] = 5.4;
   // Error—values has 10 elements with index values ranging from 0 to 9
```

If your program accesses an array through an out-of-bounds index, there is often no visible error message. Instead, the program may quietly (or not so quietly) corrupt some memory. Except for very short programs, in which the problem may go unnoticed, that corruption can make the program act unpredictably. Some C++ programming environments make an effort to report certain bounds errors, but they cannot detect them in all cases. Bounds errors are a serious issue (see also Computing & Society 6.1). You should develop the habit of scanning all array element accesses in your programs and asking yourself why they are valid.

Programming Tip 6.1

Use Arrays for Sequences of Related Values

Arrays are intended for storing sequences of values with the same meaning. For example, an array of test scores makes perfect sense:

```
int scores[NUMBER_OF_SCORES];
```

But an array

```
double personal_data[3];
```

that holds a person's age, bank balance, and shoe size in positions 0, 1, and 2 is bad design. It would be tedious for the programmer to remember which of these data values is stored in which array location. In this situation, it is far better to use three separate variables, or, as you will learn in Chapter 9, an object.

Computing & Society 6.1 **Computer Viruses**

In November 1988, Robert Morris, a student at Cornell University, launched a so-called virus program that infected a significant fraction of computers connected to the Internet (which was much smaller then than it is now). Morris was sentenced to three years probation, 400 hours of community service, and a $10,000 fine.

In order to attack a computer, a virus has to find a way to get its instructions executed. This particular program carried out a "buffer overrun" attack, providing an unexpectedly large input to a program on another machine. That program allocated an array of 512 characters, under the assumption that nobody would ever provide such a long input. Unfortunately, that program was written in the C programming language. C, like C++, does not check that an array index is less than the length of the array. If you write into an array using an index that is too large, you simply overwrite memory locations that belong to some other objects. C programmers are supposed to provide safety checks, but that had not happened in the program under attack. The virus program purposefully filled the 512-character array with 536 bytes. The excess 24 bytes overwrote a return address, which the attacker knew was stored just after the array. When the function that read the input was finished, it didn't return to its caller but to code supplied by the virus (see the figure). The virus was thus able to execute its code on a remote machine and infect it.

In recent years, computer attacks have intensified and the motives have become more sinister. Instead of disabling computers, viruses often take permanent residence in the attacked computers. Criminal enterprises rent out the processing power of millions of hijacked computers for sending spam e-mail. Other viruses monitor every keystroke and send those that look like credit card numbers or banking passwords to their master, or encrypt all disk files and demand a monetary ransom payment from the unfortunate user to unlock the files.

Typically, a machine gets infected because a user executes code downloaded from the Internet, clicking on an icon or link that purports to lead to something interesting, such as a game or video clip. Antivirus programs check all downloaded programs against an ever-growing list of known viruses.

When you use a computer for managing your finances, you need to be aware of the risk of infection. If a virus reads your banking password and empties your account, you will have a hard time convincing your financial institution that it wasn't your act, and you will most likely lose your money. It is a good idea to use banks that require "two-factor authentication" for major transactions, such as a callback on your cell phone.

Viruses are even used for military purposes. In 2010, a virus dubbed Stuxnet spread through Microsoft Windows and infected USB sticks. The virus looked for Siemens industrial computers and reprogrammed them in subtle ways. It appears that the virus was designed to damage the centrifuges of the Iranian nuclear enrichment operation. The computers controlling the centrifuges were not connected to the Internet, but they were configured with USB sticks, some of which were infected. Security researchers believe that the virus was developed by U.S. and Israeli intelligence agencies, and that it was successful in slowing down the Iranian nuclear program. Neither country has officially acknowledged or denied their role in the attacks.

1 Before the attack

Line buffer
(512 bytes)

Return address

2 After the attack

Overrun buffer
(536 bytes)

Malicious code

Return address

A "Buffer Overrun" Attack

6.2 Common Array Algorithms

In the following sections, we discuss some of the most common algorithms for processing sequences of values. We present the algorithms so that you can use them with fully and partially filled arrays as well as vectors (which we will introduce in Section 6.7). When we use the expression *size of* values, you should replace it with a constant or variable that yields the number of elements in the array (or the expression values.size() if values is a vector.)

6.2.1 Filling

This loop fills an array with zeroes:

```
for (int i = 0; i < size of values; i++)
{
   values[i] = 0;
}
```

Next, let us fill an array `squares` with the numbers 0, 1, 4, 9, 16, and so on. Note that the element with index 0 contains 0^2, the element with index 1 contains 1^2, and so on.

```
for (int i = 0; i < size of squares; i++)
{
   squares[i] = i * i;
}
```

6.2.2 Copying

Consider two arrays:

```
int squares[5] = { 0, 1, 4, 9, 16 };
int lucky_numbers[5];
```

To copy an array, use a loop to copy its elements to a new array.

Now suppose you want to copy all values from the first array to the second. The following assignment is an error:

```
lucky_numbers = squares; // Error
```

In C++, you cannot assign one array to another. Instead, you must use a loop to copy all elements:

```
for (int i = 0; i < 5; i++)
{
   lucky_numbers[i] = squares[i];
}
```

Figure 4   Copying Elements to Copy an Array

6.2.3 Sum and Average Value

You have already encountered this algorithm in Section 4.7.1. Here is the code for computing the sum of all elements in an array:

```
double total = 0;
for (int i = 0; i < size of values; i++)
{
   total = total + values[i];
}
```

To obtain the average, divide by the number of elements:

```
double average = total / size of values;
```

Be sure to check that the size is not zero.

6.2.4 Maximum and Minimum

© CEFutcher/iStockphoto.

Use the algorithm from Section 4.7.5 that keeps a variable for the largest element that you have encountered so far. Here is the implementation for arrays:

```
double largest = values[0];
for (int i = 1; i < size of values; i++)
{
   if (values[i] > largest)
   {
      largest = values[i];
   }
}
```

Note that the loop starts at 1 because we initialize largest with values[0].

To compute the smallest value, reverse the comparison.

These algorithms require that the array contain at least one element.

6.2.5 Element Separators

When separating elements, don't place a separator before the first element.

When you display the elements of a collection, you usually want to separate them, often with commas or vertical lines, like this:

```
1 | 4 | 9 | 16 | 25
```

Note that there is one fewer separator than there are numbers. Print the separator before each element *except the initial one* (with index 0):

```
for (int i = 0; i < size of values; i++)
{
   if (i > 0)
   {
      cout << " | ";
   }
   cout << values[i];
}
```

© trutenka/iStockphoto.

To print five elements, you need four separators.

6.2.6 Counting Matches

Suppose you are asked to count how many elements of an array match a certain criterion. Visit each element, test whether it is a match, and if so, increment a counter. For example, the following loop counts the number of elements that are at least 100:

```
int count = 0;
for (int i = 0; i < size of values; i++)
{
   if (values[i] >= 100)
   {
      count++;
   }
}
```

6.2.7 Linear Search

A linear search
inspects elements
in sequence until a
match is found.

© yekorzh/Getty Images.

*To search for a
specific element, visit
the elements and stop
when you encounter
the match.*

You often need to search for the position of an element so that you can replace or remove it. Visit all elements until you have found a match or you have come to the end of the array. Here we search for the position of the first element equal to 100.

```
int pos = 0;
bool found = false;
while (pos < size of values && !found)
{
    if (values[pos] == 100)
    {
        found = true;
    }
    else
    {
        pos++;
    }
}
```

If `found` is `true`, then `pos` is the position of the first match.

6.2.8 Removing an Element

Consider a partially filled array `values` whose current size is stored in the variable `current_size`. Suppose you want to remove the element with index `pos` from `values`. If the elements are not in any particular order, that task is easy to accomplish. Simply overwrite the element to be removed with the *last* element, then decrement the variable tracking the size. (See Figure 5.)

```
values[pos] = values[current_size - 1];
current_size--;
```

The situation is more complex if the order of the elements matters. Then you must move all elements following the element to be removed to a lower index, then decrement the variable holding the size of the array. (See Figure 6.)

```
for (int i = pos + 1; i < current_size; i++)
{
    values[i - 1] = values[i];
}
current_size--;
```

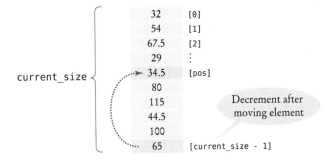

Figure 5
Removing an Element in an Unordered Array

Figure 6
Removing an Element in an Ordered Array

6.2.9 Inserting an Element

If the order of the elements does not matter, you can simply insert new elements at the end, incrementing the variable tracking the size. (See Figure 7.) For a partially filled array:

```
if (current_size < CAPACITY)
{
   current_size++;
   values[current_size - 1] = new_element;
}
```

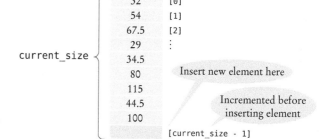

Figure 7
Inserting an Element in an
Unordered Array

> Before inserting an element, move elements to the end of the array *starting with the last one.*

It is more work to insert an element at a particular position in the middle of a sequence. First, increase the variable holding the current size. Next, move all elements above the insertion location to a higher index. Finally, insert the new element. Here is the code for a partially filled array:

```
if (current_size < CAPACITY)
{
   current_size++;
   for (int i = current_size - 1; i > pos; i--)
   {
      values[i] = values[i - 1];
   }
   values[pos] = new_element;
}
```

Note the order of the movement: When you remove an element, you first move the next element down to a lower index, then the one after that, until you finally get to the end of the array. When you insert an element, you start at the end of the array, move that element to a higher index, then move the one before that, and so on until you finally get to the insertion location (see Figure 8).

Figure 8
Inserting an Element in an
Ordered Array

6.2.10 Swapping Elements

You often need to swap elements of an array. For example, the sorting algorithm in Special Topic 6.2 sorts an array by repeatedly swapping elements.

Consider the task of swapping the elements at positions i and j of an array values. We'd like to set values[i] to values[j]. But that overwrites the value that is currently stored in values[i], so we want to save that first:

```
double temp = values[i];
values[i] = values[j];
```

Now we can set values[j] to the saved value.

```
values[j] = temp;
```

To swap two elements, you need a temporary variable.

Figure 9 shows the process.

> Use a temporary variable when swapping two elements.

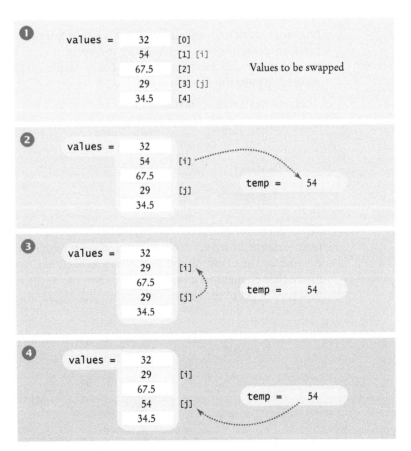

Figure 9   Swapping Array Elements

6.2.11 Reading Input

If you know how many input values the user will supply, it is simple to place them into an array:

```
double values[NUMBER_OF_INPUTS];
for (i = 0; i < NUMBER_OF_INPUTS; i++)
{
   cin >> values[i];
}
```

However, this technique does not work if you need to read an arbitrary number of inputs. In that case, add the values to an array until the end of the input has been reached.

```
double values[CAPACITY];
int current_size = 0;
double input;
while (cin >> input)
{
   if (current_size < CAPACITY)
   {
      values[current_size] = input;
      current_size++;
   }
}
```

Now values is a partially filled array, and the companion variable current_size is set to the number of input values.

This loop discards any inputs that won't fit in the array. A better approach would be to copy values to a new larger array when the capacity is reached (see Section 7.4).

The following program solves the task that we set ourselves at the beginning of this chapter, to mark the largest value in an input sequence:

sec02/largest.cpp

```
1   #include <iostream>
2
3   using namespace std;
4
5   int main()
6   {
7      const int CAPACITY = 1000;
8      double values[CAPACITY];
9      int current_size = 0;
10
11     cout << "Please enter values, Q to quit:" << endl;
12     double input;
13     while (cin >> input)
14     {
15        if (current_size < CAPACITY)
16        {
17           values[current_size] = input;
18           current_size++;
19        }
20     }
21
22     double largest = values[0];
23     for (int i = 1; i < current_size; i++)
24     {
```

```
25          if (values[i] > largest)
26          {
27             largest = values[i];
28          }
29       }
30
31       for (int i = 0; i < current_size; i++)
32       {
33          cout << values[i];
34          if (values[i] == largest)
35          {
36             cout << "  <== largest value";
37          }
38          cout << endl;
39       }
40
41       return 0;
42  }
```

Program Run

```
Please enter values, Q to quit:
34.5 80 115 44.5 Q
34.5
80
115 <== largest value
44.5
```

Special Topic 6.1

Sorting with the C++ Library

You often want to sort the elements of an array or vector. Special Topic 6.2 shows you a sorting algorithm that is relatively simple but not very efficient. Efficient sorting algorithms are significantly more complex. Fortunately, the C++ library provides an efficient sort function. To sort an array a with size elements, call

```
sort(a, a + size);
```

To sort a vector values, make this call:

```
sort(values.begin(), values.end());
```

To fully understand why the sort function is called in this way, you will need to know advanced C++ that is beyond the scope of this book. But don't hesitate to call the sort function whenever you need to sort an array or vector.

To use the sort function, include the <algorithm> header in your program.

Special Topic 6.2

A Sorting Algorithm

A *sorting algorithm* rearranges the elements of a sequence so that they are stored in sorted order. Here is a simple sorting algorithm, called **selection sort**. Consider sorting the following array values:

```
       [0] [1] [2] [3] [4]
        11  9  17   5  12
```

An obvious first step is to find the smallest element. In this case the smallest element is 5, stored in values[3]. You should move the 5 to the beginning of the array. Of course, there is already an element stored in values[0], namely 11. Therefore you cannot simply move values[3] into values[0] without moving the 11 somewhere else. You don't yet know where the 11 should end up, but you know for certain that it should not be in values[0]. Simply get it out of the way by *swapping it* with values[3]:

Now the first element is in the correct place. In the foregoing figure, the darker color indicates the portion of the array that is already sorted.

Next take the minimum of the remaining entries values[1]...values[4]. That minimum value, 9, is already in the correct place. You don't need to do anything in this case, simply extend the sorted area by one to the right:

5 9 17 11 12

Repeat the process. The minimum value of the unsorted region is 11, which needs to be swapped with the first value of the unsorted region, 17:

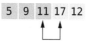

Now the unsorted region is only two elements long; keep to the same successful strategy. The minimum element is 12. Swap it with the first value, 17:

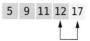

That leaves you with an unprocessed region of length 1, but of course a region of length 1 is always sorted. You are done.

Here is the C++ code:

```cpp
for (int unsorted = 0; unsorted < size - 1; unsorted++)
{
   // Find the position of the minimum
   int min_pos = unsorted;
   for (int i = unsorted + 1; i < size; i++)
   {
      if (values[i] < values[min_pos]) { min_pos = i; }
   }
   // Swap the minimum into the sorted area
   if (min_pos != unsorted)
   {
      double temp = values[min_pos];
      values[min_pos] = values[unsorted];
      values[unsorted] = temp;
   }
}
```

This algorithm is simple to understand, but it is not very efficient. Computer scientists have studied sorting algorithms extensively and discovered significantly better algorithms. The sort function of the C++ library provides one such algorithm—see Special Topic 6.1.

Special Topic 6.3
Binary Search

When an array is sorted, there is a much faster search algorithm than the linear search of Section 6.2.7.

Consider the following sorted array values:

```
[0] [1] [2] [3] [4] [5] [6] [7]
 1   5   8   9  12  17  20  32
```

We would like to see whether the value 15 is in the array. Let's narrow our search by finding whether the value is in the first or second half of the array. The last point in the first half of the data set, values[3], is 9, which is smaller than the value we are looking for. Hence, we should look in the second half of the array for a match, that is, in the sequence:

```
[0] [1] [2] [3] [4] [5] [6] [7]
 1   5   8   9  12  17  20  32
```

Now the last value of the first half of this sequence is 17; hence, the value must be located in the sequence:

```
[0] [1] [2] [3] [4] [5] [6] [7]
 1   5   8   9  12  17  20  32
```

The last value of the first half of this very short sequence is 12, which is smaller than the value that we are searching, so we must look in the second half:

```
[0] [1] [2] [3] [4] [5] [6] [7]
 1   5   8   9  12  17  20  32
```

We still don't have a match because 15 ≠ 17, and we cannot divide the subsequence further. If we wanted to insert 15 into the sequence, we would need to insert it just before values[5].

This search process is called a **binary search**, because we cut the size of the search in half in each step. That cutting in half works only because we know that the sequence of values is sorted. Here is an implementation in C++:

```cpp
bool found = false;
int low = 0;
int high = size - 1;
int pos = 0;
while (low <= high && !found)
{
   pos = (low + high) / 2; // Midpoint of the subsequence
   if (values[pos] == searched_value) { found = true; }
   else if (values[pos] < searched_value) { low = pos + 1; } // Look in second half
   else { high = pos - 1; } // Look in first half
}
if (found) { cout << "Found at position " << pos; }
else { cout << "Not found. Insert before position " << pos; }
```

6.3 Arrays and Functions

In this section, we will explore how to write functions that process arrays.

A function that processes the values in an array needs to know the number of valid elements in the array. For example, here is a sum function that computes the sum of all elements in an array:

When passing an array to a function, also pass the size of the array.

```cpp
double sum(double values[], int size)
{
   double total = 0;
   for (int i = 0; i < size; i++)
   {
```

```
            total = total + values[i];
         }
         return total;
      }
```

Note the special syntax for array parameter variables. When writing an array parameter variable, you place an empty [] behind the parameter name. Do not specify the size of the array inside the brackets.

When you call the function, supply both the name of the array and the size. For example,

```
const int NUMBER_OF_SCORES = 10;
double scores[NUMBER_OF_SCORES]
   = { 32, 54, 67.5, 29, 34.5, 80, 115, 44.5, 100, 65 };
double total_score = sum(scores, NUMBER_OF_SCORES);
```

You can also pass a smaller size to the function:

```
double partial_score = sum(scores, 5);
```

This call computes the sum of the first five elements of the scores array. Remember, the function has no way of knowing how many elements the array has. It simply relies on the size that the caller provides.

Array parameters are always reference parameters. (You will see the reason in Chapter 7.) Functions can modify array arguments, and those modifications affect the array that was passed into the function. For example, the following multiply function updates all elements in the array:

```
void multiply(double values[], int size, double factor)
{
   for (int i = 0; i < size; i++)
   {
      values[i] = values[i] * factor;
   }
}
```

> **Array parameters are always reference parameters.**

You do *not* use an & symbol to denote the reference parameter in this case.

Although arrays can be function arguments, they cannot be function return types. If a function computes multiple values, the caller of the function must provide an array parameter variable to hold the result.

> **A function's return type cannot be an array.**

```
void squares(int n, int result[])
{
   for (int i = 0; i < n; i++)
   {
      result[i] = i * i;
   }
}
```

When a function changes the size of an array, it should indicate to the caller how many elements the array has after the call. The easiest way to do this is to return the new size. Here is an example—a function that adds input values to an array:

> **When a function modifies the size of an array, it needs to tell its caller.**

```
int read_inputs(double inputs[], int capacity)
{
   int current_size = 0;
   double input;
   while (cin >> input)
   {
      if (current_size < capacity)
      {
```

```
                inputs[current_size] = input;
                current_size++;
            }
        }
        return current_size;
    }
```

Note that this function also needs to know the capacity of the array. Generally, a function that adds elements to an array needs to know its capacity. You would call this function like this:

```
const int MAXIMUM_NUMBER_OF_VALUES = 1000;
double values[MAXIMUM_NUMBER_OF_VALUES];
int current_size = read_inputs(values, MAXIMUM_NUMBER_OF_VALUES);
    // values is a partially filled array; the current_size variable specifies its size
```

Alternatively, you can pass the size as a reference parameter. This is more appropriate for functions that modify an existing array:

```
void append_inputs(double inputs[], int capacity, int& current_size)
{
    double input;
    while (cin >> input)
    {
        if (current_size < capacity)
        {
            inputs[current_size] = input;
            current_size++;
        }
    }
}
```

This function is called as

```
append_inputs(values, MAXIMUM_NUMBER_OF_VALUES, current_size);
```

After the call, the current_size variable contains the new size.

The following example program reads values from standard input, doubles them, and prints the result. The program uses three functions:

- The read_inputs function fills an array with the input values. It returns the number of elements that were read.
- The multiply function modifies the contents of the array that it receives, demonstrating that arrays are passed by reference.
- The print function does not modify the contents of the array that it receives.

sec03/functions.cpp

```
 1  #include <iostream>
 2
 3  using namespace std;
 4
 5  /**
 6      Reads a sequence of floating-point numbers.
 7      @param inputs an array containing the numbers
 8      @param capacity the capacity of that array
 9      @return the number of inputs stored in the array
10  */
11  int read_inputs(double inputs[], int capacity)
12  {
```

```
13    int current_size = 0;
14    cout << "Please enter values, Q to quit:" << endl;
15    bool more = true;
16    while (more)
17    {
18       double input;
19       cin >> input;
20       if (cin.fail())
21       {
22          more = false;
23       }
24       else if (current_size < capacity)
25       {
26          inputs[current_size] = input;
27          current_size++;
28       }
29    }
30    return current_size;
31 }
32
33 /**
34    Multiplies all elements of an array by a factor.
35    @param values a partially filled array
36    @param size the number of elements in values
37    @param factor the value with which each element is multiplied
38 */
39 void multiply(double values[], int size, double factor)
40 {
41    for (int i = 0; i < size; i++)
42    {
43       values[i] = values[i] * factor;
44    }
45 }
46
47 /**
48    Prints the elements of a vector, separated by commas.
49    @param values a partially filled array
50    @param size the number of elements in values
51 */
52 void print(double values[], int size)
53 {
54    for (int i = 0; i < size; i++)
55    {
56       if (i > 0) { cout << ", "; }
57       cout << values[i];
58    }
59    cout << endl;
60 }
61
62 int main()
63 {
64    const int CAPACITY = 1000;
65    double values[CAPACITY];
66    int size = read_inputs(values, CAPACITY);
67    multiply(values, size, 2);
68    print(values, size);
69
70    return 0;
71 }
```

Program Run

```
Please enter values, Q to quit:
12 25 20 Q
24, 50, 40
```

Special Topic 6.4

Constant Array Parameters

When a function doesn't modify an array parameter, it is considered good style to add the const reserved word, like this:

```
double sum(const double values[], int size)
```

The const reserved word helps the reader of the code, making it clear that the function keeps the array elements unchanged. If the implementation of the function tries to modify the array, the compiler issues a warning.

6.4 Problem Solving: Adapting Algorithms

By combining fundamental algorithms, you can solve complex programming tasks.

In Section 6.2, you were introduced to a number of fundamental array algorithms. These algorithms form the building blocks for many programs that process arrays. In general, it is a good problem-solving strategy to have a repertoire of fundamental algorithms that you can combine and adapt.

Consider this example problem: You are given the quiz scores of a student. You are to compute the final quiz score, which is the sum of all scores after dropping the lowest one. For example, if the scores are

```
8   7   8.5   9.5   7   4   10
```

then the final score is 50.

We do not have a ready-made algorithm for this situation. Instead, consider which algorithms may be related. These include:

- Calculating the sum (Section 6.2.3)
- Finding the minimum value (Section 6.2.4)
- Removing an element (Section 6.2.8)

Now we can formulate a plan of attack that combines these algorithms.

Find the minimum.
Remove the minimum from the array.
Calculate the sum.

Let's try it out with our example. The minimum of

[0]	[1]	[2]	[3]	[4]	[5]	[6]
8	7	8.5	9.5	7	4	10

is 4. How do we remove it?

Now we have a problem. The removal algorithm in Section 6.2.8 locates the element to be removed by using the *position* of the element, not the value.

But we have another algorithm for that:

- Linear search (Section 6.2.7)

We need to fix our plan of attack:

Find the minimum value.
Find the position of the minimum.
Remove the element at the position from the array.
Calculate the sum.

Will it work? Let's continue with our example.

We found a minimum value of 4. Linear search tells us that the value 4 occurs at position 5.

```
    [0] [1] [2] [3] [4] [5] [6]
     8   7  8.5 9.5  7   4  10
```

We remove it:

```
    [0] [1] [2] [3] [4] [5]
     8   7  8.5 9.5  7  10
```

Finally, we compute the sum: 8 + 7 + 8.5 + 9.5 + 7 + 10 = 50.

This walkthrough demonstrates that our strategy works.

Can we do better? It seems a bit inefficient to find the minimum and then make another pass through the array to obtain its position.

We can adapt the algorithm for finding the minimum to yield the position of the minimum. Here is the original algorithm:

You should be familiar with the implementation of fundamental algorithms so that you can adapt them.

```
double smallest = values[0];
for (int i = 1; i < size of values; i++)
{
   if (values[i] < smallest)
   {
      smallest = values[i];
   }
}
```

When we find the smallest value, we also want to update the position:

```
if (values[i] < smallest)
{
   smallest = values[i];
   smallest_position = i;
}
```

In fact, then there is no reason to keep track of the smallest value any longer. It is simply values[smallest_position]. With this insight, we can adapt the algorithm as follows:

```
int smallest_position = 0;
for (int i = 1; i < size of values; i++)
{
   if (values[i] < values[smallest_position])
   {
      smallest_position = i;
   }
}
```

With this adaptation, our problem is solved with the following strategy:

Find the position of the minimum.
Remove the element at the position from the array.
Calculate the sum.

EXAMPLE CODE See sec04 of your companion code for a program that implements this strategy. How To 6.1 shows an alternate approach that does not modify the array.

The next section shows you a technique for discovering a new algorithm when none of the fundamental algorithms can be adapted to a task.

HOW TO 6.1

Working with Arrays

In many data processing situations, you need to process a sequence of values. This How To walks you through the steps for storing input values in an array and carrying out computations with the array elements.

Problem Statement Consider again the problem from Section 6.4: A final quiz score is computed by adding all the scores, except for the lowest one. For example, if the scores are

8 7 8.5 9.5 7 5 10

then the final score is 50.

Thierry Dosogne/The Image Bank/Getty Images, Inc.

Step 1   Decompose your task into steps.

You will usually want to break down your task into multiple steps, such as

- Reading the data into an array.
- Processing the data in one or more steps.
- Displaying the results.

When deciding how to process the data, you should be familiar with the array algorithms in Section 6.2. Most processing tasks can be solved by using one or more of these algorithms.

In our sample problem, we will want to read the data. Then we will remove the minimum and compute the total. For example, if the input is 8 7 8.5 9.5 7 5 10, we will remove the minimum of 5, yielding 8 7 8.5 9.5 7 10. The sum of those values is the final score of 50.

Thus, we have identified three steps:

Read inputs.
Remove the minimum.
Calculate the sum.

Step 2   Determine which algorithm(s) you need.

Sometimes, a step corresponds to exactly one of the basic array algorithms in Section 6.2. That is the case with calculating the sum (Section 6.2.3) and reading the inputs (Section 6.2.11). At other times, you need to combine several algorithms. To remove the minimum value, you can find the minimum value (Section 6.2.4), find its position (Section 6.2.7), and remove the element at that position (Section 6.2.8).

We have now refined our plan as follows:

Read inputs.
Find the minimum.
Find the position of the minimum.
Remove the element at the position.
Calculate the sum.

This plan will work—see Section 6.4. But here is an alternate approach. It is easy to compute the sum and subtract the minimum. Then we don't have to find its position. The revised plan is

Read inputs.
Find the minimum.
Calculate the sum.
Subtract the minimum from the sum.

Step 3   Use functions to structure the program.

Even though it may be possible to put all steps into the main function, this is rarely a good idea. It is better to make each processing step into a separate function. In our example, we will implement three functions:

- `read_inputs`
- `sum`
- `minimum`

The main function simply calls these functions:

```
const int CAPACITY = 1000;
double scores[CAPACITY];
int scores_size = read_inputs(scores, CAPACITY);
double total = sum(scores, scores_size) - minimum(scores, scores_size);
```

For each function that processes an array, you will need to pass the array itself and the array size. For example,

```
double sum(double values[], int size)
```

If the function modifies the size, it needs to tell the caller what the new size is. The function reading inputs returns the new size:

```
int read_inputs(double inputs[], int capacity) // Returns the size
```

Step 4   Assemble and test the program.

Combine your functions into a program. Review your code and check that you handle both normal and exceptional situations. What happens with an empty array? One that contains a single element? When no match is found? When there are multiple matches? Consider these boundary conditions and make sure that your program works correctly.

In our example, it is impossible to compute the minimum if the array is empty. In that case, we should terminate the program with an error message *before* attempting to call the minimum function.

What if the minimum value occurs more than once? That means that a student had more than one test with the same low score. We subtract only one of the occurrences of that low score, and that is the desired behavior.

The following table shows test cases and their expected output:

Test Case	Expected Output	Comment
8 7 8.5 9.5 7 5 10	50	See Step 1.
8 7 7 9	24	Only one instance of the low score should be removed.
8	0	After removing the low score, no score remains.
(no inputs)	**Error**	That is not a legal input.

This main function completes the solution. Here is the complete program:

how_to_1/scores.cpp

```cpp
1  #include <iostream>
2
3  using namespace std;
4
5  /**
6      Reads a sequence of floating-point numbers.
7      @param inputs an array containing the numbers
8      @param capacity the capacity of that array
9      @return the number of inputs stored in the array
10 */
11 int read_inputs(double inputs[], int capacity)
12 {
13     int current_size = 0;
14     cout << "Please enter values, Q to quit:" << endl;
15     bool done = false;
16     while (!done)
17     {
18         double input;
19         cin >> input;
20         if (cin.fail())
21         {
22             done = true;
23         }
24         else if (current_size < capacity)
25         {
26             inputs[current_size] = input;
27             current_size++;
28         }
29     }
30     return current_size;
31 }
32
33 /**
34     Gets the minimum value from an array.
35     @param values a partially filled array of size >= 1
36     @param size the number of elements in values
37     @return the smallest element in values
38 */
39 double minimum(double values[], int size)
40 {
41     double smallest = values[0];
42     for (int i = 1; i < size; i++)
43     {
44         if (values[i] < smallest)
45         {
46             smallest = values;
47         }
48     }
49     return smallest;
50 }
51
52 /**
53     Computes the sum of the elements in an array.
54     @param values a partially filled array
55     @param size the number of elements in values
56     @return the sum of the elements in values
57 */
```

```
58  double sum(double values[], int size)
59  {
60     double total = 0;
61     for (int i = 0; i < size; i++)
62     {
63        total = total + values[i];
64     }
65     return total;
66  }
67
68  int main()
69  {
70     const int CAPACITY = 1000;
71     double scores[CAPACITY];
72     int size = read_inputs(scores, CAPACITY);
73     if (size == 0)
74     {
75        cout << "At least one score is required." << endl;
76     }
77     else
78     {
79        double final_score = sum(scores, size) - minimum(scores, size);
80        cout << "Final score: " << final_score << endl;
81     }
82     return 0;
83  }
```

EXAMPLE CODE   See how_to_1/scores_vector in your companion code for a solution using vectors instead of arrays.

WORKED EXAMPLE 6.1

Rolling the Dice

Learn how to analyze a set of die tosses to see whether the die is "fair". See your E-Text or visit wiley.com/go/bclo3.

© ktsimage/iStockphoto.

6.5 Problem Solving: Discovering Algorithms by Manipulating Physical Objects

In Section 6.4, you saw how to solve a problem by combining and adapting known algorithms. But what do you do when none of the standard algorithms is sufficient for your task? In this section, you will learn a technique for discovering algorithms by manipulating physical objects.

Consider the following task. You are given an array whose size is an even number, and you are to switch the first and the second half. For example, if the array contains the eight numbers

| 9 | 13 | 21 | 4 | 11 | 7 | 1 | 3 |

then you should change it to

| 11 | 7 | 1 | 3 | 9 | 13 | 21 | 4 |

Many students find it quite challenging to come up with an algorithm. They may know that a loop is required, and they may realize that elements should be inserted (Section 6.2.9) or swapped (Section 6.2.10), but they do not have sufficient intuition to draw diagrams, describe an algorithm, or write down pseudocode.

One useful technique for discovering an algorithm is to manipulate physical objects. Start by lining up some objects to denote an array. Coins, playing cards, or small toys are good choices.

Here we arrange eight coins.

© JenCon/iStockphoto.

Manipulating physical objects can give you ideas for discovering algorithms.

Use a sequence of coins, playing cards, or toys to visualize an array of values.

coins: © jamesbenet/iStockphoto; dollar coins: © JordiDelgado/iStockphoto.

Now let's step back and see what we can do to change the order of the coins. We can remove a coin (Section 6.2.8):

Visualizing the removal of an array element

We can insert a coin (Section 6.2.9):

Visualizing the insertion of an array element

Or we can swap two coins (Section 6.2.10).

Visualizing the swapping of two coins

Go ahead—line up some coins and try out these three operations right now so that you get a feel for them.

Now how does that help us with our problem, switching the first and the second half of the array?

Let's put the first coin into place, by swapping it with the fifth coin. However, as C++ programmers, we will say that we swap the coins in positions 0 and 4:

Next, we swap the coins in positions 1 and 5:

Two more swaps, and we are done:

Now an algorithm is becoming apparent:

```
i = 0
j = ... // We'll think about that in a minute
While // Don't know yet
    Swap elements at positions i and j.
    i++
    j++
```

Where does the variable *j* start? When we have eight coins, the coin at position zero is moved to position 4. In general, it is moved to the middle of the array, or to position *size / 2*.

And how many iterations do we make? We need to swap all coins in the first half. That is, we need to swap *size / 2* coins. The pseudocode is

```
i = 0
j = size / 2
While i < size / 2
    Swap elements at positions i and j.
    i++
    j++
```

You can use paper clips as position markers or counters.

It is a good idea to make a walkthrough of the pseudocode (see Section 4.2). You can use paper clips to denote the positions of the variables *i* and *j*. If the walkthrough is successful, then we know that there was no "off-by-one" error in the pseudocode. Exercise E6.6 asks you to translate the pseudocode to C++. Exercise R6.19 suggests a different algorithm for switching the two halves of an array, by repeatedly removing and inserting coins.

Many people find that the manipulation of physical objects is less intimidating than drawing diagrams or mentally envisioning algorithms. Give it a try when you need to design a new algorithm!

6.6 Two-Dimensional Arrays

It often happens that you want to store collections of values that have a two-dimensional layout. Such data sets commonly occur in financial and scientific applications. An arrangement consisting of rows and columns of values is called a **two-dimensional array**, or a *matrix*.

Let's explore how to store the example data shown in Figure 10: the medal counts of the figure skating competitions at the 2014 Winter Olympics.

© Trub/iStockphoto.

© technotr/iStockphoto.

	Gold	Silver	Bronze
Canada	0	3	0
Italy	0	0	1
Germany	0	0	1
Japan	1	0	0
Kazakhstan	0	0	1
Russia	3	1	1
South Korea	0	1	0
United States	1	0	1

Figure 10   Figure Skating Medal Counts

6.6.1 Defining Two-Dimensional Arrays

Use a two-dimensional array to store tabular data.

C++ uses an array with row and column index values to store a two-dimensional array. For example, here is the definition of an array with 8 rows and 3 columns, suitable for storing our medal count data:

```
const int COUNTRIES = 8;
const int MEDALS = 3;
int counts[COUNTRIES][MEDALS];
```

You can initialize the array by grouping each row, as follows:

```
int counts[COUNTRIES][MEDALS] =
   {
      { 0, 3, 0 },
      { 0, 0, 1 },
      { 0, 0, 1 },
      { 1, 0, 0 },
      { 0, 0, 1 },
      { 3, 1, 1 },
      { 0, 1, 0 }
      { 1, 0, 1 }
   };
```

Just as with one-dimensional arrays, you cannot change the size of a two-dimensional array once it has been defined.

Syntax 6.2   **Two-Dimensional Array Definition**

6.6.2 Accessing Elements

Individual elements in a two-dimensional array are accessed by using two index values, *array*[i][j].

To access a particular element in the two-dimensional array, you need to specify two index values in separate brackets to select the row and column, respectively (see Syntax 6.2 and Figure 11):

```
int value = counts[3][1];
```

Figure 11
Accessing an Element in a Two-Dimensional Array

To access all values in a two-dimensional array, you use two nested loops. For example, the following loop prints all elements of counts.

```
for (int i = 0; i < COUNTRIES; i++)
{
   // Process the ith row
   for (int j = 0; j < MEDALS; j++)
   {
      // Process the jth column in the ith row
      cout << setw(8) << counts[i][j];
   }
   cout << endl; // Start a new line at the end of the row
}
```

6.6.3 Locating Neighboring Elements

Some programs that work with two-dimensional arrays need to locate the elements that are adjacent to an element. This task is particularly common in games. Figure 12 shows how to compute the index values of the neighbors of an element.

For example, the neighbors of counts[3][1] to the left and right are counts[3][0] and counts[3][2]. The neighbors to the top and bottom are counts[2][1] and counts[4][1].

You need to be careful about computing neighbors at the boundary of the array. For example, counts[0][1] has no neighbor to the top. Consider the task of computing the sum of the neighbors to the top and bottom of the element count[i][j]. You need to check whether the element is located at the top or bottom of the array:

```
int total = 0;
if (i > 0) { total = total + counts[i - 1][j]; }
if (i < ROWS - 1) { total = total + counts[i + 1][j]; }
```

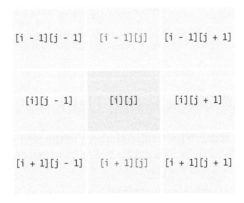

Figure 12　Neighboring Locations in a Two-Dimensional Array

6.6.4 Computing Row and Column Totals

A common task is to compute row or column totals. In our example, the row totals give us the total number of medals won by a particular country.

Finding the right index values is a bit tricky, and it is a good idea to make a quick sketch. To compute the total of row i, we need to visit the following elements:

As you can see, we need to compute the sum of counts[i][j], where j ranges from 0 to MEDALS - 1. The following loop computes the total:

```
int total = 0;
for (int j = 0; j < MEDALS; j++)
{
    total = total + counts[i][j];
}
```

Computing column totals is similar. Form the sum of counts[i][j], where i ranges from 0 to COUNTRIES - 1.

```
int total = 0;
for (int i = 0; i < COUNTRIES; i++)
{
    total = total + counts[i][j];
}
```

6.6.5 Two-Dimensional Array Parameters

A two-dimensional array parameter must have a fixed number of columns.

When defining a function with a two-dimensional array parameter, you must specify the number of columns *as a constant* with the parameter type. For example, this function computes the total of a given row:

```
const int COLUMNS = 3;

int row_total(int table[][COLUMNS], int row)
{
   int total = 0;
   for (int j = 0; j < COLUMNS; j++)
   {
      total = total + table[row][j];
   }
   return total;
}
```

This function can compute row totals of a two-dimensional array with an arbitrary number of rows, but the array must have 3 columns. You have to write a different function if you want to compute row totals of a two-dimensional array with 4 columns.

To understand this limitation, you need to know how the array elements are stored in memory. Although the array appears to be two-dimensional, the elements are still stored as a linear sequence. Figure 13 shows how the counts array is stored, row by row.

Figure 13   A Two-Dimensional Array is Stored as a Sequence of Rows

For example, to reach

```
counts[3][1]
```

the program must first skip past rows 0, 1, and 2 and then locate offset 1 in row 3. The offset from the start of the array is

$$3 \times \textit{number of columns} + 1$$

Now consider the row_total function. The compiler generates code to find the element

```
table[i][j]
```

by computing the offset

```
i * COLUMNS + j
```

The compiler uses the value that you supplied in the second pair of brackets when declaring the parameter:

```
int row_total(int table[][COLUMNS], int row)
```

Note that the first pair of brackets should be empty, just as with one-dimensional arrays.

The `row_total` function did not need to know the number of rows of the array. If the number of rows is required, pass it as a variable, as in this example:

```cpp
int column_total(int table[][COLUMNS], int rows, int column)
{
   int total = 0;
   for (int i = 0; i < rows; i++)
   {
      total = total + table[i][column];
   }
   return total;
}
```

Working with two-dimensional arrays is illustrated in the following program. The program prints out the medal counts and the row totals.

sec06/medals.cpp

```cpp
1  #include <iostream>
2  #include <iomanip>
3  #include <string>
4
5  using namespace std;
6
7  const int COLUMNS = 3;
8
9  /**
10    Computes the total of a row in a table.
11    @param table a table with 3 columns
12    @param row the row that needs to be totaled
13    @return the sum of all elements in the given row
14  */
15  double row_total(int table[][COLUMNS], int row)
16  {
17     int total = 0;
18     for (int j = 0; j < COLUMNS; j++)
19     {
20        total = total + table[row][j];
21     }
22     return total;
23  }
24
25  int main()
26  {
27     const int COUNTRIES = 8;
28     const int MEDALS = 3;
29
30     string countries[] =
31        {
32           "Canada",
33           "Italy",
34           "Germany",
35           "Japan",
36           "Kazakhstan",
37           "Russia",
38           "South Korea",
39           "United States"
40        };
41
```

```
42    int counts[COUNTRIES][MEDALS] =
43    {
44       { 0, 3, 0 },
45       { 0, 0, 1 },
46       { 0, 0, 1 },
47       { 1, 0, 0 },
48       { 0, 0, 1 },
49       { 3, 1, 1 },
50       { 0, 1, 0 },
51       { 1, 0, 1 }
52    };
53
54    cout << "        Country    Gold  Silver  Bronze   Total" << endl;
55
56    // Print countries, counts, and row totals
57    for (int i = 0; i < COUNTRIES; i++)
58    {
59       cout << setw(15) << countries[i];
60       // Process the ith row
61       for (int j = 0; j < MEDALS; j++)
62       {
63          cout << setw(8) << counts[i][j];
64       }
65       int total = row_total(counts, i);
66       cout << setw(8) << total << endl;
67    }
68
69    return 0;
70 }
```

Program Run

Country	Gold	Silver	Bronze	Total
Canada	0	3	0	3
Italy	0	0	1	1
Germany	0	0	1	1
Japan	1	0	0	1
Kazakhstan	0	0	1	1
Russia	3	1	1	5
South Korea	0	1	0	1
United States	1	0	1	2

Common Error 6.2

Omitting the Column Size of a Two-Dimensional Array Parameter

When passing a one-dimensional array to a function, you specify the size of the array as a separate parameter variable:

```
void print(double values[], int size)
```

This function can print arrays of any size. However, for two-dimensional arrays you cannot simply pass the numbers of rows and columns as parameter variables:

```
void print(double table[][], int rows, int cols) // NO!
```

The function must know *at compile time* how many columns the two-dimensional array has. You must specify the number of columns with the array parameter variable. This number must be a constant:

```
const int COLUMNS = 3;
void print(const double table[][COLUMNS], int rows) // OK
```

This function can print tables with any number of rows, but the column size is fixed.

WORKED EXAMPLE 6.2

A World Population Table

Learn how to print world population data in a table with row and column headers, and with totals for each of the data columns. See your E-Text or visit wiley.com/go/bclo3.

6.7 Vectors

A vector stores a sequence of values whose size can change.

When you write a program that collects values from user input, you don't always know how many values you will have. Unfortunately, the size of the array has to be known *when the program is compiled*.

In Section 6.1.3, you saw how you can address this problem with partially filled arrays. The **vector** construct, which we discuss in the following sections, offers a more convenient solution. A vector collects a sequence of values, just like an array does, but its size can change.

© Michael Brake/iStockphoto.

A vector expands to hold as many elements as needed.

Syntax 6.3   Defining a Vector

```
                Element type    Name  Initial size
                       /         /      /
              vector<double> values(10);
```
If you omit the size and the parentheses, the vector has initial size 0.

```
              vector<double> values = { 32, 54, 67.5, 29, 34.5 };
```
If you specify initial values, you don't provide the size.

Use brackets to access an element.
```
                        values[i] = 0;
```
The index must be ≥ 0 and < values.size().

6.7.1 Defining Vectors

When you define a vector, you specify the type of the elements in angle brackets, like this:

```
vector<double> values;
```

You can optionally specify the initial size. For example, here is a definition of a vector whose initial size is 10:

```
vector<double> values(10);
```

If you define a vector without an initial size, it has size 0. While there would be no point in defining an array of size zero, it is often useful to have vectors with *initial* size zero, and then grow them as needed.

With C++ 11 and above, you can specify initial values for a vector, using the same notation as for arrays:

```
vector<double> values = { 32, 54, 67.5, 29, 34.5 };
```

In order to use vectors in your program, you need to include the `<vector>` header.

You access the vector elements as `values[i]`, just as you do with arrays.

The `size` member function returns the current size of a vector. In a loop that visits all vector elements, use the `size` member function like this:

> Use the size member function to obtain the current size of a vector.

```
for (int i = 0; i < values.size(); i++)
{
    cout << values[i] << endl;
}
```

Table 2 **Defining Vectors**	
`vector<int> numbers(10);`	A vector of ten integers.
`vector<string> names(3);`	A vector of three strings.
`vector<double> values;`	A vector of size 0.
`vector<double> values();`	**Error:** Does not define a vector; it declares a function returning a vector.

`vector<int> numbers;`
`for (int i = 1; i <= 10; i++)`
`{`
`    numbers.push_back(i);`
`}`
	A vector of ten integers, filled with 1, 2, 3, ..., 10.

`vector<int> numbers(10);`
`for (int i = 0; i < numbers.size(); i++)`
`{`
`    numbers[i] = i + 1;`
`}`
	Another way of defining a vector of ten integers and filling it with 1, 2, 3, ..., 10.

`vector<int> numbers =` `    { 1, 2, 3, 4, 5, 6, 7, 8, 9, 10 };`	This syntax is supported with C++ 11 and above.

6.7.2 Growing and Shrinking Vectors

If you need additional elements, you use the push_back function to add an element to
the end of the vector, thereby increasing its size by 1. The push_back function is a member function that you must call with the dot notation, like this:

```
values.push_back(37.5);
```

Suppose the vector values had size 2 and elements 32 and 54 before the call to push_back
(see Figure 14). After the call, the vector has size 3, and values[2] contains the value
37.5.

Figure 14   Adding an Element with push_back

A common use for the push_back member function is to fill a vector with input values.

```
vector<double> values;   // Initially empty

double input;
while (cin >> input)
{
   values.push_back(input);
}
```

Note how this input loop is *much* simpler than the one in Section 6.2.11.

Another member function, pop_back, removes the last element of a vector, shrink-
ing its size by one (see Figure 15):

```
values.pop_back();
```

❶ Before pop_back

```
values =    32
            54
            37.5
```
} 3

This element
to be removed

❷ After pop_back   Size decreased

```
values =    32
            54
```
} 2

Figure 15   Removing an Element with pop_back

6.7.3 Vectors and Functions

Vectors can occur as function arguments and return values.

You can use vectors as function arguments in exactly the same way as any other values. For example, the following function computes the sum of a vector of floating-point numbers:

```
double sum(vector<double> values)
{
   double total = 0;
   for (int i = 0; i < values.size(); i++)
   {
      total = total + values[i];
   }
   return total;
}
```

Use a reference parameter to modify the contents of a vector.

This function visits the vector elements, but it does not modify them. If your function modifies the elements, use a reference parameter. The following function multiplies all values of a vector with a given factor.

```
void multiply(vector<double>& values, double factor) // Note the &
{
   for (int i = 0; i < values.size(); i++)
   {
      values[i] = values[i] * factor;
   }
}
```

It is a good idea to use a constant reference (see Special Topic 5.2) for vector parameters that are not modified, for example:

```
double sum(const vector<double>& values) // const & added for efficiency
```

A function can return a vector.

A function can return a vector. Again, vectors are no different from any other values in this regard. Simply build up the result in the function and return it. In this example, the squares function returns a vector of squares from 0^2 up to $(n-1)^2$:

```
vector<int> squares(int n)
{
   vector<int> result;
   for (int i = 0; i < n; i++)
   {
      result.push_back(i * i);
   }
   return result;
}
```

As you can see, it is easy to use vectors with functions—there are no special rules to keep in mind.

EXAMPLE CODE   See sec07_03 of your companion code for a program that demonstrates vectors and functions.

6.7.4 Vector Algorithms

Most of the algorithms in Section 6.2 apply without change to vectors—simply replace *size of* values with values.size(). In this section, we discuss which of the algorithms are different for vectors.

Copying

As discussed in Section 6.2.2, you need an explicit loop to make a copy of an array. It is much easier to make a copy of a vector. You simply assign it to another vector. Consider this example:

```
vector<int> squares;
for (int i = 0; i < 5; i++) { squares.push_back(i * i); }
vector<int> lucky_numbers; // Initially empty
lucky_numbers = squares; // Now lucky_numbers contains the same elements as squares
```

Finding Matches

Section 6.2.7 shows you how to find the first match, but sometimes you want to have all matches. This is tedious with arrays, but simple using a vector that collects the matches. Here we collect all elements that are greater than 100:

```
vector<double> matches;
for (int i = 0; i < values.size(); i++)
{
   if (values[i] > 100)
   {
      matches.push_back(values[i]);
   }
}
```

Removing an Element

When you remove an element from a vector, you want to adjust the size of the vector by calling the pop_back member function. Here is the code for removing an element at [pos] when the order doesn't matter.

```
int last_pos = values.size() - 1;
values[pos] = values[last_pos]; // Replace element at pos with last element
values.pop_back(); // Delete last element
```

When removing an element from an ordered vector, first move the elements, then reduce the size:

```
for (int i = pos + 1; i < values.size(); i++)
{
   values[i - 1] = values[i];
}
values.pop_back();
```

Inserting an Element

Inserting an element at the end of a vector requires no special code. Simply use the push_back member function.

When you insert an element in the middle, you still want to call push_back so that the size of the vector is increased. Use the following code:

```
int last_pos = values.size() - 1;
values.push_back(values[last_pos]);
for (int i = last_pos; i > pos; i--)
{
   values[i] = values[i - 1];
}
values[pos] = new_element;
```

EXAMPLE CODE See sec07_04 of your companion code for a program that uses vectors to solve the problem posed in Section 6.1.

6.7.5 Two-Dimensional Vectors

There are no two-dimensional vectors, but if you want to store rows and columns, you can use a vector of vectors. For example, the medal counts of Section 6.6 can be stored in this variable:

```
vector<vector<int>> counts;
```

Think of counts as a vector of rows. Each row is a vector<int>.

You need to initialize such a vector of vectors, to make sure there are rows and columns for all the elements.

```
for (int i = 0; i < COUNTRIES; i++)
{
    vector<int> row(MEDALS);
    counts.push_back(row);
}
```

Now you can simply access counts[i][j] in the same way as with two-dimensional arrays. The expression counts[i] denotes the ith row, and counts[i][j] is the value in the jth column of that row.

Vectors of vectors have an advantage over two-dimensional arrays. The row and column sizes don't have to be fixed at compile time. Suppose you don't know the number of countries and medal types at the outset. You can still construct the table of counts:

```
int countries = . . .;
int medals = . . .;
vector<vector<int>> counts;
for (int i = 0; i < countries; i++)
{
    vector<int> row(medals);
    counts.push_back(row);
}
```

In contrast, you would not be able to declare an array int[countries][medals] because the bounds are not constant.

When you process a vector of vectors, you find the number of rows and columns like this:

```
vector<vector<int>> values = . . .;
int rows = values.size();
int columns = values[0].size();
```

Remember that each element of values is a row. Therefore, values.size() is the number of rows. The size of any one of the rows gives you the number of columns.

It is also possible to declare vectors of vectors in which the row size varies. For example, to achieve a triangular shape, such as

```
t[0][0]
t[1][0] t[1][1]
t[2][0] t[2][1] t[2][2]
t[3][0] t[3][1] t[3][2] t[3][3]
```

you add rows of the appropriate sizes, like this:

```
vector<vector<int>> t;
for (int i = 0; i < 3; i++)
{
    vector<int> row(i + 1);
    t.push_back(row);
```

```
}
```

You still access each array element as t[i][j]. The expression t[i] selects the ith row, and the [j] operator selects the jth element in that row.

Programming Tip 6.2
Prefer Vectors over Arrays

For most programming tasks, vectors are easier to use than arrays. Vectors can grow and shrink. Even if a vector always stays the same size, it is convenient that a vector remembers its size. For a beginner, the sole advantage of an array is the initialization syntax. Advanced programmers sometimes prefer arrays because they are a bit more efficient. Moreover, you need to know how to use arrays if you work with older programs.

Special Topic 6.5
The Range-Based for Loop

C++ 11 introduces a convenient syntax for visiting all elements in a "range" or sequence of elements. This loop displays all elements in a vector:

```
vector<int> values = {1, 4, 9, 16, 25, 36};
for (int v : values)
{
    cout << v << " ";
}
```

In each iteration of the loop, v is set to an element of the vector. Note that you do not use an index variable. The value of v is the element, not the index of the element.

If you want to modify elements, declare the loop variable as a reference:

```
for (int& v : values)
{
    v++;
}
```

This loop increments all elements of the vector.

You can use the reserved word auto, which was introduced in Special Topic 2.3, for the type of the element variable:

```
for (auto v : values) { cout << v << " "; }
```

The range-based for loop also works for arrays:

```
int primes[] = { 2, 3, 5, 7, 11, 13 };
for (int p : primes)
{
    cout << p << " ";
}
```

The range-based for loop is a convenient shortcut for visiting or updating all elements of a vector or an array. This book doesn't use it because one can achieve the same result by looping over index values. But if you like the more concise form, and use C++ 11 or later, you should certainly consider using it.

EXAMPLE CODE See special_topic_5 of your companion code for a program that demonstrates the range-based for loop.

CHAPTER SUMMARY

Use arrays for collecting values.

- Use an array to collect a sequence of values of the same type.
- Individual elements in an array *values* are accessed by an integer index i, using the notation *values*[i].
- An array element can be used like any variable.
- An array index must be at least zero and less than the size of the array.
- A bounds error, which occurs if you supply an invalid array index, can data or cause your program to terminate.
- With a partially filled array, keep a companion variable for the current size.

Be able to use common array algorithms.

- To copy an array, use a loop to copy its elements to a new array.
- When separating elements, don't place a separator before the first element.
- A linear search inspects elements in sequence until a match is found.
- Before inserting an element, move elements to the end of the array *starting with the last one.*
- Use a temporary variable when swapping two elements.

Implement functions that process arrays.

- When passing an array to a function, also pass the size of the array.
- Array parameters are always reference parameters.
- A function's return type cannot be an array.
- When a function modifies the size of an array, it needs to tell its caller.
- A function that adds elements to an array needs to know its capacity.

Be able to combine and adapt algorithms for solving a programming problem.

- By combining fundamental algorithms, you can solve complex programming tasks.
- You should be familiar with the implementation of fundamental algorithms so that you can adapt them.

Discover algorithms by manipulating physical objects.

- Use a sequence of coins, playing cards, or toys to visualize an array of values.
- You can use paper clips as position markers or counters.

Use two-dimensional arrays for data that is arranged in rows and columns.

- Use a two-dimensional array to store tabular data.
- Individual elements in a two-dimensional array are accessed by using two index values, *array*[i][j].
- A two-dimensional array parameter must have a fixed number of columns.

Use vectors for managing collections whose size can change.

- A vector stores a sequence of values whose size can change.
- Use the size member function to obtain the current size of a vector.
- Use the push_back member function to add more elements to a vector. Use pop_back to reduce the size.
- Vectors can occur as function arguments and return values.
- Use a reference parameter to modify the contents of a vector.
- A function can return a vector.

REVIEW EXERCISES

■■ **R6.1** Carry out the following tasks with an array:

    a. Allocate an array a of ten integers.
    b. Put the number 17 as the initial element of the array.
    c. Put the number 29 as the last element of the array.
    d. Fill the remaining elements with –1.
    e. Add 1 to each element of the array.
    f. Print all elements of the array, one per line.
    g. Print all elements of the array in a single line, separated by commas.

■■ **R6.2** Write code that fills an array `double values[10]` with each set of values below.

    a. 1 2 3 4 5 6 7 8 9 10
    b. 0 2 4 6 8 10 12 14 16 18 20
    c. 1 4 9 16 25 36 49 64 81 100
    d. 0 0 0 0 0 0 0 0 0 0
    e. 1 4 9 16 9 7 4 9 11
    f. 0 1 0 1 0 1 0 1 0 1
    g. 0 1 2 3 4 0 1 2 3 4

■■ **R6.3** Consider the following array:

```
int a[] = { 1, 2, 3, 4, 5, 4, 3, 2, 1, 0 };
```

What is the value of total after the following loops complete?

```
a. int total = 0;
   for (int i = 0; i < 10; i++) { total = total + a[i]; }
b. int total = 0;
   for (int i = 0; i < 10; i = i + 2) { total = total + a[i]; }
c. int total = 0;
   for (int i = 1; i < 10; i = i + 2) { total = total + a[i]; }
d. int total = 0;
   for (int i = 2; i <= 10; i++) { total = total + a[i]; }
e. int total = 0;
   for (int i = 1; i < 10; i = 2 * i) { total = total + a[i]; }
f. int total = 0;
   for (int i = 9; i >= 0; i--) { total = total + a[i]; }
g. int total = 0;
   for (int i = 9; i >= 0; i = i - 2) { total = total + a[i]; }
h. int total = 0;
   for (int i = 0; i < 10; i++) { total = a[i] - total; }
```

■■ **R6.4** Consider the following array:

```
int a[] = { 1, 2, 3, 4, 5, 4, 3, 2, 1, 0 };
```

What are the contents of the array a after the following loops complete?

```
a. for (int i = 1; i < 10; i++) { a[i] = a[i - 1]; }
b. for (int i = 9; i > 0; i--) { a[i] = a[i - 1]; }
c. for (int i = 0; i < 9; i++) { a[i] = a[i + 1]; }
```

d. `for (int i = 8; i >= 0; i--) { a[i] = a[i + 1]; }`
e. `for (int i = 1; i < 10; i++) { a[i] = a[i] + a[i - 1]; }`
f. `for (int i = 1; i < 10; i = i + 2) { a[i] = 0; }`
g. `for (int i = 0; i < 5; i++) { a[i + 5] = a[i]; }`
h. `for (int i = 1; i < 5; i++) { a[i] = a[9 - i]; }`

■■■ **R6.5** Write a loop that fills an array `int values[10]` with ten random numbers between 1 and 100. Write code for two nested loops that fill `values` with ten *different* random numbers between 1 and 100.

■■ **R6.6** Write C++ code for a loop that simultaneously computes both the maximum and minimum of an array.

■ **R6.7** What is wrong with the following loop?

```
int values[10];
for (int i = 1; i <= 10; i++)
{
    values[i] = i * i;
}
```

Explain two ways of fixing the error.

■ **R6.8** What is an index of an array? What are the legal index values? What is a bounds error?

■ **R6.9** Write a program that contains a bounds error. Run the program. What happens on your computer?

■ **R6.10** Write a loop that reads ten numbers and a second loop that displays them in the opposite order from which they were entered.

■ **R6.11** Trace the flow of the element separator loop in Section 6.2.5 with the given example. Show two columns, one with the value of `i` and one with the output.

■ **R6.12** Trace the flow of the finding matches loop in Section 6.7.4, where `values` contains the elements 110 90 100 120 80. Show two columns, for `i` and `matches`.

■ **R6.13** Trace the flow of the linear search loop in Section 6.2.7, where `values` contains the elements 80 90 100 120 110. Show two columns, for `pos` and `found`. Repeat the trace when `values` contains 80 90 100 70.

■ **R6.14** Trace both mechanisms for removing an element described in Section 6.2.8. Use an array `values` with elements 110 90 100 120 80, and remove the element at index 2.

■ **R6.15** Consider the following loop for collecting all elements that match a condition; in this case, that the element is larger than 100.

```
vector<double> matches;
for (int i = 0; i < values.size(); i++)
{
    if (values[i] > 100)
    {
        matches.add(values[i]);
    }
}
```

Trace the flow of the loop, where `values` contains the elements 110 90 100 120 80. Show two columns, for `element` and `matches`.

R6.16 For the operations on partially filled arrays below, provide the header of a function.

   a. Sort the elements in decreasing order.

   b. Print all elements, separated by a given string.

   c. Count how many elements are less than a given value.

   d. Remove all elements that are less than a given value.

   e. Place all elements that are less than a given value in another array.

Do not implement the functions.

R6.17 You are given two arrays denoting x- and y-coordinates of a set of points in the plane. For plotting the point set, we need to know the x- and y-coordinates of the smallest rectangle containing the points.

How can you obtain these values from the fundamental algorithms in Section 6.2?

R6.18 Solve the problem described in Section 6.4 by sorting the array first. How do you need to modify the algorithm for computing the total?

R6.19 Solve the task described in Section 6.5 using an algorithm that removes and inserts elements instead of switching them. Write the pseudocode for the algorithm, assuming that functions for removal and insertion exist. Act out the algorithm with a sequence of coins and explain why it is less efficient than the swapping algorithm developed in Section 6.5.

R6.20 Develop an algorithm for finding the most frequently occurring value in an array of numbers. Use a sequence of coins. Place paper clips below each coin that count how many other coins of the same value are in the sequence. Give the pseudocode for an algorithm that yields the correct answer, and describe how using the coins and paper clips helped you find the algorithm.

R6.21 Write C++ statements for performing the following tasks with an array declared as

```
int values[ROWS][COLUMNS];
```

- Fill all entries with 0.
- Fill elements alternately with 0s and 1s in a checkerboard pattern.
- Fill only the elements in the top and bottom rows with zeroes.
- Compute the sum of all elements.
- Print the array in tabular form.

R6.22 Give pseudocode for a function that rotates the elements of an array by one position, moving the initial element to the end of the array, like this:

2	3	5	7	11	13

3	5	7	11	13	2

■■ **R6.23** Give pseudocode for a function that removes all negative values from a partially filled array, preserving the order of the remaining elements.

■■ **R6.24** Suppose values is a *sorted* partially filled array of integers. Give pseudocode that describes how a new value can be inserted in its proper position so that the resulting array stays sorted.

■■■ **R6.25** A *run* is a sequence of adjacent repeated values. Give pseudocode for computing the length of the longest run in an array. For example, the longest run in the array with following elements has length 4

1 2 5 5 3 1 2 4 3 2 2 2 2 3 6 5 5 6 3 1

■■ **R6.26** Write pseudocode for an algorithm that fills the first and last column as well as the first and last row of a two-dimensional array of integers with –1.

■■ **R6.27** True or false?

a. All elements of an array are of the same type.

b. Arrays cannot contain strings as elements.

c. Two-dimensional arrays always have the same number of rows and columns.

d. Elements of different columns in a two-dimensional array can have different types.

e. A function cannot return a two-dimensional array.

f. All array parameters are reference parameters.

g. A function cannot change the dimensions of a two-dimensional array that is passed as a parameter.

■■ **R6.28** How do you perform the following tasks with vectors in C++?

a. Test that two vectors contain the same elements in the same order.

b. Copy one vector to another.

c. Fill a vector with zeroes, overwriting all elements in it.

d. Remove all elements from a vector.

■ **R6.29** True or false?

a. All elements of a vector are of the same type.

b. A vector index can be negative.

c. Vectors cannot contain strings as elements.

d. Vectors cannot use strings as index values.

e. All vector parameters are reference parameters.

f. A function cannot return a vector.

g. A function cannot change the length of a vector that is a reference parameter.

PRACTICE EXERCISES

■■ **E6.1** Write a program that initializes an array with ten random integers and then prints four lines of output, containing

- Every element at an even index.
- Every even element.

- All elements in reverse order.
- Only the first and last element.

E6.2 Write array functions that carry out the following tasks for an array of integers. For each function, provide a test program.

a. Swap the first and last element in an array.

b. Shift all elements by one to the right and move the last element into the first position. For example, 1 4 9 16 25 would be transformed into 25 1 4 9 16.

c. Replace all even elements with 0.

d. Replace each element except the first and last by the larger of its two neighbors.

e. Remove the middle element if the array length is odd, or the middle two elements if the length is even.

f. Move all even elements to the front, otherwise preserving the order of the elements.

g. Return true if all elements of the array are identical.

h. Return the second-largest element in the array.

i. Return true if the array is currently sorted in increasing order.

j. Return true if the array contains two adjacent duplicate values.

k. Return true if the array contains duplicate values (which need not be adjacent).

E6.3 Modify the largest.cpp program to mark both the smallest and the largest element.

E6.4 Write a function void remove_min that removes the minimum value from a partially filled array without calling other functions.

E6.5 Write a function that computes the *alternating sum* of all elements in an array. For example, if alternating_sum is called with an array containing

$$1 \quad 4 \quad 9 \quad 16 \quad 9 \quad 7 \quad 4 \quad 9 \quad 11$$

then it computes

$$1 - 4 + 9 - 16 + 9 - 7 + 4 - 9 + 11 = -2$$

E6.6 Write a function that implements the algorithm developed in Section 6.5.

E6.7 Write a function reverse that reverses the sequence of elements in an array. For example, if reverse is called with an array containing

$$1 \quad 4 \quad 9 \quad 16 \quad 9 \quad 7 \quad 4 \quad 9 \quad 11$$

then the array is changed to

$$11 \quad 9 \quad 4 \quad 7 \quad 9 \quad 16 \quad 9 \quad 4 \quad 1$$

E6.8 Write a function

```
bool equals(int a[], int a_size, int b[], int b_size)
```

that checks whether two arrays have the same elements in the same order.

E6.9 Write a function

```
bool same_set(int a[], int a_size, int b[], int b_size)
```

that checks whether two vectors have the same elements in some order, ignoring duplicates. For example, the two arrays

$$1 \quad 4 \quad 9 \quad 16 \quad 9 \quad 7 \quad 4 \quad 9 \quad 11$$

and

$$11 \quad 11 \quad 7 \quad 9 \quad 16 \quad 4 \quad 1$$

would be considered identical. You will probably need one or more helper functions.

■■■ **E6.10** Write a function

```
bool same_elements(int a[], int b[], int size)
```

that checks whether two arrays have the same elements in some order, with the same multiplicities. For example,

$$1 \quad 4 \quad 9 \quad 16 \quad 9 \quad 7 \quad 4 \quad 9 \quad 11$$

and

$$11 \quad 1 \quad 4 \quad 9 \quad 16 \quad 9 \quad 7 \quad 4 \quad 9$$

would be considered identical, but

$$1 \quad 4 \quad 9 \quad 16 \quad 9 \quad 7 \quad 4 \quad 9 \quad 11$$

and

$$11 \quad 11 \quad 7 \quad 9 \quad 16 \quad 4 \quad 1 \quad 4 \quad 9$$

would not. You will probably need one or more helper functions.

■■ **E6.11** Write a function that removes duplicates from an array. For example, if remove_duplicates is called with an array containing

$$1 \quad 4 \quad 9 \quad 16 \quad 9 \quad 7 \quad 4 \quad 9 \quad 11$$

then the array is changed to

$$1 \quad 4 \quad 9 \quad 16 \quad 7 \quad 11$$

Your function should have a reference parameter for the array size that is updated when removing the duplicates.

■■ **E6.12** Write a program that generates a sequence of 20 random values between 0 and 99, prints the sequence, sorts it, and prints the sorted sequence. Use the sort function from the standard C++ library.

■■ **E6.13** Write a function that computes the average of the neighbors of a two-dimensional array element in the eight directions shown in Figure 12.

```
double neighbor_average(int values[][], int row, int column)
```

However, if the element is located at the boundary of the array, only include the neighbors that are in the array. For example, if row and column are both 0, there are only three neighbors.

■■ **E6.14** Write a function

```
void bar_chart(double values[], int size)
```

that displays a bar chart of the values in values, using asterisks, like this:

```
**********************
*************************************
****************************
***************************
*************
```

You may assume that all values in values are positive. First figure out the maximum value in values. That value's bar should be drawn with 40 asterisks. Shorter bars should use proportionally fewer asterisks.

■■■ **E6.15** Repeat Exercise E6.14, but make the bars vertical, with the tallest bar twenty asterisks high.

■■■ **E6.16** Improve the bar_chart function of Exercise E6.14 to work correctly when values contains negative values.

■■■ **E6.17** Improve the bar_chart function of Exercise E6.14 by adding an array of captions for each bar. The output should look like this:

```
      Egypt *********************
     France ****************************************
      Japan ***************************
    Uruguay **************************
Switzerland **************
```

■ **E6.18** Write a function

```
vector<int> append(vector<int> a, vector<int> b)
```

that appends one vector after another. For example, if a is

$$1 \quad 4 \quad 9 \quad 16$$

and b is

$$9 \quad 7 \quad 4 \quad 9 \quad 11$$

then append returns the vector

$$1 \quad 4 \quad 9 \quad 16 \quad 9 \quad 7 \quad 4 \quad 9 \quad 11$$

■■ **E6.19** Write a function

```
vector<int> merge(vector<int> a, vector<int> b)
```

that merges two vectors, alternating elements from both vectors. If one vector is shorter than the other, then alternate as long as you can and then append the remaining elements from the longer vector.

For example, if a is

$$1 \quad 4 \quad 9 \quad 16$$

and b is

$$9 \quad 7 \quad 4 \quad 9 \quad 11$$

then merge returns the vector

$$1 \quad 9 \quad 4 \quad 7 \quad 9 \quad 4 \quad 16 \quad 9 \quad 11$$

■■ **E6.20** Write a function

```
vector<int> merge_sorted(vector<int> a, vector<int> b)
```

that merges two *sorted* vectors, producing a new sorted vector. Keep an index into each vector, indicating how much of it has been processed already. Each time, append the smallest unprocessed element from either vector, then advance the index. For example, if a is

1   4   9   16

and b is

4   7   9   9   11

then merge_sorted returns the vector

1   4   4   7   9   9   9   11   16

■ **E6.21** Write a function that modifies a vector<string>, moving all strings starting with an uppercase letter to the front, without otherwise changing the order of the elements.

■■ **E6.22** Write a function that counts the number of distinct elements in a vector<string>. Do not modify the vector.

■ **E6.23** Write a function that finds the first occurrence of a value in a two-dimensional array. Return an int array of length 2 with the row and column, or null if the value was not found.

■ **E6.24** Write a function that checks whether all elements in a two-dimensional array are identical.

■■ **E6.25** Write a function that checks whether all elements in a two-dimensional array are distinct.

■■ **E6.26** Write a function that checks whether two two-dimensional arrays are equal; that is, whether they have the same number of rows and columns, and corresponding elements are equal.

■ **E6.27** Write a function that swaps two rows of a two-dimensional array.

■ **E6.28** Write a function that swaps two columns of a two-dimensional array.

PROGRAMMING PROJECTS

■■ **P6.1** A *run* is a sequence of adjacent repeated values. Write a program that generates a sequence of 20 random die tosses and prints the die values, marking the runs by including them in parentheses, like this:

```
1 2 (5 5) 3 1 2 4 3 (2 2 2 2) 3 6 (5 5) 6 3 1
```

Use the following pseudocode:

> *in_run = false*
> *For each valid index i in the array*
>   *If in_run*
>   *If values[i] is different from the preceding value*
>   *Print).*
>   *in_run = false*

```
If not in_run
    If values[i] is the same as the following value
        Print (.
        in_run = true
    Print values[i].
    If in_run, print ).
```

■■ **P6.2** Write a program that generates a sequence of 20 random die tosses and that prints the die values, marking only the longest run, like this:

    1 2 5 5 3 1 2 4 3 (2 2 2 2) 3 6 5 5 6 3 1

If there is more than one run of maximum length, mark the first one.

■■■ **P6.3** Write a program that produces ten random permutations of the numbers 1 to 10. To generate a random permutation, you need to fill an array with the numbers 1 to 10 so that no two elements have the same contents. You could do it by brute force, by generating random values until you have a value that is not yet in the array. But that is inefficient. Instead, follow this algorithm:

```
Make a second array and fill it with the numbers 1 to 10.
Repeat 10 times
    Pick a random position in the second array.
    Remove the element at the position from the second array.
    Append the removed element to the permutation array.
```

■■ **P6.4** It is a well-researched fact that men in a restroom generally prefer to maximize their distance from already occupied stalls, by occupying the middle of the longest sequence of unoccupied places.

For example, consider the situation where all ten stalls are empty.

    _ _ _ _ _ _ _ _ _ _

The first visitor will occupy a middle position:

    _ _ _ _ X _ _ _ _ _

The next visitor will be in the middle of the empty area at the right.

    _ _ _ _ X _ _ X _ _

Given an array of bool values, where true indicates an occupied stall, find the position for the next visitor. Your computation should be placed in a function

```
next_visitor(bool occupied[], int stalls)
```

■■■ **P6.5** In this assignment, you will model the game of *Bulgarian Solitaire*. The game starts with 45 cards. (They need not be playing cards. Unmarked index cards work just as well.) Randomly divide them into some number of piles of random size. For example, you might start with piles of size 20, 5, 1, 9, and 10. In each round, you take one card from each pile, forming a new pile with these cards. For example, the sample starting configuration would be transformed into piles of size 19, 4, 8, 9, and 5. The solitaire is over when the piles have size 1, 2, 3, 4, 5, 6, 7, 8, and 9, in some order. (It can be shown that you always end up with such a configuration.)

In your program, produce a random starting configuration and print it. Then keep applying the solitaire step and print the result. Stop when the solitaire final configuration is reached.

•••P6.6 *Magic squares.* An $n \times n$ matrix that is filled with the numbers 1, 2, 3, . . ., n^2 is a magic square if the sum of the elements in each row, in each column, and in the two diagonals is the same value.

Write a program that reads in 16 values from the keyboard and tests whether they form a magic square when put into a 4×4 array. You need to test two features:

16	3	2	13
5	10	11	8
9	6	7	12
4	15	14	1

1. Does each of the numbers 1, 2, ..., 16 occur in the user input?

2. When the numbers are put into a square, are the sums of the rows, columns, and diagonals equal to each other?

•••P6.7 Implement the following algorithm to construct magic $n \times n$ squares; it works only if n is odd.

> Set row = $n - 1$, column = $n / 2$.
> For k = 1 . . . n *n
>   Place k at [row][column].
>   Increment row and column.
>   If the row or column is n, replace it with 0.
>   If the element at [row][column] has already been filled
>   Set row and column to their previous value.
>   Decrement row.

Here is the 5×5 square that you get if you follow this method:

11	18	25	2	9
10	12	19	21	3
4	6	13	20	22
23	5	7	14	16
17	24	1	8	15

Write a program whose input is the number n and whose output is the magic square of order n if n is odd.

••P6.8 A theater seating chart is implemented as a two-dimensional array of ticket prices, like this:

```
10 10 10 10 10 10 10 10 10 10
10 10 10 10 10 10 10 10 10 10
10 10 10 10 10 10 10 10 10 10
10 10 20 20 20 20 20 20 10 10
10 10 20 20 20 20 20 20 10 10
10 10 20 20 20 20 20 20 10 10
20 20 30 30 40 40 30 30 20 20
20 30 30 40 50 50 40 30 30 20
30 40 50 50 50 50 50 50 40 30
```

Write a program that prompts users to pick either a seat or a price. Mark sold seats by changing the price to 0. When a user specifies a seat, make sure it is available. When a user specifies a price, find any seat with that price.

© lepas2004/iStockphoto.

•••P6.9 Write a program that plays tic-tac-toe. The tic-tac-toe game is played on a 3×3 grid as in the photo at right.

The game is played by two players, who take turns. The first player marks moves with a circle, the second with a cross. The player who has formed a horizontal, vertical, or diagonal sequence of three marks wins. Your program should print the game board, ask the user for the coordinates of the next mark, change the players after every successful move, and pronounce the winner.

© KathyMuller/iStockphoto.

■■■ **P6.10** *The Game of Life* is a well-known mathematical game that gives rise to amazingly complex behavior, although it can be specified by a few simple rules. (It is not actually a game in the traditional sense, with players competing for a win.) Here are the rules. The game is played on a rectangular board. Each square can be either empty or occupied. At the beginning, you can specify empty and occupied cells in some way; then the game runs automatically. In each *generation*, the next generation is computed. A new cell is born on an empty square if it is surrounded by exactly three occupied neighbor cells. A cell dies of overcrowding if it is surrounded by four or more neighbors, and it dies of loneliness if it is surrounded by zero or one neighbor. A neighbor is an occupant of an adjacent square to the left, right, top, or bottom or in a diagonal direction. Figure 16 shows a cell and its neighbor cells.

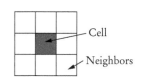

Figure 16
Neighborhood of a Cell

Many configurations show interesting behavior when subjected to these rules. Figure 17 shows a *glider*, observed over five generations. After four generations, it is transformed into the identical shape, but located one square to the right and below.

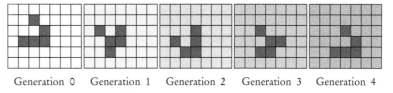

Generation 0   Generation 1   Generation 2   Generation 3   Generation 4

Figure 17   Glider

One of the more amazing configurations is the glider gun: a complex collection of cells that, after 30 moves, turns back into itself and a glider (see Figure 18).

Program the game to eliminate the drudgery of computing successive generations by hand. Use a two-dimensional array to store the rectangular configuration. Write a program that shows successive generations of the game. Ask the user to specify the original configuration, by typing in a configuration of spaces and o characters.

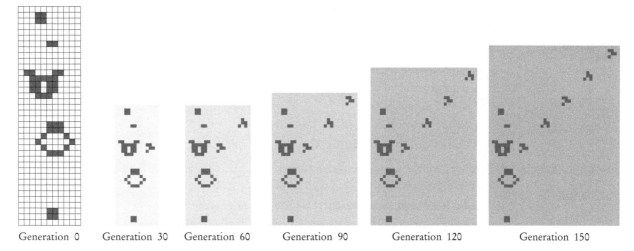

Generation 0   Generation 30   Generation 60   Generation 90   Generation 120   Generation 150

Figure 18   Glider Gun

■■ **Business P6.11** A pet shop wants to give a discount to its clients if they buy one or more pets and at least five other items. The discount is equal to 20 percent of the cost of the other items, but not the pets. Implement a function

```
void discount(double prices[], bool is_pet[], int n_items)
```

The function receives information about a particular sale. For the ith item, `prices[i]` is the price before any discount, and `is_pet[i]` is true if the item is a pet.

© joshblake/iStockphoto.

Write a program that prompts a cashier to enter each price and then a Y for a pet or N for another item. Use a price of –1 as a sentinel. Save the inputs in an array. Call the function that you implemented, and display the discount.

■■ **Business P6.12** A supermarket wants to reward its best customer of each day, showing the customer's name on a screen in the supermarket. For that purpose, the customer's purchase amount is stored in a `vector<double>` and the customer's name is stored in a corresponding `vector<string>`.

Implement a function

```
string name_of_best_customer(vector<double> sales,
     vector<string> customers)
```

that returns the name of the customer with the largest sale.

Write a program that prompts the cashier to enter all prices and names, adds them to two vectors, calls the function that you implemented, and displays the result. Use a price of 0 as a sentinel.

■■■ **Business P6.13** Improve the program of Exercise P6.12 so that it displays the top customers, that is, the `top_n` customers with the largest sales, where `top_n` is a value that the user of the program supplies.

Implement a function

```
vector<string> name_of_best_customers(vector<double> sales,
     vector<string> customers, int top_n)
```

If there were fewer than `top_n` customers, include all of them.

■■ **Engineering P6.14** Sample values from an experiment often need to be smoothed out. One simple approach is to replace each value in an array with the average of the value and its two neighboring values (or one neighboring value if it is at either end of the array). Implement a function

```
void smooth(double values[], int size)
```

that carries out this operation. You should not create another array in your solution.

■■■ **Engineering P6.15** You are given a two-dimensional array of values that give the height of a terrain at different points in a square. Write a function

```
void flood_map(double heights[10][10], double water_level)
```

that prints out a flood map, showing which of the points in the terrain would be flooded if the water level was the given value. In the flood map, print a * for each flooded point and a space for each point that is not flooded.

Here is a sample map:

```
* * * *              * *
* * * * *          * * *
* * * *              * *
* * *                * * *
* * * *        *   * * *
* * * * * * * * * * *
* *          * * *
*              * * * *      *
                      * *
                    * * *
```

© nicolamargaret/iStockphoto.

Then write a program that reads one hundred terrain height values and shows how the terrain gets flooded when the water level increases in ten steps from the lowest point in the terrain to the highest.

■■■ **Engineering P6.16** Write a program that models the movement of an object with mass m that is attached to an oscillating spring. When a spring is displaced from its equilibrium position by an amount x, Hooke's law states that the restoring force is

$$F = -kx$$

where k is a constant that depends on the spring. (Use 10 N/m for this simulation.)

Start with a given displacement x (say, 0.5 meter). Set the initial velocity v to 0. Compute the acceleration a from Newton's law ($F = ma$) and Hooke's law, using a mass of 1 kg. Use a small time interval $\Delta t = 0.01$ second. Update the velocity—it changes by $a\Delta t$. Update the displacement—it changes by $v\Delta t$.

Every ten iterations, plot the spring displacement as a bar, where 1 pixel represents 1 cm. Use the Picture class from the media/picture directory of the companion code for creating an image.

■■ **Media P6.17** Sounds can be represented by an array of "sample values" that describe the intensity of the sound at a point in time. The code in the media/sound directory of the companion code allows you to modify a sound file. Your task is to introduce an echo. For each sound value, add the value from 0.2 seconds ago. Scale the result so that no value is larger than 32767.

© GordonHeeley/iStockphoto.

■■ **Media P6.18** Using the sound processing code from the media/sound directory of the companion code, write a program that reverses the sample values in a sound file.

■■ **Media P6.19** Using the sound processing code from the media/sound directory of the companion code, write a program that computes the average and maximum sample value of a sound file, then replaces all values that are less than the average with zero, and all values that are greater than the average with the maximum. Try your program with a sound file containing human speech.

■■ **Media P6.20** Using the sound processing code from the media/sound directory of the companion code, write a program that increases the volume in the first half, gradually going from the original volume to twice the original, and then gradually decreases the volume in the second half to go back to the original.

■■ **Media P6.21** Using the Picture class from the media/picture directory of the companion code, write a program that reads an image file, obtains the two-dimensional vector of grayscale values, flips it vertically, and writes the result.

© Deejpilot/E+/Getty Images.

■■ **Media P6.22** Using the Picture class from the media/picture directory of the companion code, write a program that reads an image file, obtains the two-dimensional vector of grayscale values, flips it horizontally, and writes the result.

© tomprout/iStock/Getty Images.

■■ **Media P6.23** Using the Picture class from the media/picture directory of the companion code, write a program that reads an image file, obtains the two-dimensional vector of grayscale values, rotates it clockwise by 90 degrees, and writes the result.

■■ **Media P6.24** Using the Picture class from the media/picture directory of the companion code, write a program that reads an image file, obtains the two-dimensional vector of grayscale values, changes each pixel to a 2 × 2 array of the same color, and writes the result.

■■ **Media P6.25** Using the Picture class from the media/picture directory of the companion code, write a program that reads an image file, obtains the two-dimensional vector of grayscale values, detects edges, and writes the result. Use the following algorithm. For each pixel, calculate the average gray value of the neighbors to the east, south, and southeast. If the pixel differs by more than 10 from that average, color it black. Otherwise, color it white. Color the last row and column white.

■■ **Media P6.26** Using the Picture class from the media/picture directory of the companion code, write a program that reads an image file, obtains the two-dimensional vector of grayscale values, detects edges, and writes the result. Use the following algorithm. For each pixel, calculate the average gray value of the neighbors in all eight compass directions. If the pixel differs by more than 10 from that average, color it black. Otherwise, color it white. You will need a separate two-dimensional vector for the result.

■■ **Media P6.27** Using the Picture class from the media/picture directory of the companion code, write a program that reads two image files, obtains the two-dimensional vectors of grayscale values, and superimposes them. Average the values that are present in both images, and use gray (127) where neither image contributes pixels.

■■ **Media P6.28** Using the `Picture` class from the `media/picture` directory of the companion code, write a program that reads an image file, obtains the two-dimensional vectors of grayscale values, and colors every seventh pixel black, starting at the top left corner.

■■ **Media P6.29** Use the `Picture` class from the `media/picture` directory of the companion code to generate the image of a checkerboard.

■■ **Media P6.30** Use the code in the `media/animation` directory of the companion code, show a rectangle that travels from the left of the image to the right and then back to the left.

■■■ **Media P6.31** Using the code in the `media/animation` directory of the companion code, show an animation of the oscillating spring described in Exercise P6.16. Just draw a straight line and a square weight, but accurately update the displacement.

■■■ **Media P6.32** Using the code in the `media/animation` directory of the companion code, show an animation of a bouncing ball. The ball is dropped from an initial height, and its velocity is accelerated by the gravitational force, as described in Exercise P4.23. When the ball hits the ground, the velocity is reversed but dampened by a small percentage.

■ **Media P6.33** Use the `Picture` class from the `media/picture` directory of the companion code to generate the image of a sine wave. Draw a line of pixels for every five degrees.

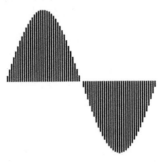

■■ **Media P6.34** Using the code in the `media/animation` directory of the companion code, show an animated sine wave. In the ith frame, shift the sine wave by $5 \times i$ degrees.

CHAPTER 7

POINTERS AND STRUCTURES

© Suzanne Tucker/Shutterstock.

CHAPTER GOALS

To be able to declare, initialize, and use pointers

To understand the relationship between arrays and pointers

To be able to convert between string objects and character pointers

To become familiar with dynamic memory allocation and deallocation

To use structures to aggregate data items

CHAPTER CONTENTS

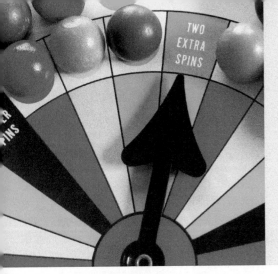

In the game in the photo, the spinner's pointer moves to an item. A player follows the pointer and handles the item to which it points—by taking the ball or following the instructions written in the space. C++ also has pointers that can point to different values throughout a program run. Pointers let you work with data whose locations change or whose size is variable. In the second part of this chapter, you will learn how to use structures. Unlike arrays, structures can be used to group values of different types together. Finally, you will see how to use pointers and structures to model interconnected data.

7.1 Defining and Using Pointers

With a variable, you can access a value at a fixed location. With a pointer, the location can vary. This capability has many useful applications. Pointers can be used to share values among different parts of a program. Pointers allow allocation of values on demand. Furthermore, as you will see in Chapter 10, pointers are necessary for implementing programs that manipulate objects of multiple related types. In the first half of this chapter, you will learn how to define pointers and access the values to which they point.

7.1.1 Defining Pointers

Consider a person who wants a program for making bank deposits and withdrawals, but who may not always use the same bank account. By using a pointer, it is possible to switch to a different account without modifying the code for deposits and withdrawals.

Let's start with a variable for storing an account balance:

```
double harrys_account = 0;
```

Now suppose that we want to write an algorithm that manipulates a bank account, but we anticipate that we may sometimes want to use harrys_account, sometimes another account. Using a pointer gives us that flexibility. A pointer tells you *where* a value is located, not what the value is.

Like a pointer that points to different locations on a blackboard, a C++ pointer can point to different memory locations.

© Alexey Chuvarkov/iStockphoto.

224

Figure 1 Pointers and Values in Memory

Here is the definition of a pointer variable. The pointer variable is initialized with the location (also called the **address**) of the variable harrys_account (see Figure 1):

A pointer denotes the location of a variable in memory.

```
double* account_pointer = &harrys_account;    ①
```

The type double*, or "pointer to double", denotes the location of a double variable. The & operator, also called the *address operator*, yields the location of a variable. Taking the address of a double variable yields a value of type double*.

The type T* denotes a pointer to a variable of type T.

Thinking about pointers can be rather abstract, but you can use a simple trick to make it more tangible. Every variable in a computer program is located in a specific memory location. You don't know where each variable is stored, but you can pretend you do. Let's pretend that we know that harrys_account is stored in location 20300. (That is just a made-up value.) As shown in Figure 1, the value of harrys_account is 0, but the value of &harrys_account is 20300. The value of account_pointer is also 20300. In our diagrams, we will draw an arrow from a pointer to the location, but of course the computer doesn't store arrows, just numbers.

The & operator yields the location of a variable.

By using a pointer, you can switch to a different account at any time. To access a different account, simply change the pointer value:

```
account_pointer = &joint_account;    ②
```

7.1.2 Accessing Variables Through Pointers

When you have a pointer, you will want to access the variable to which it points. The * operator is used to read or update the variable to which a pointer points. When used with pointers, the * operator has no relationship with multiplication. In the C++ standard, this operator is called the *indirection operator*, but it is also commonly called the *dereferencing operator*.

The * operator accesses the variable to which a pointer points.

This statement makes an initial deposit into the account to which account_pointer points (see Figure 2):

```
*account_pointer = 1000;    ①
```

Figure 2 Pointer Variables Can be on Either Side of an Assignment

In other words, you can use `*account_pointer` in exactly the same way as `harrys_account` or `joint_account`. Which account is used depends on the value of the pointer. When the program executes this statement, it fetches the address stored in `account_pointer`. It then uses the variable at that address, as shown in Figure 2.

An expression such as `*account_pointer` can be on the left or the right of an assignment. When it occurs on the left, then the value on the right is stored in the location to which the pointer refers. When it occurs on the right, then the value is fetched from the location and assigned to the variable on the left. For example, the following statement reads the variable to which `account_pointer` currently points, and places its contents into the `balance` variable:

    balance = *account_pointer; ❷

You can have `*account_pointer` on both sides of an assignment. The following statement withdraws $100:

    *account_pointer = *account_pointer - 100;

Syntax 7.1 Pointer Syntax

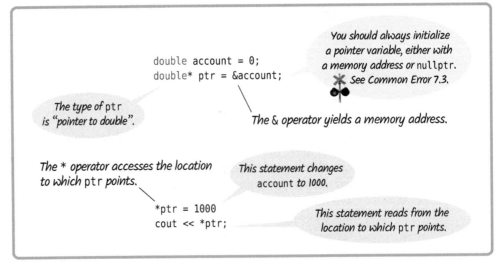

Table 1 contains additional pointer examples.

Table 1 Pointer Syntax Examples

Assume the following declarations:
```
int m = 10; // Assumed to be at address 20300
int n = 20; // Assumed to be at address 20304
int* p = &m;
```

Expression	Value	Comment
p	20300	The address of m.
*p	10	The value stored at that address.
&n	20304	The address of n.
p = &n;		Set p to the address of n.
*p	20	The value stored at the changed address.
m = *p;		Stores 20 into m.
🚫 m = p;	**Error**	m is an int value; p is an int* pointer. The types are not compatible.
🚫 &10	**Error**	You can only take the address of a variable.
&p	The address of p, perhaps 20308	This is the location of a pointer variable, not the location of an integer.
🚫 double x = 0; p = &x;	**Error**	p has type int*, &x has type double*. These types are incompatible.

7.1.3 Initializing Pointers

With pointers, it is particularly important that you pay attention to proper initialization.

When you initialize a pointer, be sure that the pointer and the memory address have the same type. For example, the following initialization would be an error:

```
int balance = 1000;
double* account_pointer = &balance; // Error!
```

The address &balance is a pointer to an int value, that is, an expression of type int*. It is never legal to initialize a double* pointer with an int*.

It is an error to use an uninitialized pointer.

If you define a pointer variable without providing an initial variable, the pointer contains a random address. Using that random address is an error. In practice, your program will likely crash or mysteriously misbehave if you use an uninitialized pointer:

```
double* account_pointer;
    // Forgot to initialize
*account_pointer = 1000;
    // NO! account_pointer contains an unpredictable value
```

The nullptr pointer
does not point to
any object.

There is a special value, nullptr, that you should use to indicate a pointer that doesn't point anywhere. If you define a pointer variable and are not ready to initialize it quite yet, set it to nullptr.

```
double* account_pointer = nullptr; // Will set later
```

You can later test whether the pointer is still nullptr. If it is, don't use it.

```
if (account_pointer != nullptr) { cout << *account_pointer; } // OK
```

Trying to access data through a nullptr pointer is illegal, and it will cause your program to terminate.

The reserved word nullptr was introduced in C++ 11. If you use an older version of C++, use the NULL constant instead.

The following program demonstrates the behavior of pointers. We execute the same withdrawal statement twice, but with different values for account_pointer. Each time, a different account is modified.

sec01/accounts.cpp

```
1  #include <iostream>
2
3  using namespace std;
4
5  int main()
6  {
7     double harrys_account = 0;
8     double joint_account = 2000;
9     double* account_pointer = &harrys_account;
10
11    *account_pointer = 1000; // Initial deposit
12
13    *account_pointer = *account_pointer - 100; // Withdraw $100
14    cout << "Balance: " << *account_pointer << endl; // Print balance
15
16    // Change the pointer value
17    account_pointer = &joint_account;
18
19    // The same statements affect a different account
20    *account_pointer = *account_pointer - 100; // Withdraw $100
21    cout << "Balance: " << *account_pointer << endl; // Print balance
22
23    return 0;
24 }
```

Program Run

```
Balance: 900
Balance: 1900
```

Common Error 7.1

Confusing Pointers with the Data to Which They Point

A pointer is a memory address—a number that tells where a value is located in memory. It is a common error to confuse the pointer with the variable to which it points:

```
double* account_pointer = &joint_account;
account_pointer = 1000; // Error
```

The assignment statement does not set the joint account balance to 1000. Instead, it sets the pointer to point to memory address 1000. The pointer account_pointer only describes *where* the joint account variable is, and it almost certainly is not located at address 1000. Most compilers will report an error for this assignment.

To actually access the variable, use *account_pointer:

```
*account_pointer = 1000; // OK
```

Programming Tip 7.1

Use a Separate Definition for Each Pointer Variable

It is legal in C++ to define multiple variables together, like this:

```
int i = 0, j = 1;
```

This style can lead to problems when used with pointers. The following declaration is not correct:

```
double* p = &i, q = &j;
```

The * associates only with the first variable. That is, p is a double* pointer, and q is a double value.

It is legal to define multiple pointers together like this:

```
double *p = &i, *q = &j;
```

That means that both p and q are variables and that *p and *q are double values. In other words, p and q are both pointers to double. Some programmers find this syntax hard to understand.

To avoid any confusion, it is best to define each pointer variable separately:

```
double* p = &i;
double* q = &j;
```

Special Topic 7.1

Pointers and References

In Section 5.9, you saw how reference parameters enable a function to modify variables that are passed as arguments. Here is an example of a function with a reference parameter:

```
void withdraw(double& balance, double amount)
{
   if (balance >= amount)
   {
      balance = balance - amount;
   }
}
```

If you call

```
withdraw(harrys_checking, 1000);
```

then $1000 is withdrawn from harrys_checking, provided that sufficient funds are available.

You can use pointers to achieve the same effect:

```
void withdraw(double* balance, double amount)
{
   if (*balance >= amount)
   {
      *balance = *balance - amount;
   }
}
```

However, then you need to call the function with the *address* of the account:

```
withdraw(&harrys_checking, 1000);
```

These solutions are equivalent. Behind the scenes, the compiler translates reference parameters into pointers.

7.2 Arrays and Pointers

Pointers are particularly useful for understanding the peculiarities of arrays. In the following sections, we describe the relationship between arrays and pointers in C++.

7.2.1 Arrays as Pointers

Consider this declaration of an array:

```
double a[10];
```

As you know, a[3] denotes an array element. The array name *without* brackets denotes a pointer to the starting element (see Figure 3).

You can capture that pointer in a variable:

```
double* p = a; // Now p points to a[0]
```

The name of an array variable is a pointer to the starting element of the array.

You can also use the array name as a pointer in expressions. The statement

```
cout << *a;
```

has the same effect as the statement

```
cout << a[0];
```

Figure 3 Pointers into an Array

7.2.2 Pointer Arithmetic

Pointers into arrays support *pointer arithmetic*. You can add an integer offset to the pointer to point to another array location. For example, suppose p points to the beginning of an array:

```
double a[10];
double* p = a;
```

Then the expression

```
p + 3
```

is a pointer to the array element with index 3, and

```
*(p + 3)
```

is that array element.

As you saw in the preceding section, we can use the array name as a pointer. That is, a + 3 is a pointer to the array element with index 3, and *(a + 3) has exactly the same meaning as a[3].

In fact, for any integer n, it is true that

```
a[n]  is the same as  *(a + n)
```

This relationship is called the *array/pointer duality law*.

This law explains why all C++ arrays start with an index of zero. The pointer a (or a + 0) points to the starting element of the array. That element must therefore be a[0].

To better understand pointer arithmetic, let's again pretend that we know actual memory addresses. Suppose the array a starts at address 20300. The array contains ten values of type double. A double value occupies 8 bytes of memory. Therefore, the array occupies 80 bytes, from 20300 to 20379. The starting value is located at address 20300, the next one at address 20308, and so on (see Figure 3). For example, the value of a + 3 is $20300 + 3 \times 8 = 20324$. (In general, if p is a pointer to a type T, then the address p + n is obtained by adding n × the size of a T value to the address p.)

Table 2 shows pointer arithmetic and the array/pointer duality using this example.

Table 2 Arrays and Pointers

Expression	Value	Comment
a	20300	The starting address of the array, here assumed to be 20300.
*a	0	The value stored at that address. (The array contains values 0, 1, 4, 9, ...)
a + 1	20308	The address of the next double value in the array. A double occupies 8 bytes.
a + 3	20324	The address of the element with index 3, obtained by skipping past 3 × 8 bytes.
*(a + 3)	9	The value stored at address 20324.
a[3]	9	The same as *(a + 3) by array/pointer duality.
*a + 3	3	The sum of *a and 3. Because there are no parentheses, the * refers only to a.
&a[3]	20324	The address of the element with index 3, the same as a + 3.

7.2.3 Array Parameter Variables Are Pointers

Once you understand the connection between arrays and pointers, it becomes clear why array parameter variables are different from other parameter types. As an example, consider this function that computes the sum of all values in an array:

```cpp
double sum(double values[], int size)
{
   double total = 0;
   for (int i = 0; i < size; i++)
   {
      total = total + values[i];
   }
   return total;
}
```

Here is a call to the function (see Figure 4):

```cpp
double a[10];
. . . // Initialize a
double s = sum(a, 10);
```

The value a is passed to the sum function. It is actually a pointer of type double*, pointing to the starting element of the array. One would therefore expect that the function is declared as

```cpp
double sum(double* values, int size)
```

When passing an array to a function, only the starting address is passed.

However, if you look closely at the function definition, you will see that the parameter variable is declared as an array with empty bounds:

```cpp
double sum(double values[], int size)
```

As viewed by the C++ compiler, these parameter declarations are completely equivalent. The [] notation is "syntactic sugar" for declaring a pointer. (Computer scientists use the term "syntactic sugar" to describe a notation that is easy to read for humans and that masks a complex implementation detail.) The array notation gives human

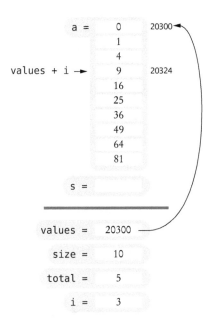

Figure 4
Passing an Array to a Function

readers the illusion that an entire array is passed to the function, but in fact the function receives only the starting address for the array.

Now consider this statement in the body of the function:

```
total = total + values[i];
```

The C++ compiler considers `values` to be a *pointer*, not an array. The expression `values[i]` is syntactic sugar for `*(values + i)`. That expression denotes the storage location that is `i` elements away from the address stored in the variable `values`. Figure 4 shows how `values[i]` is accessed when `i` is 3.

You can now understand why it is always necessary to pass the size of the array. The function receives a single memory address, which tells it where the array starts. That memory address enables the function to locate the values in the array. But the function also needs to know where to stop.

EXAMPLE CODE   See sec02 of your companion code for a program that demonstrates pointer values.

Special Topic 7.2

Using a Pointer to Step Through an Array

Consider again the `sum` function of Section 7.2.3. Now that you know that the first parameter variable of the `sum` function is a pointer, you can implement the function in a slightly different way. Rather than incrementing an integer index, you can increment a pointer variable to visit all array elements in turn:

```
double sum(double* values, int size)
{
   double total = 0;
   double* p = values; // p starts at the beginning of the array
   for (int i = 0; i < size; i++)
   {
      total = total + *p; // Add the value to which p points
      p++; // Advance p to the next array element
   }
   return total;
}
```

Initially, the pointer p points to the element `values[0]`. The increment

```
p++;
```

moves it to point to the next element (see Figure 5).

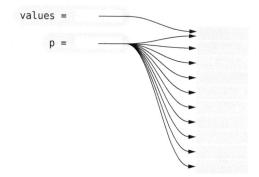

Figure 5   A Pointer Variable Traversing the Elements of an Array

It is a tiny bit more efficient to use and increment a pointer than to access an array element as values[i]. For this reason, some programmers routinely use pointers instead of indexes to access array elements.

Common Error 7.2

Returning a Pointer to a Local Variable

Consider this function that tries to return a pointer to an array containing two elements, the first and the last values of an array:

```
double* firstlast(double values[], int size)
{
   double result[2];
   result[0] = values[0];
   result[1] = values[size - 1];
   return result; // Error!
}
```

The function returns a pointer to the starting element of the result array. However, that array is a local variable of the firstlast function. The local variable no longer exists when the function exits. Its contents will soon be overwritten by other function calls.

You can solve this problem by passing an array to hold the answer:

```
void firstlast(const double values[], int size, double result[])
{
   result[0] = values[0];
   result[1] = values[size - 1];
}
```

Then it is the responsibility of the caller to allocate an array to hold the result.

Programming Tip 7.2

Program Clearly, Not Cleverly

Some programmers take great pride in minimizing the number of instructions, even if the resulting code is hard to understand. For example, here is a legal implementation of the sum function:

```
double sum(double* values, int size)
{
   double total = 0;
   while (size-- > 0) // Loop size times
   {
      total = total + *values++; // Add the value to which values points; increment values
   }
   return total;
}
```

This implementation uses two tricks. First, the function parameter variables values and size are variables, and it is legal to modify them. Moreover, the expressions size-- and values++ mean "decrement or increment the variable and return the old value". In other words, the expression

```
size-- > 0
```

combines two tasks: to decrement size, and to test whether size was positive before the decrement. Similarly, the expression

```
*values++
```

increments the pointer to the next element, and it returns the element to which it pointed before the increment.

Please do not use this programming style. Your job as a programmer is not to dazzle other programmers with your cleverness, but to write code that is easy to understand and maintain.

Special Topic 7.3
Constant Pointers

The following definition specifies a constant pointer:

```
const double* p = &balance;
```

You cannot modify the value to which p points. That is, the following statement is illegal:

```
*p = 0; // Error
```

Of course, you can read the value:

```
cout << *p; // OK
```

A constant array parameter variable is equivalent to a constant pointer. For example, consider the function

```
double sum(const double values[], int size)
```

Recall from Section 7.2.3 that values is a pointer. The function could have been defined as

```
double sum(const double* values, int size)
```

The function can use the pointer values to read the array elements, but it cannot modify them.

7.3 C and C++ Strings

C++ has two mechanisms for manipulating strings. The string class supports character sequences of arbitrary length and provides convenient operations such as concatenation and string comparison. However, C++ also inherits a more primitive level of string handling from the C language, in which strings are represented as arrays of char values. In this sections, we will discuss the relationships between these types.

7.3.1 The char Type

A value of type char denotes an individual character. Character literals are enclosed in single quotes.

The char type denotes an individual character. Character literals are delimited by single quotes; for example,

```
char input = 'y';
```

© slpix/iStockphoto.

Each character is actually encoded as an integer value. (See Appendix C for the encoding using the ASCII code, which is used on the majority of computers today.)

Note that 'y' is a single character, which is quite different from "y", a string containing the 'y' character.

Table 3 shows typical character literals.

Table 3	Character Literals
'y'	The character y
'0'	The character for the digit 0. In the ASCII code, '0' has the value 48.
' '	The space character
'\n'	The newline character
'\t'	The tab character
'\0'	The null terminator of a string
🚫 "y"	**Error:** Not a char value

Letters from foreign alphabets and special symbols may require multiple char values. See Chapter 8 for more information.

7.3.2 C Strings

A literal string (enclosed in double quotes) is an array of char values with a zero terminator.

In the C programming language, strings are always represented as character arrays. C++ programmers often refer to arrays of char values as "C strings".

In particular, a literal string, such as "Harry", is *not* an object of type string. Instead, it is an array of char values. As with all arrays, a string literal can be assigned to a pointer variable that points to the initial character in the array:

```
const char* char_pointer = "Harry"; // Points to 'H'
```

The string is declared as const because you are not supposed to modify a literal string. (See Special Topic 7.3 for more information on constant pointers.)

A C string is terminated by a special character, called a *null terminator*, denoted '\0'. For example, the C string "Harry" contains *six* characters, namely 'H', 'a', 'r', 'r', 'y' and '\0' (See Figure 6.)

The terminator is a character that is encoded as the number zero—this is different from the character '0', the character denoting the zero digit. (Under the ASCII encoding scheme, the character denoting the zero digit is encoded as the number 48.)

Functions that operate on C strings rely on this terminator. Here is a typical example, the strlen function declared in the <cstring> header that computes the length of a character array. The function counts the number of characters until it reaches the terminator.

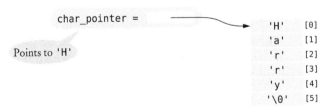

Figure 6 A Character Array

```
int strlen(const char s[])
{
   int i = 0;
   while (s[i] != '\0') { i++; } // Count characters before the null terminator
   return i;
}
```

The call strlen("Harry") returns 5.

7.3.3 Character Arrays

A literal string such as "Harry" is a constant. You are not allowed to modify its characters. If you want to modify the characters in a string, define a character array instead. For example:

```
char char_array[] = "Harry"; // An array of 6 characters
```

The char_array variable is an array of 6 characters, initialized with 'H', 'a', 'r', 'r', 'y', and a null terminator. The compiler counts the characters in the string that is used for initializing the array, including the null terminator.

You can modify the characters in the array:

```
char_array[0] = 'L';
```

7.3.4 Converting Between C and C++ Strings

Many library functions use pointers of type char*.

Before the C++ string class became widely available, direct manipulation of character arrays was common, but also quite challenging (see Special Topic 7.4). If you use functions that receive or return C strings, you need to know how to convert between C strings and string objects.

For example, the <cstdlib> header declares a useful function

```
int atoi(const char s[])
```

The atoi function converts a character array containing digits into its integer value:

```
char year[] = "2020";
int y = atoi(year); // Now y is the integer 2020
```

The c_str member function yields a char* pointer from a string object.

In older versions of C++, this functionality was missing from the string class. The c_str member function of the string class offers an "escape hatch". If s is a string, then s.c_str() yields a char* pointer to the characters in the string. Here is how you use that member function to call the atoi function:

```
string year = "2020";
int y = atoi(year.c_str());
```

You can initialize C++ string variables with C strings.

Conversely, converting from a C string to a C++ string is very easy. Simply initialize a string variable with any value of type char*, such as a string literal or character array. For example, the definition

```
string name = "Harry";
```

initializes the C++ string object name with the C string "Harry".

7.3.5 C++ Strings and the [ ] Operator

Up to this point, we have always used the substr member function to access individual characters in a C++ string. For example, if a string variable is defined as

```cpp
string name = "Harry";
```

the expression

```cpp
name.substr(3, 1)
```

yields a string of length 1 containing the character at index 3.

You can access individual characters with the [] operator:

```cpp
name[0] = 'L';
```

> You can access characters in a C++ string object with the [] operator.

Now the string is "Larry". The [] operator is more convenient than the substr function if you want to visit a string one character at a time.

Here is a useful example. The following function makes a copy of a string and changes all characters to uppercase:

```cpp
/**
    Makes an uppercase version of a string.
    @param str a string
    @return a string with the characters in str converted to uppercase
*/
string uppercase(string str)
{
    string result = str; // Make a copy of str
    for (int i = 0; i < result.length(); i++)
    {
        result[i] = toupper(result[i]); // Convert each character to uppercase
    }
    return result;
}
```

For example, uppercase("Harry") returns a string with the characters "HARRY".

The toupper function is defined in the <cctype> header. It converts lowercase characters to uppercase. (The tolower function does the opposite.)

EXAMPLE CODE   See sec03 of your companion code for a program that demonstrates string processing.

Special Topic 7.4

Working with C Strings

Before the string class became widely available, it was common to work with character arrays directly.

Table 4 shows several commonly used functions for manipulating C strings. All of these functions are declared in the <cstring> header.

Consider the task of concatenating a first name and a last name into a string. The string class makes this very easy:

```cpp
string first = "Harry";
string last = "Smith";
string name = first + " " + last;
```

Let us implement this task with C strings. Allocate an array of characters for the result:

```
const int NAME_SIZE = 40;
char name[NAME_SIZE];
```

This array can hold strings with a length of at most 39, because one character is required for the null terminator.

Now copy the first name, using strncpy:

```
strncpy(name, first, NAME_SIZE - 1);
```

You must be careful not to overrun the target array. It is unlikely that a first name is longer than 39 characters, but a hacker could supply a longer input in order to overwrite memory.

Now, if there is still room, add a space and the last name, again being careful not to overrun the array boundaries.

```
int length = strlen(name);
if (length < NAME_SIZE - 1)
{
   strcat(name, " ");
   int n = NAME_SIZE - 2 - length; // Leave room for space, null terminator
   if (n > 0)
   {
      strncat(name, last, n);
   }
}
```

As you can see, the C string code is over three times as long as the code using C++ strings, and it is not as capable—if the target array is not long enough to hold the result, it is truncated.

Table 4 C String Functions

In this table, s and t are character arrays; n is an integer.

Function	Description
strlen(s)	Returns the length of s.
strcpy(t, s)	Copies the characters from s into t.
strncpy(t, s, n)	Copies at most n characters from s into t.
strcat(t, s)	Appends the characters from s after the end of the characters in t.
strncat(t, s, n)	Appends at most n characters from s after the end of the characters in t.
strcmp(s, t)	Returns 0 if s and t have the same contents, a negative integer if s comes before t in lexicographic order, a positive integer otherwise.

7.4 Dynamic Memory Allocation

Use dynamic memory allocation if you do not know in advance how many values you need.

In many programming situations, you do not know beforehand how many values you need. To solve this problem, you can use **dynamic allocation** and ask the C++ run-time system to create new values whenever you need them. The run-time system keeps a large storage area, called the **free store**, that can allocate values and arrays of any type. When you ask for a

```
new double
```

then a storage location of type double is located on the free store, and a pointer to that location is returned.

More usefully, the expression

The new operator allocates memory from the free store.

```
new double[n]
```

allocates an array of size n, and yields a pointer to the starting element. (Here n need *not* be a constant.)

You will want to capture that pointer in a variable:

```
double* account_pointer = new double;
double* account_array = new double[n];
```

You now use the pointer as described previously in this chapter. If you allocated an array, the magic of array/pointer duality lets you use the array notation account_array[i] to access the ith element.

You must reclaim dynamically allocated objects with the delete or delete[] operator.

When your program no longer needs memory that you previously allocated with the new operator, you must return it to the free store, using the delete operator:

```
delete account_pointer;
```

However, if you allocated an array, you must use the delete[] operator:

```
delete[] account_array;
```

Syntax 7.2   **Dynamic Memory Allocation**

Capture the pointer in a variable.

The new operator yields a pointer to a memory block of the given type.

```
int* var_ptr = new int;
...
```

Use the memory.

```
*var_ptr = 1000;
...
```

Delete the memory when you are done.

```
delete var_ptr;
```

Use this form to allocate an array of the given size (size need not be a constant).

```
int* array_ptr = new int[size];
...
array_ptr[i] = 1000;
...
delete[] array_ptr;
```

Use the pointer as if it were an array.

Remember to use delete[] when deallocating the array.

This operator reminds the free store that the pointer points to an array, not a single value.

After you delete a memory block, you can no longer use it. The storage space may already be used elsewhere.

```
delete[] account_array;
account_array[0] = 1000; // NO! You no longer own the memory of account_array
```

Arrays that are allocated on the free store have one significant advantage over array variables. If you declare an array variable, you must specify a fixed array size when you compile the program. But when you allocate an array on the free store, you can choose the size at run time.

Moreover, if you later need more elements, you are not stuck. You can allocate a bigger array on the free store, copy the elements from the smaller array into the bigger array, and delete the smaller array (see Figure 7):

```
double* bigger_array = new double[2 * n];
for (int i = 0; i < n; i++)
{
   bigger_array[i] = account_array[i];
}
delete[] account_array;
account_array = bigger_array;
n = 2 * n;
```

This is exactly what a vector does behind the scenes.

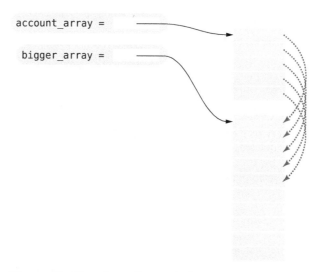

Figure 7   Growing a Dynamic Array

Dynamic allocation is a powerful feature, but you must be very careful to follow all rules precisely:

- Every call to new must be matched by exactly one call to delete.
- Use delete[] to delete arrays.
- Don't access a memory block after it has been deleted.

If you don't follow these rules, your program can crash or run unpredictably. Table 5 shows common errors.

Table 5 Common Memory Allocation Errors

Statements	Error

```int* p;```
```*p = 5;```
```delete p;```
	There is no call to new int.

```int* p = new int;```
```*p = 5;```
```p = new int;```
	The first allocated memory block was never deleted.

```int* p = new int[10];```
```*p = 5;```
```delete p;```
	The delete[] operator should have been used.

```int* p = new int[10];```
```int* q = p;```
```q[0] = 5;```
```delete p;```
```delete q;```
	The same memory block was deleted twice.

```int n = 4;```
```int* p = &n;```
```*p = 5;```
```delete p;```
	You can only delete memory blocks that you obtained from calling new.

EXAMPLE CODE   See sec04 of your companion code for a program that demonstrates dynamic memory allocation.

Common Error 7.3

Dangling Pointers

A very common pointer error is to use a pointer that points to memory that has already been deleted. Such a pointer is called a **dangling pointer**. Because the freed memory will be reused for other purposes, you can create real damage by using a dangling pointer. Consider this example:

```
int* values = new int[n];
// Process values
delete[] values;
// Some other work
values[0] = 42;
```

Using a dangling pointer (a pointer that points to memory that has been deleted) is a serious programming error.

This code will compile because the compiler does not track whether a pointer points to a valid memory location. However, the program may run with unpredictable results. If the program calls the new operator anywhere after deleting values, that call may allocate the same memory again. Now some other part of your program accesses the memory to which values points, and that program part will malfunction when you overwrite the memory. This can happen even if you don't see any call to new—such calls may occur in library functions.

Never use a pointer that has been deleted. Some programmers take the precaution of setting all deleted pointers to nullptr:

```
delete[] values;
values = nullptr;
```

This is not perfect protection—you might have saved values into another pointer variable— but it is a reasonable precaution.

Common Error 7.4

Memory Leaks

Another very common pointer error is to allocate memory on the free store and never deallocate it. A memory block that is never deallocated is called a **memory leak**.

If you allocate a few small blocks of memory and forget to deallocate them, this is not a huge problem. When the program exits, all allocated memory is returned to the operating system.

But if your program runs for a long time, or if it allocates lots of memory (perhaps in a loop), then it can run out of memory. Memory exhaustion will cause your program to crash. In extreme cases, the computer may freeze up if your program exhausted all available memory. Avoiding memory leaks is particularly important in programs that need to run for months or years, without restarting, and in programs that run on resource-constrained devices such as cell phones.

> Every call to new should have a matching call to delete.

Be sure to recycle any free store memory that your program no longer needs.

Even if you write short-lived programs, you should make it a habit to avoid memory leaks. Make sure that every call to the new operator has a corresponding call to the delete operator.

7.5 Arrays and Vectors of Pointers

When you have a sequence of pointers, you can place them into an array or vector. An array and a vector of ten int* pointers are defined as

```
int* pointer_array[10];
vector<int*> pointer_vector(10);
```

The expression pointer_array[i] or pointer_vector[i] denotes the pointer with index i in the sequence.

One application of such pointer sequences are two-dimensional arrays in which each row has a different length, such as the triangular array shown in Figure 8.

pointer_array =

Figure 8 A Triangular Array

In this situation, it would not be very efficient to use a two-dimensional array, because almost half of the elements would be wasted.

We will develop a program that uses such an array for simulating a *Galton board* (Figure 9). A Galton board consists of a pyramidal arrangement of pegs, and a row of bins at the bottom. Balls are dropped onto the top peg and travel toward the bins. At each peg, there is a 50 percent chance of moving left or right. The balls in the bins approximate a bell-curve distribution.

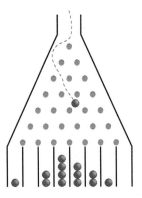

Figure 9   A Galton Board

The Galton board can only show the balls in the bins, but we can do better by keeping a counter for each peg, incrementing it as a ball travels past it.

We will simulate a board with ten rows of pegs. Each row requires an array of counters.

The following statements initialize the triangular array:

```
int* counts[10];
for (int i = 0; i < 10; i++)
{
    counts[i] = new int[i + 1];
}
```

Note that the first element counts[0] contains a pointer to an array of length 1, and the last element counts[9] contains a pointer to an array of length 10.

Before doing the simulation, let us consider how to print out the values. The element counts[i] points to an array. The element at index j of that array is

```
counts[i][j]
```

This loop prints all elements in the ith row:

```
for (int j = 0; j <= i; j++)
{
    cout << setw(4) << counts[i][j];
}
cout << endl;
```

Now let's simulate a falling ball. The movements to the left and right in Figure 9 correspond to movements to the next row, either straight down or to the right, in Figure 10. More precisely, if the ball is currently at row i and column j, then it will go to row i + 1 and, with a 50 percent chance, either stay in column j or go to column j + 1.

row i ⟶
row i + 1 ⟶

column
j

column
j + 1

Figure 10   Movement of a Ball in the Galton Board Array

The program below has the details. In the sample program run, notice how 1,000 balls have hit the top peg, and how the bottommost row of pegs approximates a bell-curve distribution.

sec05/galton.cpp

```
1   #include <iostream>
2   #include <iomanip>
3   #include <cstdlib>
4   #include <ctime>
5
6   using namespace std;
7
8   int main()
9   {
10      srand(time(0));
11      const int SIZE = 10;
12
13      int* counts[SIZE];
14
15      // Allocate the rows
16      for (int i = 0; i < SIZE; i++)
17      {
18         counts[i] = new int[i + 1];
19         for (int j = 0; j <= i; j++)
20         {
21            counts[i][j] = 0;
22         }
23      }
24
25      const int RUNS = 1000;
26
27      // Simulate 1,000 balls
28      for (int run = 0; run < RUNS; run++)
29      {
30         // Add a ball to the top
31         counts[0][0]++;
32         // Have the ball run to the bottom
33         int j = 0;
34         for (int i = 1; i < 10; i++)
35         {
36            int r = rand() % 2;
37            // If r is even, move down, otherwise to the right
38            if (r == 1)
39            {
```

```
40                j++;
41            }
42          counts[i][j]++;
43        }
44    }
45
46    // Print all counts
47    for (int i = 0; i < SIZE; i++)
48    {
49        for (int j = 0; j <= i; j++)
50        {
51            cout << setw(4) << counts[i][j];
52        }
53        cout << endl;
54    }
55
56    // Deallocate the rows
57    for (int i = 0; i < SIZE; i++)
58    {
59        delete[] counts[i];
60    }
61
62    return 0;
63 }
```

Program Run

```
1000
 480 520
 241 500 259
 124 345 411 120
  68 232 365 271   64
  32 164 283 329  161   31
  16  88 229 303  254   88   22
   9  47 147 277  273  190   44   13
   5  24 103 203  288  228  113   33    3
   1  18  64 149  239  265  186   61   15    2
```

7.6 Problem Solving: Draw a Picture

When designing programs that use pointers, you want to visualize how the pointers connect the data that you are working with. In most situations, it is essential that you draw a diagram that shows the connections.

Start with the data that will be accessed or modified through the pointers. These may be account balances, counters, character strings, or other items. Focus on what is being pointed at.

Draw the data that is being processed, then draw the pointer variables. When drawing the pointer arrows, illustrate a typical situation.

Then draw the variable or variables that contain the pointers. These will be the front-end to your system. Processing usually starts with a pointer, then locates the actual data.

Finally, draw the pointers as arrows. If the pointers will vary as the program executes, draw a typical arrangement. It can also be useful to draw several diagrams that show how the pointers change.

Consider the following problem: The media center of a university loans out equipment, such as microphones, cables, and so on, to faculty and students. We want to track the name of each item, and the name of the user who checked it out.

In this case, the data that are being accessed are item and user names. We will store all names in a long array of characters, adding new names to the end as needed. If a name is already present, we don't store it twice. This is an efficient way of storing strings, provided that few strings need to be removed. Here is a section of the character array:

Microphone TX-10\0 Smith, Diane\0 Lee, Tim\0 Tape recorder\0 Mini DVI cable\0 ...

Next, let us draw the pointers to the item names. They are stored in an array of pointers called items. Some items may have the same name. In the example below, we have two microphones with the same name.

Finally, there is a parallel array checked_out_to of pointers to user names. Sometimes, items can be checked out to the same user. Other items aren't checked out at all—the user name pointer is nullptr. When you draw a diagram, try to include examples of all scenarios.

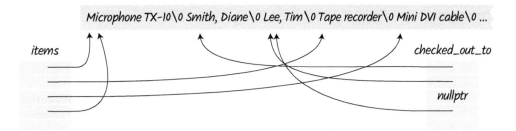

Now that you have a pointer diagram, you can use it to visualize operations on the data. Suppose we want to print a report of all items that are currently checked out. This can be achieved by visiting all pointers in both arrays. The pointer items[i] gives the name of the item, and checked_out_to[i] is either nullptr, in which case we do not want to include this item, or it is the name of the user.

Because programming with pointers is complex, you should always draw diagrams whenever you use pointers.

HOW TO 7.1

Working with Pointers

You use pointers because you want flexibility in your program: the ability to change the relationships between data. This How To walks you through the decision-making process for using pointers.

Problem Statement   We will illustrate the steps with the task of simulating a portion of the control logic for a departmental photocopier. A person making a copy enters a user number. There are 100 different users, with numbers 0 to 99. Each user is linked to a copy account, either the master account or one of ten project accounts. That linkage is maintained by the administrator, and it can change as users work on different projects. When copies are made, the appropriate account should be incremented.

© Bartosz Liszkowski/iStockphoto.

Users identify themselves on the copier control panel. Using pointers, the relationships between users and copy accounts can be flexible.

Step 1   Draw a picture.

As described in Section 7.6, it is a good idea to draw a picture that shows the pointers in your program.

In our example, we need to track the copy accounts: a master account and ten project accounts. For each user, we need a pointer to the copy account:

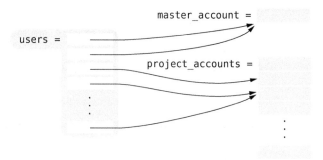

Step 2   Declare pointer variables.

This step is usually easy. With numerical data, you will have pointers of type int* or double*. If you manipulate character arrays, you use char* pointers. In Chapter 10, you will use pointers to objects.

How many pointer variables do you have? If you only have one or two, just declare variables such as

```
double* account_pointer;
```

If you have a sequence of pointers, use a vector or array, such as

```
vector<char*> lines;
```

In our example, the purpose is to manipulate copy counters. Therefore, our data are integers and the pointers have type int*. We know that we will have exactly 100 pointers, one for each user. Therefore, we can choose an array

```
int* users[100];
```

Step 3   Initialize the pointers with variable addresses or free store memory.

Will you allocate variables and then take their addresses with the & operator? That is fine if you have a fixed amount of data that you want to reach through the pointers. Otherwise, use the new operator to allocate memory dynamically. Be sure to deallocate the memory when you are done, using the delete or delete[] operator.

In our example, there is no need for dynamic allocation, so we will just take addresses of variables.

```
int master_account;
int project_accounts[10];
for (int i = 0; i < 100; i++)
{
    users[i] = &master_account;
}
// Here we reassign several users to project accounts.
// The following code is a simulation of the actions that would
// occur in an administration interface, which we do not implement.
users[2] = project_accounts + 1
users[3] = project_accounts + 2
users[99] = project_accounts + 2
```

Step 4   Use the * or [] operator to access your data.

When you access a single variable through a pointer, use the * operator to read or write the variable. For example,

```
*account_pointer = *account_pointer + 20;
```

When you have a pointer to an array, use the [] notation. Simply think of the pointer as the array:

```
account_array[i] = account_array[i] + 20;
```

If you have an array or vector of pointers, then you need brackets to get at an individual pointer. Then supply another * or [] to get at the value. You saw an example in the Galton board simulator where a count was accessed as

```
counts[i][j]
```

Implement your algorithm, keeping these access rules in mind.

In our example, we read the user ID and number of copies. Then we increment the copy account:

```
cin >> id >> copies;
*users[id] = *users[id] + copies;
```

Exercise P7.2 asks you to complete this simulation.

WORKED EXAMPLE 7.1

Producing a Mass Mailing

Learn how to use pointers to create a template for a mass mailing. See your E-Text or visit wiley.com/go/bclo3.

Computing & Society 7.1 **Embedded Systems**

An **embedded system** is a computer system that controls a device. The device contains a processor and other hardware and is controlled by a computer program. Unlike a personal computer, which has been designed to be flexible and run many different computer programs, the hardware and software of an embedded system are tailored to a specific device. Computer controlled devices are becoming increasingly common, ranging from washing machines to medical equipment, cell phones, automobile engines, and spacecraft.

Several challenges are specific to programming embedded systems. Most importantly, a much higher standard of quality control applies. Vendors are often unconcerned about bugs in personal computer software, because they can always make you install a patch or upgrade to the next version. But in an embedded system, that is not an option. Few consumers would feel comfortable upgrading the software in their washing machines or automobile engines. If you ever handed in a programming assignment that you believed to be correct, only to have the instructor or grader find bugs in it, then you know how hard it is to write software that can reliably do its task for many years without a chance of changing it. Quality standards are especially important in devices whose failure would destroy property or endanger human life. Many personal computer purchasers buy computers that are fast and have a lot of storage, because the investment is paid back over time when many programs are run on the same equipment. But the hardware for an embedded device is not shared—it is dedicated to one device. A separate processor, memory, and so on, are built for every copy of the device. If it is possible to shave a few pennies off the manufacturing cost of every unit, the savings can add up quickly for devices that are pro-duced in large volumes. Thus, the pro-grammer of an embedded system has a much larger economic incentive to conserve resources than the desktop software programmer. Unfortunately, trying to conserve resources usually makes it harder to write programs that work correctly.

C and C++ are commonly used languages for developing embedded systems.

© Courtesy of Professor Prabal Dutta.

The Controller of an Embedded System

7.7 Structures

In C++, you use arrays or vectors to collect values of the same type. If you want to group values of different types together, you use a structured type instead. In the following sections, you will learn how to define structured types and how to work with values of these types.

7.7.1 Structured Types

A structure combines member values into a single value.

Consider a street address that is composed of a house number and a street name. A **structure** named StreetAddress can be defined to combine these two values into a single entity.

In C++, we define a structure with the struct reserved word:

```
struct StreetAddress
{
    int house_number;
    string street_name;
};
```

© Joel Carillet/iStockphoto.

Syntax 7.3 Defining a Structure

The structure definition defines this type.

```
struct StreetAddress
{
    int house_number;
    string street_name;
};
```

Each variable of the structure type has these members.

Don't forget this semicolon!

Type *Variable name*

```
StreetAddress home;
home.house_number = 123;
```

Use the dot operator to access a member.

This definition yields a new type, StreetAddress, that you can use for declaring variables:

```
StreetAddress white_house;
```

You use the dot notation to access members of a structure.

The variable white_house has two named parts, called *members*, house_number and street_name. You use the "dot notation" to access each member, like this:

```
white_house.house_number = 1600;
white_house.street_name = "Pennsylvania Avenue";
```

StreetAddress	
house_number =	1600
street_name =	Penn. Ave.

Figure 11 A Structure Value

7.7.2 Structure Assignment and Comparison

When you assign one structure value to another, all members are assigned.

You can use the = operator to assign one structure value to another. All members are assigned simultaneously. For example, if we declare a structure value

```
StreetAddress destination;
```

then the assignment

```
destination = white_house;
```

is equivalent to

```
destination.house_number = white_house.house_number;
destination.street_name = white_house.street_name;
```

However, you cannot compare two structures for equality. That is,

```
if (destination == white_house) // Error
```

is not legal. You need to compare each member separately:

```
if (destination.house_number == white_house.house_number
    && destination.street_name == white_house.street_name) // Ok
```

7.7.3 Functions and Structures

Structures can be function arguments and return values. You simply specify the structure type as the parameter variable or return type, as you would with any other type.

For example, the following function has a parameter variable of type StreetAddress:

```
void print_address(StreetAddress address)
{
    cout << address.house_number << " " << address.street_name;
}
```

A function can return a structure. For example, the following function returns a random address on Main Street:

```
StreetAddress make_random_address()
{
    StreetAddress result;
    result.house_number = 100 + rand() % 100;
    result.street_name = "Main Street";
    return result;
}
```

7.7.4 Arrays of Structures

If you need to collect many addresses, you can put them into an array. For example, here is a variable delivery_route that is an array of street addresses:

```
StreetAddress delivery_route[ROUTE_LENGTH];
```

Figure 12
An Array of Structures

To access a member of the structure, you first access the element in the array with the bracket operator, and then use the dot operator:

```
delivery_route[0].house_number = 123;
delivery_route[0].street_name = "Main Street";
```

You can also access a structure value in its entirety, like this:

```
StreetAddress start = delivery_route[0];
```

Of course, you can also form vectors of structures:

```
vector<StreetAddress> tour_destinations;
tour_destinations.push_back(white_house);
```

7.7.5 Structures with Array Members

Structure members can contain arrays. For example, here is a structure that describes monthly temperatures at a given location. The temperature values are stored in an array.

```
struct MonthlyTemperatures
{
    string location;
    double values[12];
};
```

To access an array element, you first select the array member with the dot notation, then use brackets:

```
MonthlyTemperatures death_valley_noon;
death_valley_noon.values[2] = 82;
```

Figure 13 A Structure Containing an Array

7.7.6 Nested Structures

A structure can have a member that is another structure. For example, a person has a name and a street address. Because we already have a structure that describes street addresses, we can use it inside a Person structure.

```
struct Person
{
   string name;
   StreetAddress work_address;
};
```

You can access the nested member in its entirety, like this:

```
Person theodore;
theodore.work_address = white_house;
```

Alternatively, if you want to select a member of a member, use the dot operator twice:

```
theodore.work_address.street_name = "Pennsylvania Avenue";
```

A structure can have multiple members that are structures. For example, Person can also have a home address that again has type StreetAddress:

```
struct Person
{
   string name;
   StreetAddress home_address;
   StreetAddress work_address;
};
```

Figure 14   A Structure Containing Another Structure

EXAMPLE CODE   See sec07 of your companion code for a program that shows structures in use.

7.8 Pointers and Structures

7.8.1 Pointers to Structures

It is common to allocate structure values dynamically. As with all dynamic allocations, you use the new operator:

```
StreetAddress* address_pointer = new StreetAddress;
```

Now suppose you want to set the house number of the structure to which address_ pointer points. As always when you have a pointer, you can use the * operator for accessing the data to which the pointer points. However, you have to be careful. Consider the following attempt:

```
*address_pointer.house_number = 1600; // Error
```

Unfortunately, that is a syntax error. The dot operator has a higher precedence than the * operator. That is, the compiler thinks that you mean

```
*(address_pointer.house_number) = 1600; // Error
```

However, `address_pointer` is a pointer, not a structure. You can't apply the dot (.) operator to a pointer, and the compiler reports an error. Instead, you must make it clear that you first want to apply the * operator, then the dot:

```
(*address_pointer).house_number = 1600; // OK
```

Use the -> operator to access a structure member through a pointer.

Because this is such a common situation, the designers of C++ supply an operator to abbreviate the "follow pointer and access member" operation. That operator is written -> and usually pronounced "arrow".

```
address_pointer->house_number = 1600; // OK
```

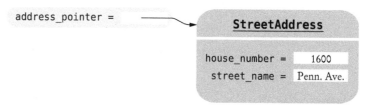

Figure 15   A Pointer to a Structure

7.8.2 Structures with Pointer Members

A member of a structure can be a pointer. This situation commonly arises when information is shared among structure values. Consider this example. In an organization with multiple offices, each employee has a name and an office location:

```
struct Employee
{
   string name;
   StreetAddress* office;
};
```

Here, we define two employees who both work for the accounting office:

```
StreetAddress accounting;
accounting.house_number = 1729;
accounting.street_name = "Park Avenue";

Employee harry;
harry.name = "Smith, Harry";
harry.office = &accounting;
Employee sally;
sally.name = "Lee, Sally";
sally.office = &accounting;
```

Figure 16 shows how these structures are related.

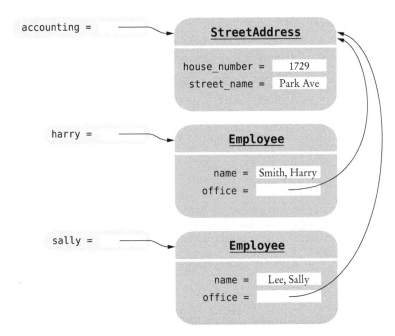

Figure 16   Two Pointers to a Shared Structure

This sharing of information has an important benefit. Suppose the accounting office moves across the street:

```
accounting.house_number = 1720;
```

Now both Harry's and Sally's office addresses are automatically updated.

EXAMPLE CODE   See sec08 of your companion code for a program that shows dynamically-allocated structures.

Special Topic 7.5

Smart Pointers

As you saw in Section 7.4, it can be a signifcant burden for programmers to allocate and deal-locate memory. C++ 11 introduces a shared_ptr type that can automatically reclaim memory that is no longer used. Consider, for example, the Employee structure from Section 7.8.2. We can change the StreetAddress* pointers to shared pointers:

```
shared_ptr<StreetAddress> accounting(new StreetAddress);
accounting->house_number = 1729;
accounting->street_name = "Park Avenue";
Employee sally;
sally.name = "Lee, Sally";
sally.office = accounting;
```

Now the StreetAddress structure describing the accounting office has two shared pointers pointing to it: accounting and sally.office. When both of these variables go away, then the structure memory is automatically deleted.

We will discuss additional strategies for memory management in C++ in Chapter 13.

EXAMPLE CODE   See special_topic_5 of your companion code for a program that uses shared pointers.

CHAPTER SUMMARY

Define and use pointer variables.

- A pointer denotes the location of a variable in memory.
- The type T* denotes a pointer to a variable of type T.
- The & operator yields the location of a variable.
- The * operator accesses the variable to which a pointer points.
- It is an error to use an uninitialized pointer.
- The nullptr pointer does not point to any object.

Understand the relationship between arrays and pointers in C++.

- The name of an array variable is a pointer to the starting element of the array.
- Pointer arithmetic means adding an integer offset to an array pointer, yielding a pointer that skips past the given number of elements.
- The array/pointer duality law states that a[n] is identical to *(a + n), where a is a pointer into an array and n is an integer offset.
- When passing an array to a function, only the starting address is passed.

Use C++ string objects with functions that process character arrays.

- A value of type char denotes an individual character. Character literals are enclosed in single quotes.
- A literal string (enclosed in double quotes) is an array of char values with a zero terminator.
- Many library functions use pointers of type char*.
- The c_str member function yields a char* pointer from a string object.
- You can initialize C++ string variables with C strings.
- You can access characters in a C++ string object with the [] operator.

Allocate and deallocate memory in programs whose memory requirements aren't known until run time.

- Use dynamic memory allocation if you do not know in advance how many values you need.
- The new operator allocates memory from the free store.
- You must reclaim dynamically allocated objects with the delete or delete[] operator.
- Using a dangling pointer (a pointer that points to memory that has been deleted) is a serious programming error.
- Every call to new should have a matching call to delete.

Work with arrays and vectors of pointers.

Draw diagrams for visualizing pointers and the data to which they point.

- Draw the data that is being processed, then draw the pointer variables. When drawing the pointer arrows, illustrate a typical situation.

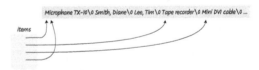

Use structures to aggregate data items.

- A structure combines member values into a single value.
- You use the dot notation to access members of a structure.
- When you assign one structure value to another, all members are assigned.

Work with pointers to structures.

- Use the -> operator to access a structure member through a pointer.

REVIEW EXERCISES

■ **R7.1** Trace the following code. Assume that a and b are stored at 20300 and 20308. Your trace table should have entries for a, b, and p.

```
double a = 1000;
double b = 2000;
double* p = &a;
*p = 3000;
p = &b;
a = *p * 2;
```

■ **R7.2** Trace the following code. Assume that a and b are stored at 20300 and 20308. Your trace table should have entries for a, b, p, and q.

```
double a = 1000;
double b = 2000;
double* p = &a;
double* q = &b;
*p = *q;
p = q;
*p = 3000;
```

■ **R7.3** What does the following code print?

```
double a = 1000;
double b = 2000;
double* p = &a;
double* q = p;
b = *q;
p = &b;
a = *p + *q;
cout << a << " " << b << endl;
```

■ **R7.4** Explain the mistakes in the following code. Not all lines contain mistakes. Each line depends on the lines preceding it.

```
1  double a = 1000;
2  double* p = a;
3  int* p = &a;
4  double* q;
5  *q = 2000;
6  int* r = nullptr;
7  *r = 3000;
```

■■ **R7.5** Suppose that a system allows the use of any string as a password, even the empty string. However, when a user connects to the system for the first time, no password has been assigned. Describe how you can use a string* variable and the nullptr pointer to distinguish unassigned passwords from empty ones.

■■ **R7.6** Given the definitions

```
double primes[] = { 2, 3, 5, 7, 11, 13 };
double* p = primes + 3;
```

draw a diagram that explains the meanings of the following expressions:

a. primes[1]

b. primes + 1

c. *(primes + 1)

d. p[1]

e. p + 1

■ **R7.7** Suppose the array `primes`, defined as

```
double primes[] = { 2, 3, 5, 7, 11, 13 };
```

starts at memory location 20300. What are the values of

   a. `primes`
   b. `*primes`
   c. `primes + 4`
   d. `*(primes + 4)`
   e. `primes[4]`
   f. `&primes[4]`

■ **R7.8** Suppose the array `primes` is defined as

```
double primes[] = { 2, 3, 5, 7, 11, 13 };
```

Consider the `sum` function discussed in Section 7.2.3. What are the values of

   a. `sum(primes, 6);`
   b. `sum(primes, 4);`
   c. `sum(primes + 2, 4);`
   d. `sum(primes, 0);`
   e. `sum(nullptr, 4);`

■■ **R7.9** Suppose the array `primes`, defined as

```
double primes[] = { 2, 3, 5, 7, 11, 13 };
```

starts at memory location 20300. Trace the function call `sum(primes, 4)`, using the definition of `sum` from Special Topic 7.2. In your trace table, show the values for `a`, `size`, `total`, `p`, and `i`.

■■■ **R7.10** Pointers are addresses and have a numerical value. You can print out the value of a pointer as `cout << (unsigned)(p)`. Write a program to compare `p`, `p + 1`, `q`, and `q + 1`, where `p` is an `int*` and `q` is a `double*`. Explain the results.

■■ **R7.11** A pointer variable can contain a pointer to a single variable, a pointer to an array, `nullptr`, or a random value. Write code that creates and sets four pointer variables `a`, `b`, `c`, and `d` to show each of these possibilities.

■■ **R7.12** Implement a function `firstlast` that obtains the first and last values in an array of integers and stores the result in an array *parameter*.

■ **R7.13** Explain the meanings of the following expressions:

   a. `"Harry" + 1`
   b. `*("Harry" + 2)`
   c. `"Harry"[3]`
   d. `[4]"Harry"`

■ **R7.14** What is the difference between the following two variable definitions?

   a. `char a[6] = "Hello";`
   b. `char* b = "Hello";`

■ **R7.15** What is the difference between the following three variable definitions?

   a. `char* p = nullptr;`
   b. `char* q = "";`
   c. `char r[1] = { '\0' };`

R7.16 Consider this program segment:

```
char a[] = "Mary had a little lamb";
char* p = a;
int count = 0;
while (*p != '\0')
{
   count++;
   while (*p != ' ' && *p != '\0') { p++; }
   while (*p == ' ') { p++; }
}
```

What is the value of count at the end of the outer while loop?

R7.17 Consider the following code that repeats a C++ string three times.

```
string a = "Hello";
string b = a + a + a;
```

Suppose s is a C string, and t is declared as

```
char t[100];
```

Write the equivalent code for C strings that stores the threefold repetition of s (or as much of it as will fit) into t.

R7.18 Which of the following assignments are legal in C++?

```
void f(int p[])
{
   int* q;
   const int* r;
   int s[10];
   p = q;  // 1
   p = r;  // 2
   p = s;  // 3
   q = p;  // 4
   q = r;  // 5
   q = s;  // 6
   r = p;  // 7
   r = q;  // 8
   r = s;  // 9
   s = p;  // 10
   s = q;  // 11
   s = r;  // 12
}
```

R7.19 What happens if you forget to delete an object that you obtained from the free store? What happens if you delete it twice?

R7.20 Write a program that accesses a deleted pointer, an uninitialized pointer, and a nullptr. What happens when you run your program?

R7.21 Find the mistakes in the following code. Not all lines contain mistakes. Each line depends on the lines preceding it. Watch out for uninitialized pointers, nullptr pointers, pointers to deleted objects, and confusing pointers with objects.

```
1  int* p = new int;
2  p = 5;
3  *p = *p + 5;
4  string s = "Harry";
5  *s = "Sally";
6  delete &s;
```

```
 7  int* a = new int[10];
 8  *a = 5;
 9  a[10] = 5;
10  delete a;
11  int* q;
12  *q = 5;
13  q = p;
14  delete q;
15  delete p;
```

■■ **R7.22** How do you define a triangular two-dimensional array using just vectors, not arrays or pointers?

■ **R7.23** Rewrite the statements in Section 7.8.2 so that the street address and employee structures are allocated on the free store.

■ **R7.24** What is a key difference between a structure and an array?

■■ **R7.25** For each of the following, should you use an array of structures, a structure containing one or more arrays, or a structure containing another structure?

    a. A course with multiple students

    b. An assignment with a due date

    c. A student with grades for each assignment

    d. An instructor with multiple courses

■■■ **R7.26** How could you implement the delivery route from Section 7.7.4 as a structure containing arrays? Which implementation is better? Why?

■■ **R7.27** Design a structure type Person that contains the name of a person and pointers to the person's father and mother. Write statements that define a structure value for yourself and your parents, correctly establishing the pointer links. (Use nullptr for your parents' parents.)

■ **R7.28** Assuming the following declarations, write C++ expressions to set all integer values of b's members to 42.

```
struct A { int m1[2]; }
struct B { A a1; A a2; int m2; }
B b;
```

■ **R7.29** Assuming the following declarations, write C++ expressions to set all integer values of b to 42.

```
struct A { int m1[2]; }
struct B { A a1; A* a2; int m2; }
B* b = new B;
```

■ **R7.30** Assuming the following declarations, find the mistakes in the statements below.

```
struct A { int m1[2]; int m2; }
struct B { A a1; A* a2; int m3; }
A a;
B b[2];
```

    a. b[0].a2 = a;

    b. b[1].m2 = 42;

    c. b[2].a2 = new A;

    d. b[0].a1.m1 = 42;

    e. b[1].a2->m2 = 42;

■■■ R7.31 Draw a figure showing the result of a call to the maximum function in Exercise E7.4.

■■■ R7.32 Draw a figure showing the pointers in the lines array in Exercise P7.3 after reading a few lines.

■■ R7.33 Section 7.6 described an arrangement where each item had a pointer to the user who had checked out the item. This makes it difficult to find out the items that a particular user checked out. To solve this problem, have an array of strings user_names and a parallel array loaned_items. loaned_items[i] points to an array of char* pointers, each of which is a name of an item that the ith user checked out. If the ith user didn't check out any items, then loaned_items[i] is nullptr. Draw a picture of this arrangement.

PRACTICE EXERCISES

■ E7.1 Write a function

```
void sort2(double* p, double* q)
```

that receives two pointers and sorts the values to which they point. If you call

```
sort2(&x, &y)
```

then x <= y after the call.

■ E7.2 Write a function

```
double replace_if_greater(double* p, double x)
```

that replaces the value to which p points with x if x is greater. Return the old value to which p pointed.

■ E7.3 Write a function that computes the average value of an array of floating-point data:

```
double average(double* a, int size)
```

In the function, use a pointer variable, not an integer index, to traverse the array elements.

■ E7.4 Write a function that returns a pointer to the maximum value of an array of floating-point data:

```
double* maximum(double* a, int size)
```

If size is 0, return nullptr.

■ E7.5 Write a function that returns a pointer to the first occurrence of the character c in the string s, or nullptr if there is no match.

```
char* find(char s[], char c)
```

■ E7.6 Write a function that returns a pointer to the last occurrence of the character c in the string s, or nullptr if there is no match.

```
char* find_last(char s[], char c)
```

■■ E7.7 Write a function that returns a pointer to the nth occurrence of the character c in the string s, or nullptr if there is no match.

```
char* find_last(char s[], char c, int n)
```

■■ E7.8 Write a function that returns a pointer to the first occurrence of the substring t in the string s, or nullptr if there is no match.

```
char* find(char s[], char t[])
```

■■ **E7.9** Write a function that, given strings s, t, and u, returns a string (allocated with the new operator) in which all occurrences of t in s are replaced with u:

```
char* replace_all(const char s[], const char t[], const char u[])
```

■■ **E7.10** Write a function that reverses the values of an array of floating-point data:

```
void reverse(double* a, int size)
```

In the function, use two pointer variables, not integer indexes, to traverse the array elements.

■■ **E7.11** Implement the strncpy function of the standard library.

■■■ **E7.12** Implement the standard library function

```
int strspn(const char s[], const char t[])
```

that returns the length of the initial portion of s consisting only of characters contained in t (in any order). For example, if all of the characters in s are in t, the function returns the length of s; if the first character in s is not in t, the function returns zero.

■■ **E7.13** Write a function

```
void reverse(char s[])
```

that reverses a character string. For example, "Harry" becomes "yrraH".

■■■ **E7.14** Using the strncpy and strncat functions, implement a function

```
void safe_concat(const char a[], const char b[], char result[],
   int result_maxlength)
```

that concatenates the strings a and b to the buffer result. Be sure not to overrun the buffer. It can hold result_maxlength characters, not counting the '\0' terminator. (That is, the buffer has result_maxlength + 1 bytes available.)

■■■ **E7.15** Write a function int* read_data(int& size) that reads data from cin until the user terminates input by entering Q. The function should set the size reference parameter to the number of numeric inputs. Return a pointer to an array on the free store. That array should have exactly size elements. Of course, you won't know at the outset how many elements the user will enter. Start with an array of 10 elements, and double the size whenever the array fills up. At the end, allocate an array of the correct size and copy all inputs into it. Be sure to delete any intermediate arrays.

■ **E7.16** Define a structure Point. A point has an x- and a y-coordinate. Write a function double distance(Point a, Point b) that computes the distance from a to b. Write a program that reads the coordinates of the points, calls your function, and displays the result.

■ **E7.17** Using the Point structure from Exercise E7.16, write a function Point midpoint(Point a, Point b) that computes the point that is halfway between a and b. Write a program that reads the coordinates of the points, calls your function, and displays the result.

■■ **E7.18** Define a structure Triangle that contains three Point members. Write a function that computes the perimeter of a Triangle. Write a program that reads the coordinates of the points, calls your function, and displays the result.

■■ **E7.19** Reimplement the Triangle structure and the perimeter function of Exercise E7.18 so that it contains two arrays of three double values each, one for the x-coordinates and one for the y-coordinates.

- **E7.20** Define an Employee structure with a name and an Employee* pointer to the employee's manager. For the CEO, that pointer will be a nullptr. Write a program that defines several employees and their managers. For each employee, print the chain of superiors.

PROGRAMMING PROJECTS

- ■■ **P7.1** Enhance the Galton board simulation by printing a bar chart of the bottommost counters. Draw the bars vertically, below the last row of numbers.

```
 1  18  64 149 239 265 186  61  15   2
     *   *   *   *   *   *   *   *
         *   *   *   *   *   *
         *   *   *   *   *   *
             *   *   *   *
             *   *   *   *
             *   *   *   *
             *   *   *   *
                 *   *   *
                 *   *   *
                 *   *
                 *   *
                 *   *
                     *
```

- ■■■ **P7.2** Complete the copier simulation of How To 7.1. Your program should first show the main menu:

  ```
  U)ser A)dministrator Q)uit
  ```

  For a user, prompt for the ID and the number of copies, increment the appropriate account, and return to the main menu.

  For an administrator, show this menu:

  ```
  B)alance M)aster P)roject
  ```

  In the balance option, show the balances of the master account and the ten project accounts. In the master option, prompt for a user ID and link it to the master account. In the project option, prompt for user and project IDs. Afterward, return to the main menu.

- ■■ **P7.3** Write a program that reads lines of text and appends them to a char buffer[1000]. Read one character at a time by calling cin.get(ch), where ch is a variable of type char. Use input redirection (Special Topic 4.3). Stop after reading 1,000 characters. As you read in the text, replace all newline characters '\n' with '\0' terminators. Establish an array char* lines[100], so that the pointers in that array point to the beginnings of the lines in the text. Consider only 100 input lines if the input has more lines. Then display the lines in reverse order, starting with the last input line.

- ■■■ **P7.4** The program in Exercise P7.3 is limited by the fact that it can only handle inputs of 1,000 characters or 100 lines. Remove this limitation as follows. Concatenate the input in one long string object. Use the c_str member function to obtain a char* into the string's character buffer. Store the beginnings of the lines as a vector<char*>.

- ■■ **P7.5** Exercise P7.4 demonstrated how to use the string and vector classes to implement resizable arrays. In this exercise, you should implement that capability manually. Allocate a buffer of 1,000 characters from the free store (new char[1000]). Whenever the buffer fills up, allocate a buffer of twice the size, copy the buffer contents, and delete the old buffer. Do the same for the array of char* pointers — start with a new char*[100] and keep doubling the size.

■■■ P7.6   Modify Exercise P7.3 so that you first print the lines in the order that they were entered, then print them in sorted order. When you sort the lines, only rearrange the pointers in the lines array.

■■■ P7.7   When you read a long document, there is a good chance that many words occur multiple times. Instead of storing each word, it may be beneficial to only store unique words, and to represent the document as a vector of pointers to the unique words. Write a program that implements this strategy. Read a word at a time from cin. Keep a vector<char*> of words. If the new word is not contained in this vector, allocate memory, copy the word into it, and append a pointer to the new memory. If the word is already present, then append a pointer to the existing word.

■ P7.8   Define a structure Student with a first name, last name, and course grade (A, B, C, D, or F). Write a program that reads input in which each line has the first and last name and course grade, separated by spaces. Upon reading the input, your program should print all students with grade A, then all students with grade B, and so on.

■■ P7.9   Enhance the program in Exercise P7.8 so that each student has ten quiz scores. The input contains the student names and quiz scores but no course grades. The program should compute the course grade. If the sum of the quiz scores is at least 90, the grade is an A. If the sum is at least 80, the grade is a B, and so on. Then print all students with grade A together with their individual quiz scores, followed by all students with grade B, and so on.

■■■ P7.10   Define a structure Student with a name and a vector<Course*> of courses. Define a structure Course with a name and a vector<Student*> of enrolled students. Then define these functions:

- void print_student(Student* s) that prints the name of a student and the names of all courses that the student takes.
- void print_course(Course* c) that prints the name of a course and the names of all students in that course.
- void enroll(Student* s, Course* c) that enrolls the given student in the given course, updating both vectors.

In your main function, define several students and courses, and enroll students in the courses. Then call print_student for all students and print_course for all courses.

■■ Engineering P7.11   Write a program that simulates a device that gathers measurements and processes them.

A gather function gathers data values (which you should simulate with random integers between 0 and 100) and places them in an array. When the array is full, the gather function calls a function new_array to request a new array to fill.

A process function processes a data value (for this exercise, it simply updates global variables for computing the maximum, minimum, and average). When it has reached the end of the array, it calls a function next_array to request a new array to process.

Because the gather function may fill arrays faster than the process function processes them, store the pointers to the filled arrays in another array. The new_array and next_array functions need to maintain that array of pointers.

In a real device, data gathering and processing happen in parallel. Simulate this by calling the gather and process functions randomly from main.

■■■ **Engineering P7.12** Write a program that simulates the control software for a "people mover" system, a set of driverless trains that move in two concentric circular tracks. A set of switches allows trains to switch tracks.

In your program, the outer and inner tracks should each be divided into ten segments. Each track segment can contain a train that moves either clockwise or counterclockwise. A train moves to an adjacent segment in its track or, if that segment is occupied, to the adjacent segment in the other track.

Define a Segment structure. Each segment has a pointer to the next and previous

© TexPhoto/iStockphoto.

segments in its track, a pointer to the next and previous segments in the other track, and a train indicator that is 0 (empty), +1 (train moving clockwise), or −1 (train moving counterclockwise). Populate the system with four trains at random segments, two in each direction. Display the tracks and trains in each step, like this:

The two rectangles indicate the tracks. Each switch that allows a train to switch between the outer and inner track is indicated by an x. Each train is drawn as a > or <, indicating its current direction. Your program should show fifty rounds. In each round, all trains move once.

CHAPTER 8

STREAMS

James King-Holmes/Bletchley Park Trust/Photo Researchers, Inc.

CHAPTER GOALS

To be able to read and write files

To convert between strings and numbers using string streams

To process command line arguments

To understand the concepts of sequential and random access

CHAPTER CONTENTS

In this chapter, you will learn how to read and write files using the C++ stream library—a very useful skill for processing real world data. As an application, you will learn how to encrypt data. (The Enigma machine shown in the photo is an encryption device used by Germany in World War II. Pioneering British computer scientists broke the code and were able to intercept encoded messages, which was a significant help in winning the war.) Later in the chapter, you will learn to process binary files, such as those that store image data.

8.1 Reading and Writing Text Files

The C++ input/output library is based on the concept of **streams**. An **input stream** is a source of data, and an **output stream** is a destination for data. The most common sources and destinations for data are the files on your hard disk.

To access a file, you use a file stream. There are three types of file streams: `ifstream` (for input), `ofstream` (for output), and `fstream` (for both input and output). Include the `<fstream>` header when you use any of these file streams.

In the following sections, you will learn how to process data from files. File processing is a very useful skill in many disciplines because it is exceedingly common to analyze large data sets stored in files.

> To read or write files, you use variables of type `fstream`, `ifstream`, or `ofstream`.

© nullplus/iStockphoto.

Data arrive in an input stream just like items on a conveyor belt, one at a time.

8.1.1 Opening a Stream

To read anything from a file stream, you need to *open* it. When you open a stream, you give the name of the file stored on disk. Suppose you want to read data from a file named `input.dat`, located in the same directory as the program. Then you use the following function call to open the file:

> When opening a file stream, you supply the name of the file stored on disk.

```
in_file.open("input.dat");
```

This statement associates the variable `in_file` with the file named `input.dat`.

Note that all streams are objects, and you use the dot notation for calling functions that manipulate them.

To open a file for writing, you use an `ofstream` variable. To open the same file for both reading and writing, you use an `fstream` variable.

File names can contain directory path information, such as

```
~/homework/input.dat (UNIX)
c:\homework\input.dat (Windows)
```

When you specify the file name as a string literal, and the name contains backslash characters (as in a Windows filename), you must supply each backslash *twice*:

```
in_file.open("c:\\homework\\input.dat");
```

Recall that a single backslash inside a string literal is an **escape character** that is combined with another character to form a special meaning, such as \n for a newline character. The \\ combination denotes a single backslash.

In older versions of C++, you must be careful when opening a file with a name that is stored in a string variable. Use the c_str function to convert the C++ string to a C string:

```
cout << "Please enter the file name:";
string filename;
cin >> filename;
ifstream in_file;
in_file.open(filename.c_str()); // Before C++ 11
```

If it is not possible to open a stream, then the stream variable is set to a failed state. You can test for that condition:

```
in_file.open("input.dat");
if (in_file.fail())
{
    cout << "Cannot read from input.dat" << endl;
}
else
{
    Read input.
}
```

When the program ends, all streams that you have opened will be automatically closed. You can also manually close a stream with the close member function:

```
in_file.close();
```

Manual closing is only necessary if you want to use the stream variable again to process another file.

8.1.2 Reading from a File

Read from a file stream with the same operations that you use with cin.

Reading data from a file stream is completely straightforward: You simply use the same functions that you have always used for reading from cin:

```
string name;
double value;
in_file >> name >> value;
```

The fail function tells you whether input has failed. You have already used this function with cin, to check for errors in console input. File streams behave in the same way. When you try to read a number from a file, and the next data item is not a properly formatted number, then the stream fails. After reading data, you should test for success before processing:

```
if (!in_file.fail())
{
    Process input.
}
```

When you read input from a file, number format errors are not the only reason for failure. Suppose you have consumed all of the data contained in a file and try to read more items. A file stream enters the failed state, whereas `cin` would just wait for more user input. Moreover, if you open a file and the name is invalid, or if there is no file of that name, then the file stream is also in a failed state. It is a good idea to test for failure immediately after calling `open`.

Syntax 8.1   Working with File Streams

8.1.3 Writing to a File

Write to a file stream with the same operations that you use with cout.

In order to write to a file, you define an `ofstream` or `fstream` variable and open it. Then you send information to the output file, using the same operations that you used with `cout`:

```
ofstream out_file;
out_file.open("output.txt");
out_file << name << " " << value << endl;
```

8.1.4 A File Processing Example

Here is a typical example of processing data in a file. The Social Security Administration publishes lists of the most popular baby names on their web site, http://www.ssa.gov/OACT/babynames/. If you query the 1,000 most popular names for a given decade, the browser displays the result on the screen (see Figure 1).

To save the data as text, simply select it and paste the result into a file. This book's companion code contains a file called babynames.txt with the data for the 1990s.

Each line in the file contains seven entries:

- The rank (from 1 to 1,000)

- The name, frequency, and percentage of the male name of that rank

- The name, frequency, and percentage of the female name of that rank

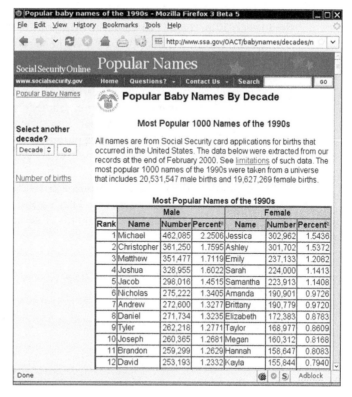

Figure 1   Querying Baby Names

For example, the line

```
10   Joseph   260365   1.2681   Megan   160312   0.8168
```

shows that the 10th most common boy's name was Joseph, with 260,365 births, or 1.2681 percent of all births during that period. The 10th most common girl's name was Megan. Why are there many more Josephs than Megans? Parents seem to use a wider set of girl's names, making each one of them less frequent.

Let us test that conjecture, by determining the names given to the top 50 percent of boys and girls in the list.

To process each line, we first read the rank:

```
int rank;
in_file >> rank;
```

We then read a set of three values for the boy's name:

```
string name;
int count;
double percent;
in_file >> name >> count >> percent;
```

Then we repeat that step for girls. Because the actions are identical, we supply a helper function `process_name` for that purpose. To stop

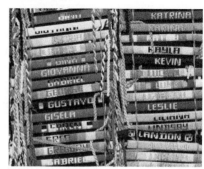

© Nancy Ross/iStockphoto.

Sellers of personalized items can find trends in popular names by processing data files from the Social Security Administration.

processing after reaching 50 percent, we can add up the frequencies and stop when they reach 50 percent. However, it turns out to be a bit simpler to initialize a total with 50 and subtract the frequencies. We need separate totals for boys and girls. When a total falls below 0, we stop printing. When both totals fall below 0, we stop reading.

Note that the in_file parameter variable of the process_name function in the code below is a reference parameter. Reading or writing modifies a stream variable. The stream variable monitors how many characters have been read or written so far. Any read or write operation changes that data. For that reason, you must always make stream parameter variables reference parameters.

The complete program is shown below. As you can see, reading from a file is just as easy as reading keyboard input.

Have a look at the program output. Remarkably, only 69 boy names and 153 girl names account for half of all births. That's good news for those who are in the business of producing personalized doodads. Exercise P8.3 asks you to study how this distribution has changed over the years.

> Always use a reference parameter for a stream.

sec01/babynames.cpp

```
1   #include <iostream>
2   #include <fstream>
3   #include <string>
4
5   using namespace std;
6
7   /**
8      Reads name information, prints the name if total >= 0, and adjusts the total.
9      @param in_file the input stream
10     @param total the total percentage that should still be processed
11  */
12  void process_name(ifstream& in_file, double& total)
13  {
14     string name;
15     int count;
16     double percent;
17     in_file >> name >> count >> percent;
18
19     if (in_file.fail()) { return; } // Check for failure after each input
20     if (total > 0) { cout << name << " "; }
21     total = total - percent;
22  }
23
24  int main()
25  {
26     ifstream in_file;
27     in_file.open("babynames.txt");
28     if (in_file.fail()) { return 0; } // Check for failure after opening
29
30     double boy_total = 50;
31     double girl_total = 50;
32
33     while (boy_total > 0 || girl_total > 0)
34     {
35        int rank;
36        in_file >> rank;
37        if (in_file.fail()) { return 0; }
38
39        cout << rank << " ";
```

```
40
41        process_name(in_file, boy_total);
42        process_name(in_file, girl_total);
43
44        cout << endl;
45    }
46
47    return 0;
48 }
```

Program Run

```
 1 Michael Jessica
 2 Christopher Ashley
 3 Matthew Emily
 4 Joshua Sarah
 5 Jacob Samantha
 6 Nicholas Amanda
 7 Andrew Brittany
 8 Daniel Elizabeth
 9 Tyler Taylor
10 Joseph Megan
. . .
68 Dustin Gabrielle
69 Noah Katie
70 Caitlin
71 Lindsey
. . .
150 Hayley
151 Rebekah
152 Jocelyn
153 Cassidy
```

8.2 Reading Text Input

In the following sections, you will learn how to process text with complex contents such as that which often occurs in real-life situations.

8.2.1 Reading Words

You already know how to read the next word from a stream, using the >> operator.

```
string word;
in_file >> word;
```

When reading a string with the >> operator, the white space between words is consumed.

Here is precisely what happens when that operation is executed. First, any input characters that are white space are removed from the stream, but they are not added to the word. White space includes spaces, tab characters, and the newline characters that separate lines. The first character that is not white space becomes the first character in the string word. More characters are added until either another white space character occurs, or the end of the file has been reached. The white space after the word is not removed from the stream.

8.2.2 Reading Characters

Instead of reading an entire word, you can read one character at a time by calling the get function:

```
char ch;
in_file.get(ch);
```

The get function returns the "not failed" condition. The following loop processes all characters in a file:

```
while (in_file.get(ch))
{
    Process the character ch.
}
```

The get function reads white space characters. This is useful if you need to process characters such as spaces, tabs, or newlines. On the other hand, if you are not interested in white space, use the >> operator instead.

```
in_file >> ch; // ch is set to the next non-white space character
```

You can get individual characters from a stream and unget the last one.

If you read a character and you regretted it, you can *unget* it, so that the next input operation can read it again. However, you can unget only the last character. This is called *one-character lookahead.* You get a chance to look at the next character in the input stream, and you can make a decision whether you want to consume it or put it back.

A typical situation for lookahead is to look for numbers:

```
char ch;
in_file.get(ch);
if (isdigit(ch))
{
    in_file.unget(); // Put the digit back so that it is part of the number
    int n;
    in_file >> n; // Read integer starting with ch
}
```

The isdigit function is one of several useful functions that categorize characters—see Table 1. All return true or false as to whether the argument passes the test. You must include the <cctype> header to use these functions.

Table 1	Character Functions in <cctype>
Function	Accepted Characters
isdigit	0 ... 9
isalpha	a ... z, A ... Z
islower	a ... z
isupper	A ... Z
isalnum	a ... z, A ... Z, 0 ... 9
isspace	White space (space, tab, newline, and the rarely used carriage return, form feed, and vertical tab)

If you read a character from a stream and you don't like what you get, you can unget it.

© altrendo images/Getty Images.

8.2.3 Reading Lines

When each line of a file is a data record, it is often best to read entire lines with the getline function:

```
string line;
getline(in_file, line);
```

The next input line (without the newline character) is placed into the string line.

The getline function returns the "not failed" condition. You can use the following loop to process each line in a file:

> You can read a line of input with the getline function and then process it further.

```
while (getline(in_file, line))
{
    Process line.
}
```

Note that getline is not a member function, but an ordinary function that is not called with the dot notation.

Here is a typical example of processing lines in a file. A file with population data from the CIA World Factbook site (https://www.cia.gov/library/publications/the-world-factbook/index.html) contains lines such as the following:

```
China  1330044605
India  1147995898
United States 303824646
. . .
```

Because each line is a data record, it is natural to use the getline function for reading lines into a string variable. To extract the data from that string, you need to find out where the name ends and the number starts.

Locate the first digit:

```
int i = 0;
while (!isdigit(line[i])) { i++; }
```

Then go backward and skip white space:

```
int j = i - 1;
while (isspace(line[j])) { j--; }
```

i starts here   i ends here

U	n	i	t	e	d		S	t	a	t	e	s		3	0	3	8	2	4	6	4	6
0	1	2	3	4	5	6	7	8	9	10	11	12	13	14	15	16	17	18	19	20	21	22

j ends here   j starts here

length j + 1

Finally, extract the country name and population:

```
string country_name = line.substr(0, j + 1);
string population = line.substr(i);
```

There is just one problem. The population is stored in a string, not a number. You will see in Section 8.4 how to extract the population number as a number.

Common Error 8.1

Mixing >> and `getline` Input

It is tricky to mix >> and `getline` input. Suppose we place country names and populations on separate lines:

```
China
1330044605
India
1147995898
United States
303824646
```

Now we can use `getline` to read each country name without worrying about spaces:

```
getline(in, country_name);
in >> population;
```

The `getline` function reads an entire line of input, including the newline character at the end of the line. It places all characters except for that newline character into the string `country_name`. The >> operator reads all white space (that is, spaces, tabs, and newlines) until it reaches a number. Then it reads only the characters in that number. It does not consume the character following the number, typically a newline. This is a problem when a call to `getline` immediately follows a call to >>. Then the call to `getline` reads only the newline, considering it as the end of an empty line.

Perhaps an example will make this clearer. Consider the first input lines of the product descriptions. Calling `getline` consumes the darker-colored characters.

in = C h i n a \n 1 3 3 0 0 4 4 6 0 5 \n I n d i a \n

After the call to `getline`, the first line has been read completely, including the newline at the end. Next, the call to `in >> population` reads the digits.

in = 1 3 3 0 0 4 4 6 0 5 \n I n d i a \n

After the call to `in >> population`, the digits of the number have been read, but the newline is still unread, because the >> operator never reads any more characters than absolutely necessary. Now we have a problem. The next call to `getline` reads a blank line.

in = \n I n d i a \n

This is a problem whenever an input with the >> operator is followed by a call to `getline`. The intention, of course, is to skip the rest of the current line and have `getline` read the next line. This purpose is achieved by the following statements, which must be inserted after the last call to the >> operator:

```
string remainder; // Read remainder of line
getline(in, remainder);
// Now you are ready to call getline again
```

Stream Failure Checking

Given a stream variable, for example,

```
istream in_file;
```

you know that you can use the fail member function to check whether the stream has failed:

```
if (in_file.fail())
{
    Report error.
}
else
{
    Process input.
}
```

Alternatively, you can use the stream variable itself as a condition. The C++ compiler converts the stream to a bool value that is true if the stream has *not* failed, and false if it has failed. Therefore, you can achieve the same effect with the following statement:

```
if (in_file)
{
    Process input.
}
else
{
    Report error.
}
```

This alternative is particularly attractive with input operations that return a stream. In Section 4.5.2, you saw that you can read a sequence of values with the loop

```
cout << "Enter values, Q to quit: ";
int value;
while (cin >> value)
{
    Process value.
}
```

When the user enters a Q, or any other input that is not an integer, the stream state fails.

You can chain the >> operators. Consider this example:

```
while (in_file >> name >> value)
{
    Process the name and value.
}
```

When evaluating the expression

```
in_file >> name >> value;
```

the subexpression in_file >> name executes first, and it returns in_file. Next, the expression in_file >> value executes and again returns in_file. The in_file object is then converted to a bool value and tested in the condition.

As you saw in Section 8.2.1 and Section 8.2.3, you can also use expressions

```
in_file.get(ch)
```

and

```
get_line(in_file, line)
```

as conditions. This works for the same reason. The get and get_line functions return the input stream, and it is converted to a bool value.

8.3 Writing Text Output

You use the << operator to send strings and numbers to a stream. To write a single character to a stream, use

```
out_file.put(ch);
```

To control how the output is formatted, you use stream *manipulators*. A manipulator is a value that affects the behavior of the stream. It is sent to a stream using the << operator. The setw manipulator, which you have already used, is a typical example. The statement

```
out_file << setw(10);
```

Use the setw manipulator to set the width of the next output.

does not cause any immediate output, but when the next item is written, it is padded with sufficient spaces so that the output spans ten characters. (If a value does not fit into the given width, it is not truncated.)

Occasionally, you need to pad numbers with leading zeroes, for example to print hours and minutes as 09:01. This is achieved with the setfill manipulator:

```
out_file << setfill('0') << setw(2) << hours
    << ":" << setw(2) << minutes << setfill(' ');
```

Now, a zero is used to pad the field. Afterward, the space is restored as the fill character.

By default, the fill characters appear before the item:

```
out_file << setw(10) << 123 << endl << setw(10) << 4567;
```

produces

```
       123
      4567
```

The numbers line up to the right. That alignment works well for numbers, but not for strings. Usually, you want strings to line up at the left. You use the left and right manipulators to set the alignment. The following example uses left alignment for a string and then switches back to right alignment for a number:

```
out_file << left << setw(10) << word << right << setw(10) << number;
```

The *default floating-point format* displays as many digits as are specified by the *precision* (6 by default), switching to scientific notation for large and small numbers. For example,

```
out_file << 12.3456789 << " " << 123456789.0 << " " << 0.0000123456789;
```

yields

```
12.3457 1.23457e+08 1.23457e-05
```

A manipulator is like a control button on a sound mixer. It doesn't produce an output, but it affects how the output looks.

© iStockphoto.

The *fixed* format prints all values with the same number of digits after the decimal point. In the fixed format, the same numbers are displayed as

```
12.345679 123456789.000000 0.000012
```

Use the `fixed` manipulator to select that format, and the `setprecision` manipulator to change the precision.

For example,

```
out_file << fixed << setprecision(2) << 1.2 << " " << 1.235
```

yields

```
1.20 1.24
```

Table 2 summarizes the stream manipulators. Note that all manipulators set the state of the stream object for all subsequent operations, with the exception of `setw`. After each output operation, the field width is reset to 0. To use any of these manipulators, include the `<iomanip>` header.

Table 2 Stream Manipulators

Manipulator	Purpose	Example	Output

setw	Sets the field width of the next item only.	`out_file << setw(6) << 123 << endl`
		`   << 123 << endl`
		`   << setw(6) << 12345678;`
			`   123`
			`123`
			`12345678`

setfill	Sets the fill character for padding a field. (The default character is a space.)	`out_file << setfill('0') << setw(6)` `   << 123;`	`000123`
left	Selects left alignment.	`out_file << left << setw(6) << 123;`	`123`
right	Selects right alignment (default).	`out_file << right << setw(6) << 123;`	`   123`
fixed	Selects fixed format for floating-point numbers.	`double x = 123.4567;` `out_file << x << endl << fixed << x;`	`123.457` `123.456700`

setprecision	Sets the number of significant digits for the default floating-point format, the number of digits after the decimal point for fixed format.	`double x = 123.4567;`
		`out_file << fixed << x << endl`
		`   << setprecision(2) << x;`
			`123.456700`
			`123.46`

scientific	Selects scientific floating-point format, with one digit before the decimal point and an exponent.	`out_file << scientific` `   << setprecision(3) << 123.4567;`	`1.235e+02`

defaultfloat	(Since C++ 11) Switches back to the default floating-point format.	`double x = 123.4567;`
		`out_file << fixed << x << endl`
		`   << defaultfloat << x;`
			`123.456700`
			`123.457`

Special Topic 8.2

Unicode, UTF-8, and C++ Strings

As described in Computing & Society 2.2, the **Unicode** standard encodes alphabets from many languages. Each Unicode character has a unique 21-bit code that is written using the hexadecimal number system. For example, é (Latin small letter e with acute accent) has the code U+OOE9 and 🚄 (high speed train) has the code U+1F684. However, it would be inefficient to use these codes when characters are saved in files or transmitted over the Internet. Instead, a character encoding is used that represents each Unicode character as a sequence of one or more bytes.

If you process English text, you don't need to worry about character encodings because English characters are encoded with a single byte. The situation is more complex if you want to process text that contains characters such as é or 🚄. Nowadays, most data on the Internet uses the UTF-8 encoding. As it happens, the UTF-8 encoding of the string é takes up two bytes, and the UTF-8 encoding of 🚄 takes four bytes (see Appendix C). Therefore, the text

    San José 🚄

with two spaces, six English characters and these two characters, consists of 14 bytes when encoded with UTF-8.

When you read this text into a C++ string value, you get a string object of length 14, even though it only contains ten Unicode characters. It is not fruitful to look at the individual char values in isolation. Instead, work with substrings that are made up of one or more Unicode characters.

For example, suppose you want to find the position of the é. Form a string containing a single Unicode character.

If your C++ compiler uses the UTF-8 encoding, you can make such a string as

```
string e_acute = u8"é";
string high_speed_train = u8"🚄";
```

The u8 prefix indicates that you want to use the UTF-8 encoding. However, to make sure that your source file is portable to any system, it is a good idea to provide the Unicode value for the letter instead. You can use the \U prefix followed by eight hexadecimal digits:

```
string e_acute = u8"\U000000e9";
string high_speed_train = u8"\U0001f684";
```

Now that you know how to specify a string containing an arbitrary Unicode character, you can use the find member function to check whether the Unicode character occurs in a given string. We haven't covered this member function before because it is a bit fussy to use. Here is what you need to do:

```
string message = . . .;
size_t pos = message.find(e_acute);
if (pos != string::npos)
{
    // Message has e_acute starting at position pos
}
```

The size_t type indicates a non-negative position, and string::npos is a special value that denotes no position.

The locale library, which we don't cover in this book, gives you additional mechanisms to process UTF-8 strings. Exercise P8.11 provides a simple way of accessing individual characters.

EXAMPLE CODE   See special_topic_2 of your companion code for a sample program using UTF-8 encoding.

8.4 Parsing and Formatting Strings

In the preceding sections, you saw how file streams read characters from a file and write characters to a file. The `istringstream` class reads characters from a string, and the `ostringstream` class writes characters to a string. That doesn't sound so exciting—we already know how to access and change the characters of a string. However, the string stream classes have the same **public interface** as the other stream classes. In particular, you can use the familiar >> and << operators to read and write numbers that are contained in strings. For that reason, the `istringstream` and `ostringstream` classes are called *adapters*—they adapt strings to the stream interface. Include the <sstream> header when you use string streams.

© iStockphoto.

Like an adapter that converts your power plugs to international outlets, the string stream adapters allow you to access strings as streams.

> Use an `istringstream` to convert the numbers inside a string to integers or floating-point numbers.

Here is a typical example. Suppose the string `date` contains a date such as `"January 24, 1973"`, and we want to separate it into month, day, and year. First, construct an `istringstream` object. Then use the `str` function to set the stream to the string that you want to read:

```
istringstream strm;
strm.str("January 24, 1973");
```

Next, simply use the >> operator to read the month name, the day, the comma separator, and the year:

```
string month;
int day;
string comma;
int year;
strm >> month >> day >> comma >> year;
```

Now `month` is `"January"`, `day` is `24`, and `year` is `1973`. Note that this input statement yields `day` and `year` as *integers*. Had we taken the string apart with `substr`, we would have obtained only strings, not numbers.

If you only need to convert a single string to its `int` or `double` value, you can instead use the functions `stoi` and `stod`:

```
string year = "1973";
int y = stoi(year); // Sets y to the integer 1973
```

These functions are available since C++ 11. If you have an older version of C++, use a helper function for this purpose:

```
int string_to_int(string s)
{
   istringstream strm;
   strm.str(s);
   int n = 0;
   strm >> n;
   return n;
}
```

Use an ostringstream to convert numeric values to strings.

By writing to a string stream, you can convert integers or floating-point numbers to strings. First construct an `ostringstream` object:

```
ostringstream strm;
```

Next, use the `<<` operator to add a number to the stream. The number is converted into a sequence of characters:

```
strm << fixed << setprecision(5) << 10.0 / 3;
```

Now the stream contains the string `"3.33333"`. To obtain that string from the stream, call the `str` member function:

```
string output = strm.str();
```

You can build up more complex strings in the same way. Here we build a data string of the month, day, and year:

```
string month = "January";
int day = 4;
int year = 1973;
ostringstream strm;
strm << month << " " << setw(2) << setfill('0') << day << ", " << year;
string output = strm.str();
```

Now `output` is the string `"January 04, 1973"`. Note that we converted the *integers* `day` and `year` into a string.

If you don't need formatting, you can use the `to_string` function to convert numbers to strings. For example, `to_string(1973)` is the string `"1973"`.

You can produce a formatted date, without a leading zero for days less than ten, like this:

```
string output = month + " " + to_string(day) + ", " + to_string(year);
```

This function is available since C++ 11. Here is an implementation that you can use with older versions:

```
string int_to_string(int n)
{
   ostringstream strm;
   strm << n;
   return strm.str();
}
```

8.5 Command Line Arguments

Depending on the operating system and C++ development environment used, there are different methods of starting a program—for example, by selecting "Run" in the compilation environment, by clicking on an icon, or by typing the name of the program at a prompt in a command shell window. The latter method is called "invoking the program from the **command line**". When you use this method, you must type the name of the program, of course, but you can also type in additional information that the program can use. These additional strings are called **command line arguments**. For example, if you start a program with the command line

```
prog -v input.dat
```

then the program receives two command line arguments: the strings `"-v"` and `"input. dat"`. It is entirely up to the program what to do with these strings. It is customary to interpret strings starting with a hyphen (-) as options and other strings as file names.

To receive command line arguments, you need to define the `main` function in a different way. You define two parameter variables: an integer and an array of string literals of type `char*`.

```cpp
int main(int argc, char* argv[])
{
   . . .
}
```

Here `argc` is the count of arguments, and `argv` contains the values of the arguments. In our example, `argc` is 3, and `argv` contains the three strings

```
argv[0]:   "prog"
argv[1]:   "-v"
argv[2]:   "input.dat"
```

Note that `argv[0]` is always the name of the program and that `argc` is always at least 1.

Let's write a program that *encrypts* a file—that is, scrambles it so that it is unreadable except to those who know the decryption method. Ignoring 2,000 years of progress in the field of encryption, we will use a method familiar to Julius Caesar, replacing an A with a D, a B with an E, and so on. That is, each character c is replaced with $c + 3$ (see Figure 2).

The program takes the following command line arguments:

- An optional `-d` flag to indicate decryption instead of encryption
- The input file name
- The output file name

For example,

```
caesar input.txt encrypt.txt
```

encrypts the file `input.txt` and places the result into `encrypt.txt`.

```
caesar -d encrypt.txt output.txt
```

decrypts the file `encrypt.txt` and places the result into `output.txt`.

© xyno/iStockphoto.

The emperor Julius Caesar used a simple scheme to encrypt messages.

Figure 2 Caesar Cipher

sec05/caesar.cpp

```cpp
1  #include <iostream>
2  #include <fstream>
3  #include <string>
4  #include <sstream>
5
6  using namespace std;
7
8  /**
9     Encrypts a stream using the Caesar cipher.
```

```
10      @param in the stream to read from
11      @param out the stream to write to
12      @param k the encryption key
13   */
14   void encrypt_file(ifstream& in, ofstream& out, int k)
15   {
16      char ch;
17      while (in.get(ch))
18      {
19         out.put(ch + k);
20      }
21   }
22
23   int main(int argc, char* argv[])
24   {
25      int key = 3;
26      int file_count = 0; // The number of files specified
27      ifstream in_file;
28      ofstream out_file;
29
30      for (int i = 1; i < argc; i++) // Process all command-line arguments
31      {
32         string arg = argv[i]; // The currently processed argument
33         if (arg == "-d") // The decryption option
34         {
35            key = -3;
36         }
37         else // It is a file name
38         {
39            file_count++;
40            if (file_count == 1) // The first file name
41            {
42               in_file.open(arg);
43               if (in_file.fail()) // Exit the program if opening failed
44               {
45                  cout << "Error opening input file " << arg << endl;
46                  return 1;
47               }
48            }
49            else if (file_count == 2) // The second file name
50            {
51               out_file.open(arg);
52               if (out_file.fail())
53               {
54                  cout << "Error opening output file " << arg << endl;
55                  return 1;
56               }
57            }
58         }
59      }
60
61      if (file_count != 2) // Exit if the user didn't specify two files
62      {
63         cout << "Usage: " << argv[0] << " [-d] infile outfile" << endl;
64         return 1;
65      }
66
67      encrypt_file(in_file, out_file, key);
68      return 0;
69   }
```

Computing & Society 8.1   Encryption Algorithms

The exercises at the end of this chapter give a few algorithms to encrypt text. Don't actually use any of those methods to send secret messages to your lover. Any skilled cryptographer can *break* these schemes in a very short time—that is, reconstruct the original text without knowing the secret keyword.

In 1978 Ron Rivest, Adi Shamir, and Leonard Adleman introduced an encryption method that is much more powerful. The method is called *RSA encryption*, after the last names of its inventors. The exact scheme is too complicated to present here, but it is not actually difficult to follow. You can find the details in `http://people.csail.mit.edu/rivest/Rsapaper.pdf`.

RSA is a remarkable encryption method. There are two keys: a public key and a private key. (See the figure.) You can print the public key on your business card (or in your e-mail signature block) and give it to anyone. Then anyone can send you messages that only you can decrypt. Even though everyone else knows the public key, and even if they intercept all the messages coming to you, they cannot break the scheme and actually read the messages. In 1994, hundreds of researchers, collaborating over the Internet, cracked an RSA message encrypted with a 129-digit key. Messages encrypted with a key of 230 digits or more are expected to be secure.

The inventors of the algorithm obtained a *patent* for it. A patent is a deal that society makes with an inventor. For a period of 20 years, the inventor has an exclusive right for its commercialization, may collect royalties from others wishing to manufacture the invention, and may even stop competitors from using it altogether. In return, the inventor must publish the invention, so that others may learn from it, and must relinquish all claim to it after the monopoly period ends. The presumption is that in the absence

Alice — The message is encrypted with Bob's public key — Bob

Meet me at the toga party

Plain text

Xwya Txu% *(Wt &93ya =9

Encrypted text

Meet me at the toga party

Decrypted text

The message is decrypted with Bob's matching private key

(mobile phone) © Anna Khomulo/iStockphoto.

Public-Key Encryption

of patent law, inventors would be reluctant to go through the trouble of inventing, or they would try to cloak their techniques to prevent others from copying their devices.

There has been some controversy about the RSA patent. Had there not been patent protection, would the inventors have published the method anyway, thereby giving the benefit to society without the cost of the 20-year monopoly? In this case, the answer is probably yes. The inventors were academic researchers, who live on salaries rather than sales receipts and are usually rewarded for their discoveries by a boost in their reputation and careers. Would their followers have been as active in discovering (and patenting) improvements? There is no way of knowing, of course. Is an algorithm even patentable, or is it a mathematical fact that belongs to nobody? The patent office did take the latter attitude for a long time. The RSA inventors and many others described their inventions in terms of imaginary electronic devices, rather than algorithms, to circumvent that restriction.

Nowadays, the patent office will award software patents.

There is another interesting aspect to the RSA story. A programmer, Phil Zimmermann, developed a program called PGP (for *Pretty Good Privacy*) that is based on RSA. Anyone can use the program to encrypt messages, and decryption is not feasible even with the most powerful computers. You can get a copy of a free PGP implementation from the GNU project (`http://www.gnupg.org`). The existence of strong encryption methods bothers the United States government to no end. Criminals and foreign agents can send communications that the police and intelligence agencies cannot decipher. The government considered charging Zimmermann with breaching a law that forbids the unauthorized export of munitions, arguing that he should have known that his program would appear on the Internet. There have been serious proposals to make it illegal for private citizens to use these encryption methods, or to keep the keys secret from law enforcement.

HOW TO 8.1

Processing Text Files

Processing text files that contain real data can be surprisingly challenging. This How To gives you step-by-step guidance.

Problem Statement As an example, we will consider this task: Read two country data files, worldpop.txt and worldarea.txt (supplied with the book's companion code). Both files contain the same countries in the same order. Write a file world_pop_density.txt that contains country names and population densities (people per square km), with the country names aligned left and the numbers aligned right:

```
Afghanistan              50.56
Akrotiri                127.64
Albania                 125.91
Algeria                  14.18
American Samoa          288.92
. . .
```

© Oksana Perkins/iStockphoto.

Singapore is one of the most densely populated countries in the world.

Step 1 Understand the processing task.

As always, you need to have a clear understanding of the task before designing a solution. Can you carry out the task by hand (perhaps with smaller input files)? If not, get more information about the problem.

The following pseudocode describes our processing task:

> *While there are more lines to be read*
> *   Read a line from each file.*
> *   Extract the country name.*
> *   population = number following the country name in the first line*
> *   area = number following the country name in the second line*
> *   If area != 0*
> *   density = population / area*
> *   Print country name and density.*

Step 2 Determine which files you need to read and write.

This should be clear from the problem. In our example, there are two input files, the population data and the area data, and one output file.

Step 3 Choose a method for obtaining the file names.

There are three options:

- Hard-coding the file names (such as "worldpop.txt")
- Asking the user:
  ```
  cout << "Enter filename: ";
  cin >> filename;
  in_file.open(filename);
  ```
- Using command-line arguments for the file names

In our example, we use hard-coded file names for simplicity.

Step 4 Choose between line, word, and character-based input.

As a rule of thumb, read lines if the input data is grouped by lines. That is the case with tabular data, as in our example, or when you need to report line numbers.

When gathering data that can be distributed over several lines, then it makes more sense to read words. Keep in mind that you lose all white space when you read words.

Reading characters is mostly useful for tasks that require access to individual characters. Examples include analyzing character frequencies, changing tabs to spaces, or encryption.

Step 5 With line-oriented input, extract the required data.

It is simple to read a line of input with the `getline` function. Then you need to get the data out of that line. You can extract substrings, as described in Section 8.2. Alternatively, you can turn the line into an `istringstream` and extract its components with the `>>` operator. The latter approach is easier when the number of items on each line is constant. In our example, that is not the case—country names can consist of more than one string. Therefore, we choose to extract substrings from each input line.

If you need any of the substrings as numbers, you must convert them (see Section 8.4).

Step 6 Place repeatedly occurring tasks into functions.

Processing input files usually has repetitive tasks, such as skipping over white space or extracting numbers from strings. It really pays off to develop a set of functions to handle these tedious operations.

In our example, we have a common task that calls for a helper function: extracting the country name and the value that follows. This task can be implemented in a helper function

```
void read_line(string line, string& country, double& value)
```

We also need a helper function `string_to_double` to convert the population and area values to floating-point numbers. This function is similar to `string_to_int` that was developed in Section 8.4.

Step 7 If required, use manipulators to format the output.

If you are asked to format your output, use manipulators, as described in Section 8.3. Usually, you want to switch to fixed format for the output and set the precision. Then use `setw` before every value, and use `left` for aligning strings and `right` for aligning numbers:

```
out << setw(40) << left << country << setw(15) << right << density << endl;
```

Here is the complete program:

how_to_1/popdensity.cpp

```cpp
 1  #include <cctype>
 2  #include <fstream>
 3  #include <iostream>
 4  #include <iomanip>
 5  #include <sstream>
 6  #include <string>
 7
 8  using namespace std;
 9
10  /**
11      Converts a string to a floating-point number, e.g. "3.14" -> 3.14.
12      @param s a string representing a floating-point number
13      @return the equivalent floating-point number
14  */
15  double string_to_double(string s)
16  {
17      istringstream stream;
18      stream.str(s);
```

```
19    double x = 0;
20    stream >> x;
21    return x;
22 }
23
24 /**
25    Extracts the country and associated value from an input line.
26    @param line a line containing a country name, followed by a number
27    @param country the string for holding the country name
28    @param value the variable for holding the associated value
29    @return true if a line has been read, false at the end of the stream
30 */
31 void read_line(string line, string& country, double& value)
32 {
33    int i = 0; // Locate the start of the first digit
34    while (!isdigit(line[i])) { i++; }
35    int j = i - 1; // Locate the end of the preceding word
36    while (isspace(line[j])) { j--; }
37
38    country = line.substr(0, j + 1); // Extract the country name
39    value = string_to_double(line.substr(i)); // Extract the number value
40 }
41
42 int main()
43 {
44    ifstream in1;
45    ifstream in2;
46    in1.open("worldpop.txt"); // Open input files
47    in2.open("worldarea.txt");
48
49    ofstream out;
50    out.open("world_pop_density.txt"); // Open output file
51    out << fixed << setprecision(2);
52
53    string line1;
54    string line2;
55
56    // Read lines from each file
57    while (getline(in1, line1) && getline(in2, line2))
58    {
59       string country;
60       double population;
61       double area;
62
63       // Split the lines into country and associated value
64       read_line(line1, country, population);
65       read_line(line2, country, area);
66
67       // Compute and print the population density
68       double density = 0;
69       if (area != 0) // Protect against division by zero
70       {
71          density = population * 1.0 / area;
72       }
73       out << setw(40) << left << country
74          << setw(15) << right << density << endl;
75    }
76
77    return 0;
78 }
```

WORKED EXAMPLE 8.1

Looking for for Duplicates

Learn how to process a file to locate lines that contain repeated words. See your E-Text or visit wiley.com/go/bclo3.

8.6   Random Access and Binary Files

In the following sections, you will learn how to read and write data at arbitrary positions in a file, and how to edit image files.

At a sit-down dinner, food is served sequentially. At a buffet, you have "random access" to all food items.

© iStockphoto.

8.6.1   Random Access

You can access any position in a random access file by moving the *file pointer* prior to a read or write operation.

So far, you've read from a file an item at a time and written to a file an item at a time, without skipping forward or backward. That access pattern is called **sequential access**. In many applications, we would like to access specific items in a file without first having to read all preceding items. This access pattern is called **random access** (see Figure 3). There is nothing "random" about random access—the term means that you can read and modify any item stored at any location in the file.

Only file streams support random access; the cin and cout streams, which are attached to the keyboard and the terminal, do not. Each file stream has two special positions: the *get* position and the *put* position (see Figure 4). These positions determine where the next character is read or written.

Figure 3   Sequential and Random Access

Figure 4   Get and Put Positions

The following function calls move the get and put positions to a given value, counted from the beginning of the stream.

```
strm.seekg(position);
strm.seekp(position);
```

To determine the current values of the get and put positions (counted from the beginning of the file), use

```
position = strm.tellg();
position = strm.tellp();
```

Whenever you put data to the stream, the get position becomes undefined. Call seekg when you switch back to reading. Call seekp when you switch from reading to writing.

8.6.2 Binary Files

Many files, in particular those containing images and sounds, do not store information as text but as binary numbers. The numbers are represented as sequences of **bytes**, just as they are in the memory of the computer. (Each byte is a value between 0 and 255.) In binary format, a floating-point number always occupies 8 bytes. We will study random access with a binary file format for images.

We have to cover a few technical issues about binary files. To open a binary file for reading and writing, use the following command:

```
fstream strm;
strm.open(filename, ios::in | ios::out | ios::binary);
```

You read a byte with the call

```
int input = strm.get();
```

This call returns a value between 0 and 255. To read an integer, read four bytes b_0, b_1, b_2, b_3 and combine them to $b_0 + b_1 \cdot 256 + b_2 \cdot 256^2 + b_3 \cdot 256^3$. We will supply a helper function for this task.

The >> operator cannot be used to read numbers from a binary file.

8.6.3 Processing Image Files

In this section, you will learn how to write a program for editing image files in the BMP format. Unlike the more common GIF, PNG, and JPEG formats, the BMP format is quite simple because it does not use data compression. As a consequence, BMP files are huge and you will rarely find them in the wild. However, image editors can convert any image into BMP format.

There are different versions of the BMP format; we will only cover the simplest and most common one, sometimes called the 24-bit true color format. In this format, each pixel is represented as a sequence of three bytes, one each for the blue, green, and red value. For example, the color cyan (a mixture of blue and green) is 255 255 0, red is 0 0 255, and medium gray is 128 128 128.

A BMP file starts with a header that contains various pieces of information. We only need the following items:

Position	Item
2	The size of this file in bytes
10	Offset to the start of the image data
18	The width of the image in pixels
22	The height of the image in pixels

The image is stored as a sequence of pixel rows, starting with the pixels of the bottom-most row of the image. Each pixel row contains a sequence of blue/green/red triplets. The end of the row is padded with additional bytes so that the number of bytes in the row is divisible by 4. (See Figure 5.) For example, if a row consisted of merely three pixels, one cyan, one red, and one medium gray one, the row would be encoded as

```
255 255 0 0 0 255 128 128 128 x y z
```

where x y z are padding bytes to bring the row length up to 12, a multiple of 4. It is these little twists that make working with real-life file formats such a joyful experience.

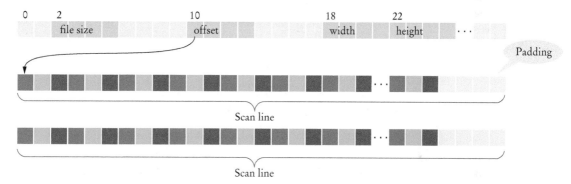

Figure 5 The BMP File Format for 24-bit True Color Images

The sample program at the end of this section reads every pixel of a BMP file and replaces it with its negative, turning white to black, cyan to red, and so on. The result is a negative image of the kind that old-fashioned film cameras used to produce (see Figure 6).

Figure 6
An Image and Its Negative   © Cay Horstmann.

To try out this program, take one of your favorite images, use an image editor to convert to BMP format (or use queen-mary.bmp from the code files for this book), then run the program and view the transformed file in an image editor. Exercises P8.16 and P8.17 ask you to produce more interesting effects.

sec06/imagemod.cpp

```cpp
1  #include <iostream>
2  #include <fstream>
3  #include <string>
4  #include <cstdlib>
5
6  using namespace std;
7
8  /**
9     Processes a pixel by forming the negative.
10     @param blue the blue value of the pixel
11     @param green the green value of the pixel
12     @param red the red value of the pixel
13  */
14  void process(int& blue, int& green, int& red)
15  {
16     blue = 255 - blue;
17     green = 255 - green;
18     red = 255 - red;
19  }
20
21  /**
22     Gets an integer from a binary stream.
23     @param stream the stream
24     @param offset the offset at which to read the integer
25     @return the integer starting at the given offset
26  */
27  int get_int(fstream& stream, int offset)
28  {
29     stream.seekg(offset);
30     int result = 0;
31     int base = 1;
32     for (int i = 0; i < 4; i++)
33     {
34        result = result + stream.get() * base;
35        base = base * 256;
36     }
37     return result;
38  }
39
40  int main()
41  {
42     cout << "Please enter the file name: ";
43     string filename;
44     cin >> filename;
45
46     fstream stream;
47     // Open as a binary file
48     stream.open(filename, ios::in | ios::out | ios::binary);
49
```

```
50    int file_size = get_int(stream, 2); // Get the image dimensions
51    int start = get_int(stream, 10);
52    int width = get_int(stream, 18);
53    int height = get_int(stream, 22);
54
55    // Scan lines must occupy multiples of four bytes
56    int scanline_size = width * 3;
57    int padding = 0;
58    if (scanline_size % 4 != 0)
59    {
60       padding = 4 - scanline_size % 4;
61    }
62
63    if (file_size != start + (scanline_size + padding) * height)
64    {
65       cout << "Not a 24-bit true color image file." << endl;
66       return 1;
67    }
68
69    int pos = start;
70
71    for (int i = 0; i < height; i++) // For each scan line
72    {
73       for (int j = 0; j < width; j++) // For each pixel
74       {
75          stream.seekg(pos); // Go to the next pixel
76          int blue = stream.get(); // Read the pixel
77          int green = stream.get();
78          int red = stream.get();
79
80          process(blue, green, red); // Process the pixel
81
82          stream.seekp(pos); // Go back to the start of the pixel
83
84          stream.put(blue); // Write the pixel
85          stream.put(green);
86          stream.put(red);
87          pos = pos + 3;
88       }
89
90       stream.seekg(padding, ios::cur); // Skip the padding
91       pos = pos + padding;
92    }
93
94    return 0;
95 }
```

Computing & Society 8.2   Databases and Privacy

Most companies use computers to keep huge data files of customer records and other business information. Databases not only lower the cost of doing business; they improve the quality of service that companies can offer. Nowadays it is almost unimaginable how time-consuming it used to be to withdraw money from a bank branch or to make travel reservations.

Today most databases are organized according to the *relational model*. Suppose a company stores your orders and payments. They will probably not repeat your name and address on every order; that would take unnecessary space. Instead, they will keep one file of all their customer names and identify each customer by a unique customer number. Only that customer number, not the entire customer information, is kept with an order record.

To print an invoice, the database program must issue a *query* against both the customer and order files and pull the necessary information (name, address, articles ordered) from both. Frequently, queries involve more than two files. For example, the company may have a file of addresses of car owners and a file of people with good payment history and may want to find all of its customers who placed an order in the last month, drive an expensive car, and pay their bills, so they can send them another catalog.

This kind of query is, of course, much faster if all customer files use the *same* key, which is why so many organizations in the United States try to collect the Social Security numbers of their customers.

Customers			Orders		
Cust. #:	Name		Order #:	Cust. #:	Item
11439	Doe, John		59673	11439	DOS for Historians
			59897	11439	Big C++
			61013	11439	C++ for Everyone

Relational Database Files

The Social Security Act of 1935 provided that each contributor be assigned a Social Security number to track contributions into the Social Security Fund. These numbers have a distinctive format, such as 078-05-1120. (This particular number was printed on sample cards that were inserted in wallets. It actually was the Social Security number of the secretary of a vice president at the wallet manufacturer. When thousands of people used it as their own, the number was voided, and the secretary received a new number.) Although they had not originally been intended for use as a universal identification number, Social Security numbers have become just that.

Some people are very concerned about the fact that just about every organization wants to store their Social Security number and other personal information. There is the possibility that companies and the government can merge multiple databases and derive information about us that we may wish they did not have or that simply may be untrue. An insurance company may deny coverage, or charge a higher premium, if it finds that you have too many relatives with a certain disease. You may be denied a job because of an inaccurate credit or medical report, and you may not even know the reason. These are very disturbing developments that have had a very negative impact for a small but growing number of people.

In many industrialized countries (but not currently in the United States), citizens have a right to control what information about themselves should be communicated to others and under what circumstances.

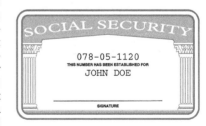

Social Security Card

CHAPTER SUMMARY

Develop programs that read and write files.

- To read or write files, you use variables of type fstream, ifstream, or ofstream.
- When opening a file stream, you supply the name of the file stored on disk.
- Read from a file stream with the same operations that you use with cin.
- Write to a file stream with the same operations that you use with cout.
- Always use a reference parameter for a stream.

Be able to process text in files.

- When reading a string with the >> operator, the white space between words is consumed.
- You can get individual characters from a stream and unget the last one.
- You can read a line of input with the getline function and then process it further.

Write programs that neatly format their output.

- Use the setw manipulator to set the width of the next output.
- Use the fixed and setprecision manipulators to format floating-point numbers with a fixed number of digits after the decimal point.

Convert between strings and numbers.

- Use an istringstream to convert the numbers inside a string to integers or floating-point numbers.
- Use an ostringstream to convert numeric values to strings.

Process the command line arguments of a C++ program.

- Programs that start from the command line can receive the name of the program and the command line arguments in the main function.

Develop programs that read and write binary files.

- You can access any position in a random access file by moving the file pointer prior to a read or write operation.

REVIEW EXERCISES

- **R8.1** When do you open a file as an ifstream, as an ofstream, or as an fstream? Could you simply open all files as an fstream?

- **R8.2** What happens if you write to a file that you only opened for reading? Try it out if you don't know.

- **R8.3** What happens if you try to open a file for reading that doesn't exist? What happens if you try to open a file for writing that doesn't exist?

- **R8.4** What happens if you try to open a file for writing, but the file or device is write-protected (sometimes called read-only)? Try it out with a short test program.

- **R8.5** How do you open a file whose name contains a backslash, such as c:\temp\output.dat?

- **R8.6** Why are the in and out parameter variables of the encrypt_file function in Section 8.5 reference parameters and not value parameters?

- **R8.7** Give an output statement to write a date and time in ISO 8601 format, such as

  ```
  2011-03-01 09:35
  ```

  Assume that the date and time are given in five integer variables year, month, day, hour, minute.

- **R8.8** Give an output statement to write one line of a table containing a product description, quantity, unit price, and total price in dollars and cents. You want the columns to line up, like this:

  ```
  Item            Qty  Price    Total
  Toaster          3   $29.92   $89.85
  Hair Dryer       1   $24.95   $24.95
  Car Vacuum       2   $19.99   $39.98
  ```

- **R8.9** How can you convert the string "3.14" into the floating-point number 3.14? How can you convert the floating-point number 3.14 into the string "3.14"? Give two ways.

- **R8.10** What is a command line? How can a program read its command line?

- **R8.11** If a program woozle is started with the command

  ```
  woozle -DNAME=Piglet -I\eeyore -v heff.cpp a.cpp lump.cpp
  ```

  what is the value of argc, and what are the values of argv[0], argv[1], and so on?

- **R8.12** What is the difference between sequential access and random access?

- **R8.13** What is the difference between a text file and a binary file?

- **R8.14** What are the get and put positions in a file? How do you move them? How do you tell their current positions?

- **R8.15** What happens if you try to move the get or put position past the end of a file? What happens if you try to move the get or put position of cin or cout? Try it out and report your results.

■ **E8.1** Write a program that carries out the following tasks:

> *Open a file with the name hello.txt.*
> *Store the message "Hello, World!" in the file.*
> *Close the file.*
> *Open the same file again.*
> *Read the message into a string variable and print it.*

■ **E8.2** Write a program that reads a text file containing floating-point numbers. Print the average of the numbers in the file. Prompt the user for the file name.

■ **E8.3** Repeat Exercise E8.2, but allow the user to specify the file name on the command-line. If the user doesn't specify any file name, then prompt the user for the name.

■ **E8.4** Write a program that reads a file containing two columns of floating-point numbers. Prompt the user for the file name. Print the average of each column.

■■ **E8.5** Write a program that reads each line in a file, reverses its characters, and writes the resulting line to another file. Suppose the user specifies input.txt and output.txt when prompted for the file names, and input.txt contains the lines

```
Mary had a little lamb
Its fleece was white as snow
And everywhere that Mary went
The lamb was sure to go.
```

After the program is finished, output.txt should contain

```
bmal elttil a dah yraM
wons sa etihw saw eceelf stI
tnew yraM taht erehwyreve dnA
.og ot erus saw bmal ehT
```

■■ **E8.6** Write a program that reads each line in a file, reverses its characters, and writes the resulting line to the same file. Use the following pseudocode:

> *While the end of the file has not been reached*
>   *pos1 = current get position*
>   *Read a line.*
>   *If the line was successfully read*
>   *pos2 = current get position*
>   *Set put position to pos1.*
>   *Write the reversed line.*
>   *Set get position to pos2.*

■■ **E8.7** Write a program that reads each line in a file, reverses its lines, and writes them to another file. Suppose the user specifies input.txt and output.txt when prompted for the file names, and input.txt contains the lines

```
Mary had a little lamb
Its fleece was white as snow
And everywhere that Mary went
The lamb was sure to go.
```

After the program is finished, output.txt should contain

```
The lamb was sure to go.
And everywhere that Mary went
Its fleece was white as snow
Mary had a little lamb
```

■■ E8.8 Write a program that asks the user for a file name and displays the number of characters, words, and lines in that file. Then have the program ask for the name of the next file. When the user enters a file that doesn't exist (such as the empty string), the program should exit.

■ E8.9 Write a program copyfile that copies one file to another. The file names are specified on the command line. For example,

```
copyfile report.txt report.sav
```

■ E8.10 Write a program that **concatenates** the contents of several files into one file. For example,

```
catfiles chapter1.txt chapter2.txt chapter3.txt book.txt
```

makes a long file book.txt that contains the contents of the files chapter1.txt, chapter2.txt, and chapter3.txt. The target file is always the last file specified on the command line.

■ E8.11 Write a program that reads a file, removes any blank lines, and writes the non-blank lines back to the same file.

■■ E8.12 Write a program that reads a file, removes any blank lines at the beginning or end of the file, and writes the remaining lines back to the same file.

PROGRAMMING PROJECTS

■■ P8.1 Write a program find that searches all files specified on the command line and prints out all lines containing a keyword. For example, if you call

```
find Tim report.txt address.txt homework.cpp
```

then the program might print

```
report.txt: discussed the results of my meeting with Tim T
address.txt: Torrey, Tim|11801 Trenton Court|Dallas|TX
address.txt: Walters, Winnie|59 Timothy Circle|Detroit|MI
homework.cpp: Time now;
```

The keyword is always the first command-line argument.

■■ P8.2 Write a program that checks the spelling of all words in a file. It should read each word of a file and check whether it is contained in a word list. A word list is available on most UNIX systems (including Linux and Mac OS X) in the file /usr/share/dict/words. (If you don't have access to a UNIX system, you can find a copy of the file on the Internet by searching for /usr/share/dict/words.) The program should print out all words that it cannot find in the word list. Follow this pseudocode:

Open the dictionary file.
Define a vector of strings called words.
For each word in the dictionary file
    Append the word to the words vector.
Open the file to be checked.
For each word in that file
    If the word is not contained in the words vector
        Print the word.

■■ P8.3 Get the data for names in prior decades from the Social Security Administration. Paste the table data in files named babynames80s.txt, etc. Modify the sec01/babynames.cpp program so that it prompts the user for a file name. The numbers in the files have comma separators, so modify the program to handle them. Can you spot a trend in the frequencies?

P8.4 Write a program that reads in sec01/babynames.txt and produces two files, boynames.txt and girlnames.txt, separating the data for the boys and girls.

P8.5 Write a program that reads a file in the same format as sec01/babynames.txt and prints all names that are both boy and girl names (such as Alexis or Morgan).

P8.6 Write a program that reads the country data in the file how_to_1/worldpop.txt (included with the book's source code). Do not edit the file. Use the following algorithm for processing each line. Add characters that are not white space to the country name. When you encounter a white space, locate the next non-white space character. If it is not a digit, add a space and that character to the country name, and keep adding characters until the next white space. If a white space is followed by a digit, unget it and read the number. Print the total of all country populations (excepting the entry for "European Union").

P8.7 *Random monoalphabet cipher.* The Caesar cipher, which shifts all letters by a fixed amount, is far too easy to crack. Here is a better idea. As the key, don't use numbers but words. Suppose the key word is FEATHER. Then first remove duplicate letters, yielding FEATHR, and append the other letters of the alphabet in reverse order:

F E A T H R Z Y X W V U S Q P O N M L K J I G D C B

Now encrypt the letters as follows:

Write a program that encrypts or decrypts a file using this cipher. For example,

```
crypt -d -kFEATHER encrypt.txt output.txt
```

decrypts a file using the keyword FEATHER. It is an error not to supply a keyword.

P8.8 *Letter frequencies.* If you encrypt a file using the cipher of Exercise P8.7, it will have all of its letters jumbled up, and will look as if there is no hope of decrypting it without knowing the keyword. Guessing the keyword seems hopeless too. There are just too many possible keywords. However, someone who is trained in decryption will be able to break this cipher in no time at all. The average letter frequencies of English letters are well known. The most common letter is E, which occurs about 13 percent of the time. Here are the average frequencies of the letters.

A	8%	H	4%	O	7%	U	3%
B	<1%	I	7%	P	3%	V	<1%
C	3%	J	<1%	Q	<1%	W	2%
D	4%	K	<1%	R	8%	X	<1%
E	13%	L	4%	S	6%	Y	2%
F	3%	M	3%	T	9%	Z	<1%
G	2%	N	8%				

Write a program that reads an input file and displays the letter frequencies in that file. Such a tool will help a code breaker. If the most frequent letters in an encrypted file are H and K, then there is an excellent chance that they are the encryptions of E and T.

Show the result in a table such as the one above, and make sure the columns line up.

•• P8.9 *Vigenère cipher.* In order to defeat a simple letter frequency analysis, the Vigenère cipher encodes a letter into one of several cipher letters, depending on its position in the input document. Choose a keyword, for example TIGER. Then encode the first letter of the input text like this:

```
A B C D E F G H I J K L M N O P Q R S T U V W X Y Z
↓ ↓ ↓ ↓ ↓ ↓ ↓ ↓ ↓ ↓ ↓ ↓ ↓ ↓ ↓ ↓ ↓ ↓ ↓ ↓ ↓ ↓ ↓ ↓ ↓ ↓
T U V W X Y Z A B C D E F G H I J K L M N O P Q R S
```

The encoded alphabet is just the regular alphabet shifted to start at T, the first letter of the keyword TIGER. The second letter is encrypted according to the following map.

```
A B C D E F G H I J K L M N O P Q R S T U V W X Y Z
↓ ↓ ↓ ↓ ↓ ↓ ↓ ↓ ↓ ↓ ↓ ↓ ↓ ↓ ↓ ↓ ↓ ↓ ↓ ↓ ↓ ↓ ↓ ↓ ↓ ↓
I J K L M N O P Q R S T U V W X Y Z A B C D E F G H
```

The third, fourth, and fifth letters in the input text are encrypted using the alphabet sequences beginning with characters G, E, and R, and so on. Because the key is only five letters long, the sixth letter of the input text is encrypted in the same way as the first.

Write a program that encrypts or decrypts an input text according to this cipher.

•• P8.10 *Playfair cipher.* Another way of thwarting a simple letter frequency analysis of an encrypted text is to encrypt *pairs* of letters together. A simple scheme to do this is the Playfair cipher. You pick a keyword and remove duplicate letters from it. Then you fill the keyword, and the remaining letters of the alphabet, into a 5 × 5 square. (Since there are only 25 squares, I and J are considered the same letter.)

Here is such an arrangement with the keyword PLAYFAIR.

```
P L A Y F
I R B C D
E G H K M
N O Q S T
U V W X Z
```

To encrypt a letter pair, say AM, look at the rectangle with corners A and M:

```
P L A Y F
I R B C D
E G H K M
N O Q S T
U V W X Z
```

The encoding of this pair is formed by looking at the other two corners of the rectangle, in this case, FH. If both letters happen to be in the same row or column, such as GO, simply swap the two letters. Decryption is done in the same way.

Write a program that encrypts or decrypts an input text according to this cipher.

■■ **P8.11** Special Topic 8.2 explains how Unicode strings are commonly encoded with the UTF-8 encoding. This exercise explores the encoding in more detail. In UTF-8, a Unicode character is either a byte < 128 (the traditional English alphabet, punctuation marks, and so on, known as ASCII), or a sequence of multiple bytes, where the first byte is ≥ 192, and subsequent bytes are between 128 and 191. Unfortunately, the char type may be signed or unsigned in any particular C++ implementation, which means that you cannot reliably compare char values to integers above 127. Instead, use the following tests:

```
if ((c & 0x80) == 0) // c is an ASCII character
else if ((c & 0xC0) == 0xC0) // c is the first byte of a multi-byte sequence
else if ((c & 0xC0) == 0x80) // c is a continuation byte of a multi-byte sequence
```

Write a program that reads a UTF-encoded file and prints the number of bytes of each Unicode character in the file. For example, if the file contains

San José ⊴

followed by a newline, your program should print

1 1 1 1 1 1 1 2 1 4 1

■■ **P8.12** Write a program that reads a UTF-8 encoded text file (see Special Topic 8.2) and prints all strings enclosed in curly quotes " " (U+201C and U+201D).

■■ **P8.13** Write a program that reads a text file and replaces all straight quotes "..." with curly quotes " " (U+201C and U+201D). Also replace double dashes -- with a Unicode em dash (U+2014).

■■■ **P8.14** The CSV (or *comma-separated values*) format is commonly used for tabular data. Each table row is a line, with columns separated by commas. Items may be enclosed in quotation marks, and they must be if they contain commas or quotation marks. Quotation marks inside quoted fields are doubled. Here is a line with four fields:

```
1729, San Francisco, "Hello, World", "He asked: ""Quo vadis?"""
```

Provide functions

```
int number_of_fields(string row)
string field(string row, int column)
```

and write a program that tests your functions with a given CSV file.

■■ **P8.15** Find an interesting data set in CSV format (or in spreadsheet format, then use a spreadsheet to save the data as CSV). Using the helper functions from Exercise P8.14, read the data and compute a summary, such as the maximum, minimum, or average of one of the columns.

■■ **P8.16** Write a program that edits an image file and reduces the blue and green values by 30 percent, giving it a "sunset" effect.

© Cay Horstmann.

P8.17 Write a program that edits an image file, turning it into grayscale.

© Cay Horstmann.

Replace each pixel with a pixel that has the same grayness level for the blue, green, and red component. The grayness level is computed by adding 30 percent of the red level, 59 percent of the green level, and 11 percent of the blue level. (The color-sensing cone cells in the human eye differ in their sensitivity for red, green, and blue light.)

P8.18 *Junk mail.* Write a program that reads in two files: a *template* and a *database*. The template file contains text and tags. The tags have the form |1| |2| |3|… and need to be replaced with the first, second, third, … field in the current database record. Your program should print out copies of the template with the tag fields replaced with database entries.

A typical database looks like this:

```
Mr.|Harry|Morgan|1105 Torre Ave.|Cupertino|CA|95014
Dr.|John|Lee|702 Ninth Street Apt. 4|San Jose|CA|95109
Miss|Evelyn|Garcia|1101 S. University Place|Ann Arbor|MI|48105
```

And here is a typical template:

```
To:
|1| |2| |3|
|4|
|5|, |6| |7|

Dear |1| |3|:

You and the |3| family may be the lucky winners of $10,000,000 in the C++ compiler
clearinghouse sweepstakes! . . .
```

P8.19 Write a program that manipulates three database files. The first file contains the names and telephone numbers of a group of people. The second file contains the names and Social Security numbers of a group of people. The third file contains the Social Security numbers and annual income of a group of people. The groups of people should overlap but need not be completely identical. Your program should ask the user for a telephone number and then print the name, Social Security number, and annual income, if it can determine that information.

P8.20 Write a program that prints out a student grade report. There is a file, classes.txt, that contains the names of all classes taught at a college, such as

classes.txt

```
CSC1
CSC2
CSC46
CSC151
MTH121
 . . .
```

For each class, there is a file with student ID numbers and grades:

csc2.txt

```
11234 A-
12547 B
16753 B+
21886 C
. . .
```

Write a program that asks for a student ID and prints out a grade report for that student, by searching all class files. Here is a sample report

```
Student ID 16753
CSC2 B+
MTH121 C+
CHN1 A
PHY50 A-
```

■■■ Engineering P8.21 After the switch in the figure below closes, the voltage (in volts) across the capacitor is represented by the equation

$$v(t) = B\left(1 - e^{-t/(RC)}\right)$$

Suppose the parameters of the electric circuit are $B = 12$ volts, $R = 500\ \Omega$, and $C = 0.25\ \mu F$. Consequently

$$v(t) = 12\left(1 - e^{-0.008t}\right)$$

where t has units of μs. Read a file params.txt (provided with your companion code) containing the values for B, R, C, and the starting and ending values for t. Write a file rc.txt of values for the time t and the corresponding capacitor voltage $v(t)$, where t goes from the given starting value to the given ending value in 100 steps. In our example, if t goes from 0 to 1,000 μs, the twelfth entry in the output file would be:

```
110  7.02261
```

■■■ Engineering P8.22 The figure below shows a plot of the capacitor voltage from the circuit shown in Exercise P8.21. The capacitor voltage increases from 0 volts to B volts. The "rise time" is defined as the time required for the capacitor voltage to change from $v_1 = 0.05 \times B$ to $v_2 = 0.95 \times B$.

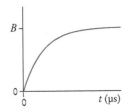

The file rc.txt contains a list of values of time t and the corresponding capacitor voltage $v(t)$. A time in μs and the corresponding voltage in volts are printed on the same line. For example, the line

    110   7.02261

indicates that the capacitor voltage is 7.02261 volts when the time is 110 μs. The time is increasing in the data file.

Write a program that reads the file rc.txt and uses the data to calculate the rise time. Approximate B by the voltage in the last line of the file, and find the data points that are closest to $0.05 \times B$ and $0.95 \times B$.

■■ Engineering P8.23 Suppose a file contains bond energies and bond lengths for covalent bonds in the following format:

© Chris Dascher/iStockphoto.

Single, double, or triple bond	Bond energy (kJ/mol)	Bond length (nm)
C|C	370	0.154
C||C	680	0.13
C|||C	890	0.12
C|H	435	0.11
C|N	305	0.15
C|O	360	0.14
C|F	450	0.14
C|Cl	340	0.18
O|H	500	0.10
O|O	220	0.15
O|Si	375	0.16
N|H	430	0.10
N|O	250	0.12
F|F	160	0.14
H|H	435	0.074

Write a program that prompts the user to enter a data item in the format of any of the columns, and prints the corresponding data from the other columns in the stored file. The program should print "No matching entries" and exit when the user types an item that does not appear in the table. If input data matches different rows, then return all matching row data. For example, a bond length input of 0.12 should return triple bond C\|\|\|C and bond energy 890 kJ/mol *and* single bond N\|O and bond energy 250 kJ/mol.

© Cameron Strathdee/iStockphoto.

CHAPTER 9

CLASSES

This chapter introduces you to object-oriented programming, an important technique for writing complex programs. In an object-oriented program, you don't simply manipulate numbers and strings, but you work with objects that are meaningful for your application. Objects with the same behavior (such as the windmills in the photo) are grouped into classes. A programmer provides the desired behavior by specifying and implementing functions for these classes. In this chapter, you will learn how to discover, specify, and implement your own classes, and how to use them in your programs.

9.1 Object-Oriented Programming

You have learned how to structure your programs by decomposing tasks into functions. This is an excellent practice, but experience shows that it does not go far enough. As programs get larger, it becomes increasingly difficult to maintain a large collection of functions.

To overcome this problem, computer scientists invented **object-oriented programming**, a programming style in which tasks are solved by collaborating objects. Each object has its own set of data, together with a set of functions that can act upon the data. (These functions are called **member functions**).

You have already experienced the object-oriented programming style when you used string objects or streams such as cin and cout. For example, you use the length and substr member functions to work with string objects. The >> and << operators that you use with streams are also implemented as member functions—see Special Topic 9.1.

> A class describes a set of objects with the same behavior.

In C++, a programmer doesn't implement a single object. Instead, the programmer provides a **class**. A class describes a set of objects with the same behavior. For example, the string class describes the behavior of all strings. The class specifies how a string stores its characters, which member functions can be used with strings, and how the member functions are implemented.

A class describes a set of objects with the same behavior. For example, a Car class describes all passenger vehicles that have a certain capacity and shape.

© Media Bakery.

You can drive a car by operating the steering wheel and pedals, without knowing how the engine works. Similarly, you use an object through its member functions. The implementation is hidden.

© Damir Cudic/iStockphoto.

When you develop an object-oriented program, you create your own classes that describe what is important in your application. For example, in a student database you might work with Student and Course classes. Of course, then you must supply member functions for these classes.

When you work with an object, you do not know how it is implemented. You need not know how a string organizes a character sequence, or how the cin object reads input from the console. All you need to know is the **public interface**: the specifications for the member functions that you can invoke. The process of providing a public interface, while hiding the implementation details, is called **encapsulation**.

You will want to use encapsulation for your own classes. When you define a class, you will specify the behavior of the public member functions, but you will hide the implementation details. Encapsulation benefits the programmers who use your classes. They can put your classes to work without having to know their implementations, just as you are able to make use of the string and stream classes without knowing their internal details.

Encapsulation is also a benefit for the implementor of a class. When working on a program that is being developed over a long period of time, it is common for implementation details to change, usually to make objects more efficient or more capable. Encapsulation is crucial to enabling these changes. When the implementation is hidden, the implementor is free to make improvements. Because the implementation is hidden, these improvements do not affect the programmers who use the objects.

> Every class has a public interface: a collection of member functions through which the objects of the class can be manipulated.

> Encapsulation is the act of providing a public interface and hiding implementation details.

> Encapsulation enables changes in the implementation without affecting users of a class.

A driver of an electric car doesn't have to learn new controls even though the car engine is very different. Neither does the programmer who uses an object with an improved implementation—as long as the same member functions are used.

© iStockphoto.com/Christian Waadt.

In this chapter, you will learn how to design and implement your own classes in C++, and how to structure your programs in an object-oriented way, using the principle of encapsulation.

9.2 Implementing a Simple Class

In this section, we look at the implementation of a very simple class. You will see how objects store their data, and how member functions access the data of an object. Knowing how a very simple class operates will help you design and implement more complex classes later in this chapter.

Our first example is a class that models a *tally counter*, a mechanical device that is used to count people—for example, to find out how many people attend a concert or board a bus (see Figure 1).

© Jasmin Awad/iStockphoto.

Figure 1   A Tally Counter

Whenever the operator pushes a button, the counter value advances by one. We model this operation with a count function. A physical counter has a display to show the current value. In our simulation, we use a get_value function instead.

Here is an example of using the Counter class. As you know from using classes such as string and ifstream, you use the class name and a variable name to define an object of the class:

```
Counter tally;
```

In Section 9.6, you will learn how to ensure that objects are properly initialized. For now, we will call a member function to ensure that the object has the correct state:

```
tally.reset();
```

Next, we invoke member functions on our object. First, we invoke the count member function twice, simulating two button pushes. Then we invoke the get_value member function to check how many times the button was pushed.

```
tally.count();
tally.count();
int result = tally.get_value(); // Sets result to 2
```

We can invoke the member functions again, and the result will be different.

```
tally.count();
tally.count();
result = tally.get_value(); // Sets result to 4
```

As you can see, the tally object remembers the effect of prior function calls.

By specifying the member functions of the Counter class, we have now specified the **behavior** of Counter objects. In order to produce this behavior, each object needs internal data, called the **state** of the object. In this simple example, the object state is very simple. It is the value that keeps track of how many times the counter has been advanced.

An object stores its state in **data members**. A data member is a storage location that is present in each object of the class.

You specify data members in the class definition:

The member functions of a class define the behavior of its objects.

An object's data members represent the state of the object.

```
class Counter
{
public:
   . . .
private:
   int value;
   . . .
};
```

A class definition has a public and private section. As you will see in the following section, we always place data members in the private section.

Each object of a class has its own set of data members. For example, if concert_counter and boarding_counter are two objects of the Counter class, then each object has its own value variable (see Figure 2).

The member functions are declared in the public section of the class.

> Each object of a class has its own set of data members.

```
class Counter
{
public:
   void reset();
   void count();
   int get_value() const;
private:
   int value;
};
```

The const reserved word denotes the fact that calling the get_value member function, unlike the other member functions, does not change the object. We will discuss this distinction in more detail in the following section.

Next, let us have a quick look at the implementation of the member functions of the Counter class. The count member function advances the counter value by 1.

```
void Counter::count()
{
   value = value + 1;
}
```

The function definition can be placed anywhere below the definition of the Counter class. The Counter:: prefix indicates that we are defining the count function of the Counter class.

Now have another look at the implementation of the Counter::count member function. Note how the body of the function increments the data member value. Which

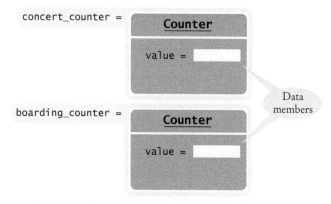

Figure 2   Data Members

data member? The one belonging to the object on which the function is called. For example, consider the call

```
concert_counter.count();
```

This call advances the value member of the concert_counter object.

The reset member function simply sets the value to zero:

```
void Counter::reset()
{
    value = 0;
}
```

Finally, the get_value member function returns the current value:

```
int Counter::get_value() const
{
    return value;
}
```

This member function is required so that users of the Counter class can find out how often a particular counter has been clicked. A user cannot simply access the value data member. That variable has been declared in the private section. The private reserved word restricts access to the member functions of the *same class*. For example, the value variable can be accessed by the count and get_value member functions of the Counter class but not by a member function of another class. Those other functions need to use the get_value member function if they want to find out the counter's value, or the count member function if they want to change it.

Private data members are an essential part of encapsulation. They allow a programmer to hide the implementation of a class from a class user.

EXAMPLE CODE   See sec02 of your companion code for a program that uses the Counter class.

9.3 Specifying the Public Interface of a Class

To define a class, we first need to specify its **public interface**. The public interface of a class consists of all member functions that a user of the class may want to apply to its objects.

Let's consider a simple example. We want to use objects that simulate cash registers. A cashier who rings up a sale presses a key to start the sale, then rings up each item. A display shows the amount owed as well as the total number of items purchased.

In our simulation, we want to carry out the following operations:

© James Richey/iStockphoto.

Our first example of a class simulates a cash register.

- Add the price of an item.
- Get the total amount of all items, and the count of items purchased.
- Clear the cash register to start a new sale.

The interface is specified in the **class definition**, summarized in Syntax 9.1. We will call our class CashRegister. (We follow the convention that the name of a programmer-

© GlobalP/iStockphoto.

defined class starts with an uppercase letter, as does each word within the name. This naming convention is called *camel case* because the uppercase letters in the middle of the name look like the humps of a camel.)

Here is the C++ syntax for the CashRegister class definition:

```cpp
class CashRegister
{
public:
   void clear();
   void add_item(double price);

   double get_total() const;
   int get_count() const;

private:
   data members—see Section 9.4
};
```

> You can use member function declarations and function comments to specify the public interface of a class.

The member functions are declared in the *public section* of the class. Any part of the program can call the member functions. The data members are defined in the *private section* of the class. Only the member functions of the class can access those data members; they are hidden from the remainder of the program.

It is legal to declare the private members before the public section, but in this book, we place the public section first. After all, most programmers reading a class are class users, not implementors, and they are more interested in the public interface than in the private implementation.

The member function declarations look similar to the declarations of regular functions. These declarations do not provide any implementation. You will see in Section 9.5 how to implement the member functions.

Syntax 9.1   Class Definition

```cpp
class CashRegister
{
public:
   void clear();
   void add_item(double price);

   double get_total() const;
   int get_count() const;

private:
   int item_count;
   double total_price;
};
```

Use CamelCase for class names.

Member functions are declared in the class and defined outside. See Syntax 9.2.

Public section

Mutator member functions

Accessor member functions

Private section

Mark accessors as const. *See Programming Tip 9.2.*

Data members should always be private. See Programming Tip 9.1.

Be sure to include this semicolon. See Common Error 9.1.

There are two kinds of member functions, called **mutators** and **accessors**. A mutator is a function that modifies the data members of the object. The CashRegister class has two mutators: clear and add_item. After you call either of these functions, the total amount and item count are changed.

> A mutator member function changes the object on which it operates.

Accessors just query the object for some information without changing it. The CashRegister class has two accessors: get_total and get_count. Applying either of these functions to a CashRegister object simply returns a value and does not modify the object. In C++, you should use the const reserved word to mark accessor functions (see Programming Tip 9.2), like this:

> An accessor member function does not change the object on which it operates. Use const with accessors.

```
double get_total() const;
```

Member functions are invoked using the dot notation that you have already seen with string and stream functions:

```
CashRegister register1; // Defines a CashRegister object
register1.clear(); // Invokes a member function
```

Now we know *what* a CashRegister object can do, but not *how* it does it. Of course, to use CashRegister objects in our programs, we don't need to know. We simply use the public interface. Figure 3 shows the interface of the CashRegister class. The mutator functions are shown with arrows pointing inside the private data to indicate that they modify the data. The accessor functions are shown with arrows pointing the other way to indicate that they just read the data.

Figure 3 The Interface of the CashRegister Class

EXAMPLE CODE   See sec03 of your companion code for the public interface of the CashRegister class.

Common Error 9.1

Forgetting a Semicolon

Braces { } are common in C++ code, and usually you do not place a semicolon after the closing brace. However, class definitions always end in };. A common error is to forget that semicolon:

```
class CashRegister
{
public:
    . . .
private:
    . . .
} // Forgot semicolon

int main()
{
```

```
    // Many compilers report the error in this line
    . . .
}
```

This error can be extremely confusing to many compilers. There is syntax, now obsolete but supported for compatibility with old code, to define class types and variables of that type simultaneously. Because the compiler doesn't know that you don't use that obsolete construction, it tries to analyze the code wrongly and ultimately reports an error. Unfortunately, it may report the error *several lines away* from the line in which you forgot the semicolon.

If the compiler reports bizarre errors in lines that you are sure are correct, check that each of the preceding class definitions is terminated by a semicolon.

9.4 Designing the Data Representation

An object holds data members that are accessed by member functions.

An object stores its data in **data members**. These are variables that are declared inside the class.

When implementing a class, you have to determine which data each object needs to store. The object needs to have all the information necessary to carry out any member function call.

Go through all member functions and consider their data requirements. It is a good idea to start with the accessor functions. For example, a CashRegister object must be able to return the correct value for the get_total function. That means, it must either store all entered prices and compute the total in the function call, or it must store the total.

Now apply the same reasoning to the get_count function. If the cash register stores all entered prices, it can count them in the get_count function. Otherwise, you need to have a variable for the count.

© migin/iStockphoto.

Like a wilderness explorer who needs to carry all items that may be needed, an object needs to store the data required for any function calls.

The add_item function receives a price as an argument, and it must record the price. If the CashRegister object stores an array of entered prices, then the add_item function appends the price. On the other hand, if we decide to store just the item total and count, then the add_item function updates these two variables.

Finally, the clear function must prepare the cash register for the next sale, either by emptying the array of prices or by setting the total and count to zero.

We have now discovered two different ways of representing the data that the object needs. Either of them will work, and we have to make a choice. We will choose the simpler one: variables for the total price and the item count. (Other options are explored in Exercises P9.6 and P9.7.)

The data members are defined in the private section of the class definition:

```
class CashRegister
{
```

```
public:
    // See Section 9.3
private:
    int item_count;
    double total_price;
};
```

Every `CashRegister` object has a separate copy of these data members (see Figure 4).

> Every object has its own set of data members.

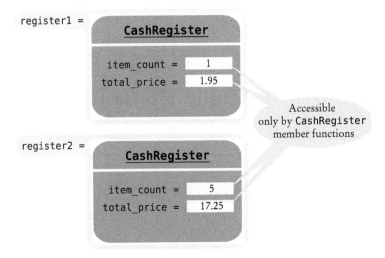

Figure 4 Data Members of `CashRegister` Objects

Because the data members are defined to be private, only the member functions of the class can access them. Programmers using the `CashRegister` class cannot access the data members directly:

```
int main()
{
    . . .
    cout << register1.item_count; // Error—use get_count() instead
    . . .
}
```

© Mark Evans/iStockphoto.

These clocks have common behavior, but each of them has a different state. Similarly, objects of a class can have their data members set to different values.

Private data
members can only
be accessed by
member functions
of the same class.

All data access must occur through the public interface. Thus, the data members of an object are effectively hidden from the programmer using the class. While it is theoretically possible in C++ to leave data members unencapsulated (by placing them into the public section), this is very uncommon in practice. We will always make all data members private in this book.

EXAMPLE CODE   See sec04 of your companion code for the CashRegister class with its data members defined.

9.5 Member Functions

The definition of a class declares its member functions. Each member function is defined separately, after the class definition. The following sections show how to define member functions.

9.5.1 Implementing Member Functions

Here is the implementation of the add_item function of the CashRegister class.

```
void CashRegister::add_item(double price)
{
   item_count++;
   total_price = total_price + price;
}
```

Use the *ClassName::*
prefix when defining
member functions.

The CashRegister:: prefix makes it clear that we are defining the add_item function of the CashRegister class. In C++ it is perfectly legal to have add_item functions in other classes as well, and it is important to specify exactly which add_item function we are defining. (See Syntax 9.2.) You use the *ClassName*::add_item syntax only when *defining* the function, not when calling it. When you call the add_item member function, the call has the form *object*.add_item(...).

When defining an accessor member function, supply the reserved word const following the closing parenthesis of the parameter list. Here is the get_count member function:

```
int CashRegister::get_count() const
{
   return item_count;
}
```

You will find the other member functions with the example program at the end of this section.

9.5.2 Implicit and Explicit Parameters

Whenever you refer to a data member, such as item_count or total_price, in a member function, it denotes the data member *of the object on which the member function was invoked*. For example, consider the call

```
register1.add_item(1.95);
```

The first statement in the CashRegister::add_item function is

```
item_count++;
```

Which item_count is incremented? In this call, it is the item_count of the register1 object. (See Figure 5.)

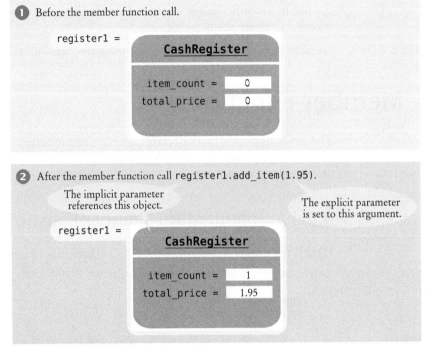

Figure 5   Implicit and Explicit Parameters

The implicit parameter is a reference to the object on which a member function is applied.

When a member function is called on an object, the **implicit parameter** is a reference to that object.

You can think of the code of the add_item function like this:

```
void CashRegister::add_item(double price)
{
    implicit parameter.item_count++;
    implicit parameter.total_price = implicit parameter.total_price + price;
}
```

In C++, you do not actually write the implicit parameter in the function definition. For that reason, the parameter is called "implicit".

When an item is added, it affects the data members of the cash register object on which the function is invoked.   © Glow Images/Getty Images, Inc.

Explicit parameters of a member function are listed in the function definition.

In contrast, parameter variables that are explicitly mentioned in the function definition, such as the price parameter variable, are called **explicit parameters**. Every member function has exactly one implicit parameter and zero or more explicit parameters.

9.5.3 Calling a Member Function from a Member Function

When calling another member function on the same object, do not use the dot notation.

When one member function calls another member function *on the same object*, you do not use the dot notation. Instead, you simply use the name of the other function. Here is an example. Suppose we want to implement a member function to add multiple instances of the same item. An easy way to implement this function is to repeatedly call the add_item function:

```cpp
void CashRegister::add_items(int quantity, double price)
{
   for (int i = 1; i <= quantity; i++)
   {
      add_item(price);
   }
}
```

Here, the add_item member function is invoked on the implicit parameter.

```cpp
for (int i = 1; i <= quantity; i++)
{
   implicit parameter.add_item(price);
}
```

That is the object on which the add_items function is invoked. For example, in the call

```cpp
register1.add_items(6, 0.95);
```

the add_item function is invoked six times on register1.

Syntax 9.2 Member Function Definition

Use *ClassName*:: before the name of the member function.

Explicit parameter

```cpp
void CashRegister::add_item(double price)
{
   item_count++;
   total_price = total_price + price;
}

int CashRegister::get_count() const
{
   return item_count;
}
```

Data members of the implicit parameter

Data member of the implicit parameter

Use const for accessor functions. See Programming Tip 9.2.

sec05/cashregister.cpp

```cpp
1  #include <iostream>
2  #include <iomanip>
3
4  using namespace std;
5
6  /**
7     A simulated cash register that tracks the item count and
8     the total amount due.
9  */
10 class CashRegister
11 {
12 public:
13    /**
14       Clears this cash register.
15    */
16    void clear();
17    /**
18       Adds an item to this cash register.
19       @param price the price of the added item
20    */
21    void add_item(double price);
22    /**
23       Gets the price of all items in the current sale.
24       @return the total amount
25    */
26    double get_total() const;
27    /**
28       Gets the number of items in the current sale.
29       @return the item count
30    */
31    int get_count() const;
32 private:
33    int item_count;
34    double total_price;
35 };
36
37 void CashRegister::clear()
38 {
39    item_count = 0;
40    total_price = 0;
41 }
42
43 void CashRegister::add_item(double price)
44 {
45    item_count++;
46    total_price = total_price + price;
47 }
48
49 double CashRegister::get_total() const
50 {
51    return total_price;
52 }
53
54 int CashRegister::get_count() const
55 {
56    return item_count;
57 }
58
```

```
59  /**
60      Displays the item count and total price of a cash register.
61      @param reg the cash register to display
62  */
63  void display(CashRegister reg)
64  {
65      cout << "Item " << reg.get_count() << ": $"
66          << fixed << setprecision(2) << reg.get_total() << endl;
67  }
68
69  int main()
70  {
71      CashRegister register1;
72      register1.clear();
73      register1.add_item(1.95);
74      display(register1);
75      register1.add_item(0.95);
76      display(register1);
77      register1.add_item(2.50);
78      display(register1);
79      return 0;
80  }
```

Program Run

```
Item 1: $1.95
Item 2: $2.90
Item 3: $5.40
```

Programming Tip 9.1

All Data Members Should Be Private; Most Member Functions Should Be Public

It is possible to define data members in the public section of a class, but you should not do that in your own code. Always use encapsulation, with private data members that are manipulated with member functions.

Generally, member functions should be public. However, sometimes you have a member function that is only used as a helper function by other member functions. In that case, you can make the helper function private. Simply declare it in the private section of the class.

Programming Tip 9.2

const **Correctness**

You should declare all accessor functions in C++ with the const reserved word. (Recall that an accessor function is a member function that does not modify its implicit parameter.)

For example, suppose you design the following class:

```
class CashRegister
{
    void display(); // Bad style—no const
    . . .
};
```

When you compile your code, no error is reported. But now suppose that another programmer uses your CashRegister class in a function:

```
void display_all(const CashRegister registers[])
{
    for (int i = 0; i < NREGISTERS; i++) { registers[i].display(); }
}
```

That programmer is conscientious and declares the registers parameter variable as const. But then the call registers[i].display() will not compile. Because CashRegister::display is not tagged as const, the compiler suspects that the call registers[i].display() may modify registers[i]. But the function promised not to modify the registers array.

If you write a program with other team members who are conscientious about const, it is very important that you do your part as well. You should therefore get into the habit of using const with all accessor member functions.

9.6 Constructors

A **constructor** is a member function that initializes the data members of an object. The constructor is automatically called whenever an object is created. By supplying a constructor, you can ensure that all data members are properly set before any member functions act on an object.

A constructor is called automatically whenever an object is created.

To understand the importance of constructors, consider the following statements:

```
CashRegister register1;
register1.add_item(1.95);
int count = register1.get_count(); // May not be 1
```

Here, the programmer forgot to call clear before adding items. Therefore, the data members of the register1 object were initialized with random values. Constructors guarantee that an object is always fully initialized when it is defined.

The name of a constructor is the same as the class name.

The name of a constructor is identical to the name of its class. You declare constructors in the class definition, for example:

```
class CashRegister
{
public:
    CashRegister(); // A constructor
    . . .
};
```

A constructor is like a set of assembly instructions for an object.

© Ann Marie Kurtz/iStockphoto.

Constructors never return values, but you do not use the void reserved word when declaring them.

Here is the definition of that constructor:

```
CashRegister::CashRegister()
{
    item_count = 0;
    total_price = 0;
}
```

In the constructor definition, the first CashRegister (before the ::) indicates that we are about to define a member function of the CashRegister class. The second CashRegister is the name of that member function.

A default constructor has no arguments.

The constructor that you just saw has no arguments. Such a constructor is called a **default constructor**. It is used whenever you define an object and do not specify any parameters for the construction. For example, if you define

```
CashRegister register1;
```

then the default constructor is called. It sets register1.item_count and register1.total_price to zero.

A class can have multiple constructors.

Many classes have more than one constructor. This allows you to define objects in different ways. Consider for example a BankAccount class that has two constructors:

```
class BankAccount
{
public:
    BankAccount(); // Sets balance to 0
    BankAccount(double initial_balance); // Sets balance to initial_balance
    // Member functions omitted
private:
    double balance;
};
```

The compiler picks the constructor that matches the construction arguments.

Both constructors have the same name as the class, BankAccount. But the default constructor has no parameter variables, whereas the second constructor has a double parameter variable. (This is an example of *overloading*—see Special Topic 9.1.)

When you construct an object, the compiler chooses the constructor that matches the arguments that you supply. For example,

```
BankAccount joes_account;
    // Uses default constructor
BankAccount lisas_account(499.95);
    // Uses BankAccount(double) constructor
```

Be sure to initialize all number and pointer data members in a constructor.

When implementing a constructor, you need to pay particular attention to all data members that are numbers or pointers. These types are not classes and therefore have no constructors. If you have a data member that is an object of a class (such as a string object), then that class has a constructor, and the object will be initialized. For example, all string objects are automatically initialized to the empty string.

Consider this class:

```
class Item
{
public:
    Item();
    // Additional member functions omitted
private:
    string description;
    double price;
```

```
};
```

In the Item constructor, you need to set price to 0, but you need not initialize the description data member. It is automatically initialized to the empty string.

As of C++ 11, you can specify default values for data members:

```
class Item
{
public:
   // No constructor
   // Member functions
private:
   string description;
   double price = 0;
};
```

If you do not initialize price in a constructor, it is set to zero.

If you do not supply any constructor for a class, the compiler automatically generates a default constructor. The automatically generated default constructor initializes the data members that have default constructors or default values, and leaves the other data members uninitialized.

EXAMPLE CODE   See sec06 of your companion code for the complete CashRegister class with a single constructor, a BankAccount class with two constructors, and an Item class with three constructors.

Common Error 9.2

Trying to Call a Constructor

The constructor is invoked only when an object is first created. You cannot invoke it again. For example, you cannot call the constructor to clear an object:

```
CashRegister register1;
. . .
register1.CashRegister(); // Error
```

It is true that the default constructor sets a *new* CashRegister object to the cleared state, but you cannot invoke a constructor on an *existing* object.

In this case, you can simply invoke the clear member function:

```
register1.clear();
```

Alternatively, you can construct a second cash register and assign it to this one:

```
CashRegister cleared_register;
register = cleared_register;
```

Special Topic 9.1

Overloading

When the same function name is used for more than one function, then the name is **overloaded**. In C++ you can overload function names provided the types of the parameter variables are different. For example, you can define two functions, both called print:

```
void print(CashRegister r)
void print(Item i)
```

When the print function is called,

```
print(x);
```

the compiler looks at the type of x. If x is a CashRegister object, the first function is called. If x is an Item object, the second function is called. If x is neither, the compiler generates an error.

It is always possible to avoid overloading by giving each function a unique name, such as print_register or print_item. However, we have no choice with constructors. C++ demands that the name of a constructor equal the name of the class. If a class has more than one constructor, then that name must be overloaded.

In addition to name overloading, C++ also supports *operator overloading*. It is possible to give new meanings to the familiar C++ operators such as +, ==, and <<. This is an advanced technique that we will discuss in Chapter 13.

Special Topic 9.2

Initializer Lists

When you construct an object whose data members are themselves objects, those objects are constructed by their class's default constructor. However, if a data member belongs to a class without a default constructor, you need to invoke the data member's constructor explicitly. Here is an example.

This Item class has no default constructor:

```
class Item
{
public:
   Item(string item_description, double item_price);
   // No other constructors
   . . .
};
```

This Order class has a data member of type Item:

```
class Order
{
public:
   Order(string customer_name, string item_description, double item_price);
   . . .
private:
   Item article;
   string customer;
};
```

The Order constructor must call the Item constructor. That is achieved with an *initializer list*. The initializer list is placed before the opening brace of the constructor. The list starts with a colon and contains names of data members with their construction arguments.

```
Order::Order(string customer_name, string item_description, double item_price)
   : article(item_description, item_price)
{
   customer = customer_name;
}
```

Initializers are separated by commas. They can also initialize a data member as a copy of a value of the same type. Here is another way of writing the Order constructor:

```
Order::Order(string customer_name, string item_description, double item_price)
   : article(item_description, item_price), customer(customer_name)
{
}
```

Special Topic 9.3

Universal and Uniform Initialization Syntax

In C++, there are several syntactic variations to initialize a variable, such as

```
double price = 19.25;
int squares[] = { 1, 4, 9, 16 };
BankAccount lisas_account(499.95);
```

C++ 11 introduces a uniform syntax, using braces and no equal sign, like this:

```
double price { 19.25 };
int squares[] { 1, 4, 9, 16 };
BankAccount lisas_account { 499.95 };
```

Use empty braces for default initialization.

```
double balance {}; // Initialized with zero
BankAccount joes_account {}; // Uses default constructor
```

The syntax is universal: it can be used in every context in which variables can be initialized. For example,

```
double* price_pointer = new double { 19.15 };
int result = sum({ 1, 4, 9, 16});
    // where sum has a parameter variable of type vector<int>
```

You can also use the uniform syntax to initialize data members in a constructor. For example, the Order constructor of Special Topic 9.2 can be written as

```
Order::Order(string customer_name, string item_description, double item_price)
  : article{item_description, item_price}, customer{customer_name}
{}
```

There is much to like about this universal and uniform syntax. However, as it is quite different from the traditional syntax, it will likely take some time before it is commonly used.

9.7 Problem Solving: Tracing Objects

You have seen how the technique of hand-tracing is useful for understanding how a program works. When your program contains objects, it is useful to adapt the technique so that you gain a better understanding about object data and encapsulation.

Use an index card or a sticky note for each object. On the front, write the member functions that the object can execute. On the back, make a table for the values of the data members.

> Write the member functions on the front of a card, and the data member values on the back.

Here is a card for a CashRegister object:

CashRegister reg1 *clear* *add_item(price)* *get_total* *get_count*	*item_count* │ *total_price*
front	*back*

In a small way, this gives you a feel for encapsulation. An object is manipulated through its public interface (on the front of the card), and the data members are hidden in the back.

When an object is constructed, fill in the initial values of the data members.

item_count	total_price
0	0

Update the values of the data members when a mutator member function is called.

Whenever a mutator member function is executed, cross out the old values and write the new ones below. Here is what happens after a call to the add_item member function:

item_count	total_price
~~0~~	~~0~~
1	19.95

If you have more than one object in your program, you will have multiple cards, one for each object:

item_count	total_price		item_count	total_price
~~0~~	~~0~~		~~0~~	~~0~~
1	19.95		1	19.95
			2	14.90

These diagrams are also useful when you design a class. Suppose you are asked to enhance the CashRegister class to compute the sales tax. Add a function get_sales_tax to the front of the card. Now turn the card over, look over the data members, and ask yourself whether the object has sufficient information to compute the answer. Remember that each object is an autonomous unit. Any data value that can be used in a computation must be

- A data member.
- A function argument.
- A global constant or variable.

To compute the sales tax, we need to know the tax rate and the total of the taxable items. (Food items are usually not subject to sales tax.) We don't have that information available. Let us introduce additional data members for the tax rate and the taxable total. The tax rate can be set in the constructor (assuming it stays fixed for the lifetime of the object). When adding an item, we need to be told whether the item is taxable. If so, we add its price to the taxable total.

For example, consider the following statements.

```
CashRegister reg2(7.5); // 7.5 percent sales tax
reg2.add_item(3.95, false); // not taxable
reg2.add_item(19.95, true); // taxable
```

When you record the effect on a card, it looks like this:

item_count	total_price	taxable_total	tax_rate
0̶	0̶	0̶	7.5
1̶	3̶.9̶5̶		
2	23.90	19.95	

With this information, it becomes easy to compute the tax. It is *taxable_total x tax_rate / 100*. Tracing the object helped us understand the need for additional data members.

HOW TO 9.1

Implementing a Class

A very common task is to implement a class whose objects can carry out a set of specified actions. This How To walks you through the necessary steps.

Problem Statement As an example, consider a class Menu. An object of this class can display a menu such as

```
1) Open new account
2) Log into existing account
3) Help
4) Quit
```

Then the menu waits for the user to supply a value. If the user does not supply a valid value, the menu is redisplayed, and the user can try again.

© Mark Evans/iStockphoto.

Step 1   Get an informal list of the responsibilities of your objects.

Be careful that you restrict yourself to features that are actually required in the problem. With real-world items, such as cash registers or bank accounts, there are potentially dozens of features that might be worth implementing. However, your job is not to faithfully model the real world. You need to determine only those responsibilities that you need for solving your specific problem.

In the case of the menu, you need to

Display the menu.
Get user input.

Now look for hidden responsibilities that aren't part of the problem description. How do objects get created? Which mundane activities need to happen, such as clearing the cash register at the beginning of each sale?

In the menu example, consider how a menu is produced. The programmer creates an empty menu object and then adds options "Open new account", "Help", and so on. There is a hidden responsibility:

Add an option.

Step 2 Specify the public interface.

Turn the list in Step 1 into a set of member functions, with specific types for the parameter variables and the return values. Be sure to mark accessors as `const`. Many programmers find this step simpler if they write out member function calls that are applied to a sample object, like this:

```
Menu main_menu;
main_menu.add_option("Open new account");
// Add more options
int input = main_menu.get_input();
```

Now we have a specific list of member functions.

- `void add_option(string option)`

- `int get_input() const`

What about displaying the menu? There is no sense in displaying the menu without also asking the user for input. However, `get_input` may need to display the menu more than once if the user provides a bad input. Thus, `display` is a good candidate for a private member function.

To complete the public interface, you need to specify the constructors. Ask yourself what information you need in order to construct an object of your class. Sometimes you will want two constructors: one that sets all data members to a default and one that sets them to user-supplied values.

In the case of the menu example, we can get by with a single constructor that creates an empty menu.

Here is the public interface:

```
class Menu
{
public:
   Menu();
   void add_option(string option);
   int get_input() const
private:
   . . .
};
```

Step 3 Document the public interface.

Supply a **documentation comment** for the class, then comment each member function.

```
/**
   A menu that is displayed on a console.
*/
class Menu
{
public:
   /**
      Constructs a menu with no options.
   */
   Menu();
```

```
/**
    Adds an option to the end of this menu.
    @param option the option to add
*/
void add_option(string option);

/**
    Displays the menu, with options numbered starting with 1,
    and prompts the user for input. Repeats until a valid input
    is supplied.
    @return the number that the user supplied
*/
int get_input() const;
private:
    . . .
};
```

Step 4   Determine data members.

Ask yourself what information an object needs to store to do its job. Remember, the member functions can be called in any order! The object needs to have enough internal memory to be able to process every member function using just its data members and the member function arguments. Go through each member function, perhaps starting with a simple one or an interesting one, and ask yourself what you need to carry out the member function's task. Make data members to store the information that the member function needs.

In the menu example, we clearly need to store the menu options so that the menu can be displayed. How should we store them? As a vector of strings? As one long string? Both approaches can be made to work. We will use a vector here. Exercise E9.6 asks you to implement the other approach.

```
class Menu
{
    . . .
private:
    . . .
    vector<string> options;
};
```

When checking for user input, we need to know the number of menu items. Because we store them in a vector, the number of menu items is simply obtained as the size of the vector. If you stored the menu items in one long string, you might want to keep another data member that stores the menu item count.

Step 5   Implement constructors and member functions.

Implement the constructors and member functions in your class, one at a time, starting with the easiest ones. For example, here is the implementation of the add_option member function:

```
void Menu::add_option(string option)
{
    options.push_back(option);
}
```

Here is the get_input member function. This member function is a bit more sophisticated. It loops until a valid input has been obtained, and it calls the private display member function to display the menu.

```
int Menu::get_input() const
{
    int input = 0;
    do
    {
        display();
        cin >> input;
```

```
      }
      while (input < 1 || input > options.size());
      return input;
   }
```

Finally, here is the display member function:

```
void Menu::display() const
{
   for (int i = 0; i < options.size(); i++)
   {
      cout << i + 1 << ") " << options[i] << endl;
   }
}
```

The Menu constructor is a bit odd. We need to construct a menu with no options. A vector is a class, and it has a default constructor. That constructor does exactly what we want, namely to construct an empty vector. Nothing else needs to be done:

```
Menu::Menu()
{
}
```

If you find that you have trouble with the implementation of some of your member functions, you may need to rethink your choice of data members. It is common for a beginner to start out with a set of data members that cannot accurately describe the state of an object. Don't hesitate to go back and rethink your implementation strategy.

Once you have completed the implementation, compile your class and fix any compiler errors.

Step 6   Test your class.

Write a short tester program and execute it. The tester program should carry out the member function calls that you found in Step 2.

```
int main()
{
   Menu main_menu;
   main_menu.add_option("Open new account");
   main_menu.add_option("Log into existing account");
   main_menu.add_option("Help");
   main_menu.add_option("Quit");
   int input = main_menu.get_input();
   cout << "Input: " << input << endl;
   return 0;
}
```

Program Run

```
1) Open new account
2) Log into existing account
3) Help
4) Quit
5
1) Open new account
2) Log into existing account
3) Help
4) Quit
3
Input: 3
```

EXAMPLE CODE   See how_to_1 of your companion code for the complete menu program.

WORKED EXAMPLE 9.1

Implementing a Bank Account Class

Learn how to develop a class that simulates a bank account. See your E-Text or visit wiley.com/
go/bclo3.

Computing & Society 9.1   Electronic Voting Machines

In the 2000 presiden-
tial elections in the
United States, votes were tallied by a
variety of machines. Some machines
processed cardboard ballots into
which voters punched holes to indicate their choices (see photo below).
When voters were not careful, remains
of paper—the now infamous "chads"—
were partially stuck in the punch
cards, causing votes to be miscounted.
A manual recount was necessary, but it
was not carried out everywhere due to
time constraints and procedural wran-
gling. The election was very close, and
there remain doubts in the minds of
many people whether the election outcome would have been different if the
voting machines had accurately
counted the intent of the voters.

© Peter Nguyen/iStockphoto.

Punch Card Ballot

Subsequently, voting machine
manufacturers have argued that electronic voting machines would avoid
the problems caused by punch cards
or optically scanned forms. In an electronic voting machine, voters indicate their preferences by pressing
buttons or touching icons on a computer screen. Typically, each voter is
presented with a summary screen for

review before casting the ballot. The
process is very similar to using an
automatic bank teller machine.

It seems plausible that these
machines make it more likely that a
vote is counted in the same way that
the voter intends. However, there
has been significant controversy surrounding some types of electronic
voting machines. If a machine simply
records the votes and prints out the
totals after the election has been completed, then how do you know that the
machine worked correctly? Inside the
machine is a computer that executes a
program, and, as you may know from
your own experience, programs can
have bugs.

In fact, some electronic voting
machines do have bugs. There have
been isolated cases where machines
reported tallies that were impossible.
When a machine reports far more or
far fewer votes than voters, then it is
clear that it malfunctioned. Unfortunately, it is then impossible to find
out the actual votes. Over time, one
would expect these bugs to be fixed
in the software. More insidiously, if the
results are plausible, nobody may ever
investigate.

Many computer scientists have
spoken out on this issue and con-
firmed that it is impossible, with
today's technology, to tell that software is error free and has not been
tampered with. Many of them recommend that electronic voting machines
should employ a *voter verifiable audit
trail*. (A good source of information is
http://verifiedvoting.org.) Typically,
a voter-verifiable machine prints out a
ballot. Each voter has a chance to
review the printout, and then deposits
it in an old-fashioned ballot box. If
there is a problem with the electronic

equipment, the printouts can be
scanned or counted by hand.

© Lisa F. Young/iStockphoto.

Touch Screen Voting Machine

As this book is written, this concept is strongly resisted both by
manufacturers of electronic voting
machines and by their customers,
the cities and counties that run elections. Manufacturers are reluctant
to increase the cost of the machines
because they may not be able to pass
the cost increase on to their customers, who tend to have tight budgets.
Election officials fear problems with
malfunctioning printers, and some of
them have publicly stated that they
actually prefer equipment that elimi-
nates bothersome recounts.

What do you think? You probably
use an automatic bank teller machine
to get cash from your bank account.
Do you review the paper record that
the machine issues? Do you check your
bank statement? Even if you don't, do
you put your faith in other people who
double-check their balances, so that

the bank won't get away with widespread cheating?

At any rate, is the integrity of banking equipment more important or less important than that of voting machines? Won't every voting process have some room for error and fraud anyway? Is the added cost for equipment, paper, and staff time reasonable to combat a potentially slight risk of malfunction and fraud? Computer scientists cannot answer these questions—an informed society must make these tradeoffs. But, like all professionals, they have an obligation to speak out and give accurate testimony about the capabilities and limitations of computing equipment.

9.8 Problem Solving: Discovering Classes

To discover classes, look for nouns in the problem description.

When you solve a problem using objects and classes, you need to determine the classes required for the implementation. You may be able to reuse existing classes, or you may need to implement new ones. One simple approach for discovering classes and member functions is to look for the nouns and verbs in the problem description. Often, nouns correspond to classes, and verbs correspond to member functions.

Concepts from the problem domain, be it science, business, or a game, often make good classes. Examples are

- Cannonball
- CashRegister
- Monster

Concepts from the problem domain are good candidates for classes.

The name for such a class should be a noun that describes the concept. Other frequently used classes represent system services such as files or menus.

What might not be a good class? If you can't tell from the class name what an object of the class is supposed to do, then you are probably not on the right track. For example, your homework assignment might ask you to write a program that prints paychecks. Suppose you start by trying to design a class PaycheckProgram. What would an object of this class do? An object of this class would have to do everything that the homework needs to do. That doesn't simplify anything. A better class would be Paycheck. Then your program can manipulate one or more Paycheck objects.

© Oleg Prikhodko/iStockphoto.

In a class scheduling system, potential classes from the problem domain include Class, LectureHall, Instructor, and Student.

Another common mistake, particularly by students who are used to writing programs that consist of functions, is to turn an action into a class. For example, if your homework assignment is to compute a paycheck, you may consider writing a class ComputePaycheck. But can you visualize a "ComputePaycheck" object? The fact that "ComputePaycheck" isn't a noun tips you off that you are on the wrong track. On the other hand, a Paycheck class makes intuitive sense. The word "paycheck" is a noun. You can visualize a paycheck object. You can then think about useful member functions of the Paycheck class, such as compute_taxes, that help you solve the assignment.

When you analyze a problem description, you often find that you need multiple classes. It is then helpful to consider how these classes are related. One of the fundamental relationships between classes is the "aggregation" relationship (which is informally known as the "has-a" relationship).

© bojan fatur/iStockphoto.

A car has a motor and tires. In object-oriented design,
this "has-a" relationship is called aggregation.

A class aggregates another if its objects contain objects of the other class.

The **aggregation** relationship states that objects of one class contain objects of another class. Consider a quiz that is made up of questions. Since each quiz has one or more questions, we say that the class Quiz aggregates the class Question. There is a standard notation, called a UML (**Unified Modeling Language**) class diagram, to describe class relationships. In the UML notation, aggregation is denoted by a line with a diamond-shaped symbol (see Figure 6).

Figure 6   Class Diagram

Finding out about aggregation is very helpful for deciding how to implement classes. For example, when you implement the Quiz class, you will want to store the questions of a quiz as a data member. Since a quiz can have any number of questions, you will choose a vector:

```
class Quiz
{
   . . .
private:
   vector<Question> questions;
};
```

In summary, when you analyze a problem description, you will want to carry out these tasks:

- Find the concepts that you need to implement as classes. Often, these will be nouns in the problem description.
- Find the responsibilities of the classes. Often, these will be verbs in the problem description.
- Find relationships between the classes that you have discovered. In this section, we described the aggregation relationship. In the next chapter, you will learn about another important relationship between classes, called inheritance.

Programming Tip 9.3
Make Parallel Vectors into Vectors of Objects

Sometimes, you find yourself using vectors of the same length, each of which stores a part of what conceptually should be an object. In that situation, it is a good idea to reorganize your program and use a single vector whose elements are objects.

For example, suppose an invoice contains a series of item descriptions and prices. One solution is to keep two vectors:

```
vector<string> descriptions;
vector<double> prices;
```

Each of the vectors will have the same length, and the ith *slice*, consisting of `descriptions[i]` and `prices[i]`, contains data that needs to be processed together. These vectors are called **parallel vectors** (see Figure 7).

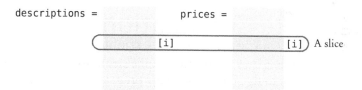

Figure 7   Parallel Vectors

Parallel vectors become a headache in larger programs. The programmer must ensure that the vectors always have the same length and that each slice is filled with values that actually belong together. Moreover, any function that operates on a slice must get all of the vectors as arguments, which is tedious to program.

The remedy is simple. Look at the slice and find the *concept* that it represents. Then make the concept into a class. In this example, each slice contains the description and price of an *item;* turn this into a class.

Avoid parallel vectors by changing them into vectors of objects.

```
class Item
{
public:
   . . .
private:
   string description;
   double price;
};
```

You can now eliminate the parallel vectors and replace them with a single vector:

```
vector<Item> items;
```

Each slot in the resulting vector corresponds to a slice in the set of parallel vectors (see Figure 8).

Parallel vectors

A vector of objects

Figure 8   Eliminating Parallel Vectors

9.9 Separate Compilation

The code of complex programs is distributed over multiple files.

When you write and compile small programs, you can place all your code into a single source file. When your programs get larger or you work in a team, that situation changes. You will want to split your code into separate source files. There are two reasons why this split becomes necessary. First, it takes time to compile a file, and it seems silly to wait for the compiler to keep translating code that doesn't change. If your code is distributed over several source files, then only those files that you change need to be recompiled. The second reason becomes apparent when you work with other programmers in a team. It would be very difficult for multiple programmers to edit a single source file simultaneously. Therefore, the program code is broken up so that each programmer is solely responsible for a separate set of files.

If your program is composed of multiple files, some of these files will define data types or functions that are needed in other files. There must be a path of communication between the files. In C++, that communication happens through the inclusion of **header files**.

A header file contains

- Definitions of classes.
- Definitions of constants.
- Declarations of nonmember functions.

The source file contains

- Definitions of member functions.
- Definitions of nonmember functions.

For the `CashRegister` class, you create a pair of files, `cashregister.h` and `cashregister.cpp`, that contain the interface and the implementation, respectively.

The header file contains the class definition:

sec09/cashregister.h

Header files contain the definitions of classes and declarations of nonmember functions.

```
 1  #ifndef CASHREGISTER_H
 2  #define CASHREGISTER_H
 3
 4  /**
 5     A simulated cash register that tracks the item count and
 6     the total amount due.
 7  */
 8  class CashRegister
 9  {
10  public:
11     /**
12        Constructs a cash register with cleared item count and total.
13     */
14     CashRegister();
15
16     /**
17        Clears the item count and the total.
18     */
19     void clear();
20
21     /**
22        Adds an item to this cash register.
23        @param price the price of this item
24     */
25     void add_item(double price);
26
27     /**
28        @return the total amount of the current sale
29     */
30     double get_total() const;
31
32     /**
33        @return the item count of the current sale
34     */
35     int get_count() const;
36
37  private:
38     int item_count;
39     double total_price;
40  };
41
42  #endif
```

You include this header file whenever the definition of the `CashRegister` class is required. Because this file is not a standard header file, you must enclose its name in quotes, not `<...>`, when you include it, like this:

```
#include "cashregister.h"
```

Note the set of directives that bracket the header file:

```
#ifndef CASHREGISTER_H
#define CASHREGISTER_H

. . .

#endif
```

Suppose a file includes two header files: cashregister.h, and another header file that itself includes cashregister.h. The effect of the directives is to skip the file when it is encountered the second time. If we did not have that check, the compiler would complain when it saw the definition for the CashRegister class twice. (Sadly, it doesn't check whether the definitions are identical.)

The source file for the CashRegister class simply contains the definitions of the member functions (including constructors).

Note that the source file cashregister.cpp includes its own header file, cashregister.h. The compiler needs to know how the CashRegister class is defined in order to compile the member functions.

Source files contain function implementations.

sec09/cashregister.cpp

```
 1  #include "cashregister.h"
 2
 3  CashRegister::CashRegister()
 4  {
 5     clear();
 6  }
 7
 8  void CashRegister::clear()
 9  {
10     item_count = 0;
11     total_price = 0;
12  }
13
14  void CashRegister::add_item(double price)
15  {
16     item_count++;
17     total_price = total_price + price;
18  }
19
20  double CashRegister::get_total() const
21  {
22     return total_price;
23  }
24
25  int CashRegister::get_count() const
26  {
27     return item_count;
28  }
```

Note that the function comments are in the header file, because comments are a part of the interface, not the implementation.

The cashregister.cpp file does *not* contain a main function. There are many potential programs that might make use of the CashRegister class. Each of these programs will need to supply its own main function, as well as other functions and classes.

Here is a simple test program that puts the CashRegister class to use. Its source file includes the cashregister.h header file.

sec09/registerdemo2.cpp

```
1  #include <iostream>
2  #include <iomanip>
3  #include "cashregister.h"
4
5  using namespace std;
6
7  /**
8     Displays the item count and total price of a cash register.
9     @param reg the cash register to display
10 */
11 void display(CashRegister reg)
12 {
13    cout << reg.get_count() << " $" << fixed << setprecision(2)
14       << reg.get_total() << endl;
15 }
16
17 int main()
18 {
19    CashRegister register1;
20    register1.clear();
21    register1.add_item(1.95);
22    display(register1);
23    register1.add_item(0.95);
24    display(register1);
25    register1.add_item(2.50);
26    display(register1);
27    return 0;
28 }
```

To build the complete program, you need to compile both the `registerdemo2.cpp` and `cashregister.cpp` source files (see Figure 9). The details depend on your compiler. For example, with the GNU compiler, you issue the command

```
g++ -o registerdemo registerdemo2.cpp cashregister.cpp
```

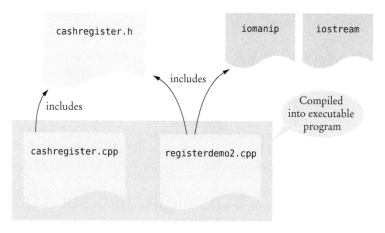

Figure 9   Compiling a Program from Multiple Source Files

You have just seen the simplest and most common case for designing header and source files. There are a few additional technical details that you should know.

- A header file should include all headers that are necessary for defining the class. For example, if a class uses the string class, include the <string> header as well. Anytime you include a header from the standard library, also include the directive

```
using namespace std;
```

item.h

```
 1  #include <string>
 2  using namespace std;
 3
 4  class Item
 5  {
 6     . . .
 7  private:
 8     string description
 9  };
```

- Place shared constants into a header file. For example,

volumes.h

```
 6  const double CAN_VOLUME = 0.355;
```

- To share a nonmember function, place the function declaration into a header file and the definition of the function into the corresponding source file.

cube.h

```
 8  double cube_volume(double side_length);
```

cube.cpp

```
 1  #include "cube.h"
 2
 3  double cube_volume(double side_length)
 4  {
 5     double volume = side_length * side_length * side_length;
 6     return volume;
 7  }
```

9.10 Pointers to Objects

It is often desirable to provide shared access to objects. This is achieved by **pointers**. A pointer provides the location of an object. When you know where an object is, you can update it without having to receive and return it. In the following sections, you will see how to use pointers for object sharing. In Chapter 10, you will see another use of pointers: for referring to objects of related classes.

9.10.1 Dynamically Allocating Objects

Suppose that we want to model two store employees who share a cash register, or two friends who share a bank account. First, we allocate the shared object on the **free**

Use the new operator to obtain an object that is located on the free store.

store, a storage area that provides memory on demand. Use the new operator together with a constructor invocation:

```
CashRegister* register_pointer = new CashRegister;
BankAccount* lisas_account_pointer = new BankAccount(1000);
```

The new operator returns a pointer to the allocated object.

The type BankAccount* denotes a pointer to a BankAccount object.

Now we can copy the pointer, without copying the object:

```
BankAccount* joes_account_pointer = lisas_account_pointer;
```

Figure 10 shows the result: two pointers that point to the same object.

When you no longer need an object that is allocated on the free store, be sure to delete it:

```
delete register_pointer;
delete lisas_account_pointer;
```

When an object allocated on the free store is no longer needed, use the delete operator to reclaim its memory.

Now the objects are no longer allocated. Be sure not to use any of the pointers afterwards.

Figure 10   Two Pointers to the Same Object

9.10.2 The -> Operator

Suppose we have a pointer to a CashRegister object:

```
CashRegister* register_pointer = new CashRegister;
```

To refer to the cash register, you can use the * operator: *register_pointer is the Cash-Register object to which register_pointer points. To invoke a member function on that object, you might call

```
(*register_pointer).add_item(1.95);
```

The parentheses are necessary because in C++ the dot operator takes precedence over the * operator. The expression without the parentheses would be a compile-time error:

```
*register_pointer.add_item(1.95); // Error—bad syntax
```

Because the dot operator has higher precedence than *, the dot would be applied to register_pointer, and * would be applied to the result of the member function call. Both of these would be syntax errors.

Use the -> operator to invoke a member function through a pointer.

Because calling a member function through a pointer is very common, there is an operator to abbreviate the "follow pointer and call member function" operation. That operator is written -> and usually pronounced as "arrow". Here is how you use the "arrow" operator:

```
register_pointer->add_item(1.95);
```

This call means: When invoking the add_item member function, set the implicit parameter to *register_pointer and the explicit parameter to 1.95.

9.10.3 The this Pointer

In a member function, the this pointer points to the implicit parameter.

Each member function has a special parameter variable, called `this`, which is a pointer to the implicit parameter. For example, consider the `CashRegister::add_item` function. If you call

```
register1.add_item(1.95)
```

then the `this` pointer has type `CashRegister*` and points to the `register1` object.

You can use the `this` pointer inside the definition of a member function. For example, you can implement the `add_item` function as

```
void CashRegister::add_item(double price)
{
    this->item_count++;
    this->total_price = this->total_price + price;
}
```

Here, the expression `this->item_count` refers to the `item_count` data member of the implicit parameter (which is `register1.item_count` in our example). Some programmers like to use the `this` pointer in this fashion to make it clear that `item_count` is a data member and not a variable.

Figure 11 The this Pointer

EXAMPLE CODE See sec10 of your companion code for a program that uses pointers to objects.

9.11 Problem Solving: Patterns for Object Data

When you design a class, you first consider the needs of the programmers who use the class. You provide the member functions that the users of your class will call when they manipulate objects. When you implement the class, you need to come up with the data members for the class. It is not always obvious how to do this. Fortunately, there is a small set of recurring patterns that you can adapt when you design your own classes. We introduce these patterns in the following sections.

9.11.1 Keeping a Total

Many classes need to keep track of a quantity that can go up or down as certain functions are called. Examples:

- A bank account has a balance that is increased by a deposit, decreased by a withdrawal.

- A cash register has a total that is increased when an item is added to the sale, cleared after the end of the sale.
- A car has gas in the tank, which is increased when fuel is added and decreased when the car drives.

In all of these cases, the implementation strategy is similar. Keep a data member that represents the current total. For example, for the cash register:

> **A data member for the total is updated in member functions that increase or decrease the total amount.**

```
double total_price;
```

Locate the member functions that affect the total. There is usually a member function to increase it by a given amount.

```
void add_item(double price)
{
   total_price = total_price + price;
}
```

Depending on the nature of the class, there may be a member function that reduces or clears the total. In the case of the cash register, there is a clear member fucntion:

```
void clear()
{
   total_price = 0;
}
```

There is usually a member function that yields the current total. It is easy to implement:

```
double get_total()
{
   return total_price;
}
```

All classes that manage a total follow the same basic pattern. Find the member functions that affect the total and provide the appropriate code for increasing or decreasing it. Find the member functions that report or use the total, and have those member functions read the current total.

9.11.2 Counting Events

> **A counter that counts events is incremented in member functions that correspond to the events.**

You often need to count how often certain events occur in the life of an object. For example:

- In a cash register, you want to know how many items have been added in a sale.
- A bank account charges a fee for each transaction; you need to count them.

Keep a counter, such as

```
int item_count;
```

Increment the counter in those member functions that correspond to the events that you want to count.

```
void add_item(double price)
{
   total_price = total_price + price;
   item_count++;
}
```

You may need to clear the counter, for example at the end of a sale or a statement period.

```
void clear()
{
   total_price = 0;
   item_count = 0;
}
```

There may or may not be a member function that reports the count to the class user. The count may only be used to compute a fee or an average. Find out which member functions in your class make use of the count, and read the current value in those member functions.

9.11.3 Collecting Values

Some objects collect numbers, strings, or other objects. For example, each multiple-choice question has a number of choices. A cash register may need to store all prices of the current sale.

Use a vector or an array to store the values. (A vector is usually simpler because you won't need to track the number of values.) For example,

© paul prescott/iStockphoto.

A shopping cart object needs to manage a collection of items.

> An object can collect other objects in an array or vector.

```
class Question
{
   . . .
private:
   vector<string> choices;
   . . .
};
```

In the constructor, we want to initialize the data member to an empty collection. The default constructor of the vector class does that automatically. Therefore, the constructor has no explicit actions:

```
Question::Question()
{
}
```

You need to supply some mechanism for adding values. It is common to provide a member function for appending a value to the collection:

```
void Question::add(string choice)
{
   choices.push_back(choice);
}
```

The user of a Question object can call this member function multiple times to add the various choices.

9.11.4 Managing Properties of an Object

A *property* is a value of an object that an object user can set and retrieve. For example, a Student object may have a name and an ID.

An object property can be accessed with a getter member function and changed with a setter member function.

Provide a data member to store the property's value and member functions to get and set it:

```cpp
class Student
{
public:
   string get_name() const;
   void set_name(string new_name);
private:
   string name;
   . . .
};
```

It is common to add error checking to the setter member function. For example, we may want to reject a blank name:

```cpp
void Student::set_name(string new_name)
{
   if (new_name.length() > 0) { name = new_name; }
}
```

Some properties should not change after they have been set in the constructor. For example, a student's ID may be fixed (unlike the student's name, which may change). In that case, don't supply a setter member function.

```cpp
class Student
{
public:
   Student(int an_id);
   string get_id() const;
   // No set_id member function
   . . .
private:
   int id;
   . . .
};
```

EXAMPLE CODE   See sec11_04 of your companion code for a class with getter and setter member functions.

9.11.5 Modeling Objects with Distinct States

If your object can have one of several states that affect the behavior, supply a data member for the current state.

Some objects have behavior that varies depending on what has happened in the past. For example, a Fish object may look for food when it is hungry and ignore food after it has eaten. Such an object would need to remember whether it has recently eaten.

Supply a data member that models the state, together with some constants for the state values:

© John Alexander/iStockphoto.

If a fish is in a hungry state, its behavior changes.

```cpp
class Fish
{
public:
   const int NOT_HUNGRY = 0;
   cont int SOMEWHAT_HUNGRY = 1;
   const int VERY_HUNGRY = 2;
private:
   int hungry;
   . . .
};
```

Determine which member functions change the state. In this example, a fish that has just eaten food won't be hungry. But as the fish moves, it will get hungrier.

```
void Fish::eat()
{
   hungry = NOT_HUNGRY;
   . . .
}

void Fish::move()
{
   . . .
   if (hungry < VERY_HUNGRY) { hungry++; }
}
```

Finally, determine where the state affects behavior. A fish that is very hungry will want to look for food first.

```
void Fish::move()
{
   if (hungry == VERY_HUNGRY)
   {
       Look for food.
   }
   . . .
}
```

EXAMPLE CODE   See sec11_05 of your companion code for the Fish class.

9.11.6 Describing the Position of an Object

Some objects move around during their lifetime, and they remember their current position. For example,

> To model a moving object, you need to store and update its position.

- A train drives along a track and keeps track of the distance from the terminus.
- A simulated bug living on a grid crawls from one grid location to the next, or makes 90 degree turns to the left or right.
- A cannonball is shot into the air, then descends as it is pulled by the gravitational force.

Such objects need to store their position. Depending on the nature of their movement, they may also need to store their orientation or velocity.

If the object moves along a line, you can represent the position as a distance from a fixed point.

```
double distance_from_terminus;
```

A bug in a grid needs to store its row, column, and direction.

If the object moves in a grid, remember its current location and direction in the grid:

```
int row;
int column;
int direction; // 0 = North, 1 = East, 2 = South, 3 = West
```

When you model a physical object such as a cannonball, you need to track both the position and the velocity, possibly in two or three dimensions. Here we model a cannonball that is shot upward into the air:

```
double z_position;
double z_velocity;
```

There will be member functions that update the position. In the simplest case, you may be told by how much the object moves:

```
void move(double distance_moved)
{
    distance_from_terminus = distance_from_terminus + distance_moved;
}
```

If the movement happens in a grid, you need to update the row or column, depending on the current orientation.

```
void move_one_unit()
{
    if (direction == NORTH) { row--; }
    else if (direction == EAST) { column++; }
    . . .
}
```

Exercise P9.21 shows you how to update the position of a physical object with known velocity.

Whenever you have a moving object, keep in mind that your program will simulate the actual movement in some way. Find out the rules of that simulation, such as movement along a line or in a grid with integer coordinates. Those rules determine how to represent the current position. Then locate the member functions that move the object, and update the positions according to the rules of the simulation.

EXAMPLE CODE   See sec11_06 of your companion code for two classes that update position data.

Computing & Society 9.2   **Open Source and Free Software**

Most companies that produce software regard the source code as a trade secret. After all, if customers or competitors had access to the source code, they could study it and create similar programs without paying the original vendor. For the same reason, customers dislike secret source code. If a company goes out of business or decides to discontinue support for a computer program, its users are left stranded. They are unable to fix bugs or adapt the program to a new operating system. Fortunately, many software packages are distributed as "open source software", giving its users the right to see, modify, and redistribute the source code of a program.

Having access to source code is not sufficient to ensure that software serves the needs of its users. Some companies have created software that spies on users or restricts access to previously purchased books, music, or videos. If that software runs on a server or in an embedded device, the user cannot change its behavior. In the article http://www.gnu.org/philosophy/free-software-even-more-important.en.html, Richard Stallman, a famous computer scientist and winner of a MacArthur "genius" grant, describes the "free software movement" that champions the right of users to control what their software does. This is an ethical position that goes beyond using open source for reasons of convenience or cost savings.

Stallman is the originator of the GNU project (http://gnu.org/gnu/the-gnu-project.html) that has produced an entirely free version of a UNIX-compatible operating system: the GNU operating system. All programs of the GNU project are licensed under the GNU General Public License (GNU GPL). The license allows you to make as many copies as you wish, make any modifications to the source, and redistribute the original and modified programs, charging nothing at all or whatever the market will bear. In return, you must agree that your modifications also fall under the license. You must give out the source code to any changes that you distribute, and anyone else can distribute them under the same conditions. The GNU GPL forms a social contract. Users of the software enjoy the freedom to use and modify the software, and in return they are obligated to share any improvements that they make available.

Some commercial software vendors have attacked the GPL as "viral" and "undermining the commercial software sector". Other companies have a more nuanced strategy, producing free or open source software, but charging for support or proprietary extensions. For example, the Java Development Kit is available under the GPL, but companies that need security updates for old versions or other support must pay Oracle.

Open source software sometimes lacks the polish of commercial software because many of the programmers are volunteers who are interested in solving their own problems, not in making a product that is easy to use by everyone. Open source software has been particularly successful in areas that are of interest to programmers, such as the Linux kernel, Web servers, and programming tools.

The open source software community can be very competitive and creative. It is quite common to see several competing projects that take ideas from each other, all rapidly becoming more capable. Having many programmers involved, all reading the source code, often means that bugs tend to get squashed quickly. Eric Raymond describes open source development in his famous article "The Cathedral and the Bazaar" (http://catb.org/~esr/writings/cathedral-bazaar/cathedral-bazaar/index.html). He writes "Given enough eyeballs, all bugs are shallow".

Courtesy of Richard Stallman published under a CC license.

Richard Stallman, a pioneer of the free source movement.

CHAPTER SUMMARY

Understand the concepts of objects and classes.

- A class describes a set of objects with the same behavior.
- Every class has a public interface: a collection of member functions through which the objects of the class can be manipulated.
- Encapsulation is the act of providing a public interface and hiding implementation details.
- Encapsulation enables changes in the implementation without affecting users of a class.

Understand data members and member functions of a simple class.

- The member functions of a class define the behavior of its objects.
- An object's data members represent the state of the object.
- Each object of a class has its own set of data members.
- A member function can access the data members of the object on which it acts.
- A private data member can only be accessed by the member functions of its own class.

Formulate the public interface of a class in C++.

- You can use member function declarations and function comments to specify the public interface of a class.
- A mutator member function changes the object on which it operates.
- An accessor member function does not change the object on which it operates. Use const with accessors.

Choose data members to represent the state of an object.

- An object holds data members that are accessed by member functions.
- Every object has its own set of data members.
- Private data members can only be accessed by member functions of the same class.

Implement member functions of a class.

- Use the *ClassName*:: prefix when defining member functions.
- The implicit parameter is a reference to the object on which a member function is applied.
- Explicit parameters of a member function are listed in the function definition.
- When calling another member function on the same object, do not use the dot notation.

Design and implement constructors.

- A constructor is called automatically whenever an object is created.
- The name of a constructor is the same as the class name.
- A default constructor has no arguments.
- A class can have multiple constructors.
- The compiler picks the constructor that matches the construction arguments.
- Be sure to initialize all number and pointer data members in a constructor.

Use the technique of object tracing for visualizing object behavior.

- Write the member functions on the front of a card, and the data member values on the back.
- Update the values of the data members when a mutator member function is called.

Discover classes that are needed for solving a programming problem.

- To discover classes, look for nouns in the problem description.
- Concepts from the problem domain are good candidates for classes.
- A class aggregates another if its objects contain objects of the other class.
- Avoid parallel vectors by changing them into vectors of objects.

Separate the interface and implementation of a class in header and source files.

- The code of complex programs is distributed over multiple files.
- Header files contain the definitions of classes and declarations of nonmember functions.
- Source files contain function implementations.

Use pointers to objects and manage dynamically allocated objects.

- Use the new operator to obtain an object that is located on the free store.
- The new operator returns a pointer to the allocated object.
- When an object allocated on the free store is no longer needed, use the delete operator to reclaim its memory.
- Use the -> operator to invoke a member function through a pointer.
- In a member function, the this pointer points to the implicit parameter.

Use patterns to design the data representation of a class.

- An data member for the total is updated in member functions that increase or decrease the total amount.
- A counter that counts events is incremented in member functions that correspond to the events.
- An object can collect other objects in an array or vector.
- An object property can be accessed with a getter member function and changed with a setter member function.
- If your object can have one of several states that affect the behavior, supply a data member for the current state.
- To model a moving object, you need to store and update its position.

- **R9.1** List all classes in the C++ library that you have encountered in this book up to this point.

- **R9.2** Consider a Date class that stores a calendar date such as November 20, 2011. Consider two possible implementations of this class: one storing the day, month, and year, and another storing the number of days since January 1, 1900. Why might an implementor prefer the second version? How does the choice affect the user of the class?

- **R9.3** Write a partial C++ class definition that contains the public interface of the Date class described in Exercise R9.2. Supply member functions for setting the date to a particular year, month, and day, for advancing the date by a given number of days, and for finding the number of days between this date and another. Pay attention to const.

- **R9.4** What value is returned by the calls reg1.get_count(), reg1.get_total(), reg2.get_count(), and reg2.get_total() after these statements?

  ```
  CashRegister reg1;
  reg1.clear();
  reg1.add_item(0.90);
  reg1.add_item(1.95);
  CashRegister reg2;
  reg2.clear();
  reg2.add_item(1.90);
  ```

- **R9.5** Consider the Menu class in How To 9.1. What is displayed when the following calls are executed?

  ```
  Menu simple_menu;
  simple_menu.add_option("Ok");
  simple_menu.add_option("Cancel");
  int response = simple_menu.get_input();
  ```

- **R9.6** What is the *interface* of a class? How does it differ from the *implementation* of a class?

- **R9.7** What is a member function, and how does it differ from a nonmember function?

- **R9.8** What is a mutator function? What is an accessor function?

- **R9.9** What happens if you forget the const in an accessor function? What happens if you accidentally supply a const in a mutator function?

- **R9.10** What is an implicit parameter? How does it differ from an explicit parameter?

- **R9.11** How many implicit parameters can a member function have? How many implicit parameters can a nonmember function have? How many explicit parameters can a function have?

- **R9.12** What is a constructor?

- **R9.13** What is a default constructor? What is the consequence if a class does not have a default constructor?

- **R9.14** How many constructors can a class have? Can you have a class with no constructors? If a class has more than one constructor, which of them gets called?

■ **R9.15** What is encapsulation? Why is it useful?

■■■ **R9.16** Data members are hidden in the private section of a class, but they aren't hidden very well at all. Anyone can read the private section. Explain to what extent the private reserved word hides the private members of a class.

■■■ **R9.17** You can read the item_count data member of the CashRegister class with the get_count accessor function. Should there be a set_count mutator function to change it? Explain why or why not.

■ **R9.18** Suppose you implement a ChessBoard class. Provide data members to store the pieces on the board and the player who has the next turn.

■■■ **R9.19** In a nonmember function, it is easy to differentiate between calls to member functions and calls to nonmember functions. How do you tell them apart? Why is it not as easy for functions that are called from a member function?

■ **R9.20** Using the object tracing technique described in Section 9.7, trace the program at the end of Section 9.5.

■■ **R9.21** Using the object tracing technique described in Section 9.7, trace the program in Worked Example 9.1.

■■■ **R9.22** Design a modification of the BankAccount class in Worked Example 9.1 in which the first five transactions per month are free and a $1 fee is charged for every additional transaction. Provide a member function that deducts the fee at the end of a month. What additional data members do you need? Using the object tracing technique described in Section 9.7, trace a scenario that shows how the fees are computed over two months.

■■ **R9.23** Consider the following problem description:

> *Users place coins in a vending machine and select a product by pushing a button. If the inserted coins are sufficient to cover the purchase price of the product, the product is dispensed and change is given. Otherwise, the inserted coins are returned to the user.*

What classes should you use to implement it?

■■ **R9.24** Consider the following problem description:

> *Employees receive their biweekly paychecks. They are paid their hourly rates for each hour worked; however, if they worked more than 40 hours per week, they are paid overtime at 150 percent of their regular wage.*

What classes should you use to implement it?

■■ **R9.25** Consider the following problem description:

> *Customers order products from a store. Invoices are generated to list the items and quantities ordered, payments received, and amounts still due. Products are shipped to the shipping address of the customer, and invoices are sent to the billing address.*

What classes should you use to implement it?

■■ **R9.26** Suppose a vending machine contains products, and users insert coins into the vending machine to purchase products. Draw a UML diagram showing the aggregation relationships between the classes VendingMachine, Coin, and Product.

■■ **R9.27** Suppose an Invoice object contains descriptions of the products ordered and the billing and shipping address of the customer. Draw a UML diagram showing the aggregation relationships between the classes Invoice, Address, Customer, and Product.

■■ **R9.28** Consider the implementation of a program that plays TicTacToe, with two classes `Player` and `TicTacToeBoard`. Each class implementation is placed in its own C++ source file and each class interface is placed in its own header file. In addition, a source file `game.cpp` contains the code for playing the game and displaying the scores of the players. Describe the contents of each header file, and determine in which files each of them is included.

■ **R9.29** What would happen if the `display` function was moved from `registerdemo2.cpp` to `cashregister.h`? Try it out if you are not sure.

■■ **R9.30** In Exercise P9.17, a `MenuItem` optionally contains a `Menu`. Generally, there are two ways for implementing an "optional" relationship. You can use a pointer that may be set to `nullptr`. Or you may use an indicator, such as a `bool` value, that specifies whether the optional item is present. Why are pointers required in this case?

■■ **R9.31** What is the `this` reference? Why would you use it?

PRACTICE EXERCISES

■ **E9.1** We want to add a button to the tally counter in Section 9.2 that allows an operator to undo an accidental button click. Provide a member function

```
void undo()
```

that simulates such a button. As an added precaution, make sure that the operator cannot click the undo button more often than the count button.

■ **E9.2** Simulate a tally counter that can be used to admit a limited number of people. First, the limit is set with a call

```
void set_limit(int maximum)
```

If the count button was clicked more often than the limit, simulate an alarm by printing out a message "Limit exceeded".

■■ **E9.3** Simulate a circuit for controlling a hallway light that has switches at both ends of the hallway. Each switch can be up or down, and the light can be on or off. Toggling either switch turns the lamp on or off. Provide member functions

```
int get_first_switch_state() // 0 for down, 1 for up
int get_second_switch_state()
int get_lamp_state() // 0 for off, 1 for on
void toggle_first_switch()
void toggle_second_switch()
```

■ **E9.4** Change the public interface of the circuit class of Exercise E9.3 so that it has the following member functions:

```
int get_switch_state(int switch_num)
int get_lamp_state()
void toggle_switch(int switch_num)
```

■ **E9.5** Implement a class `Rectangle`. Provide a constructor to construct a rectangle with a given width and height, member functions `get_perimeter` and `get_area` that compute the perimeter and area, and a member function `void resize(double factor)` that resizes the rectangle by multiplying the width and height by the given factor.

■■■ **E9.6** Reimplement the `Menu` class so that it stores all menu items in one long string. *Hint:* Keep a separate counter for the number of options. When a new option is added, append the option count, the option, and a newline character.

■■ **E9.7** Implement a class StreetAddress. An address has a house number, a street, an optional apartment number, a city, a state, and a postal code. Supply two constructors: one with an apartment number and one without. Supply a print member function that prints the address with the street (and optional apartment number) on one line and the city, state, and postal code on the next line. Supply a member function comes_before that tests whether one address comes before another when the addresses are compared by postal code.

■ **E9.8** Implement a class Student. For the purpose of this exercise, a student has a name and a total quiz score. Supply an appropriate constructor and functions get_name(), add_quiz(int score), get_total_score(), and get_average_score(). To compute the latter, you also need to store the *number of quizzes* that the student took.

■■ **E9.9** Modify the Student class of Exercise E9.8 to compute grade point averages. Member functions are needed to add a grade and get the current GPA. Specify grades as elements of a class Grade. Supply a constructor that constructs a grade from a string, such as "B+". You will also need a function that translates grades into their numeric values (for example, "B+" becomes 3.3).

■■ **E9.10** Write a class Bug that models a bug moving along a horizontal line. The bug moves either to the right or left. Initially, the bug moves to the right, but it can turn to change its direction. In each move, its position changes by one unit in the current direction. Provide a constructor

```
Bug(int initial_position)
```

and member functions

```
void turn()
void move()
int get_position()
```

Sample usage:

```
Bug bugsy(10);
bugsy.move(); //  Now the position is 11
bugsy.turn();
bugsy.move(); //  Now the position is 10
```

Your main function should construct a bug, make it move and turn a few times, and print the actual and expected positions.

■■ **E9.11** Implement a class Moth that models a moth flying along the *x*-axis. The moth has a position, the distance from a fixed origin. When the moth moves toward a point of light, its new position is halfway between its old position and the position of the light source. Supply a constructor

```
Moth(double initial_position)
```

and member functions

```
void move_to_light(double light_position)
double get_position()
```

Your main function should construct a moth, move it toward a couple of light sources, and check that the moth's position is as expected.

■■ **E9.12** Implement classes Person and StreetAddress. Each person has a street address. Provide display functions in each class for displaying their contents. Distribute your code over three source files, one for each class, and one containing the main function. Construct two Person objects and display them.

■ ■ **E9.13** Modify the Person class in Exercise E9.12 so that it contains a pointer to the street address. Construct and display two Person objects that share the same StreetAddress object.

PROGRAMMING PROJECTS

■ ■ **P9.1** A microwave control panel has four buttons: one for increasing the time by 30 seconds, one for switching between power levels 1 and 2, a reset button, and a start button. Implement a class that simulates the microwave, with a member function for each button. The member function for the start button should print a message "Cooking for ... seconds at level ...".

■ ■ **P9.2** A Person has a name (just a first name for simplicity) and friends. Store the names of the friends in a string, separated by spaces. Provide a constructor that constructs a person with a given name and no friends. Provide member functions

```
void befriend(Person p)
void unfriend(Person p)
string get_friend_names()
```

■ **P9.3** Add a member function

```
int get_friend_count()
```

to the Person class of Exercise P9.2.

■ ■ **P9.4** Reimplement the Person class from Exercise P9.2 so that the collection of a person's friends is stored in a vector<Person*>.

■ **P9.5** Write a class Battery that models a rechargeable battery. A battery has a constructor

```
Battery(double capacity)
```

where capacity is a value measured in milliampere hours. A typical AA battery has a capacity of 2000 to 3000 mAh. The member function

```
void drain(double amount)
```

drains the capacity of the battery by the given amount. The member function

```
void charge()
```

charges the battery to its original capacity.

The member function

```
double get_remaining_capacity()
```

gets the remaining capacity of the battery.

■ ■ **Business P9.6** Reimplement the CashRegister class so that it keeps track of the price of each added item in a vector<double>. Remove the item_count and total_price data members. Reimplement the clear, add_item, get_total, and get_count member functions. Add a member function display_all that displays the prices of all items in the current sale.

■ ■ **Business P9.7** Reimplement the CashRegister class so that it keeps track of the total price as an integer: the total cents of the price. For example, instead of storing 17.29, store the integer 1729. Such an implementation is commonly used because it avoids the accumulation of roundoff errors. Do not change the public interface of the class.

■ ■ **Business P9.8** Add a feature to the CashRegister class for computing sales tax. The tax rate should be supplied when constructing a CashRegister object. Add add_taxable_item and get_total_tax member functions. (Items added with add_item are not taxable.)

Business P9.9 After closing time, the store manager would like to know how much business was transacted during the day. Modify the `CashRegister` class to enable this functionality. Supply member functions `get_sales_total` and `get_sales_count` to get the total amount of all sales and the number of sales. Supply a member function `reset_sales` that resets any counters and totals so that the next day's sales start from zero.

P9.10 Implement a class `SodaCan` with member functions `get_surface_area()` and `get_volume()`. In the constructor, supply the height and radius of the can.

© Miklos Voros/
iStockphoto.

Business P9.11 Implement a class `Portfolio`. This class has two data members, `checking` and `savings`, of the type `BankAccount` that was developed in Worked Example 9.1 (`worked_example_1/account.cpp` in your code files). Implement four member functions:

```
deposit(double amount, string account)
withdraw(double amount, string account)
transfer(double amount, string account)
print_balances()
```

Here the account string is `"S"` or `"C"`. For the deposit or withdrawal, it indicates which account is affected. For a transfer, it indicates the account from which the money is taken; the money is automatically transferred to the other account.

P9.12 Define a class `Country` that stores the name of the country, its population, and its area. Using that class, write a program that reads in a set of countries and prints

- The country with the largest area.
- The country with the largest population.
- The country with the largest population density (people per square kilometer or mile).

Business P9.13 Design a class `Message` that models an e-mail message. A message has a recipient, a sender, and a message text. Support the following member functions:

- A constructor that takes the sender and recipient and sets the time stamp to the current time
- A member function `append` that appends a line of text to the message body
- A member function `to_string` that makes the message into one long string like this: `"From: Harry Hacker\nTo: Rudolf Reindeer\n . . ."`
- A member function `print` that prints the message text. *Hint:* Use `to_string`.

Write a program that uses this class to make a message and print it.

Business P9.14 Design a class `Mailbox` that stores e-mail messages, using the `Message` class of Exercise P9.13. Implement the following member functions:

```
void Mailbox::add_message(Message m)
Message Mailbox::get_message(int i) const
void Mailbox::remove_message(int i)
```

P9.15 Implement a `VotingMachine` class that can be used for a simple election. Have member functions to clear the machine state, to vote for a Democrat, to vote for a Republican, and to get the tallies for both parties.

P9.16 Provide a class for authoring a simple letter. In the constructor, supply the names of the sender and the recipient:

```
Letter(string from, string to)
```

Supply a member function

```
void add_line(string line)
```

to add a line of text to the body of the letter. Supply a member function

```
string get_text()
```

that returns the entire text of the letter. The text has the form:

Dear *recipient name*:
blank line
first line of the body
second line of the body

. . .

last line of the body
blank line
Sincerely,
blank line
sender name

Also supply a main function that prints this letter.

```
Dear John:

I am sorry we must part.
I wish you all the best.

Sincerely,

Mary
```

Construct an object of the Letter class and call add_line twice.

••• **P9.17** Reimplement the Menu class from How To 9.1 to support submenus similar to the ones in a graphical user interface.

A menu contains a sequence of menu items. Each menu item has a name and, optionally, a submenu.

Implement classes Menu and MenuItem. Supply a function to display a menu and get user input. Simply number the displayed items and have the user enter the number of the selected item. When an item with a submenu is selected, display the submenu. Otherwise simply print a message with the name of the selected item.

Note that there is a circular dependency between the two classes. To break it, first provide a declaration

```
class Menu;
```

Then define the MenuItem class and finally define the Menu class and the main function.

••• **Engineering P9.18** Define a class ComboLock that works like the combination lock in a gym locker, as shown here. The lock is constructed with a combination—three numbers between 0 and 39. The reset function resets the dial so that it points to 0. The turn_left and turn_right functions turn the dial by a given number of ticks to the left or right. The

© pixhook/iStockphoto.

open function attempts to open the lock. The lock opens if the user first turned it right to the first number in the combination, then left to the second, and then right to the third.

```
class ComboLock
{
public:
    ComboLock(int secret1, int secret2, int secret3);
    void reset();
    void turn_left(int ticks);
    void turn_right(int ticks);
    bool open() const;
private:
    . . .
};
```

■■ **Engineering P9.19** Implement a class Car with the following properties. A car has a certain fuel efficiency (measured in miles/gallon) and a certain amount of fuel in the gas tank. The efficiency is specified in the constructor, and the initial fuel level is 0. Supply a member function drive that simulates driving the car for a certain distance, reducing the fuel level in the gas tank, and member functions get_gas_level, to return the current fuel level, and add_gas, to tank up. Sample usage:

```
Car my_hybrid(50); // 50 miles per gallon
my_hybrid.add_gas(20); // Tank 20 gallons
my_hybrid.drive(100); // Drive 100 miles
cout << my_hybrid.get_gas_level() << endl; // Print fuel remaining
```

■■ **Engineering P9.20** Write a program that prints all real solutions to the quadratic equation $ax^2 + bx + c = 0$. Read in a, b, c and use the quadratic formula. You may assume that $a \neq 0$. If the *discriminant* $b^2 - 4ac$ is negative, display a message stating that there are no real solutions.

Implement a class QuadraticEquation whose constructor receives the coefficients a, b, c of the quadratic equation. Supply member functions get_solution1 and get_solution2 that get the solutions, using the quadratic formula, or 0 if no solution exists. The get_solution1 function should return the smaller of the two solutions.

Supply a function

```
bool has_solutions() const
```

that returns false if the discriminant is negative.

■■■ **Engineering P9.21** Design a class Cannonball to model a cannonball that is fired into the air. A ball has

- An x- and a y-position.
- An x- and a y-velocity.

Supply the following member functions:

- A constructor with an x-position (the y-position is initially 0)
- A member function move(double sec) that moves the ball to the next position (First compute the distance traveled in sec seconds, using the current velocities, then update the x- and y-positions; then update the y-velocity by taking into account the gravitational acceleration of –9.81 m/sec^2; the x-velocity is unchanged.) (See Exercise P4.23 for additional details.)
- A member function shoot whose parameters are the angle α and initial velocity v (Compute the x-velocity as $v \cos \alpha$ and the y-velocity as $v \sin \alpha$; then keep

calling move with a time interval of 0.1 seconds until the y-position is ≤ 0; display the (x, y) position after every move.)

Use this class in a program that prompts the user for the starting angle and the initial velocity. Then call shoot.

■■ **Engineering P9.22** The colored bands on the top-most resistor shown in the photo below indicate a resistance of 6.2 kΩ ±5%. The resistor tolerance of ±5% indicates the acceptable variation in the resistance. A 6.2 kΩ ±5% resistor could have a resistance as small as 5.89 kΩ or as large as 6.51 kΩ. We say that 6.2 kΩ is the *nominal value* of the resistance and that the actual value of the resistance can be any value between 5.89 kΩ and 6.51 kΩ.

© Maria Toutoudaki/iStockphoto.

Write a C++ program that represents a resistor as a class. Provide a single constructor that accepts values for the nominal resistance and tolerance and then determines the actual value randomly. The class should provide public member functions to get the nominal resistance, tolerance, and the actual resistance.

Write a main function for the C++ program that demonstrates that the class works properly by displaying actual resistances for ten 330 Ω ±10% resistors.

■■ **Engineering P9.23** In the Resistor class from Exercise P9.22, supply a member function that returns a string consisting of the four colors of the "color bands" for the resistance and tolerance. A resistor has four color bands:

- The first band is the first significant digit of the resistance value.
- The second band is the second significant digit of the resistance value.
- The third band is the decimal multiplier.
- The fourth band indicates the tolerance.

First band ⌐ ⌐Tolerance
Second band⌐ ⌐Multiplier

Color	Digit	Multiplier	Tolerance
Black	0	$\times 10^0$	—
Brown	1	$\times 10^1$	±1%
Red	2	$\times 10^2$	±2%
Orange	3	$\times 10^3$	—
Yellow	4	$\times 10^4$	—
Green	5	$\times 10^5$	±0.5%

Color	Digit	Multiplier	Tolerance
Blue	6	$\times 10^6$	±0.25%
Violet	7	$\times 10^7$	±0.1%
Gray	8	$\times 10^8$	±0.05%
White	9	$\times 10^9$	—
Gold	—	$\times 10^{-1}$	±5%
Silver	—	$\times 10^{-2}$	±10%
None	—	—	±20%

For example (using the values from the table as a key), a resistor with red, violet, green, and gold bands (left to right) will have 2 as the first digit, 7 as the second digit, a multiplier of 10^5, and a tolerance of ±5%, for a resistance of 2,700 kΩ, plus or minus 5%.

••• Engineering P9.24 The figure below shows a frequently used electric circuit called a "voltage divider". The input to the circuit is the voltage v_i. The output is the voltage v_o. The output of a voltage divider is proportional to the input, and the constant of proportionality is called the "gain" of the circuit. The voltage divider is represented by the equation

$$G = \frac{v_o}{v_i} = \frac{R_2}{R_1 + R_2}$$

where G is the gain and R_1 and R_2 are the resistances of the two resistors that comprise the voltage divider.

Manufacturing variations cause the actual resistance values to deviate from the nominal values, as described in Exercise P9.22. In turn, variations in the resistance values cause variations in the values of the gain of the voltage divider. We calculate the *nominal value of the gain* using the nominal resistance values and the *actual value of the gain* using actual resistance values.

Write a C++ program that contains two classes, VoltageDivider and Resistor. The Resistor class is described in Exercise P9.22. The VoltageDivider class should have two data members that are objects of the Resistor class. Provide a single constructor that accepts two Resistor objects, nominal values for their resistances, and the resistor tolerance. The class should provide public member functions to get the nominal and actual values of the voltage divider's gain.

Write a main function for the program that demonstrates that the class works properly by displaying nominal and actual gain for ten voltage dividers each consisting of 5% resistors having nominal values $R_1 = 250\ \Omega$ and $R_2 = 750\ \Omega$.

CHAPTER 10

INHERITANCE

© Lisa Thornberg/iStockphoto.

CHAPTER GOALS

To understand the concepts of inheritance and polymorphism

To learn how to inherit and override member functions

To be able to implement constructors for derived classes

To be able to design and use virtual functions

CHAPTER CONTENTS

Objects from related classes usually share common behavior. For example, shovels, rakes, and clippers all perform gardening tasks. In this chapter, you will learn how the notion of inheritance expresses the relationship between specialized and general classes. By using inheritance, you will be able to share code between classes and provide services that can be used by multiple classes.

10.1 Inheritance Hierarchies

A derived class inherits data and behavior from a base class.

In object-oriented design, **inheritance** is a relationship between a more general class (called the **base class**) and a more specialized class (called the **derived class**). The derived class inherits data and behavior from the base class. For example, consider the relationships between different kinds of vehicles depicted in Figure 1.

Cars share the common traits of all vehicles, such as the ability to transport people from one place to another. We say that the class Car *inherits* from the class Vehicle. In this relationship, the Vehicle class is the base class and the Car class is the derived class.

Informally, the inheritance relationship is called the *is-a* relationship. Contrast this relationship with the *has-a* relationship that we discussed in Section 9.8. Every car *is a* vehicle. Every vehicle *has an* engine.

The inheritance relationship is very powerful because it allows us to reuse algorithms with objects of different classes. Suppose we have an algorithm that

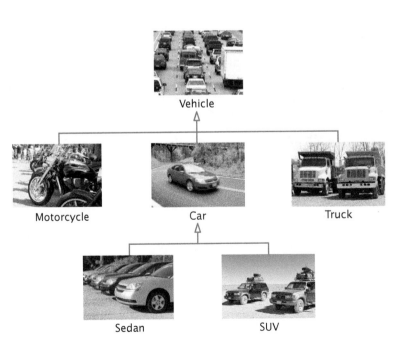

Figure 1 An Inheritance Hierarchy of Vehicle Classes

© Richard Stouffer/iStockphoto (vehicle); © Ed Hidden/iStockphoto (motorcycle); © Yin Yang/iStockphoto (car); © Robert Pernell/iStockphoto (truck); nicholas belton/iStockphoto (sedan); © Cezary Wojtkowski/Age Fotostock America (SUV).

manipulates a Vehicle object. Because a car is a special kind of vehicle, we can supply a Car object to such an algorithm, and it will work correctly. This is an example of the **substitution principle** that states that you can always use a derived-class object when a base-class object is expected.

The inheritance relationship can give rise to hierarchies where classes get ever more specialized, as shown in Figure 1. The C++ stream classes, shown in Figure 2, are another example of such a hierarchy. Figure 2 uses the UML notation for inheritance where the base and derived class are joined with an arrow that points to the base class.

As you can see, an ifstream (an input stream that reads from a file) is a special case of an istream (an input stream that reads data from any source). If you have an ifstream, it can be the argument for a function that expects an istream.

```
void process_input(istream& in) // Can call with an ifstream object
```

Why provide a function that processes istream objects instead of ifstream objects? That function is more useful because it can handle *any* kind of input stream (such as an istringstream, which is convenient for testing). This again is the substitution principle at work.

In this chapter, we will consider a simple hierarchy of classes. Most likely, you have taken computer-graded quizzes. A quiz consists of questions, and there are different kinds of questions:

© paul kline/iStockphoto.

We will develop a simple but flexible quiz-taking program to illustrate inheritance.

- Fill-in-the-blank

- Choice (single or multiple)

- Numeric (where an approximate answer is ok; e.g., 1.33 when the actual answer is 4/3)

- Free response

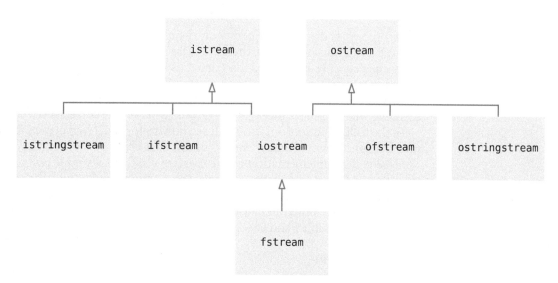

Figure 2 The Inheritance Hierarchy of Stream Classes

Figure 3 shows an inheritance hierarchy for these question types.

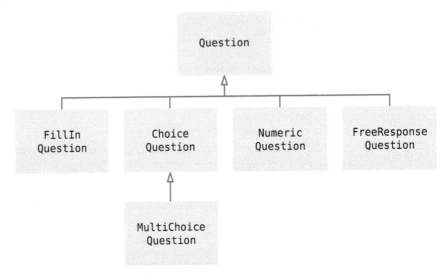

Figure 3   Inheritance Hierarchy of Question Types

At the root of this hierarchy is the Question type. A question can display its text, and it can check whether a given response is a correct answer:

```
class Question
{
public:
    Question();
    void set_text(string question_text);
    void set_answer(string correct_response);
    bool check_answer(string response) const;
    void display() const;
private:
    string text;
    string answer;
};
```

How the text is displayed depends on the question type. Later in this chapter, you will see some variations, but the base class simply sends the question text to cout. How the response is checked also depends on the question type. As already mentioned, a numeric question might accept approximate answers (see Exercise E10.1). In Exercise E10.3, you will see another way of checking the response. But in the base class, we will simply require that the response match the correct answer exactly.

In the following sections, you will see how to form derived classes that inherit the member functions and data members of this base class.

Here is the implementation of the Question class and a simple test program. Note that the Question class constructor needs to do no work because the text and answer data members are automatically set to the empty string. The boolalpha stream manipulator in the main function causes Boolean values to be displayed as true and false instead of the default 1 and 0.

sec01/demo.cpp

```
1  #include <iostream>
2  #include <sstream>
```

```cpp
3   #include <string>
4
5   using namespace std;
6
7   class Question
8   {
9   public:
10     /**
11        Constructs a question with empty text and answer.
12     */
13     Question();
14
15     /**
16        @param question_text the text of this question
17     */
18     void set_text(string question_text);
19
20     /**
21        @param correct_response the answer for this question
22     */
23     void set_answer(string correct_response);
24
25     /**
26        @param response the response to check
27        @return true if the response was correct, false otherwise
28     */
29     bool check_answer(string response) const;
30
31     /**
32        Displays this question.
33     */
34     void display() const;
35
36  private:
37     string text;
38     string answer;
39  };
40
41  Question::Question()
42  {
43  }
44
45  void Question::set_text(string question_text)
46  {
47     text = question_text;
48  }
49
50  void Question::set_answer(string correct_response)
51  {
52     answer = correct_response;
53  }
54
55  bool Question::check_answer(string response) const
56  {
57     return response == answer;
58  }
59
60  void Question::display() const
61  {
62     cout << text << endl;
```

```
63 }
64
65 int main()
66 {
67    string response;
68    cout << boolalpha; // Show Boolean values as true, false
69
70    Question q1;
71    q1.set_text("Who was the inventor of C++?");
72    q1.set_answer("Bjarne Stroustrup");
73
74    q1.display();
75    cout << "Your answer: ";
76    getline(cin, response);
77    cout << q1.check_answer(response) << endl;
78
79    return 0;
80 }
```

Program Run

```
Who was the inventor of C++?
Your answer: Bjarne Stroustrup
true
```

10.2 Implementing Derived Classes

In C++, you form a derived class from a base class by specifying what makes the derived class different. You define the member functions that are new to the derived class. The derived class inherits all member functions from the base class, but you can change the implementation if the inherited behavior is not appropriate.

The derived class automatically inherits all data members from the base class. You only define the added data members.

Here is the syntax for the definition of a derived class:

```
class ChoiceQuestion : public Question
{
public:
    New and changed member functions
private:
    Additional data members
};
```

The : symbol denotes inheritance. The reserved word public is required for a technical reason (see Common Error 10.1).

Like the manufacturer of a stretch limo, who starts with a regular car and modifies it, a programmer makes a derived class by modifying another class.

Media Bakery.

A ChoiceQuestion object differs from a Question object in three ways:

- Its objects store the various choices for the answer.
- There is a member function for adding another choice.
- The display function of the ChoiceQuestion class shows these choices so that the respondent can choose one of them.

When the ChoiceQuestion class inherits from the Question class, it needs only to spell out these three differences:

```cpp
class ChoiceQuestion : public Question
{
public:
   ChoiceQuestion();
   void add_choice(string choice, bool correct);
   void display() const;
private:
   vector<string> choices;
};
```

Figure 4 shows the layout of a ChoiceQuestion object. It inherits the text and answer data members from the Question base object, and it adds an additional data member: the choices vector.

Figure 4   Data Layout of a Derived-Class Object

A derived class can override a base-class function by providing a new implementation.

The add_choice function is specific to the ChoiceQuestion class. You can only apply it to ChoiceQuestion objects, not general Question objects. However, the display function is a redefinition of a function that exists in the base class; it is redefined to take into account the special needs of the derived class. We say that the derived class **overrides** this function. You will see how in Section 10.3.

The derived class inherits all data members and all functions that it does not override.

In the ChoiceQuestion class definition you specify only new member functions and data members. All other member functions and data members of the Question class are automatically inherited by the Question class. For example, each ChoiceQuestion object still has text and answer data members, and set_text, set_answer, and check_answer member functions.

You can call the inherited member functions on a derived-class object:

```cpp
choice_question.set_answer("2");
```

However, the inherited data members are inaccessible. Because these members are private data of the base class, only the base class has access to them. The derived class has no more access rights than any other class.

In particular, the ChoiceQuestion member functions cannot directly access the answer member. These member functions must use the public interface of the Question class to access its private data, just like every other function.

Syntax 10.1   **Derived-Class Definition**

The : symbol denotes inheritance.

Always place public *after the* :. *See Common Error 10.1.*

Derived class   *Base class*

```
class ChoiceQuestion : public Question
{
public:
   ChoiceQuestion();
   void add_choice(string choice, bool correct);
   void display() const;

private:
   vector<string> choices;
};
```

Declare functions that are added to the derived class.

Declare functions that the derived class overrides.

Define data members that are added to the derived class.

To illustrate this point, let us implement the add_choice member function. The function has two parameters: the choice to be added (which is appended to the vector of choices), and a Boolean value to indicate whether this choice is correct. If it is true, set the answer to the current choice number. (We use the to_string function to convert the number to a string—see Section 8.4 for details.)

```
void ChoiceQuestion::add_choice(string choice, bool correct)
{
   choices.push_back(choice);
   if (correct)
   {
      // Convert choices.size() to string
      string num_str = to_string(choices.size());
      // Set num_str as the answer
      . . .
   }
}
```

You can't just access the answer member in the base class. Fortunately, the Question class has a set_answer member function. You can call that member function. On which object? The question that you are currently modifying—that is, the implicit parameter of the ChoiceQuestion::add_choice function. As you saw in Chapter 9, if you invoke a member function on the implicit parameter, you don't specify the parameter but just write the member function name:

```
set_answer(num_str);
```

The compiler interprets this call as

```
implicit parameter.set_answer(num_str);
```

Private Inheritance

It is a common error to forget the reserved word `public` that must follow the colon after the derived-class name.

```cpp
class ChoiceQuestion : Question // Error
{
    . . .
};
```

The class definition will compile. The `ChoiceQuestion` still inherits from `Question`, but it inherits *privately*. That is, only the member functions of `ChoiceQuestion` get to call member functions of `Question`. Whenever another function invokes a `Question` member function on a `ChoiceQuestion` object, the compiler will flag this as an error:

```cpp
int main()
{
    ChoiceQuestion q;
    . . .
    cout << q.check_answer(response); // Error
}
```

This private inheritance is rarely useful. In fact, it violates the spirit of using inheritance in the first place—namely, to create objects that are usable just like the base-class objects. You should always use public inheritance and remember to supply the `public` reserved word in the definition of the derived class.

Replicating Base-Class Members

A derived class has no access to the data members of the base class.

```cpp
ChoiceQuestion::ChoiceQuestion(string question_text)
{
    text = question_text; // Error—tries to access private base-class member
}
```

When faced with a compiler error, beginners commonly "solve" this issue by adding *another* data member with the same name to the derived class:

```cpp
class ChoiceQuestion : public Question
{
    . . .
private:
    vector<string> choices;
    string text; // Don't!
}
```

Sure, now the constructor compiles, but it doesn't set the correct text! Such a Choice-Question object has two data members, both named `text`. The constructor sets one of them, and the `display` member function displays the other.

Instead of uselessly replicating a base-class data member, you need to call a member function that updates the base-class member, such as the `set_text` function in our example.

Programming Tip 10.1

Use a Single Class for Variation in Values, Inheritance for Variation in Behavior

The purpose of inheritance is to model objects with different *behavior*. When students first learn about inheritance, they have a tendency to overuse it, by creating multiple classes even though the variation could be expressed with a simple data member.

Consider a program that tracks the fuel efficiency of a fleet of cars by logging the distance traveled and the refueling amounts. Some cars in the fleet are hybrids. Should you create a derived class HybridCar? Not in this application. Hybrids don't behave any differently than other cars when it comes to driving and refueling. They just have a better fuel efficiency. A single Car class with a data member

```
double miles_per_gallon;
```

is entirely sufficient.

However, if you write a program that shows how to repair different kinds of vehicles, then it makes sense to have a separate class HybridCar. When it comes to repairs, hybrid cars behave differently from other cars.

Special Topic 10.1

Calling the Base-Class Constructor

Consider the process of constructing a derived-class object. A derived-class constructor can only initialize the data members of the derived class. But the base-class data members also need to be initialized. Unless you specify otherwise, the base-class data members are initialized with the default constructor of the base class.

Unless specified otherwise, the base-class data members are initialized with the default constructor.

In order to specify another constructor, you use an *initializer list*, as described in Special Topic 9.2. Specify the name of the base class and the construction arguments in the initializer list. For example, suppose the Question base class had a constructor for setting the question text. Here is how a derived-class constructor could call that base-class constructor:

```
ChoiceQuestion::ChoiceQuestion(string question_text)
   : Question(question_text)
{
}
```

The constructor of a derived class can supply arguments to a base-class constructor.

The derived-class constructor calls the base-class constructor before executing the code inside the { }.

In our example program, we used the default constructor of the base class. However, if a base class has no default constructor, you must use the initializer list syntax.

Syntax 10.2   Constructor with Base-Class Initializer

The base-class constructor is called first.

```
ChoiceQuestion::ChoiceQuestion(string question_text)
   : Question(question_text)
{
```

This block can contain additional statements.

```
}
```

If you omit the base-class constructor call, the default constructor is invoked.

10.3 Overriding Member Functions

The derived class inherits the member functions from the base class. If you are not satisfied with the behavior of the inherited member function, you can **override** it by specifying a new implementation in the derived class.

Consider the display function of the ChoiceQuestion class. It needs to override the base-class display function in order to show the choices for the answer. Specifically, the derived-class function needs to

- *Display the question text.*
- *Display the answer choices.*

The second part is easy because the answer choices are a data member of the derived class.

```
void ChoiceQuestion::display() const
{
   // Display the question text
   . . .
   // Display the answer choices
   for (int i = 0; i < choices.size(); i++)
   {
      cout << i + 1 << ": " << choices[i] << endl;
   }
}
```

But how do you get the question text? You can't access the text member of the base class directly because it is private.

Instead, you can call the display function of the base class.

```
void ChoiceQuestion::display() const
{
   // Display the question text
   display(); // Invokes implicit parameter.display()
   // Display the answer choices
   . . .
}
```

However, this won't quite work. Because the implicit parameter of ChoiceQuestion::display is of type ChoiceQuestion, and there is a function named display in the ChoiceQuestion class, that function will be called—but that is just the function you are currently writing! The function would call itself over and over.

To display the question text, you must be more specific about which function named display you want to call. You want Question::display:

```
void ChoiceQuestion::display() const
{
   // Display the question text
   Question::display(); // OK
   // Display the answer choices
   . . .
}
```

When you override a function, you usually want to *extend* the functionality of the base-class version. Therefore, you often need to invoke the base-class version before extending it. To invoke it, you need to use the *BaseClass::function* notation. However, you have no obligation to call the base-class function. Occasionally, a derived class overrides a base-class function and specifies an entirely different functionality.

A derived class can inherit a function from the base class, or it can override it by providing another implementation.

Use BaseClass::function notation to explicitly call a base-class function.

Here is the complete program that displays a plain `Question` object and a `Choice-Question` object. (The definition of the `Question` class, which you have already seen, is placed into `question.h`, and the implementation is in `question.cpp`.) This example shows how you can use inheritance to form a more specialized class from a base class.

sec03/demo.cpp

```cpp
1   #include <iostream>
2   #include <sstream>
3   #include <vector>
4   #include "question.h"
5
6   class ChoiceQuestion : public Question
7   {
8   public:
9      /**
10         Constructs a choice question with no choices.
11      */
12      ChoiceQuestion();
13
14      /**
15         Adds an answer choice to this question.
16         @param choice the choice to add
17         @param correct true if this is the correct choice, false otherwise
18      */
19      void add_choice(string choice, bool correct);
20
21      void display() const;
22   private:
23      vector<string> choices;
24   };
25
26   ChoiceQuestion::ChoiceQuestion()
27   {
28   }
29
30   void ChoiceQuestion::add_choice(string choice, bool correct)
31   {
32      choices.push_back(choice);
33      if (correct)
34      {
35         // Convert choices.size() to string
36         string num_str = to_string(choices.size());
37         set_answer(num_str);
38      }
39   }
40
41   void ChoiceQuestion::display() const
42   {
43      // Display the question text
44      Question::display();
45      // Display the answer choices
46      for (int i = 0; i < choices.size(); i++)
47      {
48         cout << i + 1 << ": " << choices[i] << endl;
49      }
50   }
51
```

```
52  int main()
53
54     string response;
55     cout << boolalpha;
56
57     // Ask a basic question
58
59     Question q1;
60     q1.set_text("Who was the inventor of C++?");
61     q1.set_answer("Bjarne Stroustrup");
62
63     q1.display();
64     cout << "Your answer: ";
65     getline(cin, response);
66     cout << q1.check_answer(response) << endl;
67
68     // Ask a choice question
69
70     ChoiceQuestion q2;
71     q2.set_text("In which country was the inventor of C++ born?");
72     q2.add_choice("Australia", false);
73     q2.add_choice("Denmark", true);
74     q2.add_choice("Korea", false);
75     q2.add_choice("United States", false);
76
77     q2.display();
78     cout << "Your answer: ";
79     getline(cin, response);
80     cout << q2.check_answer(response) << endl;
81
82     return 0;
83  }
```

Program Run

```
Who was the inventor of C++?
Your answer: Bjarne Stroustrup
true
In which country was the inventor of C++ born?
1: Australia
2: Denmark
3: Korea
4: United States
Your answer: 2
true
```

Common Error 10.3

Forgetting the Base-Class Name

A common error in extending the functionality of a base-class function is to forget the base-class name. For example, to compute the salary of a manager, get the salary of the underlying Employee object and add a bonus:

```
double Manager::get_salary() const
{
   double base_salary = get_salary();
      // Error—should be Employee::get_salary()
```

```
        return base_salary + bonus;
    }
```

Here get_salary() refers to the get_salary function applied to the implicit parameter of the member function. The implicit parameter is of type Manager, and there is a Manager::get_salary function, so that function is called. Of course, that is a recursive call to the function that we are writing. Instead, you must specify which get_salary function you want to call. In this case, you need to call Employee::get_salary explicitly.

Whenever you call a base-class function from a derived-class function with the same name, be sure to give the full name of the function, including the base-class name.

10.4 Virtual Functions and Polymorphism

In the preceding sections you saw one important use of inheritance: to form a more specialized class from a base class. In the following sections you will see an even more powerful application of inheritance: to work with objects whose type and behavior can vary at run time. This variation of behavior is achieved with **virtual functions**. When you invoke a virtual function on an object, the C++ run-time system determines which actual member function to call, depending on the class to which the object belongs.

In the following sections, you will see why you need to use pointers to access objects whose class can vary at run-time, and how a virtual function selects the member function that is appropriate for a given object.

10.4.1 The Slicing Problem

In this section, we will discuss a problem that commonly arises when you work with a collection of objects that belong to different classes in a class hierarchy.

If you look into the main function of sec03/demo.cpp, you will find that there is some repetitive code to display each question and check the responses. It would be nicer if all questions were collected in an array and one could use a loop to present them to the user:

```
const int QUIZZES = 2;
Question quiz[QUIZZES];
quiz[0].set_text("Who was the inventor of C++?");
quiz[0].set_answer("Bjarne Stroustrup");
ChoiceQuestion cq;
cq.set_text("In which country was the inventor of C++ born?");
cq.add_choice("Australia", false);
. . .
quiz[1] = cq;

for (int i = 0; i < QUIZZES; i++)
{
    quiz[i].display();
    cout << "Your answer: ";
    getline(cin, response);
    cout << quiz[i].check_answer(response) << endl;
}
```

The array `quiz` holds objects of type `Question`. The compiler realizes that a `ChoiceQuestion` is a special case of a `Question`. Thus it permits the assignment from a choice question to a question:

```
quiz[1] = cq;
```

However, a `ChoiceQuestion` object has three data members, whereas a `Question` object has just two. There is no room to store the derived-class data. That data simply gets *sliced away* when you assign a derived-class object to a base-class variable (see Figure 5).

If you run the resulting program, the options are not displayed:

```
Who was the inventor of C++?
Your answer: Bjarne Stroustrup
true
In which country was the inventor of C++ born?
Your answer:
```

When converting a derived-class object to a base class, the derived-class data is sliced away.

This problem is very typical of code that needs to manipulate objects from a mixture of classes in an inheritance hierarchy. Derived-class objects are usually bigger than base-class objects, and objects of different derived classes have different sizes. An array of objects cannot deal with this variation in sizes.

Instead, you need to store the actual objects elsewhere and collect their locations in an array by storing pointers. We will discuss the use of pointers in the next section.

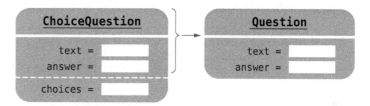

Figure 5 Slicing Away Derived-Class Data

10.4.2 Pointers to Base and Derived Classes

To access objects from different classes in a class hierarchy, use pointers. Pointers to the various objects all have the same size—namely, the size of a memory address—even though the objects themselves may have different sizes.

Here is the code to set up the array of pointers (see Figure 6):

```
Question* quiz[2];
quiz[0] = new Question;
quiz[0]->set_text("Who was the inventor of C++?");
quiz[0]->set_answer("Bjarne Stroustrup");
ChoiceQuestion* cq_pointer = new ChoiceQuestion;
cq_pointer->set_text("In which country was the inventor of C++ born?");
cq_pointer->add_choice("Australia", false);
. . .
quiz[1] = cq_pointer;
```

As the highlighted code shows, you simply define the array to hold pointers, allocate all objects by calling `new`, and use the `->` operator instead of the dot operator.

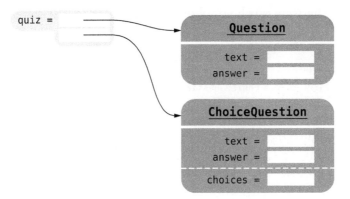

Figure 6 An Array of Pointers Can Store Objects from Different Classes

A derived-class
pointer can be
converted to a base-
class pointer.

Note that the last assignment assigns a derived-class pointer of type `ChoiceQuestion*` to a base-class pointer of type `Question*`. This is perfectly legal. A pointer is the starting address of an object. Because every `ChoiceQuestion` is a special case of a `Question`, the starting address of a `ChoiceQuestion` object is, in particular, the starting address of a `Question` object. The reverse assignment—from a base-class pointer to a derived-class pointer—is an error.

The code to present all questions is

```
for (int i = 0; i < QUIZZES; i++)
{
   quiz[i]->display();
   cout << "Your answer: ";
   getline(cin, response);
   cout << quiz[i]->check_answer(response) << endl;
}
```

Again, note the use of the `->` operator because `quiz[i]` is a pointer.

10.4.3 Virtual Functions

When you collect objects of different classes in a class hierarchy, and then invoke a member function, you want the appropriate member function to be applied. For example, when you call the `display` member function on a `Question*` pointer that happens to point to a `ChoiceQuestion`, you want the choices to be displayed.

For reasons of efficiency, this is not the default in C++. By default, a call

```
quiz[i]->display();
```

always calls `Question::display` because the type of `quiz[i]` is `Question*`.

However, in this case you really want to determine the actual type of the object to which `quiz[i]` points, which can be either a `Question` or a `ChoiceQuestion` object, and then call the appropriate function. In C++, you must alert the compiler that the function call needs to be preceded by the appropriate function selection, which can be a different one for every iteration in the loop. You use the `virtual` reserved word for this purpose:

```
class Question
{
```

```
public:
   Question();
   void set_text(string question_text);
   void set_answer(string correct_response);
   virtual bool check_answer(string response) const;
   virtual void display() const;
private:
   . . .
};
```

The `virtual` reserved word must be used in the *base class*. All functions with the same name and parameter variable types in derived classes are then automatically virtual. However, it is considered good taste to supply the `virtual` reserved word for the derived-class functions as well.

```
class ChoiceQuestion : public Question
{
public:
   ChoiceQuestion();
   void add_choice(string choice, bool correct);
   virtual void display() const;
private:
   . . .
};
```

You do not supply the reserved word `virtual` in the function definition:

```
void Question::display() const // No virtual reserved word
{
   cout << text << endl;
}
```

When a virtual function is called, the version belonging to the actual type of the implicit parameter is invoked.

Whenever a virtual function is called, the compiler determines the type of the implicit parameter in the particular call at run time. The appropriate function for that object is then called. For example, when the `display` function is declared virtual, the call

```
quiz[i]->display();
```

always calls the function belonging to the actual type of the object to which `quiz[i]` points—either `Question::display` or `ChoiceQuestion::display`.

10.4.4 Polymorphism

Polymorphism (literally, "having multiple shapes") describes objects that share a set of tasks and execute them in different ways.

The `quiz` array collects a mixture of both kinds of questions. Such a collection is called **polymorphic** (literally, "of multiple shapes"). Objects in a polymorphic collection have some commonality but are not necessarily of the same type. Inheritance is used to express this commonality, and virtual functions enable variations in behavior.

Virtual functions give programs a great deal of flexibility. The question presentation loop describes only the general mechanism: "Display the question, get a response, and check it". Each object knows on its own how to carry out the specific tasks: "Display the question" and "Check a response".

Using virtual functions makes programs *easily extensible*. Suppose we want to have a new kind of question for calculations, where we are willing to accept an approximate answer. All we need to do is to define a new class `NumericQuestion`, with its own `check_answer` function. Then we can populate the `quiz` array with a mixture of plain questions, choice questions, and numeric questions. The code that presents the questions need not be changed at all! The calls to the virtual functions automatically select the correct member functions of the newly defined classes.

© Alpophoto/iStockphoto.

In the same way that vehicles can differ in their method of locomotion, polymorphic objects carry out tasks in different ways.

Here is the final version of the quiz program, using pointers and virtual functions. When you run the program, you will find that the appropriate versions of the virtual functions are called. (The files question.cpp and choicequestion.cpp are included in your book's companion code.)

sec04/question.h

```
1  #ifndef QUESTION_H
2  #define QUESTION_H
3
4  #include <string>
5
6  using namespace std;
7
8  class Question
9  {
10 public:
11    /**
12       Constructs a question with empty question and answer.
13    */
14    Question();
15
16    /**
17       @param question_text the text of this question
18    */
19    void set_text(string question_text);
20
21    /**
22       @param correct_response the answer for this question
23    */
24    void set_answer(string correct_response);
25
26    /**
27       @param response the response to check
28       @return true if the response was correct, false otherwise
29    */
30    virtual bool check_answer(string response) const;
31
32    /**
33       Displays this question.
```

```
34      */
35      virtual void display() const;
36   private:
37      string text;
38      string answer;
39   };
40
41   #endif
```

sec04/choicequestion.h

```
1   #ifndef CHOICEQUESTION_H
2   #define CHOICEQUESTION_H
3
4   #include <vector>
5   #include "question.h"
6
7   class ChoiceQuestion : public Question
8   {
9   public:
10      /**
11         Constructs a choice question with no choices.
12      */
13      ChoiceQuestion();
14
15      /**
16         Adds an answer choice to this question.
17         @param choice the choice to add
18         @param correct true if this is the correct choice, false otherwise
19      */
20      void add_choice(string choice, bool correct);
21
22      virtual void display() const;
23   private:
24      vector<string> choices;
25   };
26
27   #endif
```

sec04/demo.cpp

```
1   #include <iostream>
2   #include "question.h"
3   #include "choicequestion.h"
4
5   int main()
6   {
7      string response;
8      cout << boolalpha;
9
10     // Make a quiz with two questions
11     const int QUIZZES = 2;
12     Question* quiz[QUIZZES];
13     quiz[0] = new Question;
14     quiz[0]->set_text("Who was the inventor of C++?");
15     quiz[0]->set_answer("Bjarne Stroustrup");
16
17     ChoiceQuestion* cq_pointer = new ChoiceQuestion;
18     cq_pointer->set_text(
19        "In which country was the inventor of C++ born?");
```

```
20     cq_pointer->add_choice("Australia", false);
21     cq_pointer->add_choice("Denmark", true);
22     cq_pointer->add_choice("Korea", false);
23     cq_pointer->add_choice("United States", false);
24     quiz[1] = cq_pointer;
25
26     // Check answers for all questions
27     for (int i = 0; i < QUIZZES; i++)
28     {
29        quiz[i]->display();
30        cout << "Your answer: ";
31        getline(cin, response);
32        cout << quiz[i]->check_answer(response) << endl;
33     }
34
35     return 0;
36  }
```

Programming Tip 10.2

Don't Use Type Tags

Some programmers build inheritance hierarchies in which each object has a tag that indicates its type, commonly a string. They then query that string:

```
if (q->get_type() == "Question")
{
   // Do something
}
else if (q->get_type() == "ChoiceQuestion")
{
   // Do something else
}
```

This is a poor strategy. If a new class is added, then all these queries need to be revised. In contrast, consider the addition of a class NumericQuestion to our quiz program. *Nothing* needs to change in that program because it uses virtual functions, not type tags.

Whenever you find yourself adding a type tag to a hierarchy of classes, reconsider and use virtual functions instead.

Common Error 10.4

Slicing an Object

In C++ it is legal to copy a derived-class object into a base-class variable. However, any derived-class information is lost in the process. For example, when a Manager object is assigned to a variable of type Employee, the result is only the employee portion of the manager data:

```
Manager m;
. . .
Employee e = m; // Holds only the Employee base data of m
```

Any information that is particular to managers is sliced off, because it would not fit into a variable of type Employee. To avoid **slicing**, you can use pointers.

The slicing problem commonly occurs when a function has a polymorphic parameter (that is, a parameter that can belong to a base class or a derived class). In that case, the parameter variable must be a pointer or a reference. Consider this example:

```
void ask(Question q) // Error
{
```

```
        q.display();
        cout << "Your answer: ";
        getline(cin, response);
        cout << q.check_answer(response) << endl;
}
```

If you call this function with a ChoiceQuestion object, then the parameter variable q is initialized with a copy of that object. But q is a Question object; the derived-class information is sliced away. The simplest remedy is to use a reference:

```
void ask(const Question& q)
```

Now only the *address* is passed to the function. A reference is really a pointer in disguise. No slicing occurs, and virtual functions work correctly.

Common Error 10.5

Failing to Override a Virtual Function

In C++, two functions can have the same name, provided they differ in their parameter types. For example, you can define two member functions called display in the Question class:

```
class Question
{
public:
    virtual void display() const;
    virtual void display(ostream& out) const;
    . . .
};
```

These are different functions, each with its own implementation. The C++ compiler considers them to be completely unrelated. We say that the display name is *overloaded*. This is different from overriding, where a derived class function provides an implementation of a base class function with the same name and the same parameter types.

It is a common error to accidentally provide an overloaded function when you actually mean to override a function. Consider this scary example:

```
class ChoiceQuestion : public Question
{
public:
    void display(); // Does not override Question::display() const
    . . .
};
```

The display member function in the Question class has subtly different parameter types: the this pointer that points to the implicit parameter (see Section 9.10.3) has type const Question*, whereas in the ChoiceQuestion class, the this pointer is not const.

In C++ 11, you can use the reserved word override to tag any member function that should override a virtual function:

```
class ChoiceQuestion : public Question
{
public:
    void display() override;
    . . .
};
```

If the member function does not actually override a virtual function, the compiler generates an error. This is good, because you can then have a closer look and add the missing const reserved word.

The compiler also generates an error if you forget to declare the base class member function as virtual. If you use C++ 11, it is a good idea to take advantage of the override reserved word.

Special Topic 10.2

Virtual Self-Calls

Suppose we add the following function to the `Question` class:

```
void Question::ask() const
{
   display();
   cout << "Your answer: ";
   getline(cin, response);
   cout << check_answer(response) << endl;
}
```

Now consider the call

```
ChoiceQuestion cq;
cq.set_text("In which country was the inventor of C++ born?");
. . .
cq.ask();
```

Which `display` and `check_answer` function will the ask function call? If you look inside the code of the `Question::ask` function, you can see that these functions are executed on the implicit parameter:

```
void Question::ask() const
{
   implicit parameter.display();
   cout << "Your answer: ";
   getline(cin, response);
   cout << implicit parameter.check_answer(response) << endl;
}
```

The implicit parameter in our call is `cq`, an object of type `ChoiceQuestion`. Because the `display` and `check_answer` functions are virtual, the `ChoiceQuestion` versions of the functions are called automatically. This happens even though the ask function is defined in the `Question` class, which has *no knowledge* of the `ChoiceQuestion` class.

   As you can see, virtual functions are a very powerful mechanism. The `Question` class supplies an ask function that specifies the common nature of asking a question, namely to display it and check the response. How the displaying and checking are carried out is left to the derived classes.

HOW TO 10.1

Developing an Inheritance Hierarchy

When you work with a set of classes, some of which are more general and others more specialized, you want to organize them into an inheritance hierarchy. This enables you to process objects of different classes in a uniform way.

Problem Statement   As an example, we will consider a bank that offers its customers the following account types:

- A savings account that earns interest. The interest compounds monthly and is computed on the minimum monthly balance.
- A checking account that has no interest, gives you three free withdrawals per month, and charges a $1 transaction fee for each additional withdrawal.

The program will manage a set of accounts of both types, and it should be structured so that other account types can be added without affecting the main processing loop. Supply a menu

```
D)eposit  W)ithdraw  M)onth end  Q)uit
```

For deposits and withdrawals, query the account number and amount. Print the balance of the account after each transaction.

In the "Month end" command, accumulate interest or clear the transaction counter, depending on the type of the bank account. Then print the balance of all accounts.

Step 1 List the classes that are part of the hierarchy.

In our case, the problem description yields two classes: SavingsAccount and CheckingAccount. To express the commonality between them, we will introduce a class BankAccount.

Step 2 Organize the classes into an inheritance hierarchy.

Draw a UML diagram that shows base and derived classes. Here is the diagram for our example:

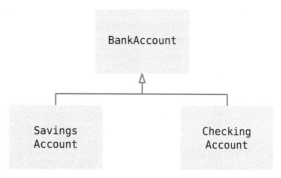

Step 3 Determine the common responsibilities.

In Step 2, you will have identified a class at the base of the hierarchy. That class needs to have sufficient responsibilities to carry out the tasks at hand. To find out what those tasks are, write pseudocode for processing the objects:

> *For each user command*
>   *If it is a deposit or withdrawal*
>   *Deposit or withdraw the amount from the specified account.*
>   *Print the balance.*
>   *If it is month end processing*
>   *For each account*
>   *Call month end processing.*
>   *Print the balance.*

From the pseudocode, we obtain the following list of common responsibilities that every bank account must carry out:

> *Deposit money.*
> *Withdraw money.*
> *Get the balance.*
> *Carry out month end processing.*

Step 4 Decide which functions are overridden in derived classes.

For each derived class and each of the common responsibilities, decide whether the behavior can be inherited or whether it needs to be overridden. Declare any functions that are overridden as virtual in the root of the hierarchy.

Getting the balance is common to all account types. Withdrawing and end of month processing are different for the derived classes, so they need to be declared `virtual`. Because it is entirely possible that some future account type will levy a fee for deposits, it seems prudent to declare the `deposit` member function virtual as well.

```cpp
class BankAccount
{
public:
   virtual void deposit(double amount);
   virtual void withdraw(double amount);
   virtual void month_end();
   double get_balance() const;
private:
   . . .
};
```

Step 5   Define the public interface of each derived class.

Typically, derived classes have responsibilities other than those of the base class. List those, as well as the member functions that need to be overridden. You also need to specify how the objects of the derived classes should be constructed.

In this example, we need a way of setting the interest rate for the savings account. In addition, we need to specify constructors and overridden functions.

```cpp
class SavingsAccount : public BankAccount
{
public:
   /**
      Constructs a savings account with a zero balance.
   */
   SavingsAccount();

   /**
      Sets the interest rate for this account.
      @param rate the monthly interest rate in percent
   */
   void set_interest_rate(double rate);

   virtual void withdraw(double amount);
   virtual void month_end();
private:
   . . .
};

class CheckingAccount : public BankAccount
{
public:
   /**
      Constructs a checking account with a zero balance.
   */
   CheckingAccount();

   virtual void withdraw(double amount);
   virtual void month_end();
private:
   . . .
};
```

Step 6   Identify data members.

List the data members for each class. If you find a data member that is common to all classes, be sure to place it in the base of the hierarchy.

All accounts have a balance. We store that value in the BankAccount base class:

```cpp
class BankAccount
{
   . . .
private:
   double balance;
};
```

The SavingsAccount class needs to store the interest rate. It also needs to store the minimum monthly balance, which must be updated by all withdrawals:

```cpp
class SavingsAccount : public BankAccount
{
   . . .
private:
   double interest_rate;
   double min_balance;
};
```

The CheckingAccount class needs to count the withdrawals, so that the charge can be applied after the free withdrawal limit is reached:

```cpp
class CheckingAccount : public BankAccount
{
   . . .
private:
   int withdrawals;
};
```

Step 7   Implement constructors and member functions.

The member functions of the BankAccount class update or return the balance:

```cpp
BankAccount::BankAccount()
{
   balance = 0;
}

void BankAccount::deposit(double amount)
{
   balance = balance + amount;
}

void BankAccount::withdraw(double amount)
{
   balance = balance - amount;
}

double BankAccount::get_balance() const
{
   return balance;
}
```

At the level of the BankAccount base class, we can say nothing about end of month processing. We choose to make that function do nothing:

```cpp
void BankAccount::month_end()
{
}
```

In the `withdraw` member function of the `SavingsAccount` class, the minimum balance is updated. Note the call to the base-class member function:

```cpp
void SavingsAccount::withdraw(double amount)
{
   BankAccount::withdraw(amount);
   double balance = get_balance();
   if (balance < min_balance)
   {
      min_balance = balance;
   }
}
```

In the `month_end` member function of the `SavingsAccount` class, the interest is deposited into the account. We must call the `deposit` member function because we have no direct access to the `balance` data member. The minimum balance is reset for the next month:

```cpp
void SavingsAccount::month_end()
{
   double interest = min_balance * interest_rate / 100;
   deposit(interest);
   min_balance = get_balance();
}
```

The `withdraw` function of the `CheckingAccount` class needs to check the withdrawal count. If there have been too many withdrawals, a charge is applied. Again, note how the function invokes the base-class function, using the `BankAccount::` syntax:

```cpp
void CheckingAccount::withdraw(double amount)
{
   const int FREE_WITHDRAWALS = 3;
   const int WITHDRAWAL_FEE = 1;

   BankAccount::withdraw(amount);
   withdrawals++;
   if (withdrawals > FREE_WITHDRAWALS)
   {
      BankAccount::withdraw(WITHDRAWAL_FEE);
   }
}
```

End of month processing for a checking account simply resets the withdrawal count:

```cpp
void CheckingAccount::month_end()
{
   withdrawals = 0;
}
```

Step 8   Allocate objects on the free store and process them.

For polymorphism (that is, variation of behavior) to work in C++, you need to call virtual functions through pointers. The easiest strategy is to allocate all polymorphic objects on the free store, using the `new` operator.

In our sample program, we allocate 5 checking accounts and 5 savings accounts and store their addresses in an array of bank account pointers. Then we accept user commands and execute deposits, withdrawals, and monthly processing.

```cpp
int main()
{
   cout << fixed << setprecision(2);

   // Create accounts
   const int ACCOUNTS_SIZE = 10;
   BankAccount* accounts[ACCOUNTS_SIZE];
```

```
for (int i = 0; i < ACCOUNTS_SIZE / 2; i++)
{
   accounts[i] = new CheckingAccount;
}
for (int i = ACCOUNTS_SIZE / 2; i < ACCOUNTS_SIZE; i++)
{
   SavingsAccount* account = new SavingsAccount;
   account->set_interest_rate(0.75);
   accounts[i] = account;
}

// Execute commands
bool more = true;
while (more)
{
   cout << "D)eposit  W)ithdraw  M)onth end  Q)uit: ";
   string input;
   cin >> input;
   if (input == "D" || input == "W")   // Deposit or withdrawal
   {
      cout << "Enter account number and amount: ";
      int num;
      double amount;
      cin >> num >> amount;

      if (input == "D") { accounts[num]->deposit(amount); }
      else { accounts[num]->withdraw(amount); }

      cout << "Balance: " << accounts[num]->get_balance() << endl;
   }
   else if (input == "M")   // Month end processing
   {
      for (int n = 0; n < ACCOUNTS_SIZE(); n++)
      {
         accounts[n]->month_end();
         cout << n << " " << accounts[n]->get_balance() << endl;
      }
   }
   else if (input == "Q")
   {
      more = false;
   }
}

return 0;
}
```

EXAMPLE CODE   See how_to_1 of your companion code for the complete program.

WORKED EXAMPLE 10.1

Implementing an Employee Hierarchy for Payroll Processing

Learn how to implement payroll processing that works for different kinds of employees. See your E-Text or visit wiley. com/go/bclo3.

Jose Luis Pelaez Inc./Getty Images, Inc.

Computing & Society 10.1   **Who Controls the Internet?**

In 1962, J.C.R. Lick-lider was head of the first computer research program at DARPA, the Defense Advanced Research Projects Agency. He wrote a series of papers describing a "galactic network" through which computer users could access data and programs from other sites. This was well before computer networks were invented. By 1969, four computers—three in California and one in Utah—were connected to the ARPANET, the precursor of the Internet. The network grew quickly, linking computers at many universities and research organizations. It was originally thought that most network users wanted to run programs on remote computers. Using remote execution, a researcher at one institution would be able to access an underutilized computer at a different site. It quickly became apparent that remote execution was not what the network was actually used for. Instead, the "killer application" was electronic mail: the transfer of messages between computer users at different locations.

In 1972, Bob Kahn proposed to extend ARPANET into the *Internet:* a collection of interoperable networks. All networks on the Internet share common *protocols* for data transmission. Kahn and Vinton Cerf developed a protocol, now called TCP/IP (Transmission Control Protocol/Internet Protocol). On January 1, 1983, all hosts on the Internet simultaneously switched to the TCP/IP protocol (which is used to this day).

Over time, researchers, computer scientists, and hobbyists published increasing amounts of information on the Internet. For example, Project Gutenberg makes available the text of important classical books, whose copyright has expired, in computer-readable form (www.gutenberg.org). In 1989, Tim Berners-Lee, a computer scientist at CERN (the European organization for nuclear research) started work on hyperlinked documents, allowing users to browse by following links to related documents. This infrastructure is now known as the World Wide Web.

The first interfaces to retrieve this information were, by today's standards, unbelievably clumsy and hard to use. In March 1993, WWW traffic was 0.1 percent of all Internet traffic. All that changed when Marc Andreesen, then a graduate student working for the National Center for Supercomputing Applications (NCSA), released Mosaic. Mosaic displayed web pages in graphical form, using images, fonts, and colors (see the figure). Andreesen went on to fame and fortune at Netscape, and Microsoft licensed the Mosaic code to create Internet Explorer. By 1996, WWW traffic accounted for more than half of the data transported on the Internet.

The Internet has a very democratic structure. Anyone can publish anything, and anyone can read whatever has been published. This does not always sit well with governments and corporations.

Many governments control the Internet infrastructure in their country. For example, an Internet user in China, searching for the Tiananmen Square massacre or air pollution in their hometown, may find nothing. Vietnam blocks access to Facebook, perhaps fearing that anti-government protesters might use it to organize themselves. The U.S. government has required publicly funded libraries and schools to install filters that block sexually-explicit and hate speech, and its security organizations have spied on the Internet usage of citizens.

When the Internet is delivered by phone or TV cable companies, those companies sometimes interfere with competing Internet offerings. Cell phone companies refused to carry Voice-over-IP services, and cable companies slowed down movie streaming. The Internet has become a powerful force for delivering information—both good and bad. It is our responsibility as citizens to demand of our government that we can control which information to access.

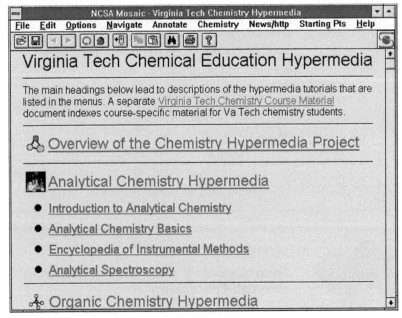

The NCSA Mosaic Browser

CHAPTER SUMMARY

Explain the notions of inheritance, base class, and derived class.

- A derived class inherits data and behavior from a base class.
- You can always use a derived-class object in place of a base-class object.

Implement derived classes in C++.

- A derived class can override a base-class function by providing a new implementation.
- The derived class inherits all data members and all functions that it does not override.
- Unless specified otherwise, the base-class data members are initialized with the default constructor.
- The constructor of a derived class can supply arguments to a base-class constructor.

Describe how a derived class can override functions from a base class.

- A derived class can inherit a function from the base class, or it can override it by providing another implementation.
- Use *BaseClass::function* notation to explicitly call a base-class function.

Describe virtual functions and polymorphism.

- When converting a derived-class object to a base class, the derived-class data is sliced away.
- A derived-class pointer can be converted to a base-class pointer.
- When a virtual function is called, the version belonging to the actual type of the implicit parameter is invoked.
- Polymorphism (literally, "having multiple shapes") describes objects that share a set of tasks and execute them in different ways.

REVIEW EXERCISES

- **R10.1** Identify the base class and the derived class in each of the following pairs of classes.
  - **a.** Employee, Manager
  - **b.** Polygon, Triangle
  - **c.** GraduateStudent, Student
  - **d.** Person, Student
  - **e.** Employee, Professor
  - **f.** BankAccount, CheckingAccount
  - **g.** Vehicle, Car
  - **h.** Vehicle, Minivan
  - **i.** Car, Minivan
  - **j.** Truck, Vehicle

- **R10.2** An object-oriented traffic simulation system has the classes listed below. Draw a UML diagram that shows the inheritance relationships between these classes.
  - Vehicle
  - Car
  - Truck
  - Sedan
  - Coupe
  - PickupTruck
  - SportUtilityVehicle
  - Minivan
  - Bicycle
  - Motorcycle

- **R10.3** What inheritance relationships would you establish among the following classes?
  - Student
  - Employee
  - Person
  - Professor
  - Secretary
  - Janitor
  - DepartmentChair

- **R10.4** Draw a UML diagram that shows the inheritance and aggregation relationships between the classes:
  - Person
  - Instructor
  - Student
  - Lecture
  - Course
  - Lab

- **R10.5** Consider a program for managing inventory in a small appliance store. Why isn't it useful to have a base class SmallAppliance and derived classes Toaster, CarVacuum, TravelIron, and so on?

- **R10.6** Which data members does the CheckingAccount class in How To 10.1 inherit from its base class? Which data members does it add?

- **R10.7** Which functions does the SavingsAccount class in How To 10.1 inherit from its base class? Which functions does it override? Which functions does it add?

- **R10.8** Design an inheritance hierarchy for geometric shapes: rectangles, squares, and circles. Draw a UML diagram. Provide a virtual function to compute the area of a shape. Provide appropriate constructors for each class. Write the class definitions but do not provide implementations of the member functions.

- **R10.9** Continue Exercise R10.8 by writing a main function that executes the following steps:

  Fill a vector of shape pointers with a rectangle, a square, and a circle.
  Print the area of each shape.
  Deallocate all objects that were allocated on the free store.

- **R10.10** Can you convert a base-class object into a derived-class object? A derived-class object into a base-class object? A base-class pointer into a derived-class pointer? A derived-class pointer into a base-class pointer? If so, give examples. If not, explain why not.

- **R10.11** Consider a function process_file(ostream& str). Objects from which of the classes in Figure 2 can be passed as parameters to this function?

- **R10.12** What does the following program print?

```cpp
class B
{
public:
    void print(int n) const;
};

void B::print(int n) const
{
    cout << n << endl;
}

class D : public B
{
public:
    void print(int n) const;
};

void D::print(int n) const
{
    if (n <= 1) { B::print(n); }
    else if (n % 2 == 0) { print(n / 2); }
    else { print(3 * n + 1); }
}

int main()
{
```

```
        D d;
        d.print(3);
        return 0;
    }
```

Determine the answer by hand, not by compiling and running the program.

■■ **R10.13** Suppose the class D inherits from B. Which of the following assignments are legal?

```
B b;
D d;
B* pb;
D* pd;
```

  a. b = d;

  b. d = b;

  c. pd = pb;

  d. pb = pd;

  e. d = pd;

  f. b = *pd;

  g. *pd = *pb;

■■ **R10.14** Suppose the class Sub is derived from the class Sandwich. Which of the following assignments are legal?

```
Sandwich* x = new Sandwich;
Sub* y = new Sub;
```

  a. x = y;

  b. y = x;

  c. y = new Sandwich;

  d. x = new Sub;

  e. *x = *y;

  f. *y = *x;

■■■ **R10.15** What does the program print? Explain your answers by tracing the flow of each call.

```
class B
{
public:
    B();
    virtual void p() const;
    void q() const;
};

B::B() {}
void B::p() const { cout << "B::p\n"; }
void B::q() const { cout << "B::q\n"; }

class D : public B
{
public:
    D();
    virtual void p() const;
    void q() const;
};

D::D() {}
void D::p() const { cout << "D::p\n"; }
void D::q() const { cout << "D::q\n"; }
```

```
int main()
{
    B b;
    D d;
    B* pb = new B;
    B* pd = new D;
    D* pd2 = new D;

    b.p(); b.q();
    d.p(); d.q();
    pb->p(); pb->q();
    pd->p(); pd->q();
    pd2->p(); pd2->q();
    return 0;
}
```

- **R10.16** In the accounts.cpp program of How To 10.1, would it be reasonable to make the get_balance function virtual? Explain your reasoning.

- **R10.17** What is the effect of declaring the display member function virtual only in the ChoiceQuestion class?

PRACTICE EXERCISES

- **E10.1** Add a class NumericQuestion to the question hierarchy of Section 10.1. If the response and the expected answer differ by no more than 0.01, then accept it as correct.

- **E10.2** Add a class FillInQuestion to the question hierarchy of Section 10.1. Such a question is constructed with a string that contains the answer, surrounded by _ _, for example, "The inventor of C++ was _Bjarne Stroustrup_". The question should be displayed as

    The inventor of C++ was _____

    Provide a main function that demonstrates your class.

- **E10.3** Modify the check_answer member function of the Question class so that it does not take into account different spaces or upper/lowercase characters. For example, the response " bjarne stroustrup" should match an answer of "Bjarne Stroustrup".

- **E10.4** Add a class MultiChoiceQuestion to the question hierarchy of Section 10.1 that allows multiple correct choices. The respondent should provide any one of the correct choices. The answer string should contain all of the correct choices, separated by spaces.

- **E10.5** Add a class ChooseAllCorrect to the question hierarchy of Section 10.1 that allows multiple correct choices. The respondent should provide all correct choices, separated by spaces.

- **E10.6** Add a member function add_text to the Question base class and provide a different implementation of ChoiceQuestion that calls add_text rather than storing a vector of choices.

- **E10.7** Implement a base class Person. Derive classes Student and Instructor from Person. A person has a name and a birthday. A student has a major, and an instructor has a salary. Write the class definitions, the constructors, and the member functions display for all classes.

E10.8 Using the Employee class from Worked Example 10.1 (worked_example_1/salaries.cpp in your companion code), form a derived class Volunteer of Employee and provide a constructor Volunteer(string name) that sets the salary to 0.

E10.9 Derive a class Programmer from Employee. Supply a constructor Programmer(string name, double salary) that calls the base-class constructor. Supply a function get_name that returns the name in the format "Hacker, Harry (Programmer)".

E10.10 Derive a class Manager from Employee. Add a data member named department of type string. Supply a function display that displays the manager's name, department, and salary. Derive a class Executive from Manager. Supply a function display that displays the string Executive, followed by the information stored in the Manager base object.

E10.11 Derive a class BasicAccount from BankAccount in How To 10.1 whose withdraw member function will not withdraw more money than is currently in the account.

E10.12 Derive a class BasicAccount from BankAccount in How To 10.1 whose withdraw member function charges a penalty of $30 for each withdrawal that results in an overdraft.

E10.13 Reimplement the CheckingAccount class from How To 10.1 so that the first overdraft in any given month incurs a $20 penalty, and any further overdrafts in the same month result in a $30 penalty.

E10.14 Change the CheckingAccount class in How To 10.1 so that a $1 fee is levied for deposits or withdrawals in excess of three free monthly transactions. Place the code for computing the fee into a private member function that you call from the deposit and withdraw member functions.

PROGRAMMING PROJECTS

P10.1 Implement a class Clock whose get_hours and get_minutes member functions return the current time at your location. To get the current time, use the following code, which requires that you include the <ctime> header:

```
time_t current_time = time(0);
tm* local_time = localtime(&current_time);
int hours = local_time->tm_hour;
int minutes = local_time->tm_min;
```

Also provide a get_time member function that returns a string with the hours and minutes by calling the get_hours and get_minutes functions. Provide a derived class WorldClock whose constructor accepts a time offset. For example, if you live in California, a new WorldClock(3) should show the time in New York, three time zones ahead. Which member functions did you override? (You should not override get_time.)

P10.2 Add an alarm feature to the Clock class of Exercise P10.1. When set_alarm(hours, minutes) is called, the clock stores the alarm. When you call get_time, and the alarm time has been reached or exceeded, return the time followed by the string "Alarm" (or, if you prefer, the string "\u23F0") and clear the alarm. What do you need to do to make the set_alarm function work for WorldClock objects?

Business P10.3 Implement a base class Appointment and derived classes Onetime, Daily, Weekly, and Monthly. An appointment has a description (for example, "see the dentist") and a date and time. Write a virtual function occurs_on(int year, int month, int day) that checks whether the appointment occurs on that date. For example, for a monthly appointment, you must check whether the day of the month matches. Then fill a vector of Appointment* with a mixture of appointments. Have the user enter a date and print out all appointments that happen on that date.

■■ **Business P10.4** Improve the appointment book program of Exercise P10.3. Give the user the option to add new appointments. The user must specify the type of the appointment, the description, and the date and time.

■■■ **Business P10.5** Improve the appointment book program of Exercises P10.3 and P10.4 by letting the user save the appointment data to a file and reload the data from a file. The saving part is straightforward: Make a virtual function save. Save out the type, description, date, and time. The loading part is not so easy. You must first determine the type of the appointment to be loaded, create an object of that type with its default constructor, and then call a virtual load function to load the remainder.

■■ **P10.6** Use polymorphism to carry out image manipulations such as those described in Exercises P8.16 and P8.17. Design a base class Effect and derived classes Sunset and Grayscale. Use a virtual function process. The file processing part of your program should repeatedly call process on an Effect* pointer, without having to know which effect is applied.

■■■ **Engineering P10.7** In this problem, you will model a circuit consisting of an arbitrary configuration of resistors. Provide a base class Circuit with a member function get_resistance. Provide a derived class Resistor representing a single resistor. Provide derived classes Serial and Parallel, each of which contains a vector<Circuit*>. A Serial circuit models a series of circuits, each of which can be a single resistor or another circuit. Similarly, a Parallel circuit models a set of circuits in parallel. For example, the following circuit is a Parallel circuit containing a single resistor and one Serial circuit.

© Maria Toutoudaki/iStockphoto.

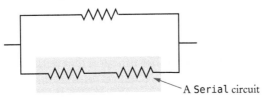

A Serial circuit

Use Ohm's law to compute the combined resistance.

■■ **Engineering P10.8** Part (a) of the figure below shows a symbolic representation of an electric circuit called an *amplifier*. The input to the amplifier is the voltage v_i and the output is the voltage v_o. The output of an amplifier is proportional to the input. The constant of proportionality is called the "gain" of the amplifier.

Parts (b), (c), and (d) show schematics of three specific types of amplifier: the *inverting amplifier*, *noninverting amplifier*, and *voltage divider amplifier*. Each of these three amplifiers consists of two resistors and an op amp. The value of the gain of each amplifier depends on the values of its resistances. In particular, the gain, g, of the inverting amplifier is given by $g = -\dfrac{R_2}{R_1}$. Similarly the gains of the noninverting amplifier and voltage divider amplifier are given by $g = 1 + \dfrac{R_2}{R_1}$ and $g = \dfrac{R_2}{R_1 + R_2}$, respectively.

(a) Amplifier

(b) Inverting amplifier

(c) Noninverting amplifier　　　　(d) Voltage divider amplifier

Write a C++ program that represents the amplifier as a base class and represents the inverting, noninverting, and voltage divider amplifiers as derived classes. Give the base class two virtual functions, get_gain and a get_description function that returns a string identifying the amplifier. Each derived class should have a constructor with two arguments, the resistances of the amplifier.

The derived classes need to override the get_gain and get_description functions of the base class.

Write a main function for the C++ program that demonstrates that the derived classes all work properly for sample values of the resistances.

■■ **Engineering P10.9** Resonant circuits are used to select a signal (e.g., a radio station or TV channel) from among other competing signals. Resonant circuits are characterized by the frequency response shown in the figure below. The resonant frequency response is completely described by three parameters: the resonant frequency, ω_o, the bandwidth, B, and the gain at the resonant frequency, k.

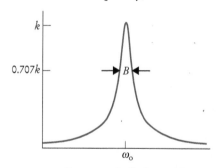

Frequency (rad/s, log scale)

Two simple resonant circuits are shown in the figure below. The circuit in (a) is called a *parallel resonant circuit*. The circuit in (b) is called a *series resonant circuit*. Both resonant circuits consist of a resistor having resistance R, a capacitor having capacitance C, and an inductor having inductance L.

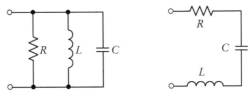

(a) Parallel resonant circuit   (b) Series resonant circuit

These circuits are designed by determining values of R, C, and L that cause the resonant frequency response to be described by specified values of ω_0, B, and k. The design equations for the parallel resonant circuit are:

$$R = k, \quad C = \frac{1}{BR}, \text{ and } \quad L = \frac{1}{\omega_0^2 C}$$

Similarly, the design equations for the series resonant circuit are:

$$R = \frac{1}{k}, \quad L = \frac{R}{B}, \text{ and } \quad C = \frac{1}{\omega_0^2 L}$$

Write a C++ program that represents ResonantCircuit as a base class and represents the SeriesResonantCircuit and ParallelResonantCircuit as derived classes. Give the base class three private data members representing the parameters ω_0, B, and k of the resonant frequency response. The base class should provide public member functions to get and set each of these members. The base class should also provide a display function that prints a description of the resonant frequency response.

Each derived class should provide a function that designs the corresponding resonant circuit. The derived classes should also override the display function of the base class to print descriptions of both the frequency response (the values of ω_0, B, and k) and the circuit (the values of R, C, and L).

All classes should provide appropriate constructors.

Write a main function for the C++ program that demonstrates that the derived classes all work properly.

RESERVED WORD SUMMARY

Reserved Word	Description	Reference Location
auto	A type that is automatically inferred	Special Topic 2.3 (C++ 11)
bool	The Boolean type	Section 3.7
break	Break out of a loop or switch	Special Topic 3.3, 4.2
case	A label in a switch statement	Special Topic 3.3
char	The character type	Section 7.3
class	Definition of a class	Section 9.2
const	Definition of a constant value, reference, member function, or pointer	Section 2.1.5, Special Topic 5.2, Special Topic 6.4, Programming Tip 9.2
default	The default case of a switch statement	Special Topic 3.3
delete	Return a memory block to the free store	Section 7.4
do	A loop that is executed at least once	Section 4.4
double	The double-precision, floating-point type	Section 2.1.2
else	The alternative clause in an if statement	Section 3.1
false	The false Boolean value	Section 3.7
float	The single-precision, floating-point type	Special Topic 2.1
for	A loop that is intended to initialize, test, and update a variable	Section 4.3
friend	Allows another class or function to access the private features of this class	Section 14.2
if	The conditional branch statement	Section 3.1
int	The integer type	Section 2.1.1
long	A modifier for the int and double types that indicates that the type may have more bytes	Special Topic 2.1
namespace	A name space for disambiguating names	Section 1.5
new	Allocate a memory block from the free store	Section 7.4
nullptr	A pointer that does not point to any value	Section 7.1.3 (C++ 11)

Reserved Word	Description	Reference Location
operator	An overloaded operator	Section 13.1
override	Declares that a member function is intended to override a virtual function	Common Error 10.5 (C++ 11)
private	Features of a class that can only be accessed by this class and its friends	Section 9.3
public	Features of a class that can be accessed by all functions	Section 9.3
return	Returns a value from a function	Section 5.4
short	A modifier for the int type that indicates that the type may have fewer bytes	Special Topic 2.1
static_cast	Convert from one type to another	Special Topic 2.4
struct	A construct for aggregating items of arbitrary types into a single value	Section 7.7
switch	A statement that selects among multiple branches, depending upon the value of an expression	Special Topic 3.3
template	Defines a parameterized type or function	Section 13.3
this	The pointer to the implicit parameter of a member function	Section 9.10.3
true	The true value of the Boolean type	Section 3.7
typename	A type parameter in a template, or a denotation that the following name is a type name	Section 13.3, Worked Example 14.2
unsigned	A modifier for the int and char types that indicates that values of the type cannot be negative	Special Topic 2.1
using	Importing a name space	Section 1.5
virtual	A member function with dynamic dispatch	Section 10.4
void	The empty type of a function or pointer	Section 5.5
while	A loop statement that is controlled by a condition	Section 4.1

The following reserved words are not covered in this book:

alignas	const_cast	inline	signed	try
alignof	continue	mutable	sizeof	typedef
asm	decltype	noexcept	static	typeid
catch	dynamic_cast	protected	static_assert	union
char16_t	explicit	register	static_cast	volatile
char32_t	enum	reinterpret_cast	thread_local	wchar_t
constexpr	goto	short	throw	

OPERATOR
SUMMARY

The operators are listed in groups of decreasing precedence in the table below. The heavy horizontal lines in the table indicate a change in operator precedence. For example, z = x - y; means z = (x - y); because = has a lower precedence than - .

The prefix unary operators and the assignment operators associate right-to-left. All other operators associate left-to-right. For example, x - y - z means (x - y) - z because - associates left-to-right, but x = y = z means x = (y = z) because = associates right-to-left.

Operator	Description	Reference Location
::	Scope resolution	Section 9.5.1
.	Access member	Section 2.5.4, Section 7.7.1
->	Dereference and access member	Section 9.10.2
[]	Vector or array index	Section 6.1, Section 6.7.1
()	Function call	Section 5.1
++	Increment	Section 2.2.2
--	Decrement	Section 2.2.2
!	Boolean *not*	Section 3.7
~	Bitwise *not*	Appendix F
+ (unary)	Positive	Section 2.2.1
- (unary)	Negative	Section 2.2.1
* (unary)	Pointer dereferencing	Section 7.1
& (unary)	Address of variable	Section 5.9, Section 7.1
new	Free store allocation	Section 7.4
delete	Free store recycling	Section 7.4
sizeof	Size of variable or type	Appendix F
(type)	Cast	not covered
.*	Access pointer to member	not covered

Operator	Description	Reference Location
->*	Dereference and access pointer to member	not covered
*	Multiplication	Section 2.2.1
/	Division or integer division	Section 2.2.1, Section 2.2.3
%	Integer remainder	Section 2.2.3
+	Addition	Section 2.2.1
-	Subtraction	Section 2.2.1
<<	Output	Section 1.5, Section 2.3.2, Appendix F
>>	Input	Section 2.3.1, Appendix F
<	Less than	Section 3.2
<=	Less than or equal	Section 3.2
>	Greater than	Section 3.2
>=	Greater than or equal	Section 3.2
==	Equal	Section 3.2
!=	Not equal	Section 3.2
&	Bitwise *and*	Appendix F
^	Bitwise *xor*	Appendix F
|	Bitwise *or*	Appendix F
&&	Boolean *and*	Section 3.7
||	Boolean *or*	Section 3.7
? :	Conditional operator	Special Topic 3.1
=	Assignment	Section 2.1.4
+= -= *= /= %= &= |= ^= >>= <<=	Combined operator and assignment	Special Topic 2.5
,	Sequencing of expressions	not covered

CHARACTER CODES

These escape sequences can occur in strings (for example, `"\n"`) and characters (for example, `'\''`) However, the `\U` escape sequences should only be used inside strings that have an encoding prefix, such as

```
string message = u8"San Jos\U000000e9 \U0001f684";
```

A string is a sequence of bytes. In the UTF-8 encoding, bytes between 0 and 127 correspond to the ASCII character range (see Table 2). Other Unicode characters are encoded into multiple bytes, where the first byte is ≥ 192, and subsequent bytes are between 128 and 191. Table 3 shows the encoding.

Table 1 **Escape Sequences**	
Escape Sequence	Description
\n	Newline
\r	Carriage return
\t	Tab
\v	Vertical tab
\b	Backspace
\f	Form feed
\a	Alert
\\	Backslash
\"	Double quote
\'	Single quote
\?	Question mark
$\backslash U h_4 h_3 h_2 h_1 h_0$	A Unicode character, which will be encoded into a sequence of bytes determined by a character encoding

Table 2 ASCII Code Table

Dec. Code	Hex Code	Char- acter	Dec. Code	Hex Code	Char- acter	Dec. Code	Hex Code	Char- acter	Dec. Code	Hex Code	Char- acter
0	00	\0	32	20	Space	64	40	@	96	60	`
1	01		33	21	!	65	41	A	97	61	a
2	02		34	22	"	66	42	B	98	62	b
3	03		35	23	#	67	43	C	99	63	c
4	04		36	24	$	68	44	D	100	64	d
5	05		37	25	%	69	45	E	101	65	e
6	06		38	26	&	70	46	F	102	66	f
7	07	\a	39	27	'	71	47	G	103	67	g
8	08	\b	40	28	(	72	48	H	104	68	h
9	09	\t	41	29	)	73	49	I	105	69	i
10	0A	\n	42	2A	*	74	4A	J	106	6A	j
11	0B	\v	43	2B	+	75	4B	K	107	6B	k
12	0C	\f	44	2C	,	76	4C	L	108	6C	l
13	0D	\r	45	2D	-	77	4D	M	109	6D	m
14	0E		46	2E	.	78	4E	N	110	6E	n
15	0F		47	2F	/	79	4F	O	111	6F	o
16	10		48	30	0	80	50	P	112	70	p
17	11		49	31	1	81	51	Q	113	71	q
18	12		50	32	2	82	52	R	114	72	r
19	13		51	33	3	83	53	S	115	73	s
20	14		52	34	4	84	54	T	116	74	t
21	15		53	35	5	85	55	U	117	75	u
22	16		54	36	6	86	56	V	118	76	v
23	17		55	37	7	87	57	W	119	77	w
24	18		56	38	8	88	58	X	120	78	x
25	19		57	39	9	89	59	Y	121	79	y
26	1A		58	3A	:	90	5A	Z	122	7A	z
27	1B		59	3B	;	91	5B	[	123	7B	{
28	1C		60	3C	<	92	5C	\	124	7C	|
29	1D		61	3D	=	93	5D	]	125	7D	}
30	1E		62	3E	>	94	5E	^	126	7E	~
31	1F		63	3F	?	95	5F	_	127	7F	

Table 3 UTF-8 Encoding	
UTF-8	Unicode
0■■■■■■■	00000 00000000 0■■■■■■■
110■■■■■ 10■■■■■■	00000 00000■■■ ■■■■■■■■
1110■■■■ 10■■■■■■ 10■■■■■■	00000 ■■■■■■■■ ■■■■■■■■
11110■■■ 10■■■■■■ 10■■■■■■ 10■■■■■■	■■■■■ ■■■■■■■■ ■■■■■■■■

C++ LIBRARY SUMMARY

Standard Code Libraries

<algorithm>

- bool **binary_search**(I begin, I end, T x)
  Function: Checks whether the value x is contained in the sorted range [begin, end).

- T **max**(T x, T y)
  Function: The maximum of x and y.

- T **min**(T x, T y)
  Function: The minimum of x and y.

- void **sort**(I begin, I end)
  Function: Sorts the elements in the range [begin, end).

<cctype>

- bool **isalnum**(char c)
  Function: Test whether c is a letter or a number.

- bool **isalpha**(char c)
  Function: Tests whether c is a letter.

- bool **isdigit**(char c)
  Function: Tests whether c is a digit.

- bool **islower**(char c)
  Function: Tests whether c is lowercase.

- bool **isspace**(char c)
  Function: Tests whether c is white space.

- bool **isupper**(char c)
  Function: Tests whether c is uppercase.

- char **tolower**(char c)
  Function: Returns the lowercase of c.

- char **toupper**(char c)
  Function: Returns the uppercase of c.

<cmath>

- int **abs**(int x)
- double **abs**(double x)
  Function: Absolute value, $|x|$

- double **cos**(double x)
  Function: Cosine, $\cos x$ (x in radians)

- double **log**(double x)
  Function: Natural log, $\log(x)$, $x > 0$

- double **log10**(double x)
  Function: Decimal log, $\log_{10}(x)$, $x > 0$

- double **pow**(double x, double y)
  Function: Power, x^y. If $x > 0$, y can be any value. If x is 0, y must be > 0. If $x < 0$, y must be an integer.

- double **sin**(double x)
  Function: Sine, $\sin x$ (x in radians)

- double **sqrt**(double x)
  Function: Square root, $\sqrt{x}$

- double **tan**(double x)
  Function: Tangent, $\tan x$ (x in radians)

<cstdlib>

- int **abs**(int x)
  Function: Absolute value, $|x|$

- void **exit**(int n)
  Function: Exits the program with status code n.

- int **rand**()
  Function: Random integer

- void **srand**(int n)
  Function: Sets the seed of the random number generator to n.

<ctime>

- time_t **time**(time_t* p)
  Function: Returns the number of seconds since January 1, 1970, 00:00:00 GMT.
  If p is not nullptr, the return value is also stored in the location to which p points.

<string>

- istream& **getline**(istream& in, string& s)
  Function: Gets the next input line from the input stream in and stores it in the string s.

- int **stoi**(const string& s) (C++ 11)
- double **stod**(const string& s) (C++ 11)
  Function: Converts the string to an integer or floating-point number.

Class string

- `const char* string::c_str() const`
  Member function: Returns a char array with the characters in this string.
- `int string::length() const`
  Member function: Returns the length of the string.
- `string string::substr(int i) const`
  Member function: Returns the substring from index i to the end of the string.
- `string string::substr(int i, int n) const`
  Member function: Returns the substring of length n starting at index i.

<iomanip>

- `boolalpha`
  Manipulator: Causes Boolean values to be displayed as true and false instead of the default 1 and 0.
- `defaultfloat`
  Manipulator: Selects the default floating-point format, which uses scientific format for very large or very small values, and fixed format for all other values.
- `fixed`
  Manipulator: Selects fixed floating-point format, with trailing zeroes.
- `left, right`
  Manipulator: Left- or right-justifies values if they are shorter than the field width.
- `scientific`
  Manipulator: Selects scientific floating-point format, such as 1.729000e+03.
- `setfill(char c)`
  Manipulator: Sets the fill character to the character c.
- `setprecision(int n)`
  Manipulator: Sets the precision of floating-point values to n digits after the decimal point in fixed and scientific formats.
- `setw(int n)`
  Manipulator: Sets the width of the next field.

<iostream>

Class istream

- `bool istream::fail() const`
  Member function: True if input has failed.
- `istream& istream::get(char& c)`
  Member function: Gets the next character and places it into c.
- `istream& istream::seekg(long p)`
  Member function: Moves the get position to position p.
- `long istream::tellg()`
  Member function: Returns the get position.
- `istream& istream::unget()`
  Member function: Puts the last character read back into the stream, to be read again in the next input operation; only one character can be put back at a time.

Class ostream

- `ostream& ostream::seekp(long p)`
  Member function: Moves the put position to position p.
- `long ostream::tellp()`
  Member function: Returns the put position.

<fstream>

Class ifstream

- `void ifstream::open(const string& n)` (C++ 11)
- `void ifstream::open(const char n[])`
  Member function: Opens a file with name n for reading.

Class ofstream

- `void ofstream::open(const string& n)` (C++ 11)
- `void ofstream::open(const char n[])`
  Member function: Opens a file with name n for writing.

Class fstream

- `void fstream::open(const string& n)` (C++ 11)
- `void fstream::open(const char n[])`
  Member function: Opens a file with name n for reading and writing.

Class fstreambase

- `void fstreambase::close()`
  Member function: Closes the file stream.
  Notes: fstreambase is the common base class of ifstream, ofstream, and fstream.
  To open a binary file n both for input and output, use f.open(n, ios::in | ios::out | ios::binary)

<strstream>

Class istringstream

- `istringstream::istringstream(string s)`
  Constructs a string stream that reads from the string s.

Class ostringstream

- `string ostringstream::`**`str`**`() const`
  Member function: Returns the string that was collected by the string stream.

  Notes: Call s = `string(out.str())` to get a string object that contains the characters collected by `ostringstream` out.

<vector>

Class vector<T>

- `vector<T>::`**`vector`**`()`
  Constructs an empty vector.

- `vector<T>::`**`vector`**`(int n)`
  Constructs a vector with n elements.

- `T& vector<T>::`**`operator`**`[](int n)`
  Member function: Accesses the element at index n.

- `void vector<T>::`**`pop_back`**`()`
  Member function: Removes (but does not return) the last element.

- `void vector<T>::`**`push_back`**`(const T& x)`
  Member function: Inserts x after the last element.

- `int vector<T>::`**`size`**`() const`
  Member function: Returns the number of elements in the container.

C++ LANGUAGE CODING GUIDELINES

Introduction

This coding style guide is a simplified version of one that has been used with good success both in industrial practice and for college courses. It lays down rules that you must follow for your programming assignments.

A style guide is a set of mandatory requirements for layout and formatting. Uniform style makes it easier for you to read code from your instructor and classmates. You will really appreciate the consistency if you do a team project. It is also easier for your instructor and your grader to grasp the essence of your programs quickly.

A style guide makes you a more productive programmer because it *reduces gratuitous choice*. If you don't have to make choices about trivial matters, you can spend your energy on the solution of real problems.

In these guidelines a number of constructs are plainly outlawed. That doesn't mean that programmers using them are evil or incompetent. It does mean that the constructs are of marginal utility and can be expressed just as well or even better with other language constructs.

If you have already programmed in C or C++, you may be initially uncomfortable about giving up some fond habits. However, it is a sign of professionalism to set aside personal preferences in minor matters and to compromise for the benefit of your group.

These guidelines are necessarily somewhat long and dull. They also mention features that you may not yet have seen in class. Here are the most important highlights:

- Tabs are set every three spaces.
- Variable and function names are lowercase.
- Constant names are uppercase. Class names start with an uppercase letter.
- There are spaces after reserved words and between binary operators.
- Braces must line up.
- No magic numbers may be used.
- Every function must have a comment.
- At most 30 lines of code may be used per function.
- No goto, continue, or break is allowed.
- At most two global variables may be used per file.

A note to the instructor: Of course, many programmers and organizations have strong feelings about coding style. If this style guide is incompatible with your own preferences or with local custom, please feel free to modify it. For that purpose, this coding style guide is available in electronic form on the companion web site for this book.

Source Files

Each program is a collection of one or more files or modules. The executable program is obtained by compiling and linking these files. Organize the material in each file as follows:

- Header comments
- `#include` statements
- Constants
- Classes
- Functions

It is common to start each file with a comment block. Here is a typical format:

```
/**
   @file invoice.cpp
   @author Jenny Koo
   @date 2022-01-24
   @version 3.14
*/
```

You may also want to include a copyright notice, such as

```
/* Copyright 2022 Jenny Koo */
```

A valid copyright notice consists of

- the copyright symbol © or the word "Copyright" or the abbreviation "Copr."
- the year of first publication of the work
- the name of the owner of the copyright

(Note: To save space, this header comment has been omitted from the programs in this book as well as the programs on disk so that the actual line numbers match those that are printed in the book.)

Next, list all included header files.

```
#include <iostream>
#include "question.h"
```

Do not embed absolute path names, such as

```
#include "c:\me\my_homework\widgets.h"  // Don't !!!
```

After the header files, list constants that are needed throughout the program file.

```
const int GRID_SIZE = 20;
const double CLOCK_RADIUS = 5;
```

Then supply the definitions of all classes.

```
class Product
{
   . . .
};
```

Order the class definitions so that a class is defined before it is used in another class.

Finally, list all functions, including member functions of classes and nonmember functions. Order the nonmember functions so that a function is defined before it is called. As a consequence, the `main` function will be the last function in your file.

Functions

Supply a comment of the following form for every function.

```
/**
    Explanation.
    @param parameter variable1    explanation
    @param parameter variable2    explanation
    . . .
    @return explanation
*/
```

The introductory explanation is required for all functions except `main`. It should start with an uppercase letter and end with a period. Some documentation tools extract the first sentence of the explanation into a summary table. Thus, if you provide an explanation that consists of multiple sentences, formulate the explanation such that the first sentence is a concise explanation of the function's purpose.

Omit the `@param` comment if the function has no parameter variables. Omit the `@return` comment for `void` functions. Here is a typical example:

```
/**
    Converts calendar date into Julian day. This algorithm is from Press
    et al., Numerical Recipes in C, 2nd ed., Cambridge University Press, 1992.
    @param year the year of the date to be converted
    @param month the month of the date to be converted
    @param day the day of the date to be converted
    @return the Julian day number that begins at noon of the given
    calendar date
*/
long dat2jul(int year, int month, int day)
{
    . . .
}
```

Parameter variable names must be explicit, especially if they are integers or Boolean.

```
Employee remove(int d, double s); // Huh?
Employee remove(int department, double severance_pay); // OK
```

Of course, for very generic functions, short names may be very appropriate.

Do not write `void` functions that return exactly one answer through a reference. Instead, make the result into a return value.

```
void find(vector<Employee> c, bool& found); // Don't!
bool find(vector<Employee> c); // OK
```

Of course, if the function computes more than one value, some or all results can be returned through reference parameters.

Functions must have at most 30 lines of code. (Comments, blank lines, and lines containing only braces are not included in this count.) Functions that consist of one long `if/else/else` statement sequence may be longer, provided each branch is 10 lines or less. This rule forces you to break up complex computations into separate functions.

Local Variables

Do not define all local variables at the beginning of a block. Define each variable just before it is used for the first time.

Every variable must be either explicitly initialized when defined or set in the immediately following statement (for example, through a >> instruction).

```
int pennies = 0;
```

or

```
int pennies;
cin >> pennies;
```

Move variables to the innermost block in which they are needed:

```
while (. . .)
{
   double xnew = (xold + a / xold) / 2;
   . . .
}
```

Do not define two variables in one statement:

```
int dimes = 0, nickels = 0; // Don't
```

When defining a pointer variable, place the * with the type, not the variable:

```
Link* p; // OK
```

not

```
Link *p; // Don't
```

Use auto only with types that are complex and not very informative, such as iterators. For example, prefer

```
unordered_map<string, int> scores = . . .;
auto pos = scores.find("Harry");
```

over

```
unordered_map<string, double>::iterator pos = scores.find("Harry");
```

Constants

In C++, do not use #define to define constants:

```
#define CLOCK_RADIUS 5 // Don't
```

Use const instead:

```
const double CLOCK_RADIUS = 5; // The radius of the clock face
```

You may not use magic numbers in your code. (A magic number is an integer constant embedded in code without a constant definition.) Any number except 0, 1, or 2 is considered magic:

```
if (p.get_x() < 10) // Don't
```

Use a const variable instead:

```
const double WINDOW_XMAX = 10;
if (p.get_x() < WINDOW_XMAX) // OK
```

Even the most reasonable cosmic constant is going to change one day. You think there are 365 days per year? Your customers on Mars are going to be pretty unhappy about your silly prejudice.

Make a constant

```
const int DAYS_PER_YEAR = 365;
```

so that you can easily produce a Martian version without trying to find all the 365's, 364's, 366's, 367's, and so on in your code.

Classes

Lay out the items of a class as follows:

```
class ClassName
{
public:
    constructors
    mutators
    accessors
private:
    data
};
```

All data members of classes must be private.

Control Flow

The for Statement

Use for loops only when a variable runs from somewhere to somewhere else with some constant increment/decrement.

```
for (i = 0; i < a.size(); i++)
{
    cout << a[i] << endl;
}
```

Do not use the for loop for weird constructs such as

```
for (xnew = a / 2; count < ITERATIONS; cout << xnew) // Don't
{
    xold = xnew;
    xnew = xold + a / xold;
    count++;
}
```

Make such a loop into a while loop, so the sequence of instructions is much clearer.

```
xnew = a / 2;
while (count < ITERATIONS) // OK
{
    xold = xnew;
    xnew = xold + a / xold;
    count++;
    cout << xnew;
}
```

Consider using the range-based `for` loop when traversing a container such as a `vector` or `list`:

```
vector<int> values = . . .;
for (int v : values)
{
   cout << v << " ";
}
```

Nonlinear Control Flow

Don't use the `switch` statement. Use `if`/`else` instead.

Do not use the `break`, `continue`, or `goto` statement. Use a `bool` variable to control the execution flow.

Lexical Issues

Naming Conventions

The following rules specify when to use upper- and lowercase letters in identifier names.

1. All variable and function names and all data members of classes are in lowercase, sometimes with an underscore in the middle. For example, `first_player`.
2. All constants are in uppercase, with an occasional underscore. For example, `CLOCK_RADIUS`.
3. All class names start with uppercase and are followed by lowercase letters, with an occasional uppercase letter in the middle. For example, `BankTeller`.

Names must be reasonably long and descriptive. Use `first_player` instead of `fp`. No drppng f vwls. Local variables that are fairly routine can be short (`ch`, `i`) as long as they are really just boring holders for an input character, a loop counter, and so on. Also, do not use `ctr`, `c`, `cntr`, `cnt`, `c2` for five counter variables in your function. Surely each of these variables has a specific purpose and can be named to remind the reader of it (for example, `ccurrent`, `cnext`, `cprevious`, `cnew`, `cresult`).

Indentation and White Space

Use tab stops every three columns. Save your file so that it contains no tabs at all. That means you will need to change the tab stop setting in your editor! In the editor, make sure to select "3 spaces per tab stop" and "save all tabs as spaces". Every programming editor has these settings. If yours doesn't, don't use tabs at all but type the correct number of spaces to achieve indentation.

Use blank lines freely to separate logically distinct parts of a function.

Use a blank space around every binary operator:

```
x1 = (-b - sqrt(b * b - 4 * a * c)) / (2 * a); // Good
x1=(-b-sqrt(b*b-4*a*c))/(2*a); // Bad
```

Leave a blank space after (and not before) each comma, semicolon, and reserved word, but not after a function name.

```
if (x == 0) . . .
f(a, b[i]);
```

Every line must fit in 80 columns. If you must break a statement, add an indentation level for the continuation:

```
a[n] = ...............................................
       + .................;
```

Braces

Opening and closing braces must line up, either horizontally or vertically.

```
while (i < n) { cout << a[i] << endl; i++; }  // OK
while (i < n)
{
   cout << a[i] << endl;
   i++;
}  // OK
```

Some programmers don't line up vertical braces but place the { *behind* the while:

```
while (i < n) {   // Don't
   cout << a[i] << endl;
   i++;
}
```

This style saves a line, but it is difficult to match the braces.

Always use braces with if, while, do, and for statements, even if the body is only a single statement.

```
if (floor > 13)
{              // OK
   floor--;
}
if (floor > 13)
   floor--;   // Don't
```

Unstable Layout

Some programmers take great pride in lining up certain columns in their code:

```
class Employee
{
   . . .
private:
   string  name;
      int  age;
   double  hourly_wage;
};
```

This is undeniably neat, and we recommend it if your editor does it for you, but *don't* do it manually. The layout is not *stable* under change. A data type that is longer than the pre-allotted number of columns requires that you move *all* entries around.

Some programmers like to start every line of a multiline comment with **:

```
/* This is a comment
** that extends over
** three source lines
*/
```

Again, this is neat if your editor has a command to add and remove the asterisks, and if you know that all programmers who will maintain your code also have such an editor. Otherwise, it can be a powerful method of *discouraging* programmers from editing the comment. If you have to choose between pretty comments and comments that reflect the current facts of the program, facts win over beauty.

GLOSSARY

Access specifier   A reserved word that indicates the accessibility of a feature, such as private or public.

Accessor function   A member function that accesses an object but does not change it.

Address   A value that specifies the location of a variable in memory.

Aggregation   The "*has-a*" relationship between classes.

Algorithm   An unambiguous, executable, and terminating specification of a way to solve a problem.

ANSI/ISO C++ Standard   The standard for the C++ language that was developed by the American National Standards Institute and the International Standards Organization.

API (Application Programming Interface)   A code library for building programs.

Argument   A value supplied in a function call, or one of the values combined by an operator.

Array   A collection of values of the same type stored in contiguous memory locations, each of which can be accessed by an integer index.

Arrow operator   The -> operator. p->m is the same as (*p).m.

ASCII code   The American Standard Code for Information Interchange, which associates code values between 0 and 127 to letters, digits, punctuation marks, and control characters.

Assignment   Placing a new value into a variable.

Assignment statement   A statement that places a new value into an existing variable.

Asymmetric bounds   Bounds that include the starting index but not the ending index.

Base class   A class from which another class is derived.

Behavior (of an object)   The actions taken by an object when its functions are invoked.

Binary file   A file in which values are stored in their binary representation and cannot be read as text.

Binary search   A fast algorithm for finding a value in a sorted array. It narrows the search down to half of the array in every step.

Bit   Binary digit; the smallest unit of information, having two possible values: 0 and 1. A data element consisting of n bits has 2^n possible values.

Black Box   A device with a given specification but unknown implementation.

Block   A group of statements bracketed by {}.

Body   All statements of a function or block.

Boolean operator   An operator that can be applied to Boolean values. C++ has three Boolean operators: &&, ||, and !.

Boolean type   A type with two possible values: true and false.

Boundary test case   A test case involving values that are at the outer boundary of the set of legal values. For example, if a function is expected to work for all nonnegative integers, then 0 is a boundary test case.

Bounds error   Trying to access an array element that is outside the legal range.

break statement   A statement that terminates a loop or switch statement.

Breakpoint   A point in a program, specified in a debugger, at which the debugger stops executing the program and lets the user inspect the program state.

Bug   A programming error.

Byte   A number made up of eight bits. Essentially all currently manufactured computers use a byte as the smallest unit of storage in memory.

Call stack   The ordered set of all functions that currently have been called but not yet terminated, starting with the current function and ending with main.

Capacity   The number of values that a data structure such as an array can potentially hold, in contrast to the size (the number of elements it currently holds).

Case sensitive   Distinguishing upper- and lowercase characters.

Cast   Explicitly converting a value from one type to a different type. For example, the cast from a floating-point number x to an integer is expressed in C++ by the static cast notation static_cast<int>(x).

Central processing unit (CPU)   The part of a computer that executes the machine instructions.

Character   A single letter, digit, or symbol.

Class   A programmer-defined data type.

Command line   The line the user types to start a program in DOS or UNIX or a command window in Windows. It consists of the program name followed by any necessary arguments.

Command line arguments   Additional strings of information provided at the command line that the program can use.

Comment   An explanation to help the human reader understand a section of a program; ignored by the compiler.

Compiler   A program that translates code in a high-level language (such as C++) to machine instructions.

Compile-time error   An error that is detected when a program is compiled.

Compound statement   A statement such as if or for that is made up of several parts (for example, condition, body).

Computer program   A sequence of instructions that is executed by a computer.

Concatenate   To place one string after another to form a new string.

Constant   A value that cannot be changed by a program. In C++, constants are marked with the reserved word const.

Construction   Setting a newly allocated object to an initial state.

Constructor   A sequence of statements for initializing a newly allocated object.

CPU (Central Processing Unit)   The part of a computer that executes the machine instructions.

Dangling pointer   A pointer that does not point to a valid location.

Data member   A variable that is present in every object of a class.

Delimiter   A character or sequence of characters used to specify the beginning or end of a text segment.

De Morgan's Law   A law about logical operations that describes how to negate expressions formed with *and* and *or* operations.

Debugger   A program that lets a user run another program one or a few steps at a time, stop execution, and inspect the variables in order to analyze it for bugs.

Declaration   A statement that announces the existence of a variable, function, or class but does not define it.

Default constructor   A constructor that can be invoked with no parameters.

#define directive   A directive that defines constant values and macros for the preprocessor. Values can be queried during the preprocessing phase with the #if and #ifndef directives. Macros are replaced by the preprocessor when they are encountered in the program file.

Definition   A statement or series of statements that fully describes a variable, a function and its implementation, a type, or a class and its properties.

delete operator   The operator that recycles memory to the free store.

Dereferencing   Locating an object when a pointer to the object is given.

Derived class   A class that modifies a base class by adding data members, adding member functions, or redefining member functions.

Directory   A structure on a disk that can hold files or other directories; also called a folder.

Documentation comment   A comment in a source file that can be automatically extracted into the program documentation by a program such as javadoc.

Dot notation   The notation *object.function(parameters)* used to invoke a member function on an object.

Dynamic memory allocation   Allocating memory as a program runs as required by the program's needs.

Editor   A program for writing and modifying text files.

Element   A storage location in an array.

Embedded system   The processor, software, and supporting circuitry that is included in a device other than a computer.

Encapsulation   The hiding of implementation details.

Escape character   A character in text that is not taken literally but has a special meaning when combined with the character or characters that follow it. The \\ character is an escape character in C++ strings.

Escape sequence   A sequence of characters that starts with an escape character, such as \\n or \\".

Exception   A class that signals a condition that prevents the program from continuing normally. When such a condition occurs, an object of the exception class is thrown.

Executable file   The file that contains a program's machine instructions.

Explicit parameter   A parameter of a member function other than the object on which the function is invoked.

Expression   A syntactical construct that is made up of constants, variables, function calls, and the operators combining them.

Extension   The last part of a file name, which specifies the file type. For example, the extension .cpp denotes a C++ file.

Failed stream state   The state of a stream after an invalid operation has been attempted, such as reading a number when the next stream position yielded a nondigit, or reading after the end of file was reached.

Fibonacci numbers   The sequence of numbers 1, 1, 2, 3, 5, 8, 13, . . . , in which every term is the sum of its two predecessors.

File   A sequence of bytes that is stored on disk.

File pointer   The position within a random-access file of the next byte to be read or written. It can be moved so as to access any byte in the file.

Flag   A type with two possible values: true and false.

Floating-point number   A number that can have a fractional part.

Folder   A structure on a disk that can hold files or other folders; also called a directory.

Free store   A reservoir of storage from which memory can be allocated when a program runs.

Function   A sequence of statements that can be invoked multiple times, with different values for its parameter variables.

Function signature   The name of a function and the types of its parameters.

Garbage collection   Automatic reclamation of memory occupied by objects that are no longer referenced. C++ does not have garbage collection

Global variable   A variable whose scope is not restricted to a single function.

grep   The "global regular expression print" search program, useful for finding all strings matching a pattern in a set of files.

Hard disk   A device that stores information on rotating platters with magnetic coating.

Hardware   The physical equipment for a computer or another device.

Header file   A file that informs the compiler of features that are available in another module or library.

High-level programming language   A programming language that provides an abstract view of a computer and allows programmers to focus on their problem domain.

HTML (Hypertext Markup Language)   The language in which web pages are described.

IDE (Integrated Development Environment)   A programming environment that includes an editor, compiler, and debugger.

#if directive   A directive to the preprocessor to include the code contained between the #if and the matching #endif if a condition is true.

Implicit parameter   The object on which a member function is invoked. For example, in the call x.f(y), the object x is the implicit parameter of the function f.

#include directive   An instruction to the preprocessor to include a header file.

Index   The position of an element in an array.

Inheritance   The "*is-a*" relationship between a general base class and a specialized derived class.

Initialization   Setting a variable to a well-defined value when it is created.

Input stream   An abstraction for a sequence of bytes from which data can be read.

Instance of a class   An object whose type is that class.

Integer   A number that cannot have a fractional part.

Integer division   Taking the quotient of two integers and discarding the remainder. In C++ the / symbol denotes integer division if both arguments are integers. For example, 11/4 is 2, not 2.75.

Integrated Development Environment (IDE)   A programming environment that includes an editor, compiler, and debugger.

Internet   A worldwide collection of networks, routing equipment, and computers using a common set of protocols that define how participants interact with each other.

Lexicographic ordering   Ordering strings in the same order as in a dictionary, by skipping all matching characters and comparing the first non-matching characters of both strings. For example, "orbit" comes before "orchid" in lexicographic ordering. Note that in C++, unlike a dictionary, the ordering is case sensitive: Z comes before a.

Library   A set of precompiled classes and functions that can be included in programs.

Linear search Searching a container (such as an array or list) for an object by inspecting each element in turn.

Linker The program that combines object and library files into an executable file.

Literal A constant value in a program that is explicitly written as a number, such as –2 or 6.02214115E23, or as a character sequence, such as "Harry".

Local variable A variable whose scope is a block.

Logic error An error in a syntactically correct program that causes it to act differently from its specification. (A form of run-time error.)

Logical operator An operator that can be applied to Boolean values. C++ has three Boolean operators: &&, ||, and !.

Loop A sequence of instructions that is executed repeatedly.

Loop and a half A loop whose termination decision is neither at the beginning nor at the end.

Machine code Instructions that can be executed directly by the CPU.

Magic number A number that appears in a program without explanation.

main function The function that is first called when a program executes.

Member function A function that is defined by a class and operates on objects of that class.

Memory The circuitry that stores code and data in a computer.

Memory location A value that specifies the location of data in computer memory.

Modulus The % operator that computes the remainder of an integer division.

Mutator function A member function that changes the state of an object.

Nested block A block that is contained inside another block.

Nested loop A loop that is contained in another loop.

new operator The operator that allocates new memory from the free store.

Newline The '\n' character, which indicates the end of a line.

null pointer The value nullptr that indicates that a pointer does not point to any object.

Number literal A constant value in a program that is explicitly written as a number, such as –2 or 6.02214115E23.

Object A value of a class type.

Object-oriented programming Designing a program by discovering objects, their properties, and their relationships.

Off-by-one error A common programming error in which a value is one larger or smaller than it should be.

Operating system The software that launches application programs and provides services (such as a file system) for those programs.

Operator A symbol denoting a mathematical or logical operation, such as + or &&.

Operator associativity The rule that governs in which order operators of the same precedence are executed. For example, in C++ the - operator is left-associative because a - b - c is interpreted as (a - b) - c, and = is right-associative because a = b = c is interpreted as a = (b = c).

Operator precedence The rule that governs which operator is evaluated first. For example, in C++ the && operator has a higher precedence than the || operator. Hence a || b && c is interpreted as a || (b && c).

Output stream An abstraction for a sequence of bytes to which data can be written.

Overloading Giving more than one meaning to a function name or operator.

Overriding Redefining a function from a base class in a derived class.

Parallel arrays Arrays of the same length, in which corresponding elements are logically related.

Parallel vectors Vectors of the same length, in which corresponding elements are logically related.

Parameter An item of information that is specified to a function when the function is called.

Parameter passing Specifying expressions to be arguments for a function when it is called.

Parameter variable A variable of a function that is initialized with a value when the function is called.

Partially filled array An array that is not filled to capacity, together with a companion variable that indicates the number of elements actually stored.

Path (to a file or directory) The sequence of directory names and, for a file, a file name at the end, that describes how to reach the file or directory from a given starting point.

Permutation   A rearrangement of a set of values.

Pointer   A value that denotes the memory location of an object.

Polymorphism   Selecting a function among several functions that have the same name on the basis of the actual type of the implicit parameter.

Postfix operator   A unary operator that is written after its argument.

Prefix operator   A unary operator that is written before its argument.

Programming   The act of designing and implementing computer programs.

Prompt   A string that tells the user to provide input.

Prototype   The declaration of a function, including its parameter types and return type.

Pseudocode   A high-level description of the actions of a program or algorithm, using a mixture of English and informal programming language syntax.

Pseudorandom number   A number that appears to be random but is generated by a mathematical formula.

Public interface   The features (functions, variables, and nested types) of a class that are accessible to all clients.

RAM (random-access memory)   Electronic circuits in a computer that can store code and data of running programs.

Random access   The ability to access any value directly without having to read the values preceding it.

Recursion   A technique for computing a result by decomposing the inputs into simpler values and applying the same function to them.

Recursive function   A function that can call itself with simpler values. It must handle the simplest values without calling itself.

Redirection   Linking the input or output of a program to a file instead of the keyboard or display.

Reference   A value that denotes the location of an object in memory.

Reference parameter   A parameter that is bound to a variable supplied in the call. Changes made to the parameter within the function affect the variable outside the function.

Regular expression   A string that defines a set of matching strings according to their content. Each part of a regular expression can be a specific required character; one of a set of permitted characters such as [abc], which can be a range such as [a-z]; any character not in a set of forbidden characters, such as [^0-9]; a repetition of one or more matches, such as [0-9]+, or zero or more, such as [ACGT]; one of a set of alternatives, such as and|et|und; or various other possibilities. For example, [A-Za-z][0-9]+ matches Cloud9 or 007 but not Jack.

Relational operator   An operator that compares two values, yielding a Boolean result.

Reserved word   A word that has a special meaning in a programming language and therefore cannot be used as a name by the programmer.

Return value   The value returned by a function through a return statement.

Roundoff error   An error introduced by the fact that the computer can store only a finite number of digits of a floating-point number.

Run-time error   An error in a syntactically correct program that causes it to act differently from its specification.

Run-time stack   The data structure that stores the local variables of all called functions as a program runs.

Scope   The part of a program in which a variable is defined.

Secondary storage   Storage that persists without electricity, e.g., a hard disk.

Sentinel   A value in input that is not to be used as an actual input value but to signal the end of input.

Sequential access   Accessing values one after another without skipping over any of them.

Shadowing   Hiding a variable by defining another one with the same name.

Shell window   A window for interacting with an operating system through textual commands.

Short-circuit evaluation   Evaluating only a part of an expression if the remainder cannot change the result.

Slicing an object   Copying an object of a derived class into a variable of the base class, thereby losing the derived-class data.

Software   The intangible instructions and data that are necessary for operating a computer or another device.

Source code   Instructions in a programming language that need to be translated before execution on a computer.

Source file   A file containing instructions in a programming language such as C++.

Stack trace   A printout of the call stack, listing all currently pending function calls.

State   The current value of an object, which is determined by the cumulative action of all functions that were invoked on it.

Statement   A syntactical unit in a program. In C++ a statement is either a simple statement, a compound statement, or a block.

Stepwise refinement   The process of solving a problem that starts out with a subdivision into steps, then continues by further subdividing those steps.

Stream   An abstraction for a sequence of bytes from which data can be read or to which data can be written.

String   A sequence of characters.

Structure   A construct for aggregating items of arbitrary types into a single value.

Stub   A function with no or minimal functionality.

Subclass   A synonym for derived class.

Substitution principle   The principle that a derived-class object can be used in place of any base-class object.

Superclass   A synonym for base class.

Symmetric bounds   Bounds that include the starting index and the ending index.

Syntax   Rules that define how to form instructions in a particular programming language.

Syntax error   An instruction that does not follow the programming language rules and is rejected by the compiler. (A form of compile-time error.)

Tab character   The '\t' character, which advances the next character on the line to the next one of a set of fixed positions known as tab stops.

Ternary operator   An operator with three arguments. C++ has one ternary operator, a ? b : c.

Test coverage   The instructions of a program that are executed when a set of test cases are run.

Test suite   A set of test cases for a program.

Text file   A file in which values are stored in their text representation.

Trace message   A message that is printed during a program run for debugging purposes.

Two-dimensional array   A tabular arrangement of elements in which an element is specified by a row and a column index.

Type   A named set of values and the operations that can be carried out with them.

Unicode   A standard code that assigns code values consisting of two bytes to characters used in scripts around the world.

Unified Modeling Language (UML)   A notation for specifying, visualizing, constructing, and documenting the artifacts of software systems.

Uninitialized variable   A variable that has not been set to a particular value. It is filled with whatever "random" bytes happen to be present in the memory location that the variable occupies.

Unit test   A test of a function by itself, isolated from the remainder of the program.

Value parameter   A function parameter whose value is copied into a parameter variable of a function. If a variable is passed as a value parameter, changes made to the parameter inside the function do not affect the original variable outside the program.

Variable   A symbol in a program that identifies a storage location that can hold different values.

Vector   The standard C++ template for a dynamically-growing array.

Virtual function   A function that can be redefined in a derived class. The actual function called depends on the type of the object on which it is invoked at run time.

void   A reserved word indicating no type or an unknown type.

Walkthrough   A step-by-step manual simulation of a computer program.

White space   Any sequence of only space, tab, and newline characters.

INDEX

Note: Page numbers followed by f indicate figures; those followed by t indicate tables. Functions and classes from the C++ library are listed by name. For functions and classes in example programs, see "applications: programs and simulations."

ILLUSTRATION CREDITS

Icons

Common Error icon: © Scott Harms/iStockphoto.
How To icon: © Steve Simzer/iStockphoto.
Paperclip: © Yvan Dubé/iStockphoto.
Programming Tip icon: © Macdaddy/Dreamstime.com.
Computing and Society icon: © Mishella/
    Dreamstime.com.
Self Check icon: © Nicholas Homrich/iStockphoto.
Special Topic icon: ©Nathan Winter/iStockphoto.
Worked Example icon: © Tom Horyn/iStockphoto.

Chapter 4

Page 130-133 (left to right, top to bottom):
Gogh, Vincent van *The Olive Orchard:* Chester Dale
    Collection 1963.10.152/National Gallery of Art.
Degas, Edgar *The Dance Lesson:* Collection of Mr. and
    Mrs. Paul Mellon 1995.47.6/National Gallery of Art.
Fragonard, Jean-Honoré *Young Girl Reading:* Gift of Mrs.
    Mellon Bruce in memory of her father, Andrew W.
    Mellon 1961.16.1/National Gallery of Art.
Gauguin, Paul *Self-Portrait:* Chester Dale Collection
    1963.10.150/National Gallery of Art.
Gauguin, Paul *Breton Girls Dancing, Pont-Aven:*
    Collection of Mr. and Mrs. Paul Mellon 1983.1.19/
    National Gallery of Art.
Guigou, Paul *Washerwomen on the Banks of the Durance:*
    Chester Dale Fund 2007.73.1/National Gallery of Art.

Guillaumin, Jean-Baptiste-Armand *The Bridge of Louis
    Philippe:* Chester Dale Collection 1963.10.155/National
    Gallery of Art.
Manet, Edouard *The Railway:* Gift of Horace Havemeyer
    in memory of his mother, Louisine W. Havemeyer
    1956.10.1/National Gallery of Art.
Manet, Edouard *Masked Ball at the Opera:* Gift of Mrs.
    Horace Havemeyer in memory of her mother-in-law,
    Louisine W. Havemeyer 1982.75.1/National Gallery
    of Art.
Manet, Edouard *The Old Musician:* Chester Dale
    Collection 1963.10.162/National Gallery of Art.
Monet, Claude *The Japanese Footbridge:* Gift of Victoria
    Nebeker Coberly, in memory of her son John W. Mudd,
    and Walter H. and Leonore Annenberg 1992.9.1/
    National Gallery of Art.
Monet, Claude *Woman with a Parasol—Madame Monet
    and Her Son:* Collection of Mr. and Mrs. Paul Mellon
    1983.1.29/National Gallery of Art.
Monet, Claude *The Bridge at Argenteuil:* Collection of Mr.
    and Mrs. Paul Mellon 1983.1.24/National Gallery of
    Art.
Monet, Claude *The Artist's Garden in Argenteuil (A
    Corner of the Garden with Dahlias):* Gift of Janice H.
    Levin, in Honor of the 50th Anniversary of the National
    Gallery of Art 1991.27.1/National Gallery of Art.